Gender, Crime, and Punishment

Kathleen Daly

Yale University Press   New Haven and London

Published with assistance from the Louis Stern Memorial Fund.

Designed by Sonia L. Scanlon.

Set in Times Roman type by DEKR Corporation, Woburn, Massachusetts.

Printed in the United States of America by BookCrafters, Inc., Chelsea, Michigan.

Library of Congress Cataloging-in-Publication Data

Daly, Kathleen, 1948–

    Gender, crime, and punishment / Kathleen Daly.

      p. cm.

    Includes bibliographical references and index.

    ISBN 0-300-05955-8 (cloth: alk. paper)

        0-300-06866-2 (pbk.: alk. paper)

    1. Sex discrimination in criminal justice administration—
Connecticut — New Haven. 2. Female offenders — Connecticut — New
Haven. 3. Women prisoners — Connecticut — New Haven. I. Title.

HV9956.N48D35 1994

364'.082—dc20   94-1582

                                             CIP

A catalogue record for this book is available from the British Library.

The paper in this book meets the guidelines for permanence
and durability of the Committee on Production Guidelines for Book
Longevity of the Council on Library Resources.

10 9 8 7 6 5 4 3 2

Contents

Appendixes

Preface

My research focuses on defendants sentenced in the New Haven, Connecticut, felony court. As described in chapter 2 and appendix 1, I first gathered case information for a "wide sample" of all the women's cases ($N=189$) and a random sample of men's cases ($N=208$) disposed of by conviction during a five-year period (1981–86). With the wide sample, I conducted a traditional disparity study, using multiple regression analyses, to determine whether there were statistically significant "sex effects" in sentencing. Also, with the wide sample, I gained an appreciation of the types of cases disposed, the racial and ethnic composition of defendants, proportions incarcerated pending trial, and other dimensions of cases. That information was essential in devising a means of selecting a smaller set of cases for closer analysis. Using a strict decision protocol and not knowing the sentencing outcome, I selected forty pairs of men and women who were accused and convicted of the same (or nearly the same) statutory offenses. I call this set of eighty cases the deep sample. It contains an assortment of all the major crime types: interpersonal violence (including homicide and aggravated assault), robbery, larceny, and drug offenses. In selecting the deep-sample pairs, I used the traditional sociolegal notion of "equal treatment." I wanted to compare the crimes and punishments of men and women whose offenses were statutorily alike. Kate and Casey, whose crimes and punishments open chapter 1, are one of the forty matched pairs.

For the deep-sample cases, I obtained two documents: the presentence investigation (PSI) report and transcripts of the remarks made in court on the day of sentencing. The PSI is a document prepared by a probation officer to guide the judge at sentencing: it describes the offense, how victims and defendants describe what happened in the incident, the defendant's previous record of arrests and convictions, and the defendant's social history. With the PSI, and at times, supplemented by the sentencing remarks, I constructed a biography of each defendant and a narrative for each crime. From the transcripts of the sentence remarks, which varied in length and detail depending on the sentencing itself, I was interested in discovering what theories of punishment judges used in justifying punishment and whether they were gender-based. In distilling and interpreting the materials, I have taken care to probe how gender constructions vary by race and class.

In chapter 1, I lay out my research questions: Do statistical studies mismeasure justice? Should punishment policy be gender-neutral or not? Chapter 2 sketches the context of the felony court's work and routines; it describes the wide sample of cases, compares features of the wide sample with the deep sample, and highlights the results of the statistical disparity study. One problem with studies of punishment is that insufficient attention is given to the circumstances and histories that bring defendants to court. Thus, part 2 (chapters 3 and 4) analyzes women's and men's pathways to court, linking biography to theories of lawbreaking and to constructions of defendants' blameworthiness. In part 3 (chapters 5 through 8), the matched pairs of men and women are examined in detail: I want to determine whether men and women, accused and convicted of statutorily similar offenses, committed crimes of similar seriousness. These chapters reveal the limits of quantification, the strengths of narrative in understanding crime "seriousness," and the subjective nature of seriousness judgments. In part 4 (chapters 9 and 10), I turn to the sentencing remarks to see whether judges used different theories of punishment when justifying punishment of men and women in court. In these chapters, I explore gender-based patterns in defendant-judge interactions and in judges' assessments of the defendant's character and potential for reform. In part 5, I present an alternative way of measuring sentence outcomes and consider the implications raised by my study. Chapter 11 opens by considering the meanings of different, disparate, and discriminatory treatment. I then describe a method of comparing sentences for the matched pairs and apply it. The results may surprise readers, as they did me. I find that for only one of the forty matched pairs was there a sentencing disparity I could not explain satisfactorily. The results of my pair-wise analysis stand at odds with the regression analysis, which shows a greater "gender gap" in sentencing. In chapter 12, I highlight major findings, expand on my measure of justice, and consider the policy questions raised.

Several appendixes document the cases in detail so that readers can make their own judgments. Some will see different elements that I overlooked in the cases; some may disagree with my determinations of the "seriousness" of men's and women's offenses, with the theories of punishment that judges invoke, and with the outcome of my pair-wise analysis of disparity. Should that occur, I shall be pleased. It will mean that discussion will take place within the scholarly ranks and by wider publics about the qualities and meanings of justice.

Acknowledgments

The Russell Sage Foundation provided funds for court transcripts and research assistance, and interest in my study early on by Alida Brill, Marshall Robinson, and Peter de Janosi was critical to getting it off the ground in 1985. A junior faculty fellowship from Yale University provided a year's leave from teaching in 1986–87. Rebecca Bordt and Molly Chaudhuri worked with me in the New Haven clerk's office in the summer of 1986, and Bordt continued to collaborate with me on the project over the next several years. I am reminded of their care and diligence whenever I examine my case files, see their distinctive handwriting, and read their research memos.

My access to the New Haven felony court was facilitated by Jack Dziekan, clerk for the court, who introduced me to Judge Frank Kinney, the presiding judge. When I first interviewed Judge Kinney in the summer of 1985, he was curious and interested. Most important, he was open to having the court studied. His sudden death a year later was a loss both to the Connecticut judiciary and to the sociolegal research community. Had it not been for Daniel Freed, a professor at the Yale Law School who ran a "Sentencing Principles" seminar, which Judge Kinney participated in, and Miriam Berkman, a member of the law school's clinical faculty, who documented the judge's responses in the seminar, there would be no detailed record of the judge's sentencing philosophy. I am indebted to Freed more generally for his thoughts on the project in its formative stages. My thanks go also to my colleagues in the sociology department at Yale, Albert J. Reiss and Kim Blankenship, for their expertise and support at various stages of the research.

Connecticut officials facilitated my gathering documents and data, and the project would not have been possible without their assistance. I appreciate the guidance and goodwill of Judge Francis Hennessy and the cooperation of Terry Capshaw, Leonard Russman, and William Pesanelli. In early and subsequent phases of the research, I benefited from conversations and interviews with New Haven prosecutors, defense attorneys, probation officers, and police officers. They include Judy Aub, Patrick Clifford, Betsy Cronin, Minna Dew, Leonard Gallo, Captain Gill, Susan Hankins, Susan Hathaway, the late Arnold Markel, Robert O'Brien, Thomas Pleckatis, Mary Tarca, and Thomas Ullman. The skill of Rose Lillo, who transcribed the notes of court reporters who were no longer working in the area, was impressive. I owe a special debt to Howard Gemeiner, a defense attorney who has worked in the court for twenty years, for reading the manuscript and for our many spirited discussions about the philosophy and psychology of sentencing.

A grant from the Rockefeller Foundation's Gender Roles Research Program, awarded in 1988, supplied me with funds for research assistance and leave from teaching. I was delighted with the Foundation's decision to have the Gender Roles Program studies compiled and some researchers videotaped by Suzanne Donovan and Valerie Gwinner of Communications Development Incorporated. Gwinner helped me to see my study's story line in preparing me for the taped interview.

A turning point in writing the manuscript was Marie-Andrée Bertrand's suggestion that I present a portion of the research at the International Conference on Women, Penal Law, and Social Control. The conference, funded in part by a grant I received from the National Science Foundation, was held in Québec in July of 1991. Laura Fishman and Christine Alder, who were discussants of my paper on women's pathways to court, provided useful criticisms, as did other conference participants who pushed me to rethink my terminology in characterizing women defendants' lives and lawbreaking. My conference coorganizers, Marie-Andrée Bertrand and Dorie Klein, have been central to me in developing a feminist analysis of crime and justice. Others who have deeply influenced my thinking and helped me over the years are Maureen Cain, Meda Chesney-Lind, Dorothy Chunn, Mary Eaton, Karlene Faith, Martha Fineman, Desirée Hansson, Frances Heidensohn, Merry Morash, Nicole Rafter, Carol Smart, and Betsy Stanko.

The summer of 1992 saw the completion of three-fourths of the manuscript and my moving from New Haven to Ann Arbor, where I began working at the University of Michigan. When circulating chapters to readers, I was richly rewarded with the comments and criticisms of a diverse group. My deepest appreciation is to David Baldus and Lisa Maher, whose queries and challenges to my thinking reflected many hours of work and sacrifice on their part. Their sharply different areas of expertise are, in some measure, what I tried to join in this book.

Baldus, a law professor, is a key figure in research on racial discrimination and the death penalty and an expert on statistical proofs of discrimination. Throughout the writing of the manuscript and today, he has given unstintingly of his critical intelligence and support. Maher, a sociologist, is writing her dissertation on drug-using, criminalized women in New York City; she draws from feminist and poststructuralist perspectives. Her careful reading of the manuscript, coupled with our continuing discussions of theory and research on gender, crime, and justice, have been invaluable and inspirational.

Other readers were instrumental in revising the manuscript. They are John Braithwaite, who prodded me to rethink the conclusion; Elizabeth Rapaport, who pushed me to address policy questions; and Lise Vogel, who provided key editorial and conceptual comments. Additional readers noted problems or asked questions, which helped to clarify my analysis. They are Shari Diamond, Roseann Greenspan, Tracy Huling, Richard Lempert, Myrna Raeder, Andrew von Hirsch, and Norma Wikler.

Students at Yale and Michigan helped me on the project. At Yale they were Rikki Abzug, Amanda Fischman, Paul Galatowitsch, Matthew Maly, and Lori Nordstrom. Ann Fitzpatrick, also at Yale, transcribed interview material with dispatch and always with great humor. At Michigan, when the manuscript was nearing completion, Valerie Wilde checked the references and Rebecca Kidder checked and gathered some last-minute source material.

I am grateful to Gladys Topkis of Yale University Press, who at an early stage in the research believed there was something worth publishing, and to Lorraine Alexson for her copyediting care and especially for querying the specialized argots of the street, the courthouse, and the social sciences.

Aida Rodriguez, a dear friend since graduate school days, has been a long-standing source of sound advice and support. Friends in Ann Arbor, New Haven, and elsewhere — Gregg Barak, Piers Beirne, Lynne Huffer, Carla Kaplan, Charlotte Pagni, Tony Platt, Robert Rosen, Vicki Shultz, and Sylvia Tesh — have been great comrades through high and low moments. My mother and female kin, Claire, Ellen, and Fran, kept me honest by reminding me of the chimerical qualities of academic life.

Finally, to the men and women defendants whose lives and lawbreaking are described here, I hope to have rendered some justice to their experiences in New Haven's "big house."

I The Problem

1 Crime, Punishment, and the Mismeasure of Justice

Compare the following two cases:

Time: February 1986, around 9 P.M.

Place: A prostitution stroll in New Haven

Crime: Kate, a white woman in her midthirties, waved down a man who was driving along the street. After exchanging a few words, another woman approached the car. Kate went to the driver's side, opened the car door, and pulled the man out. Her female accomplice put a knife to the man's back. Both women demanded his wallet and car keys. A police officer on patrol saw the three people, and recognizing Kate, stopped. As the officer approached, Kate told the victim she had a gun and put her hands in her pockets to show she had a gun. The two woman fled, the officer chased them, catching only Kate and arresting her.

Kate reported that the man had approached her seeking sex and that this affront had made her and her friend angry. The victim, described as an Arab man, said he had stopped his car because he thought Kate needed help.

Charge and prior record: Arraigned in felony court for first-degree robbery; three months later, Kate pled guilty to first-degree robbery. She had more than a dozen previous convictions and has been in and out of prison since she was twenty years old.

Punishment: Sentenced to serve two years' incarceration[1]

Time: February 1986, just after midnight

Place: An all-night convenience store in a poor New Haven neighborhood

Crime: Casey, a black man in his midtwenties, entered the store and asked the clerk, a black woman in her early twenties, for an item. When she turned around, Casey hit her on the back of the head with a blunt instrument. She was knocked to the floor. When she came to, she saw Casey at the cash register and screamed. Casey took about $55. Another female employee heard the clerk's scream, saw the intruder, and called the police. The victim was taken to the hospital and treated for neck and ear injuries. The other employee recognized Casey as being from the area and identified him from a photo.

Charge and prior record: Arraigned in felony court for first-degree robbery; three months later, Casey pled guilty to first-degree robbery. He had more than a dozen previous convictions and has been in and out of prison since his late teens.

Punishment: Sentenced to serve ten years' incarceration

Was Casey's case that much more serious than Kate's to warrant eight years more of incarceration? How do we know when punishment is too little or too much? When do we come to realize that it is disparate or unequal? These questions have long vexed philosophers, social scientists, jurists, and citizens, but there is not yet a method to assess justice. The reasons are twofold: measures of punishment are unsatisfactory, and the moral grounds of punishment are in dispute. Measurement problems arise because the detail and distinctiveness of individual cases seem to resist a uniform means of classification and quantification. Disputes about the moral basis of punishment center on why society punishes, which crimes are so much more serious than others as to warrant more punishment, and whether the same punishment for "like crimes" is desirable.[2] As social scientists confront the measurement problem and philosophers and legal scholars debate the moral issues, court officials make thousands of decisions every day about freedom, liberty, and safety.

Unlike other indicators of social and economic life, such as the unemployment rate or measures of market activity, we have no measure of justice system practices. There are measures of crime and rates of imprisonment, but the space in between is vague. The vacuum is filled by journalists' accounts, often sensationalized, that focus on dramatic and celebrated cases, crimes, trials, and death-penalty vigils. In addition, television and film supply sagas about victims and victimizers, justice officials, and innocent defendants.

In this book, I analyze cases prosecuted in the New Haven felony court to determine whether men and women prosecuted for like crimes are punished differently. That empirical determination is not in itself satisfactory, however. It must be joined with a consideration of *how* punishment practices are measured and *which* punishment principles are desirable. The approach I take combines the jurist's (as well as the citizen's and the media's) fascination with *cases* and the social scientist's depiction of *patterns of case disposition,* typically by aggregating and quantifying data. I examine cases that are routinely adjudicated in felony courts, not the celebrated cases or trials that are reported in the press or appellate reviews.

Mismeasures of Justice

Statistical studies of sentencing often show that women are treated more leniently than men (for recent reviews, see Daly and Bordt 1991; Odubekun 1992; Steffensmeier, Kramer, and Streifel 1993). Such studies challenge widely held beliefs about gender and racial discrimination, power, and punishment. On the one hand, statistical studies do not find frequent support for patterns of racial disparity favoring whites in noncapital sentencing (Hagan and Bumiller 1983; Kleck 1981). On the other hand, however, statistical studies more frequently find support for patterns of gender disparity favoring women.[3] One wonders why, in light of court defendants' stories of racism in the criminal justice system, statistical studies find little support for racial differences — and why, in light of women's subordinate status to men, studies suggest that women are favored.[4] Might these studies mismeasure justice?

A caricature of a disparity study reveals how social scientists have typically framed this form of research.[5] It begins by asking whether members of some subgroups (that is, black, young, and poor) are more likely than others to be convicted and to receive more severe punishments. Available data are sparse and incomplete: little is known about the offense, measures of the outcome or punishment are crude, and there is limited information on the defendant. Analyses are conducted in different ways, but the bottom line is to see whether there are statistically significant subgroup differences. If there are, the author concludes that disparity exists in the punishment process.[6] When there are no differences, as is frequent in research on racial differences in noncapital sentencing, the author concludes that disparity is apparently absent.[7]

In contrast to statistical studies, legal scholars and defendant advocates have focused on individual stories of disparity. Such stories or cases, which have typically centered on racial differences, were gathered from prisoners (for example, American Friends Service 1971) and by judges (for example, Frankel 1972), who may have been in a better position than social scientists to see and to document case-based disparity. Or perhaps, like journalists writing a good story, they felt less constrained by the methods of social science in documenting their claims. My sense is that it was the compelling stories of racial disparity that spawned the sentencing reform movement in the United States in the mid-1970s. The available evidence from social science research at the time had suggested little reason for change.

Neither individual stories nor statistical aggregates alone offer a meaningful measure of justice. In conducting statistical analyses of large data sets, social scientists elide moral and political questions about punishment. For example, by analyzing aggregates, social scientists do not wonder why Kate was sentenced to two years and Casey to ten years. The method does not permit a consideration of whether the crimes were sufficiently different to warrant a different response, whether the judges applied different theories of punishment in sentencing Kate and Casey, or whether the eight-year gap offends a sense of justice. Instead, moral questions are decided with reference to statistically significant differences in punishments for selected subgroups after controlling for variables such as offense severity and the defendant's prior record.

I have conducted statistical studies like these for more than a decade: if I am critical, it is because I know this method and its limits well.[8] At the same time, I am critical of the ways in which journalists and legal advocates draw from selected or celebrated cases to illustrate disparity. A good example can be seen in the American Friends Service's *Struggle for Justice* (1971, 126–28), where a table displays cases that illustrate "discretion in sentencing." No information is provided on how the cases were selected nor on how typical they were. Instead, the method is to find the most egregious cases (or, depending on one's aim, the least egregious) and to compare them. It is a deductive method whereby a conclusion is reached and then proved with selected examples. Case analyses have much to add, however; they bring depth and complexity to the meaning of crime and punishment. The problem is not, then, case analyses per se, but how particular cases are selected for analysis.

Gender and Statistical Mismeasures

If the traditional disparity analysis is limited by how crime and punishment are quantified, it is even more limited in assessing gender and punishment. The reason is that statistical protocols and theories have been derived from samples of men. Women defendants, or the "sex variable," have been inserted in analyses without considering how gender relations shape variability in lawbreaking — the perceived "seriousness" of current offenses and previous lawbreaking — or variability in such markers of conventionality as family, work, and community ties. Most disparity studies adopt an add-women-and-stir posture. In this posture, relations of gender and sexuality — their modes of domination, negotiation and resistance, and bases of inequality — are not in the frame. Also neglected is how constructs of masculinity and femininity shape what people think of themselves, how they act, and how they make sense of the behavior of others. With the add-women-and-stir stance, a researcher posits gender as if it were the same relation as class or race or age: women are merely added to the analysis as nongendered beings, or as if they were men.[9]

As a consequence, the variables used in statistical studies may not be sufficiently sensitive to gender difference. Thus, while authors claim to be holding constant such selected variables as the legal severity or type of offense charged, it is not certain that the quality of men's and women's lawbreaking is in fact being held constant. If measures of current and previous lawbreaking are not adequately controlled for, we may find a sex effect, but not know how to interpret it.

The cases of Casey and Kate show the limits of quantification. From the information available in the files of the clerk of the court, their cases could have been coded identically for a statistical analysis. They were both accused and convicted of robbery at the same level of statutory severity; they both had a prior record of a similar level of seriousness; they were both incarcerated in the pretrial period; and both were represented by public defenders. Except for race and gender, then, the two cases would appear to be the same. Few data sets contain any more detail on an offense or offender. Upon gathering additional information on these cases, I learned that Kate's robbery differed from Casey's in the following ways: Although both victimized persons they did not know, Kate's victim was not injured; Kate's accomplice, not Kate, brandished the knife; and while Kate's story and the victim's conflict, it is likely he was looking for a prostitute and thus was not viewed as a completely innocent victim. At sentencing, for example, the prosecutor described the victim's presence in the area as "perhaps somewhat suspect." By contrast, the female victim in Casey's offense suffered both physical and psychological damage, saying that she was "afraid to go back to work. I can't go anywhere near [the] store; I get physically ill." Although Kate's previous record of convictions was substantial, almost all of them were misdemeanors and prostitution-related. Casey's record, on the other hand, was composed of more serious offenses, such as robbery and assault.

The content and context of an offense, its perceived seriousness to victims and court officials, and the relation of a defendant's prior record to the current offense are not well captured by quantification. Indeed, the narrative detail resists capture and codification according to a uniform scheme.

Let me push the problem of quantification a step further. Imagine we had a better data set to analyze gender and punishment for robbery, one having variables for victim injury, victim character, and detail on prior record. If, after controlling for variability in men's and women's robberies with our new variables, we find that men are sentenced, on average, to six months more in jail, would that trouble us? The social statistician may reply, "It depends on whether the difference is statistically significant or not." Such a reply reveals the inability of the social scientist to make a moral or political judgment about group differences. Quantification thus fails us in two ways: measures of gender and punishment add women onto statistical protocols derived from studies of men, and the interpretation of group differences lacks a moral or political referent.

Compounding Mismeasures: Policy Problems
Merely adding women to disparity research has profound consequences for policy. If close to half of statistical studies suggests that women receive less severe sentences than men, holding constant a variety of case and other variables, then policymakers may try to close the gap by punishing women more harshly in the name of equality with men. The following passage by Alfred Blumstein and co-workers (1983) highlights these issues well: "If there is discrimination in sentence outcomes by sex (or by race or class), a range of "solutions" is available for eliminating discrimination. If the objective is to equalize sentences, one can shift the outcomes of the disadvantaged group to equal those of the advantaged group, or vice versa, or one can shift both groups to achieve some average of past sentencing practices" (p. 114). Before turning to the policy issues raised in this passage, I note how the authors use the terms *disadvantaged* and *advantaged*. The former term refers to those who are disadvantaged in the wider society and whose sentences are more severe. As I think Blumstein and his colleagues were aware, the assumption that disadvantaged groups in the wider society are also disadvantaged when standing accused of crime may hold for members of race and class groups, but not necessarily for gender.[10]

As Blumstein and colleagues suggest, any sentencing policy intended to close gaps is contingent on two prior elements: whether there is disparity and whether the aim is to equalize sentences before one can consider a range of solutions. Let us consider each.

Policy Issue 1: Is There Disparity?
As I have indicated, statistical evidence gives us reason to think that women may be treated more leniently than men at sentencing. But because statistical studies may mismeasure justice, we cannot be certain whether there is a disparity problem to correct. Thus, at the moment, we cannot be sure whether there is gender-based disparity.

Policy Issue 2: Is the Aim to Equalize Sentences?
Here we confront major theoretical and legal issues: foremost, whether policies should be gender-neutral or not. Feminist scholars argue that gender-neutral ("equality-based") policies ignore women's lives and force women to adopt a male standard (Fineman 1991), while gender-specific ("difference-based") policies can be used not only to provide

benefits to women but deny them (Vogel 1993, 154). The equality-difference debate has haunted women activists for more than a century. In the past decade, with an exuberant proliferation of publications and debates on the matter (for reviews and key works, see Bartlett and Kennedy 1991; Rhode 1989; Smart 1989; Vogel 1993), it is possible to characterize a somewhat settled feminist position: the equality-difference dichotomy is false and ought to be transcended. Precisely how such transcendence can be formulated in policy terms is less clear. A promising way to begin is by acknowledging that a general policy "toward women" (or gender difference) may not be feasible or desirable. Thus, gender-neutral rules may be more appropriate in one domain (such as the employment law) than another (for example, family law). How does this discussion bear on crime and punishment?

When institutions of criminal justice were established in the United States in the 1820s, they were based on a dual model of women's nature. As documented by Nicole Rafter (1982, 1990), reformatories and custodial prisons co-existed in the North and Midwest during the nineteenth century. The woman-as-misdemeanant, who could be "trained" to be domestic and less sexual, was a candidate for reformatory; the woman-as-bad (or as masculine), who was a threat and not reformable, required a strict penal regime (Rafter 1982, 243; see also Brenzel 1983; Freedman 1981).[11] The more pliable image of "woman's nature" came to dominate juvenile and criminal justice policy beginning in the first part of the twentieth century. Indeterminate sentencing had the effect of incarcerating women longer than men for certain offenses (Schlossman and Wallach 1978; see also Temin 1973). As Rafter (1990, p. xxx) suggests, the conditions of confinement for women, whether in reformatories or prisons, were "partial" in two senses of the word: apparently less harsh, and inadequate.

When considering a policy of "equalizing sentencing," we face several questions: should theories of punishment have a gender-specific component? and, should sentencing practices acknowledge the conditions surrounding women's incarceration? For theories of punishment, legal scholars have recognized that "equality of punishment" may not be just (for example, Hart 1968; Morris 1981), though their arguments invariably assume men as sentencing subjects. Under a utilitarian punishment logic,[12] sentencing practices are to reflect individual differences, not necessarily group-based differences. Yet individual qualities, which can mitigate penalties (such as "has steady employment," "has family ties," or "shows remorse"), may be present more in some groups than others. Let us consider how these issues bear on gender and sentencing.

In earlier research, I learned that court officials wanted to keep families together and not punish "innocent children." Their concern for protecting families spawned greater leniency toward those defendants I termed *familied* (that is, those caring for or supporting others) and especially toward familied women. In addition, probation officers said that women (familied or not) were more easily "scared straight" than men, meaning that some women were more impressed by the threat of jail (Daly 1987a, 1989a). Thus, for individual women who appeared more reformable or more easily deterred, court officials thought it unnecessary to punish them "the same" as men. For gender-linked *groups* of defendants (those caring for children, almost all of whom are women) court officials thought leniency may be deserved.

For conditions of confinement, group-based differences are raised but in a different way. If, as some suggest (such as Rafter 1990, 206), "The same prison sentence to a man and woman . . . condemns women to inferior treatment at the next stage in the criminal justice process," then prisons, largely sex-segregated institutions, need to be scrutinized. Although the subjective experiences of incarceration defy comparison, it is possible to compare the provision of drug or alcohol rehabilitation programs, education or training, medical and mental health services (Daly, Geballe, and Wheeler 1988; Leonard 1983; Resnik and Shaw 1980).[13]

The complexities entailed in "equalizing sentences" can be erased by proposing that punishment policy be based on retribution. Retributive (or desert-based) theory is not interested in individual- or group-based variation in potential for reform, being deterred, or caring for others. Rather it centers on punishing the crime, and in establishing punishment schemes that are proportional to the harm caused (von Hirsch 1985). Retribution-based policies are committed to "equal treatment" and uniformity in punishment. They are an important new ingredient in sentencing reform in the United States, and were proposed, in part, to reduce the appearance of racial disparity.[14] What concerns me, but what reformers may not have recognized, is that a policy of reducing racial- or class-based variability in sentencing men could increase the punishment for women.

Policy Issue 3: A Range of Solutions

Let us assume that retribution is the punishment theory and our policy objective is to equalize sentencing, how can that aim be achieved? Shall we treat women more like men? Shall we treat men more like women? Or do we split the difference? To date, sentencing schemes have embraced only two possibilities: punish women more like men (more severely) or find an average between them.[15]

In a split-the-difference approach, men's and women's average sentences are averaged together, and this new average is applied to both groups. California adopted this method in the mid-1970s, and one consequence was "to markedly increase the sentences for women, especially for violent offenses" (Blumstein et al. 1983, 114, 214–15). Split-the-difference and punishing women like men suggest that women will pay a high price in the name of uniformity and equality: they will be sentenced longer.[16] Why not, one wonders, use women as the standard? In general, men's lives and behavior are the standard in virtually all social contexts and at law. But for punishment practices, both men and women might be better off if women's lives, not men's, were the standard.[17]

Feminist Concerns about the Comparative Exercise

Leading feminist sociolegal scholars are skeptical of equal treatment studies, and for good reason: by comparing women to men, a male standard is left intact. For example, Maureen Cain (1990, 2) suggests that "equity studies do not enable us to pose the question whether or not even absolutely equal sentences might be unjust: too high or too low in themselves, or for behavior which should not . . . be subject to penalty." Carol Smart (1990, 79) argues that the "equality paradigm always reaffirms the centrality of men," as does Alison Young (1992, 42–43), who says that "women [are] measured in relation to the master-category, Man." I agree with these authors. Yet it is crucial to develop measures of justice for a variety of social sites, punishment being just one.

Feminist scholars should be well positioned to devise means of assessing punishment that do not assume that women are "Other" or that men are the master-category. Such an approach has been developed in analyzing jobs and wages. Scholars recognized that to close the gap in men's and women's wages, one had to focus on job segregation by sex, not just on comparisons of men's and women's wages for the same job. In developing a comparable worth approach to measuring pay disparities (see, for example, Blum 1991; Remick 1984), feminist researchers and policymakers developed an alternative method of making group comparisons. For justice system practices, however, it seems more difficult to make gender comparisons and to devise alternative measures. Why is this the case? One reason is that the character of the wage and prison "gaps" is markedly different. For punishment, we do not have the metaphor of "59 cents" that has defined and politicized pay disparities.

A Measure of Justice

It is crucial to devise a better means of assessing justice system practices. Policymakers may think that women are punished less than men for the "same crime" when this may not be the case. Efforts to close apparent gender gaps may lead to increasing numbers of women jailed, or jailed longer, for no other reason but numerical mismeasures of justice.

Quantification *or* case analysis alone will fail to supply an adequate measure of justice. Such a measure is possible, however, if we learn to oscillate between logico-scientific and narrative modes of reasoning. As elucidated by Laurel Richardson (1990), these modes are "irreducible to each other and complementary,"[18] each providing "a distinctive way of ordering experience and constructing reality":

> Each has its own operating principles and criteria of "well-formedness." . . . Causality plays a central role in both modes, but each defines it differently. The logico-scientific mode looks for universal truth conditions, whereas the narrative mode looks for particular connections between events. Explanation in the narrative mode is contextually embedded, whereas logico-scientific explanation is abstracted from special and temporal contexts. Both modes are "rational" ways of making meaning. (p. 118)[19]

Richardson suggests that narrative in social science should not be "used as human 'filler' to 'flesh out' statistical findings," but should be seen as "quintessential to the understanding and communication of the sociological."

The use of the word *narrative* in sociolegal studies has become popular, taking diverse forms and meanings for participants (Abrams 1991; Farber and Sherry 1993; *Michigan Law Review* 1989). I use the term in the spirit of justice system scholars such as Robert Emerson (1983), Keith Hawkins (1986), and Douglas Maynard (1982). These authors criticize logico-scientific reasoning for its flawed depictions of decision making. For example, Hawkins (1986, 1186) argues that the "rationalists presuppose and test a legal model of decisionmaking without knowing how 'factors' or 'criteria'. . . are connected with the outcome of decisions." He argues for naturalistic research, which entails a "lengthy and detailed exploration of the jungle" (p. 1242) of legal decision making. That approach contrasts with the rationalists' removal of "all the undergrowth, scrub, and saplings, leaving the broad landscape over which are dotted a number of large and important trees" (p. 1181).

Hawkins's and other scholars' pleas for better description, however well founded, do not embrace a normative stance toward the punishment process. Theirs is a descriptive exercise that calls for better and thicker description. Narrative reasoning researchers, like many judges, suggest an indeterminacy — an *impossibilism* — in judging the justice system.

Although sympathetic to narrative scholars' critiques, I am impatient with the descriptive exercise alone when consequential decisions are made daily about life and liberty. How shall we evaluate those decisions? Are they just? I would like to think it is possible to find a truce between those whose representations of the social world are numerical and logico-scientific and those whose representations take a more narrative form. Such a truce will assume some bilingualism in the strengths of statistics and storytelling in the creation of plausible truth claims. It will also take some faith by knowledge-producers in the possibility of oscillating between their familiar, or home pole, and another pole. I am proposing that a measure of justice can be found in that oscillation.

Notes

1. Kate's actual sentence was five years, suspended after two, followed by three years' probation. I report the sentences in a concise form; details are given in app. 6. *Jail* and *prison* are used interchangeably in the text to refer to any sentence involving incarceration. In the jurisdiction studied (Connecticut), the corrections system is unified as a single state system. Although the facilities for men may be called either jails or prisons, there is only one facility for women. Thus, the distinction has never applied to women in Connecticut.

2. The meaning of the term *like crimes* is explored in part 3, while the terms *differently* and *disparity* are considered in chap. 11.

3. Gary Kleck (1981) found that 9% of studies showed race effects favoring whites in noncapital sentencing. My review of the gender and sentencing literature (Daly and Bordt 1991) — using the same criteria as Kleck (1981) — found that 45% of the studies showed sex effects favoring women. It should be stressed that studies of sentencing find that the strongest predictions of outcomes are type or severity of the offense and the defendant's prior record. Compared to these variables, the defendant's race or gender contributes a relatively smaller share of explained variation (see Steffensmeier, Kramer, and Streifel's discussion on this point). Nonetheless, if subgroup differences in sentencing outcomes are significantly different (in a statistical sense), there is reason to pursue the findings further.

4. The first statistical study in the United States to compare the sentencing of men and women by race groups was published in 1984 (Gruhl, Welch, and Spohn); the few quantitative studies since then include Cassia Spohn, Susan Welch, and John Gruhl (1985), Daly (1989b), and Gayle Bickle and Ruth Peterson (1991). Candace Kruttschnitt (1980–81, 1982a, 1982b) and Mann (1984) analyzed racial differences in the response to women. Except for some conflicting results (Kruttschnitt 1980–81, 1982a), none of these studies shows significant racial variation in the sentencing of women (see Daly 1989b). From the few studies available, it appears that the gender gap may be widest for black defendants.

5. My caricature is not intended to take away from the many fine studies on sentencing, especially those conducted in the past decade. The Blumstein et al. (1983) two-volume series represented a turning point in the methodological and theoretical sophistication in this area.

6. In social science research up to the 1980s, authors used the term *discrimination* whenever statistically significant subgroup differences were found. As dis-

cussed in chap. 11, the terms *disparity* and *discrimination* have often been used loosely (see also Hagan 1977 on this point). I use the more encompassing term, *disparity,* which includes outcomes that may or may not be discriminatory. Precision in defining when a disparity is a discrimination is not possible because punishment theories, policies, and criteria vary. Moreover, precision may be misplaced in light of the political nature of punishment.

7. See reviews by John Hagan (1974), Hagan and Kristin Bumiller (1983), Kleck (1981), and William Wilbanks (1987). Racial disparity in capital punishment has been documented for the South up to 1960 (Kleck 1981). Imposition of the death penalty in the post–Furman era (Baldus, Woodworth, and Pulaski 1990) shows statistical effects based on the race of the victim: defendants convicted of killing whites were more likely to receive the death penalty than those killing blacks.

8. I should be clear on this point. Though I am critical of the data and measures used in many sentencing studies and am concerned with the overreliance researchers place on statistical significance to judge moral significance, I *am* interested in using the tools of statistical analysis in a measure of justice.

9. The same can be said for the relation of race to class in disparity research; the former is derived theoretically from the latter. Thus, subgroup comparisons may refer to relations of inequality, but they draw from vague notions of a defendants' abilities (or resources) to evade the weight of penal law or penal sanctions.

10. In 1991, women constituted 22% of arrests for the eight major "index" offenses and 11% of the index violent offenses (Flanagan and Maguire 1992, 442). (The index offenses are murder and nonnegligent manslaughter, aggravated assault, rape, robbery [which are the violent offenses], larceny, burglary, motor vehicle theft, and arson.) Women made up 13% of those convicted of felonies in state felony courts in 1988 (BJS 1990, 4). From a 1989 survey, they composed 9% of those in jail populations (ibid., 1992, 2); and in 1991, they constituted 5% of those in state prison populations (ibid., 1993). Historical studies of gender and criminal courts show variation in the female share of defendants and in punishment practices during the seventeenth through early twentieth centuries (Boritch 1992; Feeley and Little 1991; Zedner 1991).

11. Rafter (1982, 238) notes that the "reformatory style appears to have had little impact in the South . . . or in the West, which developed much of its women's prison system after the reformatory movement had passed."

12. Utilitarian theories of punishment are forward-looking and individualized: they seek to change the offender (rehabilitation), to deter the offender or others (special and general deterrence), to bring the offender back into conventional life (social reintegration), or to segregate the offender (incapacitation). Restitution may be utilitarian or nonutilitarian.

13. The more pressing need is not to build more prisons. Rather, most scholars and advocates call for alternatives to incarceration and for social and economic policies to improve schools, housing, neighborhoods, and job opportunities (see Chesney-Lind 1992).

14. Sentencing reform provisions vary widely across the United States. Some states have adopted desert-based or modified desert-based guidelines. Others have simply instituted determinate sentences.

15. Any guideline system that denies the relevance of gender-related criteria may have the effect of increasing punishment for women. Myrna Raeder (1993),

e.g., finds that the "gender-free world" of the federal sentencing guidelines and their interpretation by judges have eliminated women's care for others as a relevant consideration for departing from the guidelines. California used a split-the-difference approach, and the results are displayed in Blumstein et al. (1983, 215, table 4.7). The table shows that the average time *served* for women went from 22 to 35 months for assault and 27 to 30 months for robbery; it dropped from 20 to 16 months for second-degree burglary.

16. Although we know that sentencing reform has increased the rates of incarceration generally (Tonry 1987), we lack research on the impact of reforms for men and women separately, with some exceptions. A recent study by Barbara Meierhoefer (1992) finds that mandatory minimum terms for federal drug and firearm offenses had a greater effect on increasing incarceration for women than men and in widening the "race gap." The policing and punishment of drug offenses has been central to increasing the incarceration rates for women (Chesney-Lind 1992) and men in the United States.

17. My claim requires more discussion than I can give here. I am not suggesting that we replace a male standard with a female standard in law. Indeed, as I suggest in chap. 11, it is not clear what the male standard is in the penal context; there are several. I *am* suggesting that one way to rethink the aims and purposes of punishment is to put women, not men, in the hypothetical position of lawbreaker. For example, when imagining the circumstances leading to homicide, do sentencing reformers imagine women in relationships with violent men? In many respects, the legal categories themselves (robbery, assault, and manslaughter) need to be changed to be more descriptive of offense conduct and harm and their contexts.

18. Richardson notes, of course, that "both modes are framed in metanarratives such as 'science'. . . or 'religion.' [Thus] narrative structures are pre-operative, regardless of whether one is writing primarily in a 'narrative' or a 'logico-scientific' code" (p. 119).

19. This contrast puts each side into relief, but it may not be clear which reasoning prevails in some sociological studies. For example, what are termed qualitative methods in the social sciences draw on interviews, observations, and documentary material, but the gathering and ordering of that material may be arranged in a logico-scientific frame. Although both modes are present in the social sciences, law and legal reasoning are primarily in the narrative mode.

2 Felony Court Contexts and Statistical Outcomes

Profile of a Postmodel City

Malcolm Feeley (1979) described New Haven in the late 1970s as representing "neither the worst nor the best of American urban centers." Although he noted many problems then confronting the city — including a declining tax base, poor schools, and a growing population of unemployed minority-group residents — he also noted that the city had a civic-minded cadre of residents working to counter these problems (pp. 37–38). In setting the context for my research a decade later, I would say that the city's economic condition has not improved and that political disillusionment, and not optimism, better characterizes the 1980s.[1]

Economic and Social Indicators[2]

Three large areas of poverty exist in New Haven. In relation to the city center, they lie northeast (Dixwell-Newhallville), east (Farnham-River Street), and southwest (the Hill). Rates of joblessness are higher, and the rates of students completing high school are lower than in other parts of the city. Using the federal government's definition of poverty, the numbers of poor people increased in New Haven from 17.2 percent in 1970 to 23.2 percent in 1979. By 1990, the rate stood at 22 percent.

Those who lived in New Haven during the 1950s and 1960s say the city was different then. The postwar manufacturing boom, together with a visionary mayor (Richard C. Lee) and federal funds for this "model city," made for a sense of urban vitality. By the 1980s, according to the city's Special Commission on Poverty (1983, 37), poverty in New Haven had become "a fundamental and . . . intractable problem."

New Haven's population increased during the 1980s — from about 126,000 in 1980 to 130,500 in 1990 — but overall has declined from its peak of 164,000 in 1950. During the 1980s, the black share of the population increased from 32 to 36 percent, as did the Spanish-speaking share (8–13 percent). In 1990, the median family income was about $31,000, and that in surrounding towns was $54,000.

Crime Statistics

For some time scholars have discussed problems with official crime data gathered by the Federal Bureau of Investigation in its Uniform Crime Reports (UCR) (Black 1970; Kitsuse and Cicourel 1963; Mc-Cleary, Nienstedt, and Erven 1982; Seidman and Couzens 1974). Yet UCR data constitute the only available source for comparing the crime rates of cities. Using data for 1970, Feeley (1979, 38–39) found that the rate of crime reported to police was higher for New Haven than for other cities of its size. UCR data for 1980 show the same pattern. In that year, the number of index offenses — murder and nonnegligent manslaughter, aggravated assault, rape, robbery, larceny, burglary, motor vehicle theft, and arson — reported to the police was about 17,800; of these offenses, 11 percent were for violent offenses. In the same year, cities with a similar number of reported index offenses had populations 30 percent greater than New Haven's.[3] Although crime rates have been higher in New Haven than in other cities of its size, the relation between crime rates and punishment practices is highly mediated by political linkages and courthouse cultures in the various jurisdictions (Scheingold 1991). One indication is that incarceration rates in 1987 for those sentenced to more than a year were, on average, much lower in Connecticut than nationally and somewhat lower than in other northeastern states (Bureau of Justice Statistics 1989).[4]

Finnegan's New Haven

Journalist William Finnegan (1990) wrote a two-part series about the day-to-day life of New Haven's poor residents, which appeared in the *New Yorker*. Finnegan spent time with fifteen-year-old "Terry" and his family. He learned how Terry spent the thousands of dollars he made dealing drugs, how he evaded arrest, and his efforts to find legitimate employment when the drug scene was hot. Later, I learned from Terry's probation officer that he was "ordinary," like many other young men she has supervised in the past decade.

Finnegan's attention to detail — to the type of clothes and jewelry worn, the dialect used, and the ambience of the city and downtown shopping mall — was brilliant, as was his deftness in describing the world of a dispossessed young black male. As a lay reader, I appreciated his ability to capture the nuances of the city and the meaning of Terry's drug dealing in a biographical and social context. As a sociologist, I was troubled by the implications of Finnegan's journalistic method. As a compelling story of just *one* male adolescent, his family and friends, it could easily be transformed into a generalization. After reading Finnegan's work, my desire to analyze the stories of court cases with a broader knowledge of statistical variation became more pressing.

The New Haven Felony Court

In the spring of 1971 New Haven was at the center of a major political trial. After nearly two years of pretrial maneuvers, Black Panther members Bobby Seale and Erika Huggins were tried for conspiracy to kill another Panther member (see Freed 1973). While the trial was under way in the old courthouse on Elm Street, a new building was under construction a block away on Church Street (Brown 1976, 114).

The new courthouse is the site of my research. It is locally termed the JD court (for judicial district) and is distinguished from the "GA-6" court (for Sixth Geographical Area).[5] The JD court handles only the most serious cases, those arraigned as the most serious felonies (that is, class A or B; see appendix 1, table A-I.1). The newer courthouse also handles civil and family cases.

Maureen Mileski's (1971) and Malcolm Feeley's (1979) studies were of the GA-6 court's practices. The bustle and confusion they documented in the 1970s are still evident today. Just two changes are apparent: all defendants are now represented by attorneys, and sentencing has changed for those arrested after 1 July 1981 to "flat" (or definite) sentencing rather than sentences with minimum and maximum terms.

Compared to the worn-down conditions and noisy atmosphere of GA-6, JD courtrooms are modern and well appointed, with a church-like atmosphere. Felony court business moves far more slowly and with more decorum than in GA-6. During the years of my study (1981–86), the annual number of cases disposed of by conviction was about 420. A decade earlier, the annual number of GA-6 cases disposed was more than 6,500. For 1972, Milton Heumann (1978, 34) estimated that 2 percent of GA-6 cases were bound over to the felony court. My data suggest the same proportion during the 1980s: JD felony cases were 2–3 percent of criminal cases disposed annually.

Court Routines and the Presiding Judge
The Judge

From 1978, when he was appointed to the superior court and acted as an assistant administrative judge, to his death in September 1986, Judge Frank J. Kinney was the central actor of the New Haven court system.[6] In January 1983, when he began serving as the presiding judge for the JD court, there were more than 850 pending cases on the docket, more than 300 of which were more than a year old. Less than two years later, there were about 200 pending cases, 22 of which were more than a year old (Berkman 1986, 6). In Miriam Berkman's study and from my interviews with Judge Kinney, the pride he took in reducing the backlogged cases was obvious. How did he do it?

He was experienced and shrewd as an administrator and a lawyer.[7] Having been a defense attorney and a juvenile and adult court prosecutor, he had a good grasp of New Haven's courthouse culture. His observations of sentencing practices, modified by his beliefs, shaped his "prices" (or "going rates") for crime (ibid., 19). Although some members of the defense bar viewed him as a law-and-order judge, Kinney was widely regarded as bright, hardworking, and fair. He kept a notebook of all open cases, recording what happened as the case moved from arraignment to trial or plea and to sentencing. He studied the numbers in his notebook and on any day knew how many cases were pending and at what stage they were in the pretrial process (ibid., 6). He acted quickly and firmly on the bench and in chambers; he was impatient with ill-prepared or inexperienced attorneys.

Plea Bargaining

As presiding judge, Judge Kinney understood his job to be that of an active mediator: to negotiate pleas with counsel and propose sentencing prices. During the research period, the proportion of cases going to trial was 8 and 3 percent, respectively, for men and women. Of cases disposed by guilty plea or trial conviction, 95 and 98 percent of men and women, respectively, pled guilty. About half of the guilty pleas were taken by Judge Kinney. He established a time frame within which bargaining was to occur; failing agreement by counsel or the defendant's willingness to plead guilty, the case was assigned to the trial list, and to one of four other judges. Although the case would be assigned to the trial list, a negotiated plea with another judge typically ensued.[8]

Judge Kinney's schedule for hearing counsel in court and chambers followed the following sequence. After arraignment, the case was scheduled for a "two o'clock pretrial" for pretrial motions. Several such sessions might occur before the case was placed on a list for a 9:30 A.M. session. By then at least two months would have elapsed, a trial prosecutor would have been assigned, and counsel was more willing to bargain. At the 9:30 sessions, normally scheduled for Monday mornings in chambers, Judge Kinney would listen to the counsel for each side discuss the case. He would point out the state's evidentiary weaknesses or the inconsistencies of the defendant's alibi. These discussions occurred with other attorneys present; they had the effect of socializing prosecutors and defense attorneys to Judge Kinney's evidentiary and sentencing concerns. His open approach to what is known as sentence bargaining not only conveyed information about his going rates but also revealed a fair system, one without apparent favoritism.

Features of the Plea Process

There were two features to plea bargaining that encouraged defendants to plead guilty and helped defense attorneys to manage the plea process. One was the use of the Alford plea. Under the Alford doctrine,[9] a defendant does not admit guilt but admits that the state has sufficient evidence to find him or her guilty, should the case go to trial. During the research period, about 40 percent of women and men entered Alford pleas. This plea is not confined to the New Haven courthouse; it is used throughout Connecticut. When Kinney began as presiding judge, the Alford plea was being used with increasing frequency.[10] A second feature was how Judge Kinney decided sentences: he set sentences low enough so they would be accepted; he imposed them consistently and would not change his price once his offer had been made. In a Yale Law School seminar, Judge Kinney said his policy was "to grant an approximate one-third discount to defendants who pled guilty" (Berkman 1986, 23). This discount was based on what he thought the defendant would receive if found guilty at trial.[11]

Judicial Philosophy

Judge Kinney's punishment goals were to sentence in accordance with retributive principles and to bring order and efficiency to the process. Berkman (1986, 18) notes that unlike six other judges observed at the Yale Law School seminar, "Judge Kinney . . . maintained that the first step in considering a sentence was to evaluate the *offense alone,* unconnected to any information about the offender" (emphasis in original). She found that Judge Kinney put cases in rough crime categories, based on injury, violence, and the role of the victim. Once he assessed the gravity of the offense, he looked at the defendant's prior record. After that, he might consider whether the defendant was leading a "street life" or not (ibid., 30–36).

Connecticut Felony Courts, 1970s and 1980s

In comparing the New Haven felony court in the 1980s with Heumann's (1978) study of Connecticut plea bargaining in the early 1970s, I find certain differences. Unlike most judges Heumann interviewed, Judge Kinney imposed his conception of the right punishment into the plea bargaining process, he took a more active role in socializing new attorneys, and he placed an even greater priority on moving cases through the legal channels in a timely fashion ("moving the business") and on efficiency in court dispositions. The form and result of plea bargaining were the same, however. The form was sentencing bargaining — understood as the right way to dispose most cases. Factual guilt was rarely at issue and trial rates were low.

Presentence Investigation and Sentencing

For New Haven felony court business, the roles of probation officers are to attend revocation hearings, supervise probationers, and prepare presentence investigation reports (PSI's).[12] A PSI is a confidential document in Connecticut; normally of three to four single-spaced pages, its summary of the defendant's crime, prior record, and social history is intended to guide the judge in sentencing. In New Haven, PSI's are written after the defendant has entered a plea of guilty (or after having been found guilty at trial) and before sentencing. The document is prepared during the month before the date of sentencing.

Today, scholars view the PSI as an anachronism from the days when rehabilitative theories of punishment were in vogue (Rosecrance 1988). In some states today, the content of the PSI is thin because there is not sufficient staff to collect information and write reports. In New Haven the reports are detailed and informative. Yet because most PSI's are written *after* a sentence bargain has been struck, PSI information about the offense and the defendant's social history will not affect the sentencing decision in most cases. From time to time, a probation officer can paint a sympathetic picture of a defendant in the PSI, especially of a defendant's efforts to change during the pretrial period. This factor can move the judge to reduce the length of an incarceration sentence.[13]

The sentencing ceremony normally lasts ten to fifteen minutes. The prosecutor describes the offense, the defendant's role in it and the victim's reaction (if any), and offers a sentencing recommendation, noting its history or reason. The defense attorney then speaks, acknowledging the defendant's role in the offense, while bringing to light mitigating circumstances about the offense, the defendant's remorse, or indications of improvement in the pretrial period. In their remarks, the prosecutor and defense attorney make reference to the PSI, underscoring points or challenging phrases or interpretations. The judge then asks if the defendant wishes to speak. Upon advice of counsel, defendants typically do not speak. Then, before imposing the sentence, the judge talks about the crime and the rationale for punishment. Heumann (1978, 45) suggests that these sentencings are "a bit of charade [sic]," since court actors "know that [their advocacy or comments are] merely a formal routine." Further, he points out that judges' justifications are "absent . . . or kept to a minimum." As shown in part 4, the sentencing ceremonies in the 1980s show somewhat more drama and justification, even if Heumann's points are well taken.

A Consistent Court?

I have sketched a courthouse that was apparently ruled by one man, and in many respects it was. Judge Kinney's philosophical, legal, and managerial approach to the criminal process defined the court's routines. In half of the cases disposed, he was responsible for taking pleas and sentencing. Sixteen other judges handled cases during the research period. All were men, and all but one were white. Two (Milton Fishman and William Hadden) each disposed about 10 percent of the cases; three (Harold Mulvey, Flemming Norcott, James Higgins), about 5 percent of the cases each; the remaining judges were responsible for no more than 1–3 percent of the cases. Although these judges were independent, one attorney suggested to me that "Kinney's personality became a dominant force." My sense is that if ever a courthouse displayed consistency in sentencing, the New Haven courthouse during Kinney's tenure must have.

Research Design, Data and Documents, and Setbacks

Appendix 1 describes the stages of my fieldwork, methods of gathering data and documents, problems faced, and the limitations of my materials.

My research plan borrows from the Vera Institute of Justice study, *Felony Arrests* (1977), which presented a "wide sample" of cases that moved from the initial stages of prosecution to sentencing and focused on a smaller set of "deep-sample" cases to determine why complainants decided to dismiss charges and how court officials made decisions about prosecution, pleas, and sentencing. The Vera study analyzed case attrition; mine centers on sentencing outcomes. My wide sample is of all the women and a random sample of the men whose cases were disposed of by conviction during a five-year period (July 1981 through June 1986). I spent the summer of 1986 in the New Haven chief clerk's office, culling from the clerk's docket sheets all the relevant information on defendants and their cases. A wide-sample data set was created, the data were "cleaned" for errors, and analyzed.

In September 1986 Judge Kinney died of a heart attack; he was just 54. The impact of his death on family members, friends, and the legal establishment was great. My research was just under way, and it was my first setback. I would not be able to ask him why he sentenced apparently like cases differently or whether he held gender-based sentencing philosophies.

A crucial methodological step was to select the deep-sample cases. After considering several methods, I decided to select pairs of men and women whose charges at arraignment and conviction were the same.[14] I arrayed the cases first by the exact statutory charges for each major type of offense (such as homicide, assault, and robbery). I then devised the following selection-decision protocol: (1) Prior record (the defendant may have been on probation or parole at the time of the offense or been convicted previously in the New Haven felony court), (2) age, (3) race and ethnicity, and (4) pretrial release status. When male-female pairs had identical statutory charges, I then picked those having a prior record (or not). If the defendants had the same statutory offenses and prior record, I chose those closest in age, and so forth. Throughout the process of selecting cases, I did not know the sentence that a defendant received (see appendix 1, table A-I.3 for deep-sample details).

With the exception of one case that went to trial, all the defendants in the deep sample were convicted by a guilty plea. In New Haven, the trial tariff — or the amount of punishment for going to trial and being found guilty at trial — is great. Because more men than women go to trial, and hence, men's average sentences will be greater, I wanted to minimize this source of gender-based variation. My method of selecting the deep sample approximates how law and policy normally construe like cases. And yet, concurring with Donald Black (1979, 1989), I am skeptical of the relevance of legal categories: socially constructed notions of harm are likely to be more important.

After selecting the deep-sample cases in the summer of 1987, I began collecting two sets of documents: transcripts of the remarks made on sentencing day and the PSI report, which required overcoming more hurdles. In the spring of 1988, I prepared requests for transcripts from the court reporter's office and learned that for thirty of the eighty deep-sample cases, the notes of one stenographer, though technically available, could no longer be transcribed. Thus it was impossible to obtain transcriptions for a substantial number of cases. My research had moved to a stage where I had carried out other work with the initial eighty cases in mind. Fortunately, the remarks that could be transcribed are a good representation of the offenses and defendants adjudicated (see appendix 1, note 1).

In the summer of 1988 I began discussions with the Judicial Department about obtaining PSI's for my deep sample. These documents were essential for learning about the offense, the defendant's social history, and prior record; and they assumed even greater importance in the absence of a complete set of sentencing transcripts. Among the stipulations in my access to the PSI's, I was not permitted to photocopy them. Beginning in January 1989 and for the next three months, therefore, a research assistant and I worked in the probation department. We logged all the relevant information from the files for the deep-sample cases into portable computers.

In gathering data and documents for this project, I gained insight into the practices of the clerk's office and probation department, workers' concerns, and how records are kept. I interviewed many of the probation officers who had written the PSI's I was using, as well as several prosecutors and defense attorneys. The interview material helped me understand the court's work and to interpret selected aspects of the documents.

Felony Court Statistics

In the context of the court's routines, let us examine the statistical data on cases and outcomes. Summary information on women's and men's cases in the wide and deep sample is given in table 2.1. Turning to the wide sample first,[15] the average age of defendants was mid- to late twenties; about 60 percent were black, 30 percent white; and 10 percent were latin. Most defendants were represented by public defenders. Half of the men and one-third of the women were incarcerated in the pretrial period. My measure of prior record — whether the accused had a previous conviction in the New Haven felony court or was on probation or parole at the time of release — underestimates the number of defendants with previous convictions, whether for misdemeanors or felonies in other jurisdictions. Although this variable suggests that 20–30 percent of defendants had prior records, the proportion is higher.[16]

Women and men were convicted for different types of offenses. Drugs and larceny featured more for women than for men (52 versus 31 percent), while interpersonal violence was more prevalent for men than for women (40 versus 31 percent), as was robbery (29 percent for men versus 17 percent for women). Men faced somewhat more severe charges than women, having been arraigned on more than one count. The conviction charges for men and women were similar: most were convicted of one count, with an average potential incarceration time of 170–190 months. These data translate to convictions largely for B, C, and unclassified felonies (see appendix 1, table A-I.1). Half of the convictions were secured by a straight guilty plea, while about 40 percent were pled under the Alford doctrine. Very small proportions pled nolo contendre or were found guilty at trial.

More wide-sample men than women (73 versus 45 percent) were sentenced to serve time; for those incarcerated, men's time was longer than women's (fifty-five months versus thirty-three months).[17] Most defendants received probation, whether following incarceration (a "split sentence") or as part of a suspended sentence. Few received fines. Judge Kinney disposed of about half of the cases (and a somewhat higher share of women's than men's cases), while Judges Hadden, Fishman, and Mulvey were responsible for 7–13 percent each.

How Does the New Haven Court Compare with Other Courts?

When a single-court study is conducted, a question arises about whether one can generalize from it to other courts. I draw from reports on court processing to compare data on how convictions are secured,[18] the demographic composition of defendants, gender and race distributions in types of offenses prosecuted, types of sentences imposed, and the length of incarceration by offense.[19] New Haven is on the high side of convictions secured by a guilty plea (97 percent) rather than trial compared to national estimates (91–96 percent). Both in New Haven and nationally, women constitute about 10–15 percent of defendants. Compared to felonies prosecuted nationally, New Haven men and women were more likely to be convicted of robbery and assault; New Haven women were more likely to be convicted of homicide and drug offenses than women in a national sample. The *female share* of defendants prosecuted in the New Haven court is similar to the national share (15–20 percent for drugs and larceny and 5–10 percent for violent offenses). The *black share* of defendants prosecuted, however, is higher in New Haven (56 percent) than nationally (40 percent). New Haven women and men were less likely to be incarcerated for aggravated assault, larceny, and drug offenses compared to defendants nationally; for those incarcerated, sentence lengths were lower in New Haven. The gender gap in the rate of incarceration and length of incarceration is generally wider in New Haven, although there is an offense-based variation.

In sum, the New Haven felony court has a higher composition of black defendants and a comparatively higher share of violent offenses prosecuted than do felony courts nationally. The court uses incarceration somewhat less often, and the length of incarceration is shorter. Although sentencing is generally less punitive in New Haven, gender differences (or gaps) are wider.

A Statistical Disparity Analysis

By using a multivariate analysis, gender and race differences (or gaps) in sentencing can be examined with greater technical accuracy. The initial size of the sentencing gap is substantial, as shown in table 2.2. Overall, the gender gap is 29 percentage points, and the black-white gap is 21 percentage points in measuring the likelihood of receiving an incarceration sentence. For defendants incarcerated, the time sentenced was 13.3 months greater for men than women. For the racial-ethnic gap, however, whites were sentenced, on average, to longer terms than blacks were (2.9 months), while latins were sentenced 2.5 months longer than were whites.

Table 2.1 Summary Information for the Wide* and Deep Samples

	Women		Men	
	Wide (N = 163)	Deep (N = 40)	Wide (N = 154)	Deep (N = 40)
Age (yr)				
Median	28	25	25	27
Range	16–61	17–60	16–66	16–61
Race or Ethnicity				
Black	56%	58%	57%	65%
Latin	11	12	12	10
White	33	30	31	25
Attorney				
Public defender	69%	65%	70%	62%
Private	31	35	30	38
Pretrial Status				
Promise to appear	15%	4%	8%	8%
Out on bail	49	48	38	42
Incarcerated	36	48	54	50
Bail Amount				
Median**	$10 K	$10 K	$10 K	$10 K
Range	1–100 K	1–100 K	500–125 K	1–100 K
Prior Record				
On probation or parole or had previous New Haven felony convictions: yes	22%	20%	29%	23%
Conviction Offense				
Homicide	9%	10%	5%	10%
Assault	15	20	23	20
Risk of injury	2	7	5	7
Arson	5	5	7	5
Robbery	17	20	29	20
Drugs	38	20	22	20
Larceny	14	18	9	18
N of Counts, original charges				
One	43%	50%	28%	40%
Two	31	22	38	35
Three or more	26	28	34	25
Incarceration Time (mo), original charges				
Maximum potential time for charges at arraignment				
12–240	34%	35%	26%	30%
241–360	33	27	31	25
> 360	33	38	43	45
Mean (excludes trials)	393	464	442	446
N of Counts, convicted charges				
One	91%	83%	83%	93%
Two	9	17	15	7
Three	1	0	3	0
Severity				
Maximum potential incarceration time (mo) for charges at conviction				
3–12	7%	5%	6%	7%
13–60	10	15	13	13
61–239	43	27	30	27

(continued)

Table 2.1 (continued)

	Women		Men	
	Wide (N = 163)	Deep (N = 40)	Wide (N = 154)	Deep (N = 40)
240	33	48	40	48
> 240	7	5	11	5
Mean (excludes trials)	172	186	190	178
Form of Conviction				
Pled guilty, straight plea	55%	50%	52%	54%
Pled guilty, Alford plea	38	48	39	40
Pled nolo contendre	5	2	5	3
Found guilty at trial	2	0	4	3
Sentence: *In-Out*				
No time to serve	55%	48%	27%	37%
Time to serve	45	52	73	63
Sentence: *Time* (mo)				
None (suspended)	55%	48%	27%	37%
1–24	28	28	38	18
25–60	13	18	18	25
> 60	4	7	17	20
Mean (all cases)	15	18	40	36
Mean (only with jail)	33	35	55	58
Probation Imposed				
Yes	87%	88%	75%	70%
Probation Time (mo)				
Mean (only with probation)	39	38	38	40
Probation Conditions (of those receiving probation)				
Yes***	48%	54%	40%	39%
Fine Imposed				
Yes	7%	5%	3%	5%
Judge				
Kinney	53%	63%	46%	40%
Hadden	13	5	12	13
Fishman	9	13	10	13
Mulvey	7	0	6	0
Norcott	4	0	5	5
Higgins	4	7	4	5
Others (1%–3% of cases by Berdon, Celotto, Falsey, McKeever, Maiocco, Mancini, Purtill, Quinn, Ronan, Schaller, Testo)	14	12	17	24

*Data gathered from the clerk's docket book, police records, and penal code statutes. The reduced wide sample excludes rape, burglary, violation of probation, and other offenses (see app. 1, table A1.2).

**Bail amounts are for defendants for whom bail was set and information was in the docket book (87 men and 107 women in the reduced wide sample, and 25 men and 32 women in the deep sample).

***The conditions of probation were as follows: For the 68 women for whom conditions were imposed, there were a total of 96 conditions. The distributions were: drug treatment (27%), psychological treatment (22%), restitution (21%), alcohol treatment (8%), community service (7%), seek employment or no contact with victim (3% each), and others (9%). For the 46 men for whom conditions were imposed, there were a total of 56 conditions. Their distributions were drug treatment (27%), psychological treatment (12%), restitution (20%), alcohol treatment (20%), community service (3%), no contact with victim (7%), and others (11%).

Table 2.2   Sentence Outcomes by Gender and Race and Ethnicity

A. Percent incarcerated (*In-Out* decision)

	N of Cases	Percent Incarcerated (*In-Out*)	Size of Bivariate Gap (in percentage points)	
All women	160	44	Male-female:	+29
All men	147	73		
All blacks	173	66	Black-white:	+21
All latins	36	58	Latin-white:	+13
All whites	98	45		
Black women	89	52	Black-white:	+19
Latin women	17	41	Latin-white:	+8
White women	54	33		
Black men	84	81	Black-white:	+22
Latin men	19	74	Latin-white:	+15
White men	44	59		

B. Length of sentence (*Time*) (only those receiving an incarceration sentence)

	N of Cases	Length of Sentence (mo) (*Time*)	Size of Bivariate Gap (mo)	
All women	71	33.5	Male-female: +13.3	
All men	108	46.8		
All blacks	114	40.2	Black-white:	−2.9
All latins	21	45.6	Latin-white:	+2.5
All whites	44	43.1		
Black women	46	37.6	Black-white:	+14.2
Latin women	7	31.7	Latin-white:	+8.3
White women	18	23.4		
Black men	68	42.0	Black-white:	−14.3
Latin men	14	52.5	Latin-white:	−3.8
White men	26	56.3		

Note. Averages *exclude* defendants found guilty at trial.

A regression analysis permits us to determine whether these initial subgroup differences in the sentences received can be explained when additional case factors are considered. Thus, if interpersonal violence cases generally receive higher sentences, and if black defendants are more likely to be prosecuted for interpersonal violence than whites, then the black-white gap in the percentage of those incarcerated may become smaller after a control variable for interpersonal violence is entered.[20]

The statistical controls used in my analysis are like those in other studies. They include the statutory severity of the convicted offense, the defendant's prior record, the offense of conviction (interpersonal violence, robbery, and drugs — which are contrasted with larceny), type of attorney (public defender or not), the judge presiding (Judge Kinney or not), and whether the defendant was incarcerated in the pretrial period (see appendix 2, table A-II.1 for definitions and the distributions of these variables). One comment is in order on the pretrial status variable (termed *Detain* in the analysis). I would not usually use this variable as a control. It is, however, appropriate because (1) it augments the measure of prior record, which is weak, and (2) it gives a stringent test of disparity.

For all analyses I excluded defendants who were found guilty at trial (three women and seven men in the reduced wide sample), because their sentences are increased by a trial tariff. The numbers of men's ($N=147$) and women's ($N=160$) cases are also reduced because some men's offenses (rape and burglary) were not relevant for women. I conducted the analyses with different mixes of control variables to see their influence in reducing the statistical effects of sex, race, or ethnicity in sentencing.

A final word on statistical parlance and conventions. The term *sex effect* refers to the magnitude of gender differences in the outcome; similarly, the term *race effect* refers to the magnitude of black-white and latin-white differences. The effects of other variables refer to the strength and direction of their relation to the sentencing outcome. Statistically significant effects are denoted by an asterisk following the regression coefficients: coefficients with a double asterisk are significant at the conventional error level (.05 or less), while those with a single asterisk are significant at a more generous error level (.10 or less).[21]

Incarcerated or Not

Let us turn first to the decision to incarcerate (the *In-Out* decision). In table 2.3a, equation 1, we see that without control variables, men were 29 percent more likely to be incarcerated than women,[22] the same difference noted in table 2.2. This sex effect is reduced to 25 percentage points with the introduction of controls for the severity of the offense, prior record, and race and ethnicity (equation 2). With additional controls for the type of offense or conviction, the sex effect is reduced to 20 percentage points (equation 3), and with the addition of the pretrial status variable (*Detain*), the sex effect is narrowed to 17 percentage points (equation 4). In this last equation, we see that the type of attorney and judge had no effect on the sentence outcome. Also, equation 4 shows that black defendants were 11 percent more likely to be incarcerated than were whites. For equation 4, the sex and race effects are statistically significant (note that the coefficient is significant for latins in equation 3, but not equation 4; it is significant for blacks in both equations). The relation of type of offense to sentencing can be interpreted this way: relative to larceny (the omitted category in the analysis), those convicted of interpersonal violence and robbery were more likely to be incarcerated (note that the robbery effect is significant in equation 3 but not in equation 4, with the introduction of the *Detain* variable). There were no differences in the likelihood of receiving an incarceration sentence for those convicted of drugs and larceny.

This standard disparity analysis indicates both race and sex effects, after controlling for relevant variables: male and black defendants were more likely to receive incarceration sentences. The adjusted R-squared at the bottom of the table refers to how well the variables explain variation in the sentencing outcome. In equation 4, the R-squared (adjusted for the number of variables) is 35 percent. Sentencing studies typically show 30 percent; thus the size of the R-squared is good.

Time Incarcerated (Time Sentenced)

For the second measure of sentence, the length of time for those with sentences to serve *(Time)*, we see in table 2.3*b*, equation 1, the gender difference reported earlier: men's sentences were 13.3 months longer than women's. With controls for severity, prior record, and race or ethnicity, the sentence length gap actually increased to 15.9 months (equation 2). With additional controls for the type of offense, the gap reduces to 13.5 months (equation 3). In the last equation, the difference was 12.3 months (equation 4). The sex effect reduced little from equation 1 to equation 4, and it remained statistically significant. Unlike the *In-Out* decision, the *Time* outcome showed no race effects. Thus, black defendants were significantly more likely to be incarcerated than whites, but for those who were incarcerated, racial differences were not evident for the length of the sentence.

To probe the combined influences of gender and race on sentencing, I conducted additional analyses (see appendix 2, tables A-II.2 and A-II.3). Sex effects were statistically significant for black defendants: black men were 22 percent more likely to be incarcerated than black women (equation 4), and their mean sentence was 14.5 months longer. For white defendants, white men were 13 percent more likely to be incarcerated than white women (equation 4), and their mean sentence was 25.5 months longer. The differences for whites neared, but did not achieve statistical significance. For latin defendants there were no statistically significant differences, a finding in part attributable to the low numbers in the analysis.

Table 2.3 The Changing *Sex Effect* with Different Variables in the Equations

A. *In-Out* decision: 1 = Incarceration time to serve
0 = No time to serve

	Eq. 1	Eq. 2	Eq. 3	Eq. 4
Sex (male = 1)	.29**	.25**	.20**	.17**
Severity		.001**	.001**	.001**
Prior record		.22**	.27**	.22**
Black		.20**	.19**	.11**
Latin		.13	.14*	.09
Violence			.20**	.16**
Robbery			.18**	.13
Drugs			−.06	−.05
Attorney (PD = 1)				.03
Judge (Kinney = 1)				−.001
Detain (yes = 1)				.28**
Constant	.44	.04	.01	.003
Adjusted R²	.08	.25	.29	.35
Mean	.58	.58	.58	.58
Number of cases	307	307	307	307

**p ≤ .05
*p ≤ .10

PD = public defender

B. *Time*: Time sentenced to serve (mo) (only those receiving incarceration
sentences)

	Eq. 1	Eq. 2	Eq. 3	Eq. 4
Sex (male = 1)	13.3**	15.9**	13.5**	12.3**
Severity		0.3**	0.3**	0.3**
Prior record		17.8**	28.6**	28.1**
Black		3.5	1.7	0.2
Latin		−1.0	−2.4	−3.6
Violence			35.9**	36.7**
Robbery			23.1*	23.5**
Drugs			8.0	9.1
Attorney (PD = 1)				1.7
Judge (Kinney = 1)				1.0
Detain (yes = 1)				2.0
Constant	33.6	−35.8	−57.4	−61.4
Adjusted R²	.01	.36	.40	.39
Mean	41.6	41.6	41.6	41.6
Number of cases	179	179	179	179

**p ≤ .05
*p ≤ .10

PD = public defender

Racial and ethnic differences between men and women offer another perspective. The results of the *In-Out* decision vary, depending on whether the *Detain* variable is included. When it is in the analysis, there are no racial differences between women or between men in receiving an incarceration sentence. But when the *Detain* variable is removed, there are differences: black women and black men were 14 and 23 percent more likely than their white counterparts to receive an incarceration sentence.

Measure or Mismeasure of Justice?

The New Haven data set is not as sophisticated as others (for example, Myers 1987; Steffensmeier, Kramer, and Streifel 1993; Wheeler, Weisburd, and Bode 1982), but it is typical of the information researchers normally have available in analyzing disparity. In the New Haven felony court, the magnitude of the sex effect for the *In-Out* decision, 17–20 percentage points with statistical controls, is similar to that reported elsewhere. Specifically, from an analysis of statistical studies (Daly and Bordt 1991), the sex effect (or gender gap) for incarceration sentences ranged from 8 to 25 percentage points. For the length of sentence for those incarcerated, sex effects were also evident: men were sentenced, on average, to about a year longer than women.

These sex effects were joined with race effects for a single sentence outcome: incarceration. When the pretrial status variable is excluded, black men and women were more likely to be incarcerated than white men and women. Although the size and direction of the coefficients for latins suggest the same pattern, they were not statistically significant.

What should we make from these statistical findings? Are they evidence that women, and to some extent, whites, are accorded sentencing leniency? Or do the findings mislead us? The remaining chapters are devoted to those questions.

Notes

1. Feeley (1979, chap. 2) describes how the courts were organized and the impact of political parties on the hiring (or appointment) of professional and staff workers. Several important changes have since taken place. The superior court now handles all criminal business, both that more serious (pt. A, or felony court) and less serious (pt. B, the old circuit court). Indeterminate sentencing was abolished by the legislature in 1980, replaced in mid-1981 with definite (or "flat") sentencing. Parole was officially abolished in 1980, but the Department of Corrections exercises control in granting and supervising postprison options (e.g., supervised home release). Being on parole therefore remains a meaningful sociolegal status.

2. Information comes from three sources: the New Haven Special Commission on Poverty (1983), 1990 census data, and a four-part series in the *New Haven Register* ("City, suburbs," 14–17 June 1992) that summarized and compared relevant 1990 census data for Connecticut cities.

3. Cities such as Little Rock (Arkansas), Kansas City (Kansas), and Spokane (Washington) had a similar number of crimes reported to the police. In 1980 their populations were each between 160,000 and 170,000; New Haven's was 126,000 (see Flanagan and McLeod 1983, 350–53).

4. Connecticut's Department of Corrections is centralized (see chap. 1, n.1). Because prison counts combine jail and prison inmates in Connecticut, I have used incarceration rates for those sentenced to more than a year (this means *prison time* in most states) in order to compare Connecticut's rates to those of other states and regions. In 1987, the number of prisoners per 100,000 of the resident population was 144 in Connecticut, 169 in other northeastern states, and 228 nationally. Rates in the Midwest (184), West (214), and South (255) were higher than in the Northeast.

5. Previous research on Connecticut and New Haven courts referred to the JD and GA-6 courts as the superior and circuit courts, respectively. With a unified superior court established in 1978, these distinctions are no longer made.

6. My sketch of the judge and court contexts comes from my interviews with Judge Kinney in the summer of 1985, together with Miriam Berkman's (1986) profile of the judge for a Yale Law School seminar, "Sentencing Principles," taught by Prof. Dan Freed. Berkman's profile has been crucial to my research since she captured the logic of Judge Kinney's sentencing philosophy and judicial management style just before his unexpected death of a heart attack at age 54.

7. Kinney was born in New Haven in 1932; he graduated from Yale College and Yale Law School. He had a general law practice in New Haven from 1957 to 1972, including substantial criminal defense work. He served as a prosecutor in New Haven, first in 1963, and then for four years beginning in 1968 in the juvenile court. He was appointed to the circuit court (with jurisdiction over misdemeanors and less serious felonies) in 1972, and in 1978, when Connecticut trial courts merged, he was appointed to the superior court, working first in the GA section before moving over to JD in 1983 (details from Berkman, 1986, 3–4).

8. In interviews with a prosecutor and public defender, I learned that it was assumed that the other trial judges could be tougher, on average, than Judge Kinney. For cases disposed of by guilty plea, my sentencing analysis reveals no differences between Kinney and non-Kinney sentences.

9. U.S. Supreme Court decision, North Carolina v. Alford, 400 U.S. 25 (1970), on appeal from the Middle District of North Carolina. Alford, indicted for first-degree murder, elected to plead guilty to second-degree murder to avoid the possibility of receiving the death penalty if found guilty at trial. He protested his innocence: "I don't — I'm not guilty but I plead guilty" (91 Supreme Court Reporter, p. 163), but the Supreme Court held that where "strong evidence of guilt substantially negated defendant's claim of innocence," accepting a guilty plea and imposing criminal penalties, including prison, was constitutionally permissible. The majority opinion drew from nolo contendre cases in which defendants, though not admitting guilt, may be subject to prison terms. The theoretical difference between an Alford and nolo contendre plea is that the latter does not entail a factual basis

for determining guilt. The practical difference, at least in Connecticut courts, is that the latter plea is used when civil liability may be at issue.

10. Although it is unlikely that the guilty plea rate increased with the introduction of Alford pleas (the rate was already quite high in Connecticut, based on Heumann's research), the Alford plea was a tool that defense attorneys could use to expedite the process.

11. The time a judge imposes and the time a defendant will actually serve are, of course, different. During the research period (1981–86), prisoners would be expected to serve two-thirds of their sentence, with additional time off for "good time." I am told that by the end of the 1980s, when prison overcrowding increased, the time served would often be less than two-thirds — perhaps closer to 25%–50% for nonviolent offenses.

12. There was variation in how these tasks were accomplished. One method was to divide tasks so that one group of officers would write the PSI's and another would supervise probationers. Another was to share tasks. During the time of my research, both methods had been used at different times.

13. Plea negotiations typically ended in an "agreed recommendation" between prosecutor and defense attorney, which meant that the sentence was fixed. Beginning in the latter part of the 1980s, sentencing *caps* were more frequently used. Caps place an upper limit on the sentence, allowing defense attorneys to argue for a lesser sentence. PSI information may be more influential in a sentencing-cap context.

14. After obtaining the PSI's, I learned that two of the forty pairs were co-defendants in the same offense. Some may wonder why I did not select co-defendants. The reason is simply that my choices were made from the clerk's docket books, which lists defendants alphabetically, not by offense.

15. This is the reduced wide sample, which excludes rape and burglary, violation of probation, and a small number of other offenses (see app. 1, table A-I.2, first line of totals for the reduced wide sample on the two left-hand columns). No woman was convicted of burglary, and only one was convicted of rape during the five-year period; the information on violation-of-probation cases was not sufficiently clear on statutory charges to make meaningful comparisons.

16. The analysis of the deep-sample cases shows that two-thirds of the women and three-fourths of the men had been convicted in the past. The convictions may have been for misdemeanors or for felonies in another court.

17. These averages include defendants who were found guilty at trial. In the regression analysis, the trial cases were excluded, and the mean for the men is lower (47 months).

18. These include "Profile of Felons Convicted in State Courts, 1986" (BJS 1990), which analyzes a survey of 115 state felony courts in 37 states; "Tracking Offenders, 1988" (ibid., 1991), which describes sentences received in 14 states by offense of conviction; and "Sentencing Outcomes in Twenty-Eight Felony Courts in 1985" (ibid., 1987).

19. It is not clear what information is relevant to generalizing from one court about sentencing disparity. Some federally sponsored data-gathering efforts focus on single jurisdictions but do not compare or link findings across jurisdictions. Most statistics do not break down offenses and sentencing adequately enough by gender.

20. Here and throughout my reporting of the statistical results, I use ordinary least squares (OLS), the standard regression model. Some suggest, however, that the OLS model is inappropriate when dichotomous dependent variables (such as *In-Out*) are analyzed. I ran the *In-Out* equations using the logit model and found no substantive differences in interpreting the coefficients.

21. Adopting standard usage, the error levels are associated with *two-tailed tests* of statistical significance.

22. Strictly speaking, the terminology should be that there is a 29 percentage-point difference between men's and women's incarceration rates, with men's being higher than women's, though I have used fewer words to convey the same idea.

II Who Are the Accused?

How did the New Haven men and women get caught up in crime? Did they move into lawbreaking in different ways? In part 2, I first aim to enable readers to appreciate the circumstances that spawn violence and illegal forms of economic gain. Second, I explore gender differences in the defendants' social histories and current circumstances to determine whether women's lives contain a greater level of informal social control (such as having responsibility for others) and whether the construction of women's crimes renders them less dangerous than men.[1] Previous research suggests that to court officials women may appear to be better probation risks because of informal social controls (Daly 1987a, 1989a; Eaton 1986; Kruttschnitt 1982a, 1982b), or they may be viewed as less dangerous and more reformable than men (Allen 1987a, 1987b; Daly 1987a). Statistical analyses are often limited in that measures of informal social control, conventionality, and perceived dangerousness are only dimly captured in variables such as "is currently employed" or "cares for children." We require a way to link the defendant's past to a current offense, just as court officials do.

An effective device for linking biography and an offense is an expansive definition of *blameworthiness,* as defined by Stanton Wheeler, Kenneth Mann, and Austin Sarat (1988, 88):

> [Judges] start with events surrounding the offense itself. . . . They then move both backward and forward — backward chronologically to an assessment of the defendant's past conduct, personality, motivational structure, and many attributes of his [sic] personal and social history. The assessment may then move forward chronologically to include character readings based on the defendant's conduct after the offense [such as] . . . lying or deceitfulness, or remorse, or cooperation with the prosecution and the like.

Wheeler, Mann, and Sarat's concept of blameworthiness is broader than others. They recognize that a defendant's social history superimposes meaning on a crime.[2] The typology court officials use for classifying blameworthiness is typically male centered: there are good and bad guys. But what is the typology for women?

To sketch such a typology, I begin in chapter 3 with the feminist research on women lawbreakers and augment my analysis with research on the relation of child abuse or neglect to criminalization.

Although I describe the pathways of defendants to felony court, I cannot test theories of crime. My focus is on criminalization rather than crime causation (Nettler 1984; Vold and Bernard 1986). The latter is not an inappropriate focus of study, but it is inappropriate for the kinds of research materials I have at my disposal.

Qualifications

I have four qualifications to make about my materials and analyses. The first concerns drawing from the PSI's as a primary source, the second concerns my use of the term *biography,* and the remainder, issues of generalizability.

PSI's as a Source

I have constructed a biography for each defendant based on information contained in the PSI. My biographical sketch is thus constrained by what probation officers chose to include (or exclude) in the PSI, coupled with the dynamics of the defendant-probation officer interview itself.[3] The PSI social histories are not the defendants' stories or what defendants chose to remember or to report. They are reports generated by a probation officer from interviews with the defendant and others (Spencer 1984).

Although the PSI's have limitations, it is useful to recall the deficiencies in social science interviews of criminalized people. Matters of memory and truthfulness can affect an interview. Issues of power relations between the interviewer and interviewee are similarly present. The major difference between a social scientist's interview and that of a probation officer centers on time and trust. The social science interview may be longer; it is likely to contain more detailed information from less wary interviewees, who have little to lose by being completely candid.[4] The PSI report contains information that is not part of a social science interview, including comments by a defendant's family members, friends, teachers, or counselors, as well as other diagnostic documents. We would expect each source of interview material about defendants to yield a partial and perhaps different story.[5]

Biography

The life events reported in a PSI do not add up to or constitute a biography in the normal meaning of the term. I use *biography* here to mean a partial and selected sketch of life events. I do not use it to mean a method, an approach that has emerged with a sophisticated set of literary concepts and concerns, especially those of feminist scholars (Bell and Yalom 1990; Heilbrun 1988; Laslett 1990). It is not possible to disentangle the many relations between myself, the eighty defendants, and the seventeen probation officers who wrote the PSI's.[6] The PSI, of course, is a document constructed with a particular purpose in mind addressed to a small audience of court officials.

Generalizing from Felony Court

With respect to gender-based patterns in crime or pathways to criminal court, the main generalization issue is that these are *felony* court defendants. Such defendants typically constitute a low share of the criminal docket (and in New Haven, only 2–3 percent). The pathway categories derived from this select group of convicted felons may reflect a more toughened set of conditions or life events that propel more serious forms of harm. For the deep-sample women this was so. Women convicted of violent offenses were more likely than those convicted of larceny or drug offenses to have been abused as children, beaten by their mates, and to have psychological problems. This pattern was not evident for the men.

Generalizing from the Deep Sample

The interpersonal violence (defined here as homicide, assault, risk of injury, arson, and rape) and robbery share of women's convictions was 41, 47, and 60 percent in the initial sample, reduced wide sample, and deep sample, respectively. For men, these offenses were 63, 69, and 60 percent in the initial sample, reduced wide sample, and deep sample (see appendix 1, table A-I.2). The deep-sample women may evince a somewhat higher frequency of abuse or psychological problems than would be apparent from the wide sample or from felony court samples of women more generally. For the men, the violence share did not change appreciably, and offense-linked differences in pathways were not apparent.

Analysis and Presentation

Each of the portraits of the deep-sample women and men has two parts. The first profiles their biographies as a group, using a descriptive statistical approach. The second highlights individual pathways to the felony court, using a narrative form.

To develop the statistical portrait, I coded the PSI's with the following questions:[7] What were the men's and women's social and economic circumstances growing up? Did they run away from home or finish high school? What was their paid-employment record? Did they have children, and did they care for their children? What were their familial and economic circumstances at the time of the offense? Was there evidence of abuse in the household when they were growing up, or by current or past partners or spouses? Were they addicted to drugs and alcohol, and when did they begin using drugs? Had they been arrested or convicted before?

In presenting the biographies, I faced a problem of selection. I did not want to select just the most interesting or dramatic cases, but a wide sampling. My initial desire to present all the biographies gave way to the practicality of not wearying patient readers, and thus one-third of the biographies are presented.

A decisive analytical strategy is to present the women first, an ordering that accomplishes several objectives. First, I establish women as the standard by which to compare men, a reversal of the usual order in making gender comparisons — in social science, law, and elsewhere. Second, by taking women first, one sees how theories of gender difference may differ depending on which gender is used as the standard. For those aiming to devise reputedly general social theories, which often gloss over gender or other key social relations, the exercise of taking "the other" first may give us pause.

Notes

1. Portions of my analysis of women's pathways appeared in Daly (1992). Note that earlier (Daly 1992, 23, 45) I wrongly reported the number of black and white women as 24 and 11. The numbers and interpretation reported here are correct.

2. Definitions of blameworthiness and related terms vary in legal opinion and social science usage. At times blameworthiness is used interchangeably with culpability to mean the same thing; or blameworthiness may refer to a defendant's mental state or motive, and culpability may refer to the wider array of factors that construct the "seriousness" of an offense. In this study, I use culpability to refer to the defendant's role or actions in an offense. Blameworthiness refers to the broader linking of the defendant's biography (social history and prior record) to the offense, as defined by Wheeler, Mann, and Sarat (1988).

3. From interviews with the probation officers, I learned that the women officers felt it was easier to elicit information from women than men defendants and that women defendants were more forthcoming about themselves. In the conclusion to part 2, I consider the consequences of these dynamics for the production of knowledge about the defendants' social histories.

4. For example, Meda Chesney-Lind and Noelie Rodriguez (1983, 50) report in their interviews of incarcerated women that "there appeared to be an initial period of caution and reserve followed by a flood of information once rapport was established." The length of their interview time ranged from 2 to 6 hours. New Haven probation officers spend 1 to 2 hours interviewing defendants for the PSI. Probation officers also gather information from teachers, employers, and family members of the defendant.

5. It would be important to see how the deep-sample defendants would challenge the PSI reports of them, especially since the reports chronicle trouble, prob-

lems, and conflict. There is a third source of information about lawbreakers: their own stories, unmediated by social scientists or legal officials. Mark Devlin (1985, 230–33) reacted to a report by the superintendent of a juvenile institution where Devlin was incarcerated: "I wondered if I was in fact the sadistic criminal he suggested I was" (p. 232). Kathryn Burkhart's (1976) collection of essays by incarcerated women also show how women counter the official stories about themselves.

6. The PSI writers' and defendants' gender are as follows:

	Male Defendants	Female Defendants	Total
Male PO	13	10	23
Female PO	19	24	43
No PSI	8	6	14
Total	40	40	80

Of the 17 probation officers writing the 66 PSI's, 9 were men, but women probation officers were responsible for a substantial portion (about two-thirds) of the PSI's. With one exception, all the PSI writers were white.

7. There were eight men and six women for whom PSI's were not written, and thus I was not able to code these cases in great detail. However, there was information in the defendants' files about family, education, and prior record that I did code. For some variables I report percentages of the 40 men and 40 women; for most, the percentages are of 32 men and 34 women (see app. 3).

Little of a systematic nature is known of the circumstances that bring accused women to criminal court. Statistical studies of these defendants give a thin account, at best, of their lives. They may give the women's average age, level of education, paid-employment situation, marital status, familial situation, and their previous arrests or convictions. The profiles of incarcerated women are more detailed. A recent survey of women and men in United States jails (BJS 1992) reveals that the women are usually in their late twenties, close to half of them have never married, and about half have completed high school. Most are unemployed, use illegal drugs, are black or are Spanish-speaking, have children under eighteen, and have previously been convicted at least once. Thirty-one percent reported having been physically or sexually abused by an adult before the age of eighteen. On these and other dimensions of social history and current circumstances, the profile of New Haven women was similar (appendix 3).

Profile of the Deep-Sample Women

The women's median age was 25 and ranged from 17 to 60 years. Most women were black (58 percent), twelve were white (30 percent), and five were Puerto Rican or from Latin America (12 percent). I describe the women's situations at the time of the *instant offense,* that is, the offense for which they were prosecuted.

Familial Circumstances Growing Up

Half the women were raised in single-parent families, and half were raised in two-parent families. One-third were raised by both their biological mothers and fathers, another third were raised by their mothers alone, and the remainder lived in a mix of familial circumstances. For two-thirds of the women, biological fathers were out of the picture: unknown to the women or not contributing to the support of the families. A little more than half lived in families whose economic circumstances were precarious. Only two women grew up in middle-class households. Physical abuse of the women or their mothers and siblings while growing up was evident for one-third of the women.[1] Of women with siblings, one-third had one or more who had been arrested, convicted, or imprisoned (almost always a brother). For 9 percent, the women's parents or guardians had been arrested, convicted, or imprisoned. One-third of the women's mothers, fathers, or both were alcohol or drug abusers; one-fourth ran away from home or detention facility while growing up.

In the women's early years, then, a consistent one-third grew up in tough or difficult circumstances, emotionally and economically. Their fathers or stepfathers physically or sexually abused them and other family members. Their mothers could not care for them. About 12 percent of the women were described by mothers or female kin as being aggressive or hard to control. Whatever the cause — external circumstances, an aspect of the girl's personality, or a combination of the two — familial relations were strained for about 40 percent of the women.

Education, Employment, and Family

One-third completed high school or received a general equivalency diploma (GED). Only one woman had a four-year college degree. For those who did not complete high school, the main reason was not related to pregnancy. Instead, the PSI narrative suggests a lack of interest in school, failing grades, and high rates of absenteeism. For some women a growing disinterest in school was related to a developing drug habit. With or without a high school diploma, 30 percent of the women took skill training (such as daycare, secretarial work, and hair styling). Two-thirds had either a sporadic or no paid-employment record; at the time of the offense, more than 80 percent were not employed in a paying job.

About two-thirds of the women had one or more children, and their median age at first birth was 19–20 years. At the time of the instant offense, 35 percent of the women had dependent children (and in one case an elderly parent) for whom they cared on a regular basis, and slightly more than 40 percent were supporting themselves or their children through state aid.[2] At the time of arrest their household situations varied. The most frequent circumstance was to be living with children, whether alone, with a mother, boyfriend, or spouse (44 percent). The next most frequent arrangement was that of living with a boyfriend or spouse without children (26 percent). The rest lived with their mothers, parents, other female kin, or lived alone; for some, there was no information given in the PSI. Whether in a current or previous relationship, about 30 percent of the women had been beaten by their boyfriends or spouses.

To summarize, most women lacked a high school education, vocational training, and a stable employment record. At arrest, 20 percent had paying jobs, and 40 percent were supported by state aid. That leaves a large portion of the women without a clear means of economic support. Family members, boyfriends, and spouses helped in part, coupled with the women's earnings from prostitution, theft, or selling drugs. Most women had given birth to at least one child, but at the time of the offense, most were not caring for a child on a regular basis, either because their children had grown or because other female kin cared for them. Finally, a significant minority of women had been assaulted by boyfriends or husbands.

Substance Abuse, Psychological Problems, and Prior Record

Two-thirds of the women were addicted to alcohol, drugs, or both. Of those with substance abuse problems, 15 percent were linked to alcohol, 50 percent to drugs, and 35 percent to both. More than half began abusing alcohol or drugs at the age of twenty or younger. About one-third developed or continued their drug habits in association with a boyfriend or spouse. Although most of the addicted women (72 percent) had entered treatment programs, few were successful in quitting their habits. Half were described as having psychological problems. These included a general aggressive personality, suicidal gestures, depression, and manic depression, as well as several other unspecified emotional or nervous problems. Fifteen percent had tried to kill themselves. One-third of the women had never been arrested before, 40 percent had a moderate record of previous arrests or convictions (by *moderate* I mean one to five incidents), and 25 percent had more extensive records (six or more incidents). For those with previous arrests, the modal age of first contact with juvenile or adult authorities was 17–18 years. A minority (15 percent) were institutionalized in reform schools, mental hospitals, or state homes while in their teens.

A Feminist Composite of Women's Lawbreaking: The Street Woman

Although the sociodemographic profile gives a cross-sectional view of accused women, the biographical sketches can tell a more chronological tale. What do we expect will be the story line? From research of girls or women who have been arrested or incarcerated in the United States (Arnold 1990; Campbell 1991; Chapman 1980; Chesney-Lind 1989; Chesney-Lind and Rodriguez 1983; Gilfus 1992; Maher and Curtis 1992; Miller 1986; Romensko and Miller 1989; Rosenbaum 1981) or in England, Australia, Canada, and several European countries (Adelberg and Currie 1987; Alder 1986; Cain 1989; Carlen 1988; Carlen et al. 1985), I constructed a composite of women's lawbreaking. I term the composite *street woman,*[3] and it takes the form I now describe.

Pushed out of or running from abusive homes or becoming part of deviant milieus, some young women begin to engage in petty hustles or prostitution. Life on the street often leads to drug use and addiction, which in turn often leads to more frequent lawbreaking to support a drug habit. Young women may drop out of high school because of pregnancy, boredom and disinterest, or both. Their paid-employment record is negligible: they are not interested in working in low-paid or unskilled jobs, and making fast money is more exciting. Having a child may facilitate entry to the networks of adult women and allow a woman to support herself in part with state aid. Some women may continue lawbreaking as a result of relationships with men who are also involved in crime. These women move between the criminal justice system and welfare agencies, between time incarcerated and time trying to stay out of trouble.

Biographies of the Deep-Sample Women

Does the street woman composite apply to New Haven women? I analyzed their biographies and found that *street woman* characterized ten women, or one-fourth of my sample. There were an additional five women having street woman elements in their biography. Another route to felony court, just as frequent as that of the street woman, is what I term *harmed and harming women;* this group comprised fifteen women. I classified the remaining women as *battered* (five women), *drug-connected* (six women), and *other* (four women). Table 3.1 lists each group with their pseudonyms and the statutory offense for which they were convicted. Below I briefly describe each pathway.

Street Women
Street women were those women who ran away from abusive households or who were drawn to the excitement of the street. They eked out a living on the street, supporting a drug addiction by prostitution, theft, and selling drugs. Their arrest and conviction records were heavy, and they had been incarcerated often.

Harmed and Harming Women
These women were a diverse group, but a common experience was physical or sexual abuse or neglect. They had chaotic and difficult experiences growing up. By their teens alcohol consumption, drug addiction, or a psychological problem had amplified an "acting out" (that is, reacting with violence) or tough demeanor. I identified three subgroups: women whose violence escalated when drinking, those supporting drug habits, and those who could not cope with their immediate circumstances.

Table 3.1   Women's Pathways to Felony Court

Street Women (*N*=10): Pushed out or ran away from an abusive household and went to the street or got involved in petty hustles; became drug addicted and engaged in prostitution, theft, and selling drugs to support drug habit; well-developed record of arrests and some time incarcerated

Colleen (sale of narcotics)
Edith (larceny 1st)
Julie (sale of narcotics)
Kate (robbery 1st)
Laura (larceny 4th and criminal impersonation)
Mary (sale of narcotics)
Pamela (robbery 1st)
Pat (aiding robbery 1st)
Penny (sale of narcotics)
Stacey (attempted assault 2d and conspiracy to commit assault 2d)

Harmed and Harming Women (*N*=15): Abused or neglected as a child; identified as a "problem child" or one who acts out; gets violent when drinking alcohol; may be drug addicted and have psychological problems; unable to cope with current situation

a. Violence and alcohol (*N*=6): "Out-of-control" or violent behavior evidenced as a child or in adolescence; gets violent when drinking alcohol; may also have psychological problems

Alice (assault 2d)
Bell (robbery 3d)
Claire (manslaughter 1st)
Dee Dee (assault 1st)
Latasha (assaulting a police officer)
Nellie (assault 1st)

b. Violence and drug addiction (*N*=4): "Out-of-control" or violent behavior evidenced as a child or in adolescence; addicted to heroin or cocaine and engaged in some crime to support habit; psychological problems

Maria* (larceny 6th)
Susan (robbery 1st)
Tara* (larceny 1st)
Toni (attempted robbery 1st)

c. Psychological problems coping (*N*=5): Unable to cope with current circumstances; feels aggrieved toward parents or siblings; psychological problems

Chris (two counts of risk of injury)
Edie (manslaughter 1st)
Flo (two counts of risk of injury)
Nancy (arson 2d)
Nola (risk of injury and assault 1st)

(continued)

Table 3.1 (continued)

Battered Women ($N=5$): In a relationship with a violent man, or recently ended such a relationship

Carrie* (reckless endangerment 1st)
Dorothy (reckless burning)
Jean (manslaughter 1st)
Lonnie (manslaughter 1st)
Sharon (assault 2d)

Drug-connected Women ($N=6$): Uses or sells drugs in connection with boyfriends or family members

Kathleen* (assault 3d)
Lotty (possession of narcotics)
Marcie (sale of narcotics)
Miranda (sale of narcotics)
Wendy* (robbery 1st)
Winnie (larceny 1st)

Other ($N=4$): Immediate economic circumstance or greed; none is a street woman, a harmed and harming, or drug-connected woman

Bonnie (sale of narcotics)
June (larceny 2d)
Maggie (robbery 1st and kidnapping 1st)
Prish (larceny 1st)

*Was a street woman or is now on the pathway of becoming a street woman

Battered Women
Battered women were in relationships with violent men or had recently ended such relationships. Although 30 percent of the deep-sample women had been in relationships with violent men, the battered women were in court because they were fighting or fending off violent men, with whom they were (or had been) in relationships.

Drug-connected Women
These women used or sold drugs in their relationships with boyfriends or family members. The women's drug use was recent and experimental, and they had only minimal or no prior records.

Other Women
These women did not fit any of the profiles: none had a problem with drugs or alcohol, and none had been arrested before. Their lawbreaking seemed to arise from a desire for more money.

These pathway categories, although based on biographical elements, should not be viewed as static characterizations of the women or their lives. Harmed and harming women might eventually lead more of a street woman's life, or a woman might have appeared previously in court as a battered woman. My approach was to decide which pathway trajectory seemed most prominent in bringing a woman to felony court for the instant offense; the pathway groups thus reflect a cross section in time. They also reflect a spectrum of women's blameworthiness, by which court officials forge sentencing decisions. In the following biographical sketches, the words or phrases in quotation marks are, unless otherwise indicated, those of the probation officers writing the PSI.

Street Women

Kate, Mary, Penny, and Colleen offer a good sampling of the biographical elements and immediate contexts that bring street women to court.

Kate. The woman whose robbery opened this book fits the street woman profile in all respects. Kate is white and 35. Soon after she was born, her mother ended a twenty-year marriage to a man whom she described as "very bad" because he drank too much, gambled, and was a "womanizer." He beat her and her two sons. Although Kate's mother said her second spouse was a "good father," he too was an alcoholic. When Kate was growing up, her mother remembered her having many problems in school: she ran away from home and associated with "negative influences." Kate described herself as rebellious and unmanageable. She became distant from her family as an adolescent. She was placed in a residential program for problem children when she was 12 years old. When she was 16, Kate had a child, whom she gave up for adoption. During that same year, she was arrested for breach of peace. Since then she has been convicted a dozen times. She became part of the street life in her late teens. She drank heavily and was a heroin addict. She was in and out of prison starting from the age of 20, spending three months to more than a year incarcerated at a stretch. When she was 24, she gave birth to a second child. Around that time she tried to quit using drugs. She was able to care for her second child, and when she was 30, she gave birth to a third child. The father of her third child beat her. He left the state and assumed custody of their child. The father of her second child has been taking care of that child; he would like to reconcile with Kate if she would give up drugs and leave the life of the street. Kate's latest offense came about because she needed money to support her drug habit.[4]

Mary. Black woman and 51, Mary was convicted in felony court for selling cocaine from her apartment. She had left home at 17 to become a dancer and worked on the road for several years. She began to use heroin in her early twenties when she became involved with James. First jailed in her midtwenties on drug charges, she married James the day she was released from jail. They were together for about fifteen years. Although a regular drug user for thirty years, Mary gave birth to four children and raised three of them with James. In her early forties, she divorced James and became the sole support of her children. During this time she was convicted more than a dozen times for larceny, prostitution, forgery, and breach of peace. She was sentenced to serve time on four occasions. When not incarcerated, she cared for her children, supporting them through welfare and social security disability benefits. For the past several years, she has been on methadone maintenance. At the time of the offense she was living with her boyfriend, Lloyd, a drug addict with a criminal record.

Mary's story is somewhat noteworthy because by criminal justice standards, she is an elder defendant. More typical is a woman in her mid- to late twenties who hustles or sells drugs to support herself and a drug habit. Four of the ten street women were convicted of drug offenses; Penny and Colleen are among them.

Penny. Penny, a 25-year-old black woman, exemplifies the pull and allure of selling drugs. She was raised in a stable working-class family; her mother was the family's sole support. Although Penny did not complete high school, she obtained some vocational training. She began using drugs at 16 and was a regular cocaine user by 19. Because she sniffs heroin instead of injecting it, she views herself in control of her habit and has no interest in drug treatment. Described by the probation officer as "opting to lead a street life existence since midadolescence" and as being irresponsible because she sees "nothing wrong with her lifestyle or drug usage," Penny has sold drugs since she was 19. She said there was more money in dealing drugs than in working, and she viewed drug trafficking as a job in which she could get "the finer things of life." She claimed that on a good day she could earn as much as $2,000. Penny was more confident of herself than most deep-sample women. There was no indication she suffered abuse as a child. She felt in control of her drug habit; she was not in a relationship with a man who abused her or who was drug-addicted.

Colleen. Colleen, white and 33, and her husband were arrested for selling narcotics. Born in the South, Colleen moved with her mother to Connecticut when she was 7 and her parents had just divorced. After she completed high school, she lived with her mother while working in secretarial and factory jobs. She was first convicted of prostitution when she was 18. She began using drugs around this time and supported her habit over the next decade by prostitution. At 21 she was jailed for possessing heroin; she served time the next year for a conviction of disorderly conduct. She again served time in her late twenties when convicted for disorderly conduct and petty larceny. When she was 30, she met and married Rennie, who had an extensive criminal record. A year after their marriage Colleen entered a methadone maintenance program, where she has made good progress. Several months later, she and Rennie were arrested for the current drug charge. When Rennie was incarcerated in the pretrial period for the drug charge, Colleen visited him in jail and was arrested for trying to smuggle marijuana to him.

With the exception of Penny, each of the street women had a serious drug addiction. Each supported her addiction through prostitution, selling drugs, theft, and robbery. All but two were arrested for the first time in their late teens. For most of them, drug and alcohol use was a part of the street scene.

Harmed and Harming Women

Harmed and harming inadequately conveys the physically and emotionally harmful experiences this group of women experienced growing up and the many ways those experiences are reproduced in the harm they do to others. Although some women could be described as survivors, their friends or family members may note lingering emotional or psychological problems. Most of these women were convicted of offenses of interpersonal violence.

Violence and Alcohol

Dee Dee. Among the most desperate biographies was that of Dee Dee, a 24-year-old black woman who stabbed a female acquaintance with a knife, causing her serious injury. Dee Dee's experience growing up was brutal and chaotic. She was removed from her parents' home and placed in state-supervised care at the age of 7. Her parents were alcoholics; they did not register their children in school. Dee Dee and her three siblings were neglected, malnourished, and physically abused. They were taken from their parents and placed first in the care of an aunt, but she died when Dee Dee was 11. Dee Dee and her siblings were then placed with another aunt for several years, but because the aunt could not effectively control the children, they were moved to yet another aunt, their third caretaker. By their early teens, Dee Dee and one brother were diagnosed as emotionally disturbed. She completed eight years of schooling and began to abuse alcohol in her teens. She gave birth to her first child at about the age of 17 and to her second child when she was 23. Just before the birth of her second child, Dee Dee served time in jail for attempting to burn down the rooming house where her boyfriend lived. Soon after her release, she was convicted of assaulting the same boyfriend. (She and two male accomplices slashed the boyfriend with a mirror while he slept.) Subsequently, she and the boyfriend were arrested for fighting. Abused by her boyfriend as well as by her parents, Dee Dee often becomes violent when intoxicated. In the latest incident, she and the female victim had been drinking, and in Dee Dee's words, "My temper got over on me." Because of her drinking problem, she is unable to care for either child.

Latasha. White and 19, Latasha struck a male police officer with a baseball bat. He and two other officers had been trying to arrest her for an assault she had committed earlier in the day against the mother of her former boyfriend's new girlfriend. Latasha's father was a "severe alcoholic," and her mother said he "screwed up Latasha by using her to get back at me." Her parents separated when she was 10. Described by her mother as "incorrigible," Latasha started to abuse alcohol when she was 13. She was married for a short period in her teens. She gave birth to a child by another man when she was 18. She was convicted of assault at 17. The instant offense arose because she wanted her infant son back. Her former boyfriend and his new girlfriend were living with the child at the girlfriend's mother's house. They believed Latasha was incapable of caring for her child.

Violence and Drugs

The major difference between the "violence and alcohol" group and the "violence and drugs" group of harmed and harming women is the link between addiction to illegal drugs and crime. This latter subgroup of four women resembles the street women in many ways, except that they are younger and their time on the street has been shorter. The following biography of Susan shows themes of victimization and of victimizing others while growing up. Susan's addiction to drugs moved her to commit offenses for economic gain rather than to assault others.

Susan. A 21-year-old Puerto Rican woman, Susan committed a string of three robberies just after she was released from jail. She grew up in a family of six children. Her father was a "violent and abusive alcoholic," who beat his wife and children. A third-grade teacher described Susan as "aggressive and defiant." After completing six years of school, Susan was supposed to attend an alternative learning center, but the school refused her because of her history of assaultive behavior. She was first arrested at the age of 12 for breach of peace. As a member of a male gang, her role was having sexual relations with prospective gang members. Adjudicated delinquent at 15, she was placed in a juvenile facility, where she assaulted a staff member and two students. She ran away from this facility several times. She was then placed in a second facility, but she also ran away from there.

While at the second facility, a psychiatric evaluation described her as having "the ability to dehumanize her victims," having "no conscience," and being "violently asocial." She was placed in a third juvenile facility, where she lived more than a year. At this facility she was described by staff members as "inordinately proud of her illegal activities" and acting "cocky, arrogant, tough, and manipulative." Susan said she was asked to leave the facility because she triggered an interracial fight, which caused substantial damage. At 16 she was convicted of shooting another teenage girl who resided at the facility. Susan was in jail for two years before being released at the age of 18. She was in and out of jail for the next several years because she violated probation. She abuses both drugs and alcohol and seems to have committed her latest offenses to support a drug habit.

Toni. White and 19, Toni attempted to rob a suburban jewelry store. One of four children raised in a two-parent, middle-class family, Toni felt she did not get all the material things her siblings did. Her mother described Toni as immature and jealous of her siblings; she also said that Toni never had a good self-image and was a "manipulator, fabricated stories, wanted things handed to her without doing much to attain them herself." The only positive thing Toni's mother said about her was that she was excellent with children. Toni finished the tenth grade but did not continue school because of drug use. By the eighth grade, she was using LSD on a regular basis. She also took amphetamines and used alcohol. In the tenth grade, she jumped out of the second story of her parents' house and suffered a brain concussion and a leg fracture. She and her parents had been arguing over her drug use and absence from school. A year later, Toni was hospitalized for overdosing on drugs and alcohol. On admission, she was described as suicidal and was later diagnosed as having depressive neurosis. During a psychiatric evaluation, Toni described her shoplifting: she took pride in her abilities and boasted of stealing hundreds of dollars in items from local stores each week. While she was being prosecuted for the current offense, she married, divorced, and remarried. She described her first husband as "a bum on the street." Her second husband, though employed, beat her. She had not been arrested before.

Psychological Problems and Inability to Cope
Compared to the other harmed and harming women, the defining feature of this subgroup was (with one exception) not having been arrested before. Of the five women, two were mentally disturbed, two were under the domination of a man, and one could not handle the care of her infant.

Nola. Nola, 20 and black, was convicted of abusing her four-month-old son by throwing him on a hard mattress; he sustained a skull fracture and bruises. Nola's mother had abused her, and although her father left the household when Nola was young, he sexually abused her during the times he lived with the family, when Nola was a young child and when she was a teenager. Nola was raised by her grandmother, who died when Nola was 10. She lived with an aunt and also with her mother when she was a teen. Nola recalled her mother being an irresponsible parent and that she would place her boyfriends above Nola in importance.

Nola completed high school at 19 and married Stuart a month after graduation. She was pregnant at the time and gave birth to her first child at 19. Less than a year later, she gave birth to a second child, the child she injured. During her second pregnancy, Nola felt nervous, partly because her mother was living with her and Stuart. She thought the baby was "nervous"; Stuart described him as "feisty," while Nola described him as "cranky" and "fussy." She went to New Haven with both children for several days "to get away from problems at home." She stayed with her father, and during this time, he made "sexual advances toward her." Nola did not specify her home problems or the nature of her father's sexual advances. She believed "she may have been undergoing a nervous breakdown" at the time of the offense. A day after she threw her infant on the mattress, she brought him into the emergency room. The infant had scars from old burns on his buttocks and thighs.

Chris. Chris is an extreme example of the effects of being physically abused while growing up. She allowed her husband to sexually abuse both her nieces and her nephew, who were ages 5 to 9 at the time. White and 22 years old when she was arrested, Chris was the youngest of five children. Her parents separated when she was 5. Her father was an alcoholic who beat Chris and her siblings. During one incident, when Chris's mother tried to stop a beating of the children, her father pushed her mother down the stairs and broke her arm. The father also beat Chris's brother to the point of breaking his eardrum. The probation officer suggested that because of her father's beatings, Chris became "nervous," and her "speech was unintelligible." After being referred to a school psychologist, Chris was placed in special education classes from the second grade until she graduated from high school. Chris's mother described her as "an obedient daughter" and "easily led." Chris worked for several years before marrying when she was 21. Her husband, Bob, was 35. When they married, her mother disapproved of him so much that she did not go to the wedding. Bob was a trucker, and Chris traveled with him on the road. When they returned to the New Haven area, they cared for Chris's nieces and nephew on the weekends. It was during this time that the sexual abuse occurred. Although Bob was the person who had instigated the abuse, Chris did not stop him. Chris's account suggests that she acted with him to please him and to be loved by him.[5]

Battered Women

From media depictions of celebrated cases, as well as deserved feminist attention, one might conclude that cases of battered women who fight back against violent mates would be prevalent in felony court. They are not. But they are very much present, and the biographies and circumstances of the New Haven battered women are like those reported in social research and legal commentary (for example, Browne 1987; "Women's Self-Defense Law" 1986). The cases of Sharon and Carrie illustrate the range of this five-woman group.

Sharon. Sharon was sexually and physically assaulted as a child, and as an adult, her "crime" was fighting back against a violent intimate. Black and 28 years old, Sharon grew up in New York City. It appears that her father, an alcoholic, abused family members, including Sharon. She left home after she was raped at age 15, but the PSI gives few details about it. Although Sharon's story is classic, she did not run to the streets; instead she was able to make something of herself. She had a child at age 18, and although she had completed only eight years of schooling, she trained as a nurse's aide and was steadily employed. Her problems began in her early twenties when she began dating Tim. He had a lengthy arrest record and was described as "disruptive, assaultive, and a seriously disturbed individual." They had a child together, but during their seven-year relationship, she "lived under constant harassment" from Tim. Two years before the incident she tried to commit suicide. The circumstances that led to the current incident were that Tim came to Sharon's house drunk and threatened to harm her if she would not let him into her apartment. He came after her; she shot at him, but he survived.

Sharon had never been arrested before, had no problems with alcohol or drugs, and was not violent toward others. Several other battered women, however, had one or more of these elements in their background, as is seen from Carrie's biography.

Carrie. Carrie, black and 38, was arrested for firing a pistol at her boyfriend when he tried to hit her with his car. Raised in the South and one of twelve children, Carrie had moved to New Haven when she was 15 to live with an older sister. She finished the ninth grade, but her arrest record suggests a life on the streets soon after. Her first conviction was for larceny at age 17. She was twice convicted for breach of peace at ages 18 and 19, and she served about six weeks in jail. She married when she was 21. At 22 she was convicted for prostitution, and at 23 she was convicted for assault with a weapon and shoplifting. She was also convicted of shoplifting twice in her midtwenties. She separated from her husband, and in her late twenties she began to live with Chuck. Chuck had a record of gambling and drug convictions and had served time in jail. They lived together for ten years, and Carrie was severely beaten by him during this period. On one occasion she was hospitalized for eleven days. She began using cocaine with Chuck and had a moderate habit. She drank alcohol heavily but has since quit. In the last several years she has been turning her drug and alcohol abuse problems around. In this offense, witnesses reported that Carrie was crying and yelling at Chuck to leave her alone.

In Carrie's biography one sees that several pathway categories may describe a woman over time. In her twenties, Carrie led the life of a street woman. But by the end of her twenties and over the next decade, she was in a relationship with a violent man, who like Carrie, abused cocaine.

Drug-connected Women
The five drug-connected women in this subgroup used or sold drugs with boyfriends or family members. Court officials attributed the women's lawbreaking largely to the men in their lives.

Winnie. Winnie, white and 18, grew up in a middle-class household; she stole silverware from her parents. She said she took the silver "so I could get some money so we [her husband and herself] could be together."[6] Winnie was a model student and had no problems at home until she was 16, when she started seeing Sam. She continued to see Sam against her parents' wishes. Eventually, her parents evicted her from the house because they could not "tolerate her negative behavior."

During her relationship with Sam, Winnie began to abuse alcohol and drugs. At 17, she married Sam, moved in with his parents, and got pregnant. Sam and his parents wanted her to have the child, but her parents did not. She was hospitalized for depression for several months after she had an abortion. While married, she lived with her parents several times and stole from them to support Sam and herself. Her current arrest was the result of pawning her parents' silverware, estimated to be worth close to $30,000, for $200. Her parents said they never wanted to see her again.

Miranda. Colombian-born and 42, Miranda was arrested with her sons for selling drugs out of their house. Miranda had attended school, but her education was "terminated prematurely" after nine years. At 22 she had her first child, and by 26 she had two more children. A year after the birth of her third child, she and her family moved to New York City. Soon after, her children returned to Colombia to live with their grandparents. While in New York, Miranda was a factory worker and a seamstress. She gave birth to two more children. After her fifth child, Miranda developed a back problem that made it difficult for her to work. Her husband also died. Several years later, she returned to Colombia to live for a year. At 35, she moved to the New Haven area with her children. She was first convicted of selling drugs when she was 37. New Haven police consider Miranda and her family among the "major drug distributors" in the area.

Other Cases
Four of the women's biographies did not fit the profile of the street, harmed and harming, battered, or drug-connected women. None seemed to have a problem with drugs or alcohol. Their offenses had economic motives unrelated to a drug addiction or to a street life, as Prish's biography suggests.

Prish. White and 50 years old, Prish recalled having had a normal childhood in a working-class household. Her parents divorced when Prish was 12, and her mother soon remarried. Prish is the only woman in the deep sample to have completed a four-year college degree. She married three times but never had children. Her most recent marriage, to Michael, took place when she was in her late thirties, and was described as happy and stable. Soon after their marriage, Prish began working as a bookkeeper and office manager for a car dealership, the organizational victim in this offense. She worked there for eleven years, made a good salary, and seemed to have no gambling, drug, or other psychological problems. She has never been arrested before. Although she and her husband were building a house, they had no major debts. She embezzled more than $125,000 from her employer during the last six years of her employment. Curiously, while out on bond and awaiting trial, she secured another bookkeeping job with another car dealership in the area.

My review of the women's biographies suggests that the street woman pathway, although frequent, is only one of several routes to felony court. Allowing that the deep sample underrepresents women convicted of drug offenses — women who are likely to be street women — I estimate that no more than half of the women prosecuted in urban felony courts arrived by the street woman pathway. I would not argue that the deep-sample women's biographies topple the leading feminist scenario of women's lawbreaking. On the contrary, the street woman

Table 3.2　Women's Pathways by Race and Ethnicity

	Street	Harmed and Harming	Battered	Drug-connected	Other	Total
Black	5	7	4	4	3	23
Latin	0	3	1	1	0	5
White	5	5	0	1	1	12
Total	10	15	5	6	4	40

pathway is likely to be more common for women prosecuted in district or misdemeanor courts, where most criminal cases are disposed, than in felony courts. But I would argue for a more multidimensional explanation of why women get caught up in crime. In addition to the street woman pathway, the routes to felony court may include:

1. Having been abused or neglected when young, or defined as having a violent nature, joined in adolescence with alcohol or drug abuse and psychological problems.
2. Being (or having been) in a relationship with a violent man.
3. Being associated with boyfriends, mates, or family members who use or sell drugs. Although a minority pathway to the court, these women were pulled into lawbreaking by allowing their household to be used for drug sales or by participating with boyfriends in drug-related crime.
4. Such other reasons as wanting money to lead a more economically secure and conventional life.

Although the numbers are small, I note some racial and ethnic differences among the women (table 3.2). No white woman was classified as battered, and no latin woman was in the street women group. Apart from these differences, the proportions of black and white women in the street and battered women groups are comparable to their ratios in the deep sample. The PSI is not sufficiently detailed to determine whether Eleanor Miller's (1986) finding of black women's deviant and domestic networks applies to these New Haven women. I did find, however, that a portion of the black women in my sample grew up in households that were not only abusive but also where their mothers used drugs. Drug-using mothers were not evident in the PSI's for the white women.

My analysis of women's pathways is useful for telling us something about women and crime and for suggesting a typology of women's blameworthiness.

Women and Crime

The street woman scenario can be misleading in putting too much emphasis on the economic motives for crime, or on crime "as work." We see in the harmed and harming women's biographies a trajectory in which childhood abuse, lack of care, or psychological problems leave some women emotionally crippled, angry and abusive toward others, and getting high on drugs and alcohol frequently. At issue for these women is not just that their survival or poverty is criminalized (Carlen 1988; Chesney-Lind 1989), but that their anger or violence is criminalized.

Cathy Widom's (1989, 261) research on the relation between child abuse or neglect and adult arrest for crime shows that 16 percent of the girls who were officially adjudicated as abused or neglected were arrested as adults, while the arrest rate for the control group (girls who were not adjudicated as neglected or abused) was 9 percent.[7] Widom acknowledges problems in distinguishing those in the control group from those *adjudicated* as abused or neglected, and in using adult arrest data as an indication of lawbreaking. Her research, however, demonstrates that abused or neglected children are more likely to be arrested for crime as adults. Her study also calls attention to offense-based variation in arrest patterns for the abused or neglected and control groups of women. Specifically, she finds that as adults, abused or neglected women were not at "increased risk" of arrest for violent offenses, although they were at increased risk of arrest for property, drug, and public order offenses (ibid., 264).

The New Haven women's biographies and offenses shed light on Widom's findings for offense-based variability. Of the twenty-five women prosecuted for violent offenses (using Widom's definition of violence, which includes robbery), five were reacting to or fending off violent men. Although Widom recognizes that women may turn their aggression inward more than men do (often resulting in psychiatric hospitalization), she did not consider another dimension of women's violence. For some women, their aggression is spawned *in adulthood* in their relations with abusive and violent men, who precipitate the violence.

To the street woman scenario of hustling in the shadow of the law, we need to add those harmed and harming women (nine of fifteen) whose illegalities were not in pursuit of economic gain. Instead, these women were angry and harmed others. We also need to consider women who may not have been abused or neglected as children but who now suffer and respond to such violence at the hands of their mates. These women's experiences as victims and victimizers cannot be explained by immediate economic conditions or struggles to survive economically, but reflect a process of reproducing physical and emotional harm.

As Jack Katz (1988)   for men's subjectivities in lawbreaking, so too for women: explanations for crime grounded largely on an economic understanding of human behavior are incomplete. I disagree in part with Katz's construction of crime's "seductions." Because his analysis focuses on the immediate circumstances leading to a particular offense, he offers little biographical context in which to locate crime's putative allure, and he mainly concentrates on men's lives and the criminal consequences of masculinity. Had Katz learned more about men's lives, not just for celebrated male cases, he might have seen that crime's seductions are not only about easy money or transcending humiliation, but also include reproducing harms visited upon the lawbreakers themselves in the past.

Blameworthiness

How might the biographies and patterns of offense affect the responses of court officials toward women? In chapter 2 we learned that after taking into account the offense and the defendant's prior record, Judge Kinney might consider whether the defendant had led a street life or not. Street women are a category of disreputable defendants and are likely candidates for incarceration. Some street women, many harmed and harming women, and all the battered women, however, were either abused growing up or in their current relationships. Thus, using Mary Gilfus's (1992) term, there are *blurred boundaries* between victim and offender in describing women's biographies. That blurring is likely to produce two distinct versions of blameworthiness, especially for women prosecuted for interpersonal violence and robbery.

In one, women's violence — though spawned in the context of being harmed herself or as a product of mental imbalance — is viewed as dangerous to others. Susan's biography, together with her previous and current offenses, is an example of this modality. In another, women's violent acts may be viewed as explicable or excusable. Sharon's shooting an abusive intimate and Nola's abuse of her child would fall into this category.

For those women whose crime was carried out with a boyfriend or spouse (ten women in the deep sample), court officials may have difficulty in determining blameworthiness. They may wonder whether the woman was acting equally and autonomously or not. Chris's biography and child abuse suggests she was "controlled" by her boyfriend, and Colleen seemed more of a bystander in her husband's selling of drugs. Yet, as we shall see in part 3, there is a good deal of ambiguity surrounding these and other deep-sample crimes.

Notes

1. There were 12 women for whom evidence of childhood victimization existed in the PSI or the file; for 23 there was no evidence; and for 5, there was not sufficient information to say. The 30% figure is based on the entire deep sample (12 of 40); for those with PSI's, the percentage is 32 (11 of 34).

2. The PSI's were not often clear on the type of state benefits the defendants received.

3. The name comes, in part, from the title of Eleanor Miller's (1986) book.

4. Readers might consider whether, in light of this biographical sketch, the meaning or seriousness of Kate's robbery changed.

5. Marcia Millman's (1975) analysis of the sociological and cultural understandings of gender and deviance calls attention to the ease with which women's deviance can be explained by "falling in love with a deviant man," among other explanations. Few of the deep-sample women were characterized this way, and when they were, the role of dominating men was also part of the picture. In chap. 7, I consider these themes. See Lisa Maher's (1993) critique of the she-did-it-all-for-love thesis as it applies to women's initiation into drug use.

6. It is hard to determine whether Winnie stole the silver for drug money or to maintain her relationship with her husband. The latter was given more emphasis in the PSI.

7. Widom also finds that a higher proportion of abused or neglected black women (28%) than white women (17%) were later arrested. Figures for the control groups of black and white women were 19% and 11%, respectively. (I am reporting these differences for the oldest of four age groups in Widom's table 3, p. 263.)

4 Men's Pathways to Felony Court

What are men's routes to felony court? Although I tried to place the men's biographies in the women's pathway scheme, it was without success — not surprisingly, since the women's pathways were tailored to research on women's lawbreaking. But in my effort to determine how men fit into a women-based classification, I saw with even greater clarity why women may not fit theories of crime. Such theories, which are typically based on boys' or men's lives, do not consider certain elements: (1) the greater likelihood that young women run away from abusive households, (2) the impact and significance of becoming a mother and caring for a child, (3) women's ability to make money by forms of sex work, but being denied access to other illegitimate activities because they are for men only, (4) for women on the street, the need to form ties to men for protection, in light of male competition for control of the street;[1] and (5) gender relations in street life and in their intimate lives that put women at great risk to be battered by men they know.

For some time feminist scholars have shown that theories of crime center on male delinquency and adult men's lawbreaking (as, for example, Daly and Chesney-Lind 1988; Leonard 1982; Naffine 1987; Smart 1976); even nonfeminist scholars have pointed this out (such as Harris 1977; Reckless 1961). Such theories are also remiss in that they fail to consider the gender specificity in men's or boys' lives. With some exceptions (as Cohen 1955; Miller 1958), masculinity is ignored (see Allen 1989): it is construed as a universal condition of generic "man."

After reading the men's biographies, I devised several categories to capture a masculine specificity. These embody the "costs and excesses of masculinity" and include explosive expressions of violence, protecting one's honor or oneself from harassing men, and engaging in crime as recreational activity. I also identified masculine versions of street, harmed and harming, and drug-connected pathways.

With modifications and additions to the women's pathway scheme, the men's routes to felony court were as follows: *street* (fifteen men), *harmed and harming* (eight men), *drug-connected* (three men), the *excesses of masculinity* group, containing the explosively violent (seven men), *bad luck* (five men), and *masculine gaming* (two men). These groups are defined in the sections below. For now, I note that compared to the women, more of the men conformed to a pattern of street life, and fewer were harmed and harming.

Profile of the Deep-Sample Men and Comparisons with the Women

The men's age ranged from 16 to 61 years and averaged 27. Most were black (65 percent), 25 percent were white, and 10 percent were from Puerto Rico or a Latin American country.

Familial Circumstances Growing Up

Close to half of the men were raised by their biological parents, and 38 percent were raised by their mother alone. One man was from a middle-class household, and one-third lived in stable working-class households; most grew up in economically precarious circumstances. Half the men either knew their biological father or their father had played a role in their upbringing. Close to 10 percent grew up in a household in which he or his siblings were physically abused or neglected.

Most men were raised in large families: more than half had at least three siblings, and 38 percent were raised in families with six or more children. Only one man was an only child. Of those with siblings, 16 percent had a sibling who was involved in crime. For 9 percent, their parents or guardians had been arrested or convicted of a crime. One-fifth of the men's mothers, fathers, or both were alcohol or drug abusers. Nine percent ran away from home or a juvenile institution while growing up.

To summarize the men's early years, most grew up in economically rough circumstances; 15–20 percent were likely victims of abusive, alcoholic, or drug-addicted parents. Compared to the women, more men knew their biological fathers, and fewer seem to have been abused or neglected by a parent or guardian. While growing up, the men's caretaking arrangements were more stable than the women's, fewer of the men's siblings were involved in crime, and fewer of the men's parents were addicted to alcohol or drugs. Although the men's economic and emotional circumstances growing up were not optimal, they were better than the women's for almost all the indicators. Evidence of strained familial relations was higher for women than men (38 versus 25 percent), and a larger proportion of women than men (26 versus 9 percent) ran away from home or a juvenile facility. The men's formative years suggest less damaging and abusive family contexts than the women's.[2]

Education, Employment, and Family

Like the women, 40 percent of the men had completed high school or had their GED; only one man graduated from a four-year college. The reasons for not completing high school were related to acting out in school, high rates of absenteeism, and indications of "limited intelligence" or mental retardation. A striking gender difference is the greater frequency with which the deep-sample men were characterized as dull, slow, or limited intellectually: seven men were described in these terms, but none of the women was. Although 19 percent of the men had vocational training, 29 percent of the women did. The type of training men pursued was in electronics, welding, and industrial arts. Somewhat more than half the men had only sporadic work experience or none; at the time of the offense 70 percent were not employed in a paid job, and about 20 percent received various types of state aid.

Most of the men (60 percent) claimed not to have fathered a child.[3] Of those who had, the average age at which they first became fathers was 23. At the time of the offense, 22 percent had child dependents whom they said they supported on a regular basis. Most men lived with a mother (31 percent) or with a partner and child (if any) (34 percent). None of the men with dependent children had sole responsibility for their care. For only two men was it explicitly mentioned in the PSI that they had abused a girlfriend or spouse.

For the men's employment and familial circumstances, then, most were high school dropouts without evidence of further training in a skill. Though a strong minority (44 percent) had had a steady job in the past, at the time of the offense, 31 percent were working and 19 percent were on state aid. Thus, half the men had no clear means of economic support. Although 40 percent of the men admitted they were biological fathers, at the time of the offense, only 20 percent were supporting their children — in part, because the children had grown.

Gender differences are striking in the paid work, family, and household areas. Far more women than men claim to be biological parents (65 versus 44 percent), and twice as many women are familied (71 versus 34 percent).[4] While eleven women had *sole* responsibility for the care of their children, none of the men had such responsibilities. One woman lived with her mother alone, while ten men did. Somewhat more men than women had some form of paid employment, but most men (56 percent) and women (68 percent) had no or only sporadic paid work experience. Somewhat more women (59 percent) than men (50 percent) had some source of economic support, whether through legitimate paid jobs or state aid.

Substance Abuse, Psychological Problems, and Prior Record

A little more than half of the men abused alcohol or drugs, or both. The average age at which they began to abuse drugs or alcohol was 17–18. None of the men developed their habit in association with a partner or spouse, and a minority (20 percent) of substance abusers had at some time entered a drug treatment program. Psychological problems or mental disabilities were noted for 31 percent of the men; they included being aggressive, depressive, immature or "primitive," mentally retarded, and a "regressed sex offender." Only one man was reported to have attempted suicide.

One-fourth of the men had never been arrested before; 38 percent had up to five prior arrests or convictions, and 38 percent had been caught up in the criminal justice system six or more times. Of those with a record of arrests, the average age at first contact with penal authorities was 17–18. One-fourth of the men had been arrested by the age of 16, and 20 percent had been institutionalized in a juvenile reformatory.

Common to men and women were high levels of alcohol and drug abuse, with higher levels of women (65 percent) than men (55 percent) having a problem with alcohol or drug addiction.[5] Women's substance abuse problems developed a bit later than men's did and were more likely to have begun in association with a partner or spouse. More women than men (56 versus 31 percent) were described as having psychological problems or mental disabilities,[6] and a higher proportion of women than men (15 versus 3 percent) had attempted suicide. Men got into trouble with penal authorities at an earlier age than did the women, and their previous records of arrests and convictions were more substantial. More women than men (41 versus 25 percent) had *ever* received a psychological evaluation, but the character of men's intelligence was mentioned more often. When the men's mental abilities were characterized, more frequent reference was made to limited intelligence in comparison to the women, who if their intelligences were described, would more likely be characterized as being "higher than average."

Encapsulating details, the men's profile suggests that about one-fourth were family men with paid jobs; they had completed high school, did not abuse drugs or alcohol, and had not been arrested before. At least half the men were at the other end of the spectrum: they were high school dropouts without a regular job; they were drug or alcohol addicted, lived with their mothers, and had moderate to heavy prior records. The remaining quarter of the men fell between these poles: they moved between a law-abiding life and episodes of lawbreaking.

Compared with the men, the profile for the women suggests more abuse or neglect while growing up, and as adults a higher frequency of drug or alcohol addiction and psychological problems. The women's lives, however, also reveal more stability and purpose: they have responsibilities for the care of children, more have vocational training, and somewhat more have sources of legitimate income from state aid or paid jobs. The women thus appear more conventional in the present lives and more scarred from victimization in their recent and distant past.[7]

Biographies of the Deep-Sample Men

To afford comparisons with the women, I present the men's pathways in roughly the same order as the women's. Table 4.1 lists each group, together with the men's pseudonyms and the statutory offenses of conviction.

Street Men

There were two masculine versions of street men: standard and hardened. Common to both was an addiction to drugs and for some, alcohol. The standard street men varied in their commitment to street life: some supplemented their paid employment with lawbreaking, or they would turn to crime when seasonal jobs ended. Hardened street men had serious drug or alcohol addictions; they were hardened by both street life and time spent in prison.

Standard Street Men
Street men were like street women in that most were drug addicted or at times alcoholics, they sold drugs or committed economic crimes to support a drug habit, and they had a developing record of convictions. Some street men were not entirely committed to the street life and withdrew from it when they got regular jobs. Unlike street women, street men did not run from abusive households. Instead, they dropped out of school to work or because they did not perform well. Although it is possible that street men were initially pulled into lawbreaking by their membership in delinquent groups, this was rarely mentioned in the PSI. Eleven men's biographies and offenses correspond to the standard version of street men. Of these, Lester, Rennie, and Casey provide a good sampling.

Lester. Black and 27, Lester slashed the face of a man who refused to give him money to buy a pint of alcohol. Born in the South, one of six children, Lester was 17 when he moved to New Haven to live with his brother. He left the South soon after he was suspended from school for fighting. Although Lester completed ten years of school, the PSI writer suggests that "his speech and thought processes appear quite

Table 4.1   Men's Pathways to Felony Court

Street Men (*N*=15): Lives by petty hustles or more serious forms of lawbreaking, typically to support a drug addiction: (a) regular masculine version characterized by problems in school or developing drug use as pathway to the street (rather than running away from abusive households); (b) hardened street men involved in lawbreaking early on; spent a good deal of time incarcerated in adult facilities.

a. Regular masculine version (*N*=11)

Antonio (robbery 1st)
Carl (sale of narcotics)
Casey (robbery 1st)
Douglas (sale of narcotics)
Dylan (sale of narcotics)
Joe (larceny 1st)
Lester (assault 2d)
Rennie (sale of narcotics)
Rob (sale of narcotics)
Ron (robbery 1st)
Simon (attempted robbery 1st)

b. Hardened street men (*N*=4)*

Geoff (larceny 1st)
Pete (attempted assault 2d)
Roger (larceny 1st)
Wade (risk of injury)

Harmed and Harming Men (*N*=8): May have been physically or sexually abused or neglected while growing up; family life chaotic, had many caretaking arrangements, or alcoholic parents; defined by others as violent, aggressive, or acting out

a. Predictable link between harmed and harming elements (*N*=5)

Allen (robbery 1st)
Clarence (assault 1st)
Lennie (larceny 4th)
Victor (robbery 1st and conspiracy to commit robbery 1st)
Wayne (arson 2d)

b. Unclear link between harmed and harming elements (*N*=3)

Maurice (assault 1st)
Ralph (risk of injury)
Scott (larceny 2d)

(continued)

Table 4.1 (continued)

Costs and Excesses of Masculinity ($N=14$): Masculine-specific contexts and forms of lawbreaking

a. Explosively Violent Men ($N=7$): Anger erupts while drunk; violence is directed to others the man knows, such as intimates, family members, and children

Barry (manslaughter 1st)
Earl (manslaughter 1st)
Enrico (reckless burning)
Georges (attempted assault 1st)
Jack (risk of injury and assault 1st)
Ted (conspiracy to commit murder)
Wes (manslaughter 1st)

b. Bad Luck Men ($N=5$): In the wrong place at the wrong time, used by others, reacting to harassing men

Andrew (assaulting a police officer, 2 counts)
Darrell (larceny 1st)
Juan (sale of narcotics)
Richie (aiding robbery 1st)
Shane (assault 2d)

c. Masculine Gaming ($N=2$): Junior version of street men; street crime as recreational activity with friends

Charles** (robbery 3d)
Tyrone** (larceny 5th)

Drug-connected Men ($N=3$): Recreational drug user; not involved in street life

Carlos (possession of narcotics)
Larry (assault 3d)
Reggie (sale of narcotics)

*In addition to these men, there were six others who spent considerable time incarcerated in juvenile and adult institutions: Allen, Casey, Jack, Lennie, Rennie, and Wayne.
**On the pathway to becoming a street man

slow, giving the impression that he is intellectually limited." Soon after arriving in New Haven, Lester was arrested for breach of peace. During his twenties he was convicted seven times for carrying a dangerous weapon, petty larceny, possessing marijuana, breach of peace, and related incidents. He received short jail sentences three times. All his arrests and convictions appear to be alcohol-related. He began to live with a girlfriend in his midtwenties, and they now have two children. Some years before, he had fathered two other children by another woman. Apart from one job as a dishwasher when he was 23, Lester has no work record. He quit that job because there were "too many varied chores expected of him." He supported himself primarily from city welfare and his girlfriend. Lester's brother said Lester is "mentally slow" and that the "simple life of the family farm is [better for Lester] than the fast pace of the city."

Compared to other street men, Lester's lawbreaking was alcohol-related; more commonly, street men are drug addicted. Casey and Rennie, the street men next described, exemplify an escalating drug habit with a life almost entirely committed to lawbreaking, with no sources of income from regular jobs. Their records were heavy, and their lawbreaking a routine part of their lives.

Casey. Casey, whose robbery of a convenience store opened the book, is black and in his midtwenties. He attributes his lawbreaking to his addiction to crack, saying, "I did a lot of things to get crack that I am not proud of. One of those things is [this robbery]." Casey was the third of four children his mother had from two marriages. His parents divorced when he was 7; his younger brother was "well known" to the New Haven penal authorities. Casey completed ten years of schooling but was sent to a reformatory when he was 17 for a burglary and larceny conviction. He has been in and out of prison since. At 18 he was convicted of larceny and sentenced to serve a year; at 19 he was sentenced to sixty days for a car theft, and later that year he was sentenced to serve eighteen months for a robbery. When he was 21, he was convicted for possessing a stolen credit card and for forgery and car theft; he received more incarceration time. When he was released from prison, he was soon arrested and before the courts again, this time for disorderly conduct. A year later, and about the same time as the instant offense, he was arrested for burglary, robbery, and assaulting an elderly person.

In high school Casey was described as a marginal student who "would not apply himself." Admitting to his crack addiction, Casey told the probation officer, "I knew I would get caught. I wanted to get caught. When I came to jail . . . I knew I needed a . . . program. I needed something because using this crack was killing me. I was hurting people. This was my cry for help."

Rennie. Rennie, a black man, was 33 when he was arrested for having heroin, cocaine, and marijuana in his apartment. A heroin addict since he was 20, Rennie has accumulated a long record of arrests and convictions. Rennie's parents divorced when he was 11. His father was arrested for gambling when Rennie was an adolescent. Rennie completed high school, but when he tried to enlist in the Marines after graduation, he could not pass the test. He had no paid work during his twenties and early thirties. Most of his time was spent in and out of jail. He was first convicted at 17 for shoplifting, and at 19, for carrying a weapon and car theft, for which he received a jail sentence. At 20 he was convicted of possessing heroin and jailed. Convicted of several petty larcenies in his early twenties, he was convicted of robbery at 23 and received a sentence of five years' minimum to serve. Incarcerated between the ages of 23 and 26, out for a year, and then back on a parole violation in his late twenties, Rennie was again convicted in his early thirties on several minor charges; he was sentenced to serve a year for a burglary. All the offenses stem from his heroin addiction.

In his late twenties he fathered a child, and then married Colleen, a street woman with an extensive record of arrests for prostitution and larceny to support her drug habit (see Colleen's story, above). After Rennie got out of jail for serving time on the burglary conviction, he lived with Colleen and his son. He worked for a while, supplementing his earnings with welfare. He has been in drug treatment and was off drugs for sixteen months, but after his release from jail on the burglary conviction, he was again using heroin.

Hardened Street Men

Casey's and Rennie's biographies demonstrate a cycle of drug addiction, lawbreaking, conviction, and imprisonment. As established street men who have spent a large part of their lives in prison, their biographies shade into a second trajectory of street men: those hardened by street life and stretches of time in prison. Alcohol and drug addiction feature in these men's lives; in the following sketch of Roger, alcohol was the problem.

Roger. Roger, a white man, was 25 when he and an accomplice broke into a residence and stole items worth several thousand dollars. Roger had one of the longest criminal records of the deep-sample men: more than fifty convictions for public order offenses, bad checks, larcenies, and some burglaries, which he committed from the ages of 16 to 25. Although Roger said there were never serious family problems, he felt that his brothers received preferential treatment. At 15 he began to get into trouble; he ran away from home and lived with another family. The next year he married a fifteen-year-old; they had a child when Roger was 17 and a second child when he was 21. When he was released from prison at 22, his wife left Roger and the children, who were cared for by his parents.

Roger completed nine years of school but dropped out in the tenth grade; he was absent half the time. He began drinking at 13 and attributes much of his lawbreaking to excessive drinking. Since he was 17 he has received nine separate incarceration sentences. His pattern was to commit offenses almost immediately after being released from prison. For example, after his release in December 1978, he committed another offense in January of 1979; he was back in prison immediately. Two years after his wife left him, he married again;

he was incarcerated at the time. His wife supported herself and her two children from welfare. He tried to stop drinking alcohol on several occasions without success. Several months before the instant offense, he was on work release from an inpatient alcohol treatment center. He left the facility each morning on the pretense of working, but he never really had a job. When he was arrested for the instant offense, he was out on bond.

Harmed and Harming Men

Like their women counterparts, a common experience for the harmed and harming men is having been physically abused or neglected as a child or growing up in chaotic family circumstances in which one or both parents abused alcohol or drugs. Caretaking arrangements often shifted. Unlike harmed and harming women, the men were not characterized by family members as "out of control," nor did they exemplify alcohol-related violence as much as the women did. The eight harmed and harming men grew up in tough circumstances, emotionally and psychologically. For five, one can see a chain of events from their childhood experiences to harming others, but for three, the link was less clear. Each trajectory is illustrated in the following biographies.

Predictable Link

Victor. Among the most harrowing family histories is Victor's. Aged 17 and white, he robbed a gas station with two older men. Victor was born in New York, the oldest of five children. His mother had many boyfriends, some of whom beat Victor and his mother. His mother was unable to care for Victor or his younger siblings. A New York Protective Services case worker's report, written when Victor was 12, described his household as being "in disarray with garbage strewn about; . . . [it] lacked heat, locks on doors, bathroom facilities, and child-proof windows." Victor and his siblings wore torn and dirty clothes; they had body dirt and dirty hair. His mother is described as having "no front teeth; [she] wears her hair very teased, and wears a great deal of make-up." Further, she is depicted as leading a "disorganized and promiscuous lifestyle," which has "pushed Victor into an adult-like lifestyle prematurely."

Victor and his siblings were adjudicated neglected when he was 14. He was placed in a home, where he lived for less than two years before returning to his mother's household. He refused to attend school and has never been employed. School records suggest that he is mentally impaired. When given an educational evaluation at 16, he was described as performing at the fifth grade level. A psychiatric evaluation reported "no psychotic symptoms" but a "behavior disorder of adolescence with a history of stealing, truancy, drug abuse, and aggressivity." He is also described as "striving for pseudomasculine images for himself." An uncommon display of self-deprecation is apparent in Victor's comment about his offense: "It's terrible what I did. I'm a disgusting person. I did wrong." Several months before the robbery, Victor had been arrested for another robbery. The probation officer attributed Victor's involvement in both robberies to his identification with older men.

Clarence. Clarence, black and 29 years old, stabbed an acquaintance with a broken bottle and stole his car keys and car. The facts of the incident are cloudy because the 50-year-old victim changed his story, saying that Clarence may not have been the man who stabbed him. Clarence's biography contains less detail than Victor's, but one sees in the gaps a difficult life growing up soothed by drinking alcohol to excess. Clarence and his twin sister were born in New York City. When he was 9, his parents divorced. His mother was apparently "distraught over the divorce" and brought her children to New Haven when Clarence was 11. A year later, his mother's drinking problem was such that she was unable to care for her children. Clarence and his sister were placed in a juvenile center, and he was there for a year and a half before being sent to a training school in New Jersey. He remained there until he was 18, completing the eleventh grade, and then returned to New Haven. In the next year, Clarence was arrested for criminal mischief, and over the next three years, he was convicted of five petty alcohol-related offenses. He spent about ten days in jail during this time. Clarence had "various odd jobs" doing carpentry and masonry work, though his "periods of employment were sporadic." When not employed, Clarence received city welfare. The probation officer thinks Clarence has some potential and attributes his problem to "a lack of motivation towards constructive activity." At the time of the instant offense, Clarence was living with a girlfriend; she said they planned to marry soon.

In Victor's and Clarence's biographies, victimization in the men's early years does not translate into violent or acting out behavior as we saw for the harmed and harming women. Rather, the biographies suggest a life without purpose, using drugs or alcohol as palliatives. For three other harmed and harming men, their lives were hardened by lawbreaking and imprisonment, as shown in Wayne's life sketch.

Wayne. Wayne, black and 27, set fire to his girlfriend's apartment, causing extensive damage. He was born in the New Haven area, the youngest of ten children. His early childhood was "unstable and insecure." When he was 5, his mother and father were sentenced to serve time for selling liquor to minors and for keeping a gambling house. His father died when Wayne was 11, and several years later his family moved to New Haven, where they lived in one of the "poor, run-down, high crime areas of the city." Two siblings were involved in lawbreaking. Wayne did not finish high school, and school records suggest he is "limited intellectually." He was first convicted at 16 for car theft; in the same year, he was convicted of burglary, breach of peace, and another car theft. He was sent to a reformatory that year, spending eight months there. Soon after his release, he was convicted of robbery and returned to the reformatory. He began to use drugs in midadolescence and by age 20 was using cocaine and heroin. From then to his arrest at 27 for the instant offense, Wayne was convicted on fifteen occasions, usually for larcenies and burglaries, and was sentenced to incarceration on six separate occasions. He said he would plead guilty to crimes because he wanted help; he hoped that going to jail would force him to quit using drugs. His employment record is sparse; he worked no more than several months in unskilled jobs before quitting or being laid off. When he was 25 he began to live with the victim of the arson he had committed, but they split up six months before the incident because she could not put up with Wayne's street life, drug use, battering, and threats to kill her.

Unclear Link

For three harmed and harming men, their biographies suggest a more discontinuous path from a harmful or chaotic home life to lawbreaking. Ralph's biography reveals this circuitry.

Ralph. White and in his midforties at the time of the arrest, Ralph had sexual relations with his stepdaughter on a regular basis while she was in her teens. Born in Connecticut, the second of three children, Ralph said his early years were difficult because his parents were always arguing and because he was in the middle of their marital problems. His mother was a full-time housewife, and his father was a skilled factory worker. His father, and perhaps also his mother, had an alcohol problem. Ralph recalled being an angry child and involved in many fights. When he was 11, he set fire to the priests' vestments in a church "as an expression of his anger." He graduated from high school and went on to complete a degree in design. He was steadily employed in blue-collar jobs, married in his late twenties, and had a son several years later. After his son's birth, he and his wife divorced, apparently amicably. He began to live with another woman, Rayna, and her two children. Ralph and Rayna married and had a child. Financial woes beset Ralph in his late thirties: he was convicted of tax fraud and lost a substantial sum of money in running a franchised business. Around this time, he began to abuse alcohol and drugs and to have sexual relations with his stepdaughter.

Costs and Excesses of Masculinity

Explosively Violent Men

The explosively violent men in my sample share similarities with the harmed and harming women who abused alcohol. There was, however, little evidence in the PSI that the men were victimized by abusive or alcoholic parents while growing up. Instead, the PSI suggests that the men had developmental problems with alcohol abuse. These, in turn, were linked to "work pressures" or other life problems. The explosively violent men may have grown up in harmful or damaging contexts, but such detail was not given in the PSI. All but one man in this group abused alcohol, but the rage and violence expressed in their harms cannot be explained simply by their "drinking too much." The biographies and offenses of Wes, Georges, and Jack illustrate these elements of explosively violent men.

Wes. Black and 50 years old, Wes fatally stabbed a friend late one evening during a fight. Raised on a farm in the South, he was one of ten children. He left school after the second grade to work on his father's farm. He is illiterate. Wes married in his late teens and had a child soon after. Over the next dozen years, Wes and his wife had five more children. In his early thirties, he moved to New Haven, having separated from his wife. He began to live with another woman, Ellen, and has been with her for nearly fifteen years. Described by his supervisor as a "reliable person," Wes was steadily employed as a maintenance worker. When he first came to New Haven, he accumulated a record of alcohol-related arrests for breach of peace and driving under the influence. Although he admitted he "has a drinking problem in a way," he was able to maintain a relationship with Ellen and to keep his job. Ellen said Wes has never been violent toward her, but she would call the police so he could sleep off his drunkenness in jail.

The circumstances leading to Wes's crime were captured in a note scrawled across the top of his probation department file: "The unhappy fishing trip." Wes and his buddy, Sammy, had been fishing and drinking all day. In the evening, they argued about who should pay for their hamburgers. Apparently Sammy punched Wes while he was driving, and this caused Wes's car to veer close to an oncoming car. Wes pulled the car over and challenged Sammy to fight. Wes could not "remember exactly what happened next," but was "remorseful."

Wes was angry at his friend for putting his life in danger. His judgment was likely impaired from having been drinking all day. One badge of masculinity is to settle a dispute or defend oneself by violent means. As the next biographies reveal, another is using violence to control and dominate intimates.

Georges. White and in his midforties, Georges fired shots at his wife and daughter as they drove away from their house. No one was physically injured. Born in Québec, the fourth of twelve children, Georges grew up on a farm. Except for economic difficulties, he recalled his early family life as "average." His father, a road maintenance worker, died when Georges was 15. Georges dropped out of high school to help support the family. In his late teens, he married Andrée, and they moved to the United States about a decade later in search of "better job opportunities." Andrée said their marital troubles began when they moved. Georges began to drink too much; he abused her and was "too strict" with her. Andrée also said that Georges was not a good father and liked to play with guns. The couple separated after more than twenty years of marriage and then reunited, but Andrée "threw him out" again, about a year before the shooting incident because of Georges's drinking and abuse. Several weeks before the incident, he had put in many overtime hours in his job. It was on the morning of the incident that he appeared in court for final divorce proceedings, apparently too drunk to go forward.

Jack. Of all the explosively violent men, Jack displayed the most intensity. Although I cannot be sure, his aggressiveness and anger may be linked to teenage years spent imprisoned, and perhaps also to violent experiences growing up that are not described in the PSI. Jack is a black man who beat his five-year-old stepson, Floyd, unconscious. At the time, Jack was caring for Floyd and two other sons while his wife was away. Jack denied he beat the boy but was convicted at trial.

Born in Detroit, the second of six children, Jack was raised primarily by his mother in conditions of poverty. His father left when Jack was 10 and has had no contact with the family since. Jack completed nine years of school and said he dropped out to support the family. He was first convicted at 17 for larceny and burglary and was sentenced to serve three years. Soon after his release, he married Annette. The couple lived with her parents and had three children over the next three years. Before the birth of the third child, Jack stabbed an acquaintance in an argument, and the man died. Jack was sentenced to serve a minimum of seven years. While incarcerated, he broke up with Annette. When he was released from prison, he married Rita. They had three children, although the third child, Floyd, was not fathered by Jack. In his early thirties, Jack was accused of abusing Floyd, who was less than two years old at the time. The circumstances surrounding this earlier incident of abuse were not made clear in the PSI, and Jack was not prosecuted. Floyd, however, was placed in the custody of his maternal grandfather. When Jack was 32, an arrest warrant was issued for him because he struck Annette's boyfriend in the head with a tire iron. Jack and Rita fled to New Haven after the warrant was issued. He worked in a laundry but was fired after a year for absenteeism and coming to work drunk. When Floyd's grandfather died, Floyd moved to New Haven to live with his mother, brothers, and Jack. The abuse of Floyd occurred a month after he moved to New Haven.

Bad Luck Men

Unlike the explosively violent men, the bad luck men did not abuse drugs or alcohol. Rather, they were in the wrong place at the wrong time, had to defend themselves from harassing men, or were used by other men. They exemplify the crime-promoting consequences of simply being a man.

Andrew. Black and 19, Andrew assaulted two police officers who were attempting to arrest his friend Bo for a suspected robbery. Raised in New Haven, Andrew is the youngest of six children. His parents separated before he was born, but his father lived nearby and kept in close contact. At the time of the offense, Andrew lived with his mother and older siblings. His mother described him as "always well-behaved at home," and a high school teacher praised him as "hard working and well-behaved with an excellent attitude." He graduated from high school, was active on the basketball team, and sang in the choir. He had not been arrested before and had no problem with drugs or alcohol.

The probation officer was at a loss to explain "his sudden outburst," in light of his having "no previous arrests, his exemplary school background, and a strong supportive family." Andrew's decision to come to the aid of his friend was based on what he perceived as police brutality. On sentencing day, he said, "I had seen that two police officers had picked [my friend] up and slammed him on the ground and started beating on him. I came over and asked them to let him up, and they did not do that. So I jumped in at that time." This situation is specific to men's lives (perhaps, more specifically, to the lives of minority group men). It is unlikely that a woman would intervene in this way when witnessing police officers "subduing" a suspect. Similarly, the next man, Shane, was reacting to the taunts and harassment of male gang members. Like Andrew, Shane responded in an immediate situation not of his choosing.

Shane. Black and 17 years old, Shane fired a gun at a gang member as he was leaving school. He had been punched by gang members earlier and had been taunted by them twice in the previous week. Shane was born in the South but raised in New Haven from the age of 3 by his maternal grandmother. His mother has a "history of emotional problems," and he never knew his father. He had a close relationship with his grandmother and referred to her as his mother. Shane had never been arrested before and did not use drugs or alcohol. While in high school, he received low marks in academic subjects but good ones in industrial arts courses. The shooting incident occurred six weeks before graduation, and although Shane was expelled from school because of it, he was allowed to complete his classes and graduate by home-based instruction. For three years in high school he was an elected representative in student government. The probation officer described him as "well-mannered" and a "soft-spoken young man."

Another route of bad luck men is being used by others, as the circumstances surrounding Juan's offense and the biography show.

Juan. Born in Puerto Rico, Juan was in his midtwenties when unspecified amounts of cocaine were found in his room. His biography combines elements of bad luck and drug-connected men. Juan was one of five children his mother had by five different men. He has had no contact with his father. A year before moving to New Haven and when he was 6, Juan "fell off a cliff [in Puerto Rico], was comatose" for a day, and was hospitalized for two months. His mental impairment and seizures are explained by the fall and fractured skull. The "falling off a cliff" story strains credulity, but it may have a cultural source.[8]

Juan was first evaluated as being mentally impaired when he was 12. A psychological report at the time indicated that he set fires and had "frequent outbursts of destructive behavior" that were followed by "hiding in the corner and chewing on his clothes." A psychological examination when Juan was 19 suggested that he failed to progress after three years in special classes. His mental slowness, inability to learn English, and high absenteeism were the reasons given. He was absent more than half the time, giving illness or family problems as the reason. Some blame was also leveled at Juan's mother, described as "a well-meaning but limited woman in that she has not become fully involved in the American culture." Juan participated in a vocational rehabilitation program. Other than poor attendance, he had good evaluations. He was not addicted to drugs or alcohol, nor had he been arrested before. Apparently he was set up to sell cocaine, having little sense of the implications and making little money from his efforts. He said "someone gave it [the cocaine] to me to sell, and I sold it. They would give me $20 to $40 a week."

One cannot help but be sympathetic to the circumstances of these bad luck men. They were caught up in events or relationships with other men that pushed them into lawbreaking. For the men I describe next, one is far less sympathetic.

Masculine Gaming

The masculine gaming set considers crime as a form of recreation. The lawbreaking of two young men and their friends exemplifies street crime that is frightening to victims but nets little economic reward for the offenders. For example, Tyrone and two friends robbed a woman of $7 and ripped off her gold chain. The incident that brought Charles to court involved a purse snatch.

Charles. Black and 18 years old, Charles, with a friend, threatened a young woman in a parking lot, taking her purse and checkbook, and then attempted to cash one of the checks. Born in New Haven, the elder of two children, Charles grew up in a stable working-class family. He completed eleven years of schooling, but he dropped out in the twelfth grade; no reason was given in the PSI. After the offense and before sentencing, Charles got a job as a maintenance worker, earning $4 an hour. This job was his first. He was described by his employer as a good worker and by the probation officer as "intelligent and street-wise."

For Tyrone and Charles, this was their first offense. I interpreted their acts as a form of recreation — that is, something to do when hanging out with their male friends, a way to prove their masculine prowess and street smarts. The masculine gaming men come closest to the conceptions of traditional delinquency theorists of young men's unplanned, though serious, delinquency, for the thrill of it (Cohen 1955; Miller 1958).

Street gangs were rarely discussed in the PSI's. Only two men's incidents were gang-related in some way, and gang membership or association was not part of the PSI script. Compared to gang activity in other cities (for example, Hagedorn 1988; Horowitz 1983; Moore 1978, 1991), New Haven's criminalized men may have been less organized in the early 1980s.[9]

Drug-connected Men
Like their female counterparts, the drug-connected men were not heavily drug addicted. Their lawbreaking largely supported a part-time recreational habit. Unlike the women, the men were not linked to girlfriends or family members in selling or using drugs. Carlos exemplifies the drug-connected men's route to felony court.

Carlos. Born in Colombia, Carlos was 27 when the police forced entry into his apartment, finding several packets of cocaine. Carlos had four siblings; his parents were dead. He came to the United States in his late teens and lived on the West Coast for five years before moving to New York. He lived in New York for about six months before moving to New Haven, where he has lived for several years. While in California, he fathered a child. He worked as a musician and has not been arrested before. He completed high school in Colombia before coming to the United States.

Table 4.2 Men's Pathways by Race and Ethnicity

| | Street | Harmed and Harming | Costs and Excesses of Masculinity | | | Drug-connected | Total |
			Explosively Violent	Bad Luck	Masculine Gaming		
Black	11	5	4	3	2	1	26
Latin	1	0	1	1	0	1	4
White	3	3	2	1	0	1	10
Total	15	8	7	5	2	3	40

Discussion

One common category of male defendants in felony court is street men. Their pathway to court began by dropping out of school to support a family or because of disinterest. Leaving school, coupled with the fun of getting high on drugs or alcohol, pulled adolescent boys into petty as well as serious forms of lawbreaking. Subsequently, the boys were in and out of the criminal justice system as their problems with drugs and alcohol intensified. Some street men were hardened and toughened by incarceration, often at an early age. Once addicted to illegal drugs, the men found that getting them had become a commanding force. For the alcoholics, drinking soothed a life without direction or purpose. I classified slightly more than 40 percent of the men as street men or on their way to becoming street men.

Another common pathway for men was victimization in childhood or an inability to control explosive violence toward others. Harmed and harming men were raised in damaging contexts: parents abused them or were alcoholics; mothers were unable to care for them. Explosively violent men lashed out at others, at times because they thought their lives were in danger, but more often because they wanted to control and dominate others. Although it is likely that some explosively violent men were mistreated when they were young, the PSI gave no evidence of this. Almost all the violent men had problems with alcohol.

The two remaining pathways were populated by first-time defendants. Bad luck men were in the wrong place at the wrong time, or they were used or harassed by other men; the drug-connected men were recreational drug users who were caught selling small amounts of drugs.

For racial and ethnic variability (table 4.2), the number of latin men is too small to make a good comparison. Of ten white men, I termed half harmed and harming or explosively violent, whereas of 26 black men, one-third were so termed. For black men, the street path was more frequent.

Men and Crime

The effects of criminalizing drugs and poverty brought a large share of men to felony court. Yet reasons other than economic motives or drug use were apparent: some grew up in abusive and harmful households, and some used violence as adults to settle disputes or to control others. For that reason, Katz's (1988) notion of crime's seductions, although useful in calling attention to the noneconomic rewards of lawbreaking, misses the mark for the harmed and harming and explosively violent men. Some, like the women, are reproducing harms visited upon them in the past. Some, however, also used masculine-specific forms of domination.

Scholars often cast male lawbreakers as victimized by economic conditions, racism, and limits on masculine forms of accomplishment in ghetto enclaves. In the 1970s many British and United States deviancy and labeling theorists explained men's crime this way (see Heidensohn 1985, 125–44; Young 1988), a tradition that persists in the United States (for example, Hagedorn 1988; Sullivan 1989; Taylor 1990). Some British criminologists (feminists and "left realists") recognize that this model of economically victimized manhood was incomplete in overlooking the physical and sexual abuse many men visited on intimates and children (Gelsthorpe and Morris 1988; Matthews and Young 1986; Young 1988). That realization has not taken root in United States criminology, where studies of male delinquency and crime continue to be silent on questions of men's abuse of women.[10]

As for the women, so too for the men: we need to bring into view the harmed and harming and explosively violent men whose lawbreaking is not about forms of illegal economic gain. Rather, it is about the reproduction of social and physical harm. The biographical material in the PSI's suggests some links between victimization in childhood and criminalization in adulthood. There are, however, other sites of male victimization that are not childhood- or family-centered: developmental forms of abuse men visit on each other, on the street or in institutions, during adolescence and adulthood.

Blameworthiness

How might these pathways affect the construction of court officials of men's blameworthiness? A large share of men are in the disreputable street-man category. Compared to the women, a smaller share claimed they were victimized in childhood and more became violent for seemingly inexplicable reasons. Hence, we might expect to find that a higher proportion of men's acts are viewed by court officials as more dangerous. These and other gender comparisons are discussed in the chapter summary.

Notes

1. This element varies by city, city area, and over time. When men "control the streets," a woman may need to ally with a man for protection (Miller 1986). Other research suggests that women may act more independently of men (Miller 1993).

2. The same conclusion is drawn from a Bureau of Justice Statistics jail study (1992): higher proportions of men grew up in homes with either one or both parents present, a higher share of women's than men's siblings were involved in crime, and women's experience with physical abuse was three times more frequent. Indeed, that study and mine had almost identical percentages for the men and women who reported being abused while growing up (9% versus 29%–31%) (BJS 1992, 10). These percentages may well underestimate the prevalence of abuse experienced by male and female defendants.

3. One reader thought this percentage seemed low and speculated whether more men were fathers, but fearful that they would be forced to pay child support, they denied a fatherhood status.

4. These percentages are comparable to those in my study of a New York City court (Daly 1987b, 1989b). I developed the term *familied* to describe gender- and family-based responses to defendants. Familied men and women may or may not be married, but they do have responsibilities for the care and economic support of others. Court officials make even finer distinctions between familied men and women, and they link a defendant's family status to features of the crime and the defendant's lawbreaking history (Daly 1987a, 1989a).

5. If the rates of alcohol and drug addiction for the deep sample are applied to the wide sample, gender differences widen further. I estimate that 68% of the women and 54% of the men prosecuted in felony court were drug or alcohol addicted. Women's higher abuse of drugs and alcohol is also seen in the Bureau of Justice Statistics jail study (1992). In addition, our studies found that although drugs are the favored substance of men and women, men are more likely to abuse alcohol alone.

6. For the 19 women for whom problems were noted, all focused on psychological states. For the 10 men, 6 concerned psychological states, and 4 concerned mental deficiencies of some type.

7. What is uncertain, of course, is how much the gender differences reported are a function of what questions are asked, how willing the defendants are to report social history information and in what detail, and the dynamics of interview process between a probation officer and defendant (and others interviewed).

8. I wonder whether the "fall" was an accident and whether the mental problems were evident before it. There were several Puerto Ricans in the deep sample whose violent acts and mental problems were attributed to various head-injury accidents they had in childhood.

9. The probation officers I interviewed said that in 1991 there were eight to ten well-known New Haven gangs, but that during my research, gang activity was less apparent to them and the police.

10. Compare John Hagedorn's (1988) study of young men affiliated with gangs in Milwaukee with Miller's (1986) interviews of street women in the same city. In Hagedorn's book, there is no mention of the men's violence toward their mates or girlfriends, but in Miller's, there is repeated reference to the women's experience of physical and sexual abuse by men. Recent work by James Messerschmidt (1993) and Tim Newburn and Betsy Stanko (1994) is exceptional in focusing on masculinities and crime.

Summary

Drawing from group profiles and biographies, I introduced the deep-sample men and women. Some have been crushed by poverty, drug and alcohol abuse, sexism, and racism. Others have not. Still others drift somewhere in between. Economic explanations alone are not sufficient to understand the circumstances that bring men and women to felony court. A key noneconomic dimension is the reproduction of physical and emotional harm, which takes gender-specific forms.

The biographies suggest a panoply of problems: drug addiction, alcohol abuse, rape and physical abuse, mental impairment, psychological problems, and violence in current relationships. Whatever their sources — childhood experiences, the expression or result of "normal" male domination in families and intimate relations, or victimization in institutions or on the streets — these problems were typical.

Eliciting Information

Gender comparisons are bedeviled by gendered processes in asking questions, divulging information, and how behavior is explained and categorized. In several areas, sharp gender differences were evident in the PSI's: abuse or neglect was mentioned more often in the women's than the men's PSI's (29 versus 9 percent), as were psychological problems. The more frequent indications of victimization and mental instability for women may reflect a gender-skewed lens through which probation officers and others interpret the women's behavior. Or they may reflect something real about women's and men's lives.

I broached these questions to a portion of the PSI writers. When I asked them why they thought victimization was more often mentioned in the women's PSI's, they said the men may be "more guarded" than the women in talking about themselves. They also thought it likely that women had been victimized more than the men and that women learned to articulate their experiences better. Finally, some said they were more inclined to probe the women's family histories because the women now had families.

When I asked them why psychological problems were mentioned more frequently in women's PSI's, they were surprised to learn of this difference since they remembered men and women as similarly "troubled." Subsequently, they offered the following explanations: Women prosecuted in felony court were already a select minority, and perhaps more than the men, they were the "cream of the [troubled] crop." One officer said she might not probe further in interviewing a man if he was a "typical heroin addict," whereas she might if a woman was drug addicted. The officers also suggested that women may give more information about themselves, they may be more "self-analytical" and seek psychological counseling, and family members and teachers may respond to misbehaving girls more strictly.

Blurred Boundaries and Blameworthiness

Compared to the men, more of the women's past lives appear troubled and scarred by victimization. At the same time, more of the women's present circumstances seem somewhat more conforming. Whatever the basis for these gender differences — partly real and partly amplified or attenuated by a gendering of knowledge about experience — we should expect the court to respond to some women, especially those victimized in the past, more sympathetically. Some men may also be viewed in a sympathetic light, especially those described as mentally slow or impaired.

A somewhat higher share of women than men had responsibility for others and a somewhat higher share of women had not been arrested before. If a forward-looking approach to punishment is taken, these indicators suggest a somewhat better prognosis for women than men. A significant minority of defendants came to felony court by the street pathway, but there were even more street men whose previous lawbreaking was more serious than that of the street women. Although there were ten men whose lives I considered to be hardened by years in prison or in street life, there were just two women whose lawbreaking and time institutionalized were comparable.

Differences were apparent in the link between biography and offense. Five women fought intimates who abused them, but no man was in this situation. Some victimized bad luck men might elicit court sympathy, but the explosively violent men, whose acts seemed inexplicable, would likely not elicit sympathy. More explicit linkages were made by PSI writers between the women's experience of past victimization and the current offense. The story line went this way: the women were abused or inadequately cared for, leading to "out of control" behavior, alcoholism, or drug addiction, which in turn led to street life or violence toward others. Another theme was that of being under the control of dominating men or being mentally unbalanced. These linkages between victimization, offending, and criminalization seemed "obvious" for women, though not most women, but for four in ten.

For the men, the link between victimization and criminalization was less obvious and was made less frequently. Such a link was evident for perhaps two of ten men. Fewer men were described as growing up

Table II.1 Gender, Race and Ethnicity, and Pathways

A. Women's pathways, collapsed categories I, II, and other

	I Street, Drug-connected	II Harmed and Harming, Battered	Other	Total
Black	9	11	3	23
Latin	1	4	0	5
White	6	5	1	12
Total	16	20	4	40

B. Men's pathways, collapsed categories I, II, and other

	I Street, Masculine Gaming, Drug-connected	II Harmed and Harming; Explosively Violent	Other (bad luck)	Total
Black	14	9	3	26
Latin	2	1	1	4
White	4	5	1	10
Total	20	15	5	40

C. Men's and women's pathways combined, collapsed categories I, II, and other

	I Street (etc.)	II Harmed (etc.)	Other	Total
Black	23	20	6	49
Latin	3	5	1	9
White	10	10	2	22
Total	36	35	9	80

in abusive households or having parents unable to care for them. One problem is that other sites of the men's victimization (such as reformatory schools and jails while in their teens, or initiation requirements for adolescent male groups) are not discussed by the probation officers or the men. The costs of masculinity, such as "taking it like a man" and not showing weakness, render men less victimized than they might be and construct them as less victimized in comparison to women. Overall, then, a portion of men may be viewed as more blameworthy than women.

Gender, Race and Ethnicity, and Pathways

I venture some broad brush strokes in characterizing the multiple influences of gender and race on pathways to court (Summary, II, table 1). The numbers of latin men and women are too small to warrant solid inferences, however.

With the exception of black men and latin women, half of those coming to felony court came by the street or drug-connected routes. For black men, the street and drug-connected pathways were even more frequent; for latin women the harmed and harming and battered pathways were more frequent. Put another way, black women, white women, white men, and latin men had roughly equal proportions of (1) street or drug-connected routes and (2) harmed and harming, battered, or violent pathways. More than all the other groups, black men were characterized as leading street lives, a status that may confer a more serious quality to their acts.

III What Did They Do?

One way to assess punishment disparity is to identify like crimes and then determine whether these crimes were punished differently along dimensions deemed inappropriate or irrelevant. One immediately sees several problems with such a facile formula. First, what offenses shall be deemed "like"? What level of detail is necessary, and what criteria should be used to identify like (or unlike) harms? Second, what constitutes a "different" response? What amount of difference in punishment is sufficient to suggest a disparity that troubles us? What response dimensions are inappropriate? In part 3, I consider how to assess like harms and to compare seriousness and begin the process of comparing sentences for the matched pairs. In chapter 11, I take up a pair-wise comparative analysis more fully and address the meaning of different and disparate responses.

The Concept of Like Crimes

A short history of modern criminal law in the West might begin in the eighteenth century with Cesare Beccaria's treatise on punishment.[1] In *On Crimes and Punishments* (1764), Beccaria called for a rational punishment system based on an offense harm: punishment should be the same for the same level of harm. In the late nineteenth century, opinion and policy in the United States muddied the "likes" question considerably when both the person and the crime became the focus of punishment. The ideological focus on individualizing punishment under the rehabilitative ideal rendered the notion of like cases more opaque.

Sentencing reform during the 1970s brought renewed attention to punishing the crime. Reformers across the political spectrum have assumed that a focus on the crime as object of punishment can attenuate disparity associated with using the person as the focus of punishment. Yet, as historical studies show (for example, Garland 1985; Radzinowicz and Hood 1979) and as philosophers of contemporary punishment practices admit (such as Gross 1979), the crime and the person cannot be separated in principle or in practice. To say that one should be more important than the other is to affirm the dominant ideological posture of a specific time and place.

Today, the dominant posture is that the crime should be the primary object of punishment. Many legislative and sentencing commissions have outlined how punishment should fit the crime, but as Franklin Zimring (1981, 331) suggests, "We lack the capacity to define into formal law the nuances of situation, intent, and social harm that condition the seriousness of particular acts." Despite these difficulties, most commentators worry that "unequal sentences [are] given to different perpetrators of crimes that are indistinguishable in seriousness" (Gross 1981, 239). Or, to make the point more directly, in H. L. A. Hart's (1968, 24) words, there is "the somewhat hazy requirement that 'like cases be treated alike.'" When, then, are crimes "alike" or "indistinguishable in seriousness"? What criteria can be used to judge these qualities? Statutory and sociological features of penal harms give us some purchase on these questions.

Statutory Status of Crime Seriousness

My research design is based on an empirically open assumption: that men and women accused and convicted of statutorily similar criminal offenses have engaged in similarly serious or like offenses. The same assumption features in statistical sentencing studies when researchers say they have controlled for the severity and type of offense. But have they? At most, they have controlled for levels of statutory severity (that is, the degrees or classes of felonies and misdemeanors) and the type of offense (homicide, larceny, robbery, and so forth).[2] Some suggest that one reason for statistical sex effects favoring women in sentencing, with statutory severity and type of offense controlled, is that women are "involved in the less serious offenses within the broad [offense and statutory] categories" (Steffensmeier 1980, 348). This claim has merit, and court officials I have interviewed have made it (Daly 1987a, 1989a); but we lack evidence for it. Furthermore, as Black (1979, 24) suggests, "crime seriousness" is not a fact but rather a judgment about crime. Therefore, any measure of seriousness is a measure of the *"response* to crime, not a characteristic of crime itself" (ibid., 25, emphasis added).[3]

We do know that there are gender differences in the distributions of common crime offenses prosecuted; men are more likely to be prosecuted for violent crimes such as homicide, assault, rape, or robbery. My research on gender and white-collar offenses convicted in federal court (Daly 1989d) suggests that women's bank embezzlements, credit and mail frauds, and false claims and statements are less serious than men's. Still, we do not know the degree of gender-based variation in "crime seriousness" for statutorily similar common crimes. This is not a trivial issue: were we to find that women's first-degree robberies were generally less serious than men's, then comparing sentences of men and women convicted of first-degree robbery would be misleading.

Sociological Meaning of Crime Seriousness

Several approaches have been pursued for measuring crime seriousness: rankings of crime seriousness (Cullen, Link, and Polanzi 1982; Rossi et al. 1974; Sellin and Wolfgang 1964; Wolfgang et al. 1985), judgments of sentencing severity (Rossi, Simpson, and Miller 1985), judgments of both seriousness and sentence (Hamilton and Rytina 1980; Rose and Prell 1955), codings of offense elements (Baldus, Woodworth, and Pulaski 1990), constructions of seriousness in officials' interactions (Emerson 1983; Maynard 1982), and theoretical propositions on how crime and seriousness are variably defined by location and direction in social space (Black 1976, 1979). Researchers normally identify these elements as conferring a more serious quality: offenses involving physical violence that lead to death or serious injury, that take place among those unknown to each other, and that have vulnerable or frail victims. Other social influences are captured in the terms "aggravating" and "mitigating circumstances." Aggravating suggests gratuitous violence, planned or premeditated violence, misuse of a position of power or trust, and a history of similar lawbreaking. Mitigating includes victim provocation, a defendant's cooperation with authorities, a defendant's making restitution, and a first-time offender.

It is instructive to learn from the study of the death penalty in Georgia by David Baldus, George Woodworth, and Charles Pulaski (1990, 201) that the state justices then believed there was "no uniform method for selecting the characteristics from the death-sentence cases under review to be used for determining 'similar' cases."[4] If for a select portion of violence cases (that is, those deemed death-eligible), the Georgia Supreme Court justices found it difficult to identify like offenses, then we can expect some difficulty in nominating such qualities across a wider band of harms. One reason for the difficulty, noted by Peter Rossi, Jon Simpson, and JoAnn Miller (1985), is that a global measure of crime seriousness (such as the one constructed by Wolfgang et al. 1985) is less predictive in judgments of personal violence. Rossi, Simpson, and Miller found that when there is more detail on the consequences of an offense, observers give more weight to the offense particulars.

Other findings from Baldus, Woodworth, and Pulaski (1990), Marvin Wolfgang and colleagues (1985), and Rossi, Simpson, and Miller (1985) bear on my study. When capital offenses have female victims, defendants more often received the death penalty (Baldus, Woodworth, and

Pulaski 1990, 588). The defendant's gender was not significantly predictive, however.[5] Using citizens' judgments in hypothetical sentencing situations, Rossi, Simpson, and Miller (1985, 78) found that violence to a female victim was thought to deserve a more severe sentence and that female defendants were "consistently regarded with less severity than male" (p. 77).

Although some studies have explored the meaning of crime seriousness through a gendered lens (for example, Rossi, Simpson, and Miller 1985; Baldus, Woodworth, and Pulaski 1990), most do not. As for court practices, no one has yet examined whether men and women accused and convicted of the same statutory offenses have committed offenses of "similar seriousness."[6]

To describe the social organization of the deep-sample offenses, I coded the crime narratives using the seriousness elements identified in the literature:[7] the degree of injury, the value of property taken, the presence of weapons, the defendant's role in the offense, and victim-offender relations, among others. I want to determine not only whether men's and women's offenses are the same or different along these dimensions but also whether the coded offense elements offer a good way to compare seriousness. Narrative-oriented scholars (such as Emerson 1983 and Maynard 1982) argue for a "holistic" or "gestalt" approach to crime seriousness, which cannot be inferred from combinations of offense elements alone.

Each of the next four chapters focuses on a major form of lawbreaking. Except for violent harms such as homicide and assault, there is no research that anticipates gender differences in the social organization and contexts of offenses prosecuted. Thus my analysis of robbery, larceny, and drug-law violations breaks new ground.

One focus of the chapters is judging the seriousness of the deep-sample offenses and how we, as observers and readers of "crime facts," decide that one offense is more serious than another. From time to time, I shall prepare the reader for the pair-wise disparity analysis in chapter 11 by focusing on selected pairs that raise a question of disparity.

A related second focus are the different analytical problems that emerge in assessing punishment for the four broad classifications of crimes studied here: robbery, larceny, interpersonal violence, and drugs. Those analytical problems raise more general questions of the meaning and practice of commensurate punishment across diverse harms.

Notes

1. See Piers Beirne's (1991) revisionist history of Beccaria's ideas and their relation to classical and positivist criminology, David Matza's ([1964] 1990) effort

to transcend the classical and positivist dichotomy, and Samuel Walker's (1980) history of criminal justice policies and practices in the United States. Good summaries of shifts in sentencing practices, together with key documents, can be found in Hyman Gross and Andrew von Hirsch (1981) and von Hirsch and Andrew Ashworth (1992).

2. Few studies of gender and punishment are this fine-grained in the types of variables introduced to control for variability in the severity and type of punishment. Single-offense studies may come closest.

3. That response will vary with time and place, e.g., "getting tough on drug offenders," "cracking down on drunk drivers," and "taking domestic violence seriously."

4. The statement was for the 1973–78 time period in the study. Baldus, Woodworth, and Pulaski argued against the justices' "impossibility hypothesis" by demonstrating that it *was* possible to conduct a rigorous proportionality review of death sentences.

5. The focus of the research of Baldus, Woodworth, and Pulaski was on racial discrimination. The central finding was that the death penalty was significantly more likely to be imposed on white- than black-victim cases. The authors failed to find a statistically significant difference between black offender–white victim and white offender–white victim cases. The number of cases was too low (especially for woman offender–woman victim) to assess statistically gender-of-offender and gender-of-victim interactions.

6. Or, to be more accurate, that men and women are perceived to be engaged in offenses of similar (or more or less) seriousness. I am indebted to Otis Dudley Duncan's (1985, 185–93) discussion of the problems associated with magnitude estimation in crime seriousness scales, among them there being no standard unit and an inability to interpret group differences.

7. The "narratives" are my reconstructions of the offense from the prosecutor's sketch, coupled with the offender's and victim's versions of what happened as documented in the PSI. I also draw from sentencing remarks and police reports where these can add information. As we shall see, many incidents have ambiguous "facts." It is hard to know what really happened, and for the women's cases, what the defendant's role was.

5 Robbery

I didn't know it would be no robbery. I thought it would be minor.
They did the robbery. . . . I took the money because I said, "The
heck with it."
— Victor, Robbery Case 8

I went there to scare the guy. . . . I guess I was interested in a fast
buck along with the fast life. I was desperate, I didn't like being on
the state.
— Maggie, Robbery Case 8

To compare women's and men's robberies, I move from statistical
data to crime narratives in presenting (1) the variables coded from the
clerk's docket books, police records, and penal statutes for the wide
and deep samples, (2) the variables coded from the psi crime narratives, and (3) the crime narratives themselves.

Docket Book Variables

The men's deep-sample robberies registered a slight decrease in severity (using conviction charges) compared to those in the wide sample
(table 5.1). For women, there was no change in severity. The sentence
variables register the largest shift: from a 22 percentage-point gender
gap in receiving incarceration time in the wide sample to no such gap
in the deep sample.

Examining the men's and women's deep-sample cases, one sees
that the seriousness of the convicted charges and prior criminal history
are similar for men and women. The average seriousness of the convicted charges was 233–248 months, which translates to a conviction
on one count of first-degree robbery.[1] From information in the clerk's
docket books, one-fourth had previously been convicted or were on
probation at the time of the offense.[2] Most men and women were
represented by public defenders and most were incarcerated pending
trial; the median bail amounts ranged from $15,000 to $30,000. Although a similar proportion of men and women (75 percent) was sentenced to serve time, the average time for those sentenced to serve
was longer for men than women (sixty-one versus forty-two months).

Table 5.1 Statistical Data on Men's and Women's Robberies (from clerk's docket book, police records, and penal code statutes)

	Robbery			
	Men*		Women**	
	Wide (N = 45)	Deep (N = 8)	Wide (N = 27)	Deep (N = 8)
Age (median, yr)	21	20	24	25
Race or Ethnicity				
Black	58%	63%	44%	63%
Latin	13	12	19	12
White	29	25	37	25
Attorney				
Public defender	80%	63%	74%	75%
Private	20	37	26	25
Pretrial Status				
Incarcerated or detained	69%	63%	59%	75%
Out on bail	31	37	26	12.5
Promise to appear	0	0	15	12.5
Bail Amount (median)$^\triangle$	$10 K	$30 K	$10 K	$15 K
Pled Guilty	89%	100%	100%	100%
Prior Record				
Has been convicted in New Haven felony court or was on probation or parole at the time of the offense? yes	36%	25%***	33%	25%***
Severity				
Potential time (mo), convicted offense$^\triangle$	246	233	249	248
(std. dev.)	(70)	(81)	(64)	(113)
Sentence (*In-Out*)				
Received incarceration sentence to serve time? yes	89%	75%	67%	75%
Sentence (*Time*)				
Length of sentence (mo), only cases receiving incarceration$^\triangle$	66	61	31	42
(std. dev.)	(68)	(33)	(24)	(31)

$^\triangle$Denotes that these variables may have a smaller number of cases.

*Except where indicated by a triangle, the measures are of $N = 45$ and $N = 8$ men in the wide- and deep-robbery samples, respectively. Bail amounts were available from the clerk's records (or were relevant) for $N = 21$ and $N = 5$ men in the wide and deep samples, respectively. Convicted offense severity and incarceration time averages exclude trial cases: five in the wide sample, none in the deep sample.

**Except where indicated by a triangle, the measures are of $N = 27$ and $N = 8$ women in the wide- and deep-robbery samples, respectively. Bail amounts were available from the clerk's records (or were relevant) for $N = 15$ and $N = 6$ women in the wide and deep samples, respectively. There were no women who were found guilty at trial in the wide sample; thus, convicted offense severity and incarceration time averages are for those pleading guilty.

***From the PSI, where more complete prior criminal history was shown, the proportion of men and women previously convicted was 88% and 75%, respectively.

Coded Elements of the Robbery Narratives

The statutory severity of men's and women's robberies is similar, but how similar are the robberies? To probe variation in social organization, I coded the narratives along such dimensions as victim-offender relations, the defendant's role, the defendant's use of weapon, whether the victim was injured, and other items drawn from prior research (see appendix 4, robbery column).

With one exception, both men and women acted with friends.[3] More men than women robbed in threesomes, and with one exception the accomplices in both men's and women's robberies were men. Half the men and women robbed or attempted to rob commercial organizations, such as gas stations or convenience stores; the other half robbed people on the street or in their homes. Robbery victims were as likely to be women as men. With race and ethnic information on the victim missing for three men's cases, it was hard to compare men and women along this dimension. Most defendants did not know their victims, though more women than men knew their victims. Similar proportions of men and women used a weapon in the robbery, and the majority played an active role. Victim injury was atypical, occurring in one man's and two women's robberies. Women's robberies netted a somewhat higher amount of money (about $350) than men's (about $200). For most dimensions, the deep-sample robberies were similar to the nonlethal robberies described by Zimring and James Zuehl (1986) from Chicago police reports.[4]

Drawing from David Luckenbill's (1980) analysis of patterns of force in robberies, I found that for "threat of force," men's and women's robberies were similar. Most opened with a command; half used symbolic or physical gestures to coerce the victim's compliance, and few victims were incapacitated. For "importance of target" (or robbery victim), it was harder to make a determination from the PSI, but my impression was that somewhat more women's than men's robberies relied on victims to turn over money.[5]

The social organization of men's and women's robberies is similar for many dimensions, though two differences are apparent. First, men's robbery groups consisted of a male twosome or threesome, while for almost all the women, the group was a man and woman. Thus, when speaking of men's robberies, the reference is to an all-male group; when speaking of women's robberies, the reference is usually to a mixed-gender group. Second, more women robbed those they knew (all were men). From the research of Rossi, Simpson, and Miller (1985), we might anticipate that the deep-sample men's robberies would be perceived as somewhat more serious than the women's because their victims were unknown to them and because the men worked in all-male groups.

Robbery Narratives

My first reading of the narratives suggested that men's robberies were different from the women's *and* that the men's were more serious. From the narrative coded elements, however, I found that men's and women's robberies were similar in most dimensions — for example, women were as active as men, and they were as likely to use weapons — among the other elements I have listed above. What happened, I wondered, when moving from the crime narrative to my quantitative coding of its elements? Why did the narrative tell one story (women's robberies were less dangerous than men's; there were gender differences in organization), but my coding scheme suggest another (that men's and women's robberies were "alike")? I soon realized that my coding scheme was useful in counting up the presence or absence of certain case elements, but by itself, it could not tell me which robberies were more serious than others.[6] Examples from the crime narratives will show how this occurs.

Coded Elements and Statutory Charges Apparently Alike

I will compare Casey's robbery of the convenience store, which opened the book, with Toni's attempted robbery of a jewelry shop and with Kate's robbery of a man on the street, which also opened the book.

Casey and Toni

Comparing the coded elements of Casey's and Toni's robberies shows that these variables can give a misleading impression of crime seriousness. Both Casey and Toni acted alone, victimized a commercial establishment, used a weapon, and victimized a woman. To be sure, there were differences in their robberies: his was completed, and hers only attempted; he injured the victim and she did not. But even allowing for these differences, the coded elements do not prepare us for the far more serious quality of Casey's act. Recall that Casey, black and 26, entered a convenience store at around midnight. He struck a female clerk on the neck with a blunt instrument, knocking her to the floor. He took about $55 and left. Casey had been convicted on a dozen occasions for larcenies, burglaries, and assault, and received a sentence of ten years to serve. Compare his offense with Toni's:

Robbery Case 5, Toni
Toni, white and 19, attempted to rob a jewelry store. She came into the shop, looked at some jewelry, and left, but returned a short while later. While being shown some items, she pulled out a handgun and

demanded money from the female clerk; the clerk refused. Later, the clerk said she thought the robbery was a practical joke. Unable to get money, Toni left frustrated, but the clerk was able to identify the make of Toni's car. Toni had not been arrested before. She received a suspended sentence and three years' probation.[7]

The elements of acting alone, victimizing a commercial establishment, using a weapon, and female victim were identical in both cases, but they differed in the harms that occurred. Casey was a more experienced lawbreaker than Toni, having been incarcerated at least four times since he was 17. The convenience store clerk, whom Casey knocked to the floor, was treated at the hospital for a broken ear bone, and she had to wear a neck brace. Toni posed little threat to the female jewelry store clerk. When Toni pulled the handgun on the clerk, the clerk did not believe she would shoot, because, as the clerk reported, Toni "didn't look like the type of person" to commit a robbery. The clerk also said that she had tried to talk Toni out of committing the robbery. Casey's blow to the victim, coupled with the greater threat he posed to his victim than did Toni, constructed his crime as more serious than hers.[8]

Lynn Mather's (1979, 102–3) discussion of how public defenders in Los Angeles felony court distinguished between first-degree robberies applies here. They differentiated a "real" first-degree robbery from "the rest" of first-degree robberies this way: a real robbery has "the meanest guys . . . vicious . . . a background going . . . back to childhood with crimes of violence," whereas the rest are "a lot of amateurs . . . not really dangerous guys. Do it more out of feelings of inadequacy." Using the public defender's scheme, Casey was close to being among "the meanest." Toni may not have even reached the status of amateur.[9]

Kate and Casey

Kate is the matching case for Casey: they were both accused and convicted of first-degree robbery. Recall that in her robbery with a female accomplice, she waved down the victim, who was driving along the street. She opened the car door on the driver's side and pulled the man out while her accomplice put a knife to the man's back. Both demanded his wallet and car keys. A patrolling police officer saw the three, and recognizing Kate, he chased and arrested her. Kate had a dozen previous convictions and has been in and out of prison since she was 20 years old. She received a sentence of two years to serve.

Kate's and Casey's robberies differed in that Kate's victim was not injured and was seen as partly responsible for his victimization. Kate and Casey were street people, with a heightened level of blameworthiness attached to their acts.[10] Casey's prior record, however, suggested that he was among the "meanest guys," while Kate's suggested a "not really dangerous guy," according to the Los Angeles public defender's scheme. Anticipating the pair-wise disparity analysis in chapter 11, we may wonder whether these differences were justly translated into an eight-year gap in the term of incarceration. Kate and Casey were one of two pairs that I judged the sentencing disparity to be largely (though not fully) explained by differences in offense seriousness and prior record.

Toni and Simon

Toni's match is Simon. Simon's arraignment and conviction charges were also for attempted first-degree robbery. The circumstances of Simon's case differed markedly from Toni's.

Robbery Case 5, Simon

Simon and a male accomplice attempted to rob Wayne in an alleyway in "the projects" on the morning of Christmas Eve day. A witness reported to the police that there were two men "running around the projects with a shotgun and a handgun." The incident stemmed from a gang dispute between Simon and his accomplice, who were members of the New Haven Dogs, and Wayne, who was a member of another gang. It is not certain what the dispute was about, although a failed drug deal may have been at issue. Simon and his accomplice were 20 years old and the victim 18; all were black. Simon received a shorter sentence (four years to serve) than his accomplice (six years) because, it seems, the accomplice wielded the shotgun in the incident. At sentencing, Simon's accomplice said the incident "couldn't be avoided because they kept coming on to us."

This pair of offenses illustrates the difficulty of measuring and comparing crime seriousness. Perhaps the actions of Simon and his accomplice took on greater seriousness as a threat to public safety during a holiday period, when peace is elevated as a virtue. A concern over gang violence was also present. The same facts, however, could have been interpreted in a far less serious light by the police as a "normal" expression of ghetto violence.[11]

Toni's attempted robbery was viewed by the victim, the police, and the court as less threatening or serious. Toni was a slight woman, perhaps without the necessary demeanor to pose a threat to the jewelry store clerk. A description of her in the file said she was a "short, slender, fairly attractive, stylishly dressed female who possesses a certain toughness." Yet one could imagine that with some change in the woman's demeanor or ability to control the situation, this attempted robbery could have seemed more serious. An added element that made Simon's offense more serious than Toni's was his previous lawbreaking: he and his accomplice had been convicted the year before for a robbery and had served time, whereas Toni had not been arrested before.

Gestalt of the Harm

Having discovered that the seriousness of a robbery cannot be grasped from offense elements or from statutory severity alone, I grouped the robberies to reflect the *gestalt of the harm*. To do this, I identified the elements and variants of a "typical stickup."[12] A typical stickup occurs on the street or against a commercial establishment; the offender uses a weapon and does not know the victim. Deviations from a typical stickup are those in which the offender plays a secondary role and may or may not know the victim. I nested the typical stickup scenario within the statutory charges and identified the following groups:

1. Pairs who were convicted of the same statutory offense and whose harms were similarly serious (Susan and Ron, Pat and Richie)
2. Pairs who were convicted of somewhat different statutory offenses but whose harms were similarly serious (Victor and Wendy, Antonio and Maggie)
3. Pairs who were convicted of the same statutory offense but the men's harms were more serious than the women's (Kate and Casey, Toni and Simon, Allen and Pamela, Charles and Bell).

Same Statutory Offense and Same Seriousness

For two pairs, the men's and women's robberies were statutorily identical and comparably serious. Ron and Susan committed an armed robbery of a gas station, and each played a primary role; Pat and Richie each played a secondary role by driving the getaway car.[13]

Susan and Ron

Susan, 21 and Puerto Rican, and Ron, 21 and black, were convicted of first-degree robbery, having been arraigned on that charge and conspiracy to commit first-degree robbery.

Robbery Case 2, Susan

Susan and a male accomplice, David, robbed a gas station, taking $385 in cash and the female clerk's purse. This was one of three robberies Susan had committed in the past month with David while both were on parole. Susan used a sawed-off shotgun, pushed a female clerk, and pulled the clerk's hair. David said they had committed the robbery for money to get high. Susan had been institutionalized in juvenile facilities for several years and has a history of violent aggressiveness.

She received one of the harshest sentences for women in the deep sample: eight years to serve. David received six years.

Robbery Case 2, Ron

Ron and two black male accomplices robbed a gas station one evening. Wearing masks, the three men entered the station, said they had a gun, and announced a stickup. They fled on foot carrying a cash drawer, taking about $125. A police officer spotted them, and with the aid of a second officer, arrested them on the scene. All three men were in their early twenties. Ron received 2½ years to serve, and his accomplices received three years.

In these classic forms of armed robbery, the seriousness of the offense was similar for Susan and Ron, as was their culpability. However, Susan's previous record was more serious than Ron's, rendering her act more blameworthy. David cooperated with the police in identifying her, which likely led to his receiving a reduced sentence. Although the 5½-year sentencing gap is substantial, I was satisfied in my pair-wise comparisons that the disparity could be explained by differences in prior record.

Pat and Richie

Both protagonists in this pair played a secondary role and were convicted of aiding and abetting a first-degree robbery.

Robbery Case 4, Pat

Pat, black and 35, drove the getaway car in the robbery of an ice cream parlor late one evening. She was in the car while her male accomplice went into the shop. Brandishing a gun, he ordered two employees and a customer to the rear of the store. A total of $800 was taken. Police later spotted the car and arrested the couple. Pat says she "was drunk and asleep in the car" when the robbery occurred. She had been released from prison a month before and has the longest string of previous convictions of all the women in the deep sample. She received four years to serve; her male accomplice received nine years.

Robbery Case 4, Richie

Richie, white and 32, drove the getaway car in the robbery of a convenience store late one evening. He alleged that he was only giving his friend a ride to the store to buy some cigarettes, although they had been together for most of the evening. In robbing the store, Richie's male friend drew a knife and demanded money. When he demanded more money from another cash drawer, the female clerk refused and began to cry. The man left, taking a total of $55. Richie received a suspended sentence, while his accomplice received one year to serve.

The seriousness of Pat's and Richie's participation in driving the getaway car was comparable. Both said they were unaware that their companion was going to commit a robbery, and as in the previous pair, the woman received a harsher penalty than the man. In neither case would I interpret the more severe sentencing of the woman as arising from *evil woman* notions operating in the minds or words of sentencing officials. By *evil woman,* scholars refer to the more punitive response to women who commit *male-typed* offenses, although the meaning of that term is vague.[14] As we have seen, some women's robberies can be viewed as less serious than men's, challenging any general claim that women convicted of a male-typed offense like robbery are treated more harshly. Other men's and women's robberies may be viewed as similarly serious, but the women's more developed record of previous convictions, coupled with a more blameworthy profile, may invite a harsher sentence. Note, as well, that for Pat and Richie, both of whom played secondary roles, their penalties were less severe than those of their crime partners who played primary roles.

Somewhat Different Statutory Offense, Same Seriousness
Victor and Wendy

Victor, 17 and white, was convicted of first-degree robbery and conspiracy to commit first-degree robbery; at arraignment he was also charged with assault and kidnapping. Wendy, 25 and black, was convicted of first-degree robbery; at arraignment she was also charged with possession of a sawed-off shotgun. Although the details of their offenses differ somewhat, they are similarly serious.

Robbery Case 8, Victor

Victor and two other white males robbed a gas station at dawn during the summer. One of the accomplices tied up the middle-aged male clerk; all three were involved in stealing an unknown amount of money from the clerk and from the station's register. Victor took a knife away from the clerk and took money from his pocket. Based on the victim's description of the car, the police arrested Victor and his partners a short while later.

The day of the robbery, the three had just arrived from New York City, and the robbery seemed a spur-of-the-moment idea. Victor said he "didn't know it would be no robbery. I thought it would be minor. They did the robbery. . . . I took the money because I said, 'the heck with it.'" Victor is characterized by the probation officer as identifying with "stronger, older male figures, who are negative influences on him." His accomplices were about five years older than he. Although they received four years to serve, Victor got three years.

Robbery Case 6, Wendy

Wendy and a black male accomplice robbed a gas station at around midnight in January. On entering the store the two attempted to purchase an item. The male clerk noticed that Wendy was holding a sawed-off shotgun while her accomplice, Mo, ordered him to turn over the money. About $700 was taken. Wendy says she "did it because I wanted to get higher and needed money." She and Mo have been together for five years and have a daughter. Wendy has been convicted previously of larceny. She and Mo received the same sentence of 3½ years to serve.

Comparison of Victor and Wendy shows that although their acts differed somewhat in a statutory sense, the gestalt of their harm was similar. Each act was a typical stickup of a gas station during the late-night shift. Both victims feared for their lives. One couldn't talk to the probation officer about the incident, and the other quit his job.

Antonio and Maggie

Antonio and Maggie each committed a typical stickup but did so by threatening the occupant(s) of a household they broke into. Maggie's robbery had an added twist: she had been recently employed as a housecleaner for the victim.

Robbery Case 6, Antonio

Antonio, Puerto Rican and 29, and two male accomplices forced their way into a latin household early one evening. There were six adults and four children present. Brandishing guns and a knife, the three men demanded money and drugs, but the household members said that they had none. One adult was struck. The victims surrendered some money, and the apartment was ransacked for more. About $520 in jewelry, cash, and other household items was taken, including $5 from a baby's bank. Antonio had recently been convicted on drug charges. Although he initially denied involvement in the incident, he pled guilty, but then regretted his plea because "they gave me the same thing." He received six years to serve, while his partners received two years.

Robbery Case 8, Maggie

Wearing a ski mask and working with a male accomplice, Maggie, 21 and black, forced her way into the victim's house in the late afternoon. She knew the victim, Max, having worked for him as a housecleaner and companion several months before. (He said they had sexual relations, but she denies this.) Although Max, a white man in his sixties, tried to flee, he was slashed in the hand by the male accomplice. The two demanded bankbooks; Maggie took Max's wallet and then ransacked the house. Although she didn't speak during the incident, Max recognized her. A total of $102 was taken in cash, along with other valuables, including a mink coat. Max was forced into his car and taken to a bank to make a cash withdrawal. A bank employee noticed that something was wrong, and Maggie's partner fled with Max. Maggie and the accomplice dropped Max off on the street, and soon after he called the police. About the incident, Maggie said she "went there to scare the guy." Her accomplice "had been drinking," and Maggie said she "blocked [his] knife." She said she was "interested in a fast buck along with the fast life. I was desperate and didn't like being on the state." Maggie has not been arrested before. She received three years to serve, and her male accomplice, five years. She said the robbery was his idea. After she was arrested, she implicated him.

Both household robberies registered a similar sense of seriousness. Although the victim knew Maggie, it did not soften his outrage or desire for retribution. He reported to the probation officer that "she sent me a letter [but] I would never accept her apology. She can talk to the Pope if she wants to. She should get ten to fifteen years, the more the merrier." The element of the betrayal of trust in Maggie's offense, coupled with the fact that Max was elderly, made her offense at least as serious as Antonio's, if not more so. Although their crimes were similarly serious, Antonio's longer prison term was based in part on his prior record and in part on the fact that Maggie cooperated with the police in identifying her accomplice.

Same Statutory Offense, Men's More Serious

Two of the four pairs in this group have been described already (Kate and Casey, Toni and Simon). An important dimension in the remaining pairs is that the women knew their victims. As we learned in Maggie's case, crime seriousness is not necessarily reduced when victims and offenders know each other. An element of ambiguity exists when a woman, acting with another person, robs someone she knows: did she set the victim up, or did her accomplice take advantage of a situation? If the former is true, a woman's robbery might be viewed as more serious since a trust has been transgressed. If the latter, the woman's role may be cast in a less serious light: the accomplice, not she, instigated the robbery. Three women (Maggie, Pamela, and Bell) robbed men they knew, and for two (Maggie and Pamela), the victims were not just acquaintances but men with whom they had likely had sexual relations in the past.[15]

Women Victimizing Men They Knew

Pamela and Bell

Pamela's case suggests that a male accomplice took advantage of a situation, but I could not be sure.

Robbery Case 3, Pamela

Pamela, black and 30, met her companion, Reinhart, one evening. He was German and worked for a multinational corporation that had relocated him to the New Haven area for six months. Pamela asked if her "cousin," a black man, could join Reinhart for a ride in the car, and it is likely that Reinhart hoped to buy some marijuana from this cousin. After driving a little while, the cousin put a handgun to the back of Reinhart's head, telling him to stop the car and telling Pamela to take money from Reinhart's pocket. A total of $40–$50 was taken.

Pamela said she was only carrying out her cousin's orders because she was scared the victim would be hurt. She "knew Reinhart never carried more than $16" and that he "used credit cards. . . . I never would've robbed him. I didn't have to rob him [because] I could've asked him for money and he would've given it to me." She has been convicted on six occasions for prostitution, disorderly conduct, and on drug possession charges. Both she and her male accomplice received a suspended sentence.

Reinhart was reluctant to have Pamela prosecuted, although he thought her accomplice should be. He hoped that by reporting the incident, he would be achieving something positive: Pamela could receive drug treatment and be given the chance to "clean up her act." In contrast to Maggie's victim, Reinhart did not feel betrayed. While Pamela was awaiting trial at the women's prison, about an hour's drive from New Haven, Reinhart wrote and visited her. He said he wanted to continue seeing her and to be her friend.

The circumstances surrounding Bell's case are more sketchy than Pamela's. Like Pamela, Bell knew the man she had robbed. He said he had known Bell's family for fifteen years. Bell was convicted of third-degree robbery for the following offense:

Robbery Case 7, Bell

With a male accomplice, Bell, black and 25, robbed Effie, a black male in his thirties, on the street. Effie knew Bell and her family and described her as "an alcoholic" who hadn't "had a sober day in a long while." The male accomplice gave Effie a severe karate blow that hospitalized him for a day. Effie lost $825 of his vacation money, which, he said, he never saw again. Bell has been arrested or convicted eight times during the past five years. Almost all the incidents involved violence — by her and against her — while she was drinking. She received four months to serve and was ordered to pay half of Effie's medical expenses as a condition of probation. There was no record of what happened to her male accomplice.

In Bell's and Pamela's cases, the male victims did not report the incident right away. Reinhart could not decide whether to get Pamela into trouble, but after a week he reported the incident to the police. It also took Effie a week to report Bell's robbery, but there is little information in the file from which to infer the reasons for Effie's delay in calling the police. Effie knew Bell and her male accomplice, and it is possible that there was an ongoing money dispute.

Men Victimizing Women They Did Not Know

Allen and Charles

Compared to Bell and Pamela, the men with whom they were paired committed acts that seemed more threatening, especially to the female victims. Allen was matched with Pamela. Like her, he was convicted of first-degree robbery, and like her, he seemed to be following orders. But his harm was more sinister than hers.

Robbery Case 3, Allen

Allen, black and 20, acted as a lookout in the robbery of a white woman in her late twenties. The woman, Jodi, was coming back to her apartment at around 9:00 in the evening when Allen's accomplice, 18 and black, came up from behind her in the building hallway. The accomplice put his arm around Jodi's neck and attempted to grab her purse. After he threatened Jodi with a gun, she relinquished her purse, which contained $12. Allen netted $5 for his job as lookout. Jodi said she was "pretty petrified" after the incident and had "no sympathy for either one of them." Allen has been in trouble since he was 13. He was placed in a secure juvenile facility and later served time for burglarizing his sister's apartment when he was 17. He has been in and out of jail the past several years. He was sentenced to serve five years, but his partner received 3½ years.[16]

Robbery Case 7, Charles

In Charles's robbery, the woman victim was somewhat less frightened by the robbery, but she reported that "since the crime occurred, I have been fearful and suspicious when walking on the street." Charles, 18 and black, was convicted of third-degree robbery.

With his 20-year-old cousin, Charles "accosted" a woman (her race was not given) in a parking lot. The two men threatened her with a handgun and demanded that she give them her purse. They fled with her purse, which contained $10 in cash, a checkbook, and other items. A passerby saw the two and stopped them, but they got away. About an hour later, they attempted to cash one of the victim's checks for $300. Although the teller gave them the cash, the bank later determined that the check was forged. Charles said that he and his cousin found the checkbook in the parking lot. He has never been arrested before. He and his accomplice received a suspended sentence. The records also show that Charles was fined $1,000 and his cousin was fined $100.[17]

I judged Charles's offenses as being more serious than Bell's. Although Bell's accomplice hurt Effie and her robbery was not trivial, Effie took a week to report the incident, and he focused on Bell's need for an alcohol rehabilitation program, "where she has to stay for a while before coming back to the streets." Moreover, Effie seemed not to be concerned about news that Bell "was going to get me when she gets out — you know, revenge." In contrast, the victim of Charles's robbery expressed greater fear. Charles had never been arrested before, but Bell had a moderate record of arrests and convictions.

Racial Dynamics in Crime Seriousness

How do race relations construct crime seriousness? Four of the men's robberies were intraracial: two were black, and one each was white and latin. For three, the victims' race or ethnicity could not be determined; two of the male defendants were black, and one was white. The remaining robbery was a black offender–white victim. My sense is that the intra- or interracial composition of the men's robberies was less important in constructing seriousness than the stranger (or non-stranger) relationship, coupled with the relative vulnerability of the victims.[18] Victim vulnerability was based partly on age (older or very young) and partly on gender (women victims being more vulnerable). In the PSI crime narrative and the prosecutor's description of the offense on sentencing day, the victim's race and the racial dynamics of the incident typically were not described. This may reflect an effort by a white-dominated justice system to appear unbiased. The same erasure can be seen in crime news reporting, unless the case is a celebrated one. In contrast, neither age nor gender is erased from crime stories.

The women's robberies reveal a somewhat different set of intra- and interracial dynamics than do the men's. Five were interracial (one was a white offender and "Arab" victim, and the rest were black offenders and white victims or a mix of black and white victims). Two were intraracial (one white and one black), and in one the victim's race or ethnicity could not be determined. As in the men's robberies, the racial dynamics in the women's robberies were less important in constructing seriousness. The more salient elements were stranger (or nonstranger) relations and victim vulnerability.

Judgments of Robbery Seriousness

In comparing men's and women's robberies of the same statutory severity, at arraignment and conviction, I judged four to be comparably serious, but for four others, the men's actions seemed more threatening and serious than the women's (see the pair-wise seriousness judgments in appendix 5). I found that neither the coded elements nor statutory charges alone were sufficient in assessing crime seriousness. For only one dimension did Luckenbill's (1980) schemes of force differentiate men's and women's robberies: women were somewhat more likely to seek the victim's cooperation.

Judging the seriousness of women's and men's robberies is not straightforward. It entails a nuanced determination that consolidates lines of social relations, the place and timing of an incident, and the relation of offense to biography, especially the defendant's previous lawbreaking, which heightens or reduces blameworthiness. I was best able to group and compare the seriousness of robberies by assessing the gestalt of the harm, together with the statutory charges.

As a group, women's robberies were less serious than men's, but not for the reasons scholars normally give. Specifically, (1) women were as likely as men to brandish a knife or gun, and they pushed or restrained victims in the same proportions as men, albeit low; (2) women and men took active participatory roles. The same numbers of men and women said the robbery was an accomplice's idea, not theirs.

The more decisive elements were the gender composition of the robbery group and women's knowing their victims. Women robbed in mixed-gender groups, while men's groups were all-male; the men's robbery groups may have only seemed more fearsome, especially when robbery victims were vulnerable by age or gender. More female robbery defendants not only knew their victims, but some of the victims were less credible. Knowing a victim does not always imply a discounted harm, however — especially if it appears that a woman set up a male victim. Of the two women who had sexual relations with their victims, the men's reactions differed greatly: one wanted to remain friends, and the other wanted the woman jailed for as long as possible.

We may need to take a step beyond victim characteristics in assessing seriousness. A relational view is needed, which considers offender group size and physical stature *in relation to* those being victimized. Some male victims were vulnerable by being older and by being overpowered by offenders (Maggie's and Victor's robberies), and some male victims were vulnerable by being *younger* and overpowered (Antonio's robbery).

Although research by Rossi, Simpson, and Miller, and by Baldus and colleagues suggests that crimes with female victims are thought to be "more serious" or are punished more severely, I am not sure this holds for female lawbreakers and the contexts of their offenses.[19] By focusing on characteristics of the victim alone, we ignore the sociological significance of crime as a social relationship.

The sentences of co-defendants revealed as much variability between the men and women as between the matched pairs of men and women (see appendix 4). In light of the gestalt of the harm, the defendant's previous lawbreaking, and the defendent's cooperation with the police, the sentences seemed reasonable. There were no widely fluctuating sanctions, even when different judges sentenced co-defendants at different times.

Of the eight matched pairs, six initially raised a question of disparity in my mind. Although the pair-wise analysis is developed more fully in chapter 11, I summarize my judgments here while the crime facts and outcomes are fresh for the reader. For three cases, I judged the offense to be similarly serious, but in one, the man received a more severe penalty (Antonio and Maggie), and in two, the women received a more severe sentence (Pat and Richie, Susan and Ron). For one, I judged the man's offense to be somewhat more serious than the woman's, but her sentence was slightly higher (Bell and Charles). And in two the men's crimes were more serious and their penalties greater, but I wondered whether the sentencing gap was merited (Pamela and Allen, Casey and Kate). For all the pairs except Casey and Kate, I judged the disparity to be fully explained by the defendant's prior record, role in the offense, or the state's evidentiary problems.

Notes

1. See table A-I.1 (app. 1) for a review of the penal code.
2. In the PSI's, which give more detailed information on prior record, a higher proportion of women (75%) and men (88%) had been convicted in the past.
3. In several women's cases, the offenders may have been acting with boyfriends, but unless the PSI reported this explicitly or I could be confident in inferring this relationship, I classified the accomplice as a "friend."
4. In light of differences in sample size and site between my study and theirs, it is all the more remarkable that my robbery profile is similar to theirs. Their

much larger sample of nonlethal robberies ($N=360$) has these features: 62% were carried out by twosomes or larger groups (p. 25); weapons were used in two-thirds of the incidents, usually guns or personal force (p. 23); 87% involved those unknown to each other (p. 9); half occurred in the street, with fewer in commercial (10%) or other locations (30%), such as hallways, cars, and institutional settings (p. 8); one-third had female victims (pp. 17, 23); and in 30%, victims were injured (p. 21). One difference is that my sample has more commercial robberies, which may be attributed to the site of my analysis (court prosecution) compared to theirs (police reports). Another difference is that in my sample, more women's robbery victims were people they knew.

5. Details were lacking in the New Haven PSI's to compare the stages and sequences of moves given in another article by Luckenbill (1981). Note that although Luckenbill's (1980) article uses "his" and "her" in referring to the robbery offender, in his conclusion (p. 376), he says that the "patterns of force discussed . . . held across all subgroups — juvenile or adult, white, black, or hispanic," and whether operating solo or with others. He does not say whether the patterns of force held across gender groups. Although his terminology was gender-neutral (i.e., he used "his" and "her"), his analysis did not consider gender as an axis of robbery transactions.

6. There is a parallel here between "retelling" stories in a legal context (Delgado 1989), and the counting and classification of phenomena in the social sciences, which I have discussed in an earlier article (Daly 1991).

7. With the exception of one case, all those in the deep sample who received suspended sentences were placed on probation, usually for a term of three to five years.

8. On the racial composition of victim-offender relations, the female jewelry clerk was white, and the female clerk in the convenience store was black. Both robberies were thus intraracial. The more decisive elements of seriousness were victim injury and the defendant's threatening demeanor.

9. The public defender's "meanest" and "amateur" scheme is the quality of blameworthiness that attaches to acts. It interweaves biography and offense.

10. Here I would distinguish between the terms *culpability* and *blameworthiness*. Kate and Casey were similarly culpable in the roles they played in carrying out the offense, and they both could expect a heightened level of blameworthiness to attach to their acts. Casey's previous lawbreaking, however, increased his blameworthiness.

11. See Stuart Hall et al. (1978) for the British appropriation of the term *mugging* in the early 1970s from the United States. Public and media concern about street crime (especially robbery) was transformed to a "moral panic."

12. I am borrowing *stickup* from Katz's (1988) discussion of robbery. His analysis centers on urban black, masculine identities and subjectivities forged in the robbery encounter.

13. It is remarkable that the crime facts for these pairs were so similar. Recall that I selected cases on the basis of the statutory charges at arraignment and conviction and had no other information about the organization of the offense. Pairs like these were quite similar, whereas others were quite dissimilar.

14. The evil woman thesis has been discussed in various ways by Otto Pollak (1950), Walter Reckless and Barbara Ann Kay (1967), and Rita Simon (1975). But

like other concepts used to describe women's lawbreaking, no empirical referent is given. See Daly (1987b, 172) for a discussion of specification and interpretive problems with this thesis.

15. Note that although Maggie denied that she had had sexual relations with Max, he said that on two occasions when she came to his house, he paid her for sexual services. Maggie's account was that Max had "pushed sex" on her.

16. It appears from the PSI that the accomplice gave Allen's name to the police. Allen was originally arrested on another outstanding warrant for a robbery in Bridgeport. Although I lack complete information, I suspect that the accomplice got a sentence reduction for cooperating with the police and that Allen's arrest and conviction record was more serious than his accomplice's.

17. I suspect, but cannot verify, that this was an error in the clerk's records and that Charles's cousin was also fined $1,000.

18. I make this claim as an observer of the crime episodes and cannot know how the victims' subjectivities of race, fear, and crime seriousness were constructed.

19. For example, a female victim may not be more vulnerable in comparison to a female offender, and as we shall see in the interpersonal violence cases, many of the women's male victims had victimized the women.

6 Larceny

I seen a pocketbook to snatch, and I snatched it.
— Lennie, Larceny Case 7

This drunk guy picked me up and asked me to come over [to his apartment] and have drinks. He passed out. I was stuck there. I was loaded myself.
— Tara, Larceny Case 2

The larceny cases posed different analytical problems not present in the robberies. First, a wider range of potential behaviors and relations fell within a larceny conviction. Among the women's cases were these: pawning silver stolen from parents, embezzling more than $100,000 from an employer, burglarizing residences, and illegally receiving welfare money. Second, for the men's cases especially, some larceny convictions were for offenses that were factually robberies or burglaries.[1] The state likely had insufficient evidence to convict these defendants on robbery or burglary charges.[2] Finally, two men's cases contained separate offenses that had been consolidated into one larceny conviction; they had engaged in far more extensive lawbreaking than the one-count conviction suggested. A larceny conviction thus contained a more varied set of circumstances and behaviors than did a robbery conviction in this court.

Docket Book Variables

For the wide and deep samples, the potential incarceration time for the convicted offense was the same for men and women: 155 months, plus or minus several months (table 6.1). About half of the convictions were for first-degree larceny and the rest were for larcenies in the second, third, and fourth degrees, and so on.[3] Gender differences appeared at sentencing: the gender gap for those receiving time to serve did not narrow when moving from the wide to the deep samples: it remained at 30–40 percentage points. The average length of sentence was the same for wide-sample men and women. Only one deep-sample woman received an incarceration sentence, which was longer than the average sentence received by four deep-sample men. A higher proportion of wide-sample women than men (52 versus 29 percent) was ordered to pay restitution. This can be attributed to the larger proportion of women who defrauded state entities or businesses.[4] Men were

Table 6.1 Statistical Data on Men's and Women's Larcenies (from clerk's docket book, police records, and penal code statutes)

| | Larceny | | | |
| | Men* | | Women** | |
	Wide (N = 14)	Deep (N = 7)	Wide (N = 23)	Deep (N = 7)
Age (median, yr)	26	25	28	26
Race or Ethnicity				
Black	43%	57%	48%	29%
Latin	7	0	13	14
White	50	43	39	57
Attorney				
Public defender	64%	57%	70%	57%
Private	36	43	30	43
Pretrial Status				
Incarcerated or detained	43%	43%	26%	14%
Out on bail	43	43	35	57
Promise to appear	14	14	39	29
Bail Amount (median)$^\triangle$	$3 K	$2.5 K	$5 K	$5 K
Pled Guilty	93%	100%	96%	100%
Prior Record				
Has been convicted in New Haven felony court or was on probation or parole at the time of the offense?				
yes	50%	57%***	26%	29%***
Severity				
Potential time (mo), convicted offense$^\triangle$	155	157	160	157
(std. dev.)	(102)	(110)	(97)	(110)
Sentence (*In-Out*)				
Received incarceration sentence to serve time? yes	64%	57%	35%	14%
Sentence (*Time*)				
Length of sentence (mo), only cases receiving incarceration$^\triangle$	21	30	22	60
(std. dev.)	(17)	(21)	(18)	(0)
Ordered restitution to victim: yes	29%	29%	52%	29%

$^\triangle$Denotes that these variables may have a smaller number of cases.

*Except where indicated by a triangle, the measures are of N = 14 and N = 7 men in the wide- and deep-larceny samples, respectively. Bail amounts were shown in the clerk's records (or were relevant) for N = 7 and N = 3 men in the wide and deep samples, respectively. Convicted offense severity and incarceration time averages exclude trial cases: one in the wide sample, none in the deep sample. (Note: Deviating from the usual pattern, the one man found guilty at trial did not receive an incarceration sentence; instead he was ordered to pay $10,000 in restitution.)

**Except where indicated by a triangle, the measures are of N = 23 and N = 7 women in the wide- and deep-larceny samples, respectively. Bail amounts were shown in the clerk's records (or were relevant) for N = 11 and N = 5 women in the wide and deep samples, respectively. Convicted offense severity and incarceration time averages exclude trial cases: one in the wide sample, none in the deep sample.

***From the PSI, where a more complete prior criminal history was shown, the proportion of men and women previously convicted was 86% and 43%, respectively.

about twice as likely as women (50 and 25 percent, respectively) to have been convicted in the felony court or to be on probation or parole at the time of the offense.[5]

Coded Elements of the Larceny Narratives

For the content of men's and women's larcenies, the coded elements reveal these patterns (see appendix 4). Most men and women acted with others in carrying out the larceny and took active roles; the women's accomplices were more likely to be boyfriends or spouses. The men committed their offenses with male friends; none acted with a girlfriend or spouse. Although most women victimized someone they knew, no man did. The men burglarized residences or stole property from businesses or state entities. Only one woman carried out the larceny in the course of employment, compared to three men who did. The average value of property stolen was higher for women ($28,000, plus one car) than for men ($16,000, plus one car), but this measure can be misleading. For example, the woman who pawned her parents' silver received several hundred dollars for goods valued at $30,000. A man who stole checks and cash from a safe in a utilities company said he "burned the checks" (valued at $44,000 to the company) and spent the cash (about $3,200). Using the value of property as a measure of seriousness is also misleading in that some of the incidents were robberies (netting low amounts of money) in which defendants pled to larcenies.

Larceny Narratives

I present the narratives along three axes of variation: (1) the masking quality of the legal charges, especially for men, (2) the character of victim-offender relations, (3) and workplace crime and fraud. For some cases I present only the defendant's name and a brief mention of the offense. All the narratives are presented in appendix 6.

Masking Quality of Statutory Charges

Lennie and Laura

Lennie and Laura were each convicted on one count of "using a motor vehicle without the owner's permission," an offense included under motor vehicle theft. However, Lennie's case contained many other incidents. On the same day that he was sentenced in felony court for this offense, he was sentenced in GA-6 for others,[6] including burglaries, selling drugs, and a purse snatch. What follows is part of what Lennie, black and 19, did in a week's time.[7]

Larceny Case 7, Lennie. While driving around with his friends one evening, Lennie recalled, "I seen a parked car and took it." He drove the car back to New Haven, and the next day, while he was driving through a middle-class New Haven neighborhood, he recalled, "I seen a pocketbook to snatch, and I snatched it." The victim, a 50-year-old white woman, was getting out of her car. Lennie said, "I pulled around the corner, stopped, and went back to snatch her pocketbook. I ran up from behind and snatched it. The pocketbook fell on the ground, I picked it up and kept goin'." Lennie hit the woman on the back of the head; she fell, and he took her purse. He received one year to serve for the car theft, a sentence to run concurrently with 6½ years to serve on other charges.

About the stolen car and robbery, Lennie admitted to the probation officer, "I did it. I already regret what I did. I should've been working. There's nothing that I can do about it now. Is there anything in the world that I can do to get my time reduced?" He received a sentence reduction for cooperating with the police in identifying friends with whom he had committed other offenses during this time. Thus, although Lennie was prosecuted and convicted for stealing a car, this offense was only one of many illegalities wrapped in the larceny conviction.

Laura's primary offense was car theft, in which she and her husband stole a car [female larceny case 7]. She had previously been convicted for petty larcenies and had served time for breach of peace. She received a one-year suspended sentence, and her husband received one year to serve. In contrast to Lennie's thick file, Laura's is strikingly slim: there was as much information about her husband in her file as there was about her.[8] Lennie's acts added up to a more serious case than Laura's. Compared to her husband and accomplice, Laura seemed to be a less serious and less experienced lawbreaker.

Geoff

Another illustration of the masking qualities of men's larceny convictions is Geoff, white and 19. On five separate occasions he was variously convicted of larceny, burglary, and disorderly conduct. In his current case, he was sentenced for a series of burglaries and larcenies committed over a four-month period.

Larceny Case 3, Geoff. Geoff was convicted of seven felonies, four for stealing property from businesses and three for burglarizing residences. The four organizational thefts were from stores in the area. The items stolen included snowblowers, toy trains, color television sets, skin-diving equipment, and computers, at an estimated value of $11,000. While released on a $20,000 bond for these thefts, he and a male accomplice burglarized (or attempted to burglarize) four residences. The household victims were able to recover some of their losses (estimated at about $16,000) from their insurance, but the value of the items stolen was of less importance to them than their sense of safety and violation. For example, one couple thought that Geoff or his accomplice had poisoned their dog. About his thefts and burglaries, Geoff said to the probation officer, "I'm sorry it happened. It was my drug problem. It's too bad it was them supporting my drug habit."

In Geoff's case, the clerk's records showed seven convictions in addition to the first-degree larceny on the same sentence date. In the PSI, the one larceny offense combined the four business thefts. The judge sentenced Geoff to twelve years suspended after four years, a sentence to be served concurrently with one imposed on another docket number, which was for one of the residential burglaries. After many readings of Geoff's file, I am still not sure exactly for what Geoff was being sentenced. As important, from the clerk's records one could have assumed, wrongly, that Geoff's case was statutorily equivalent to Winnie's (described below) in that both were accused of and pled guilty to first-degree larceny. Winnie's case, though serious, contained fewer illegal acts than Geoff's. It also differed in that she stole from people she knew.

Women Victimizing People They Know
Winnie

Winnie and three other women in the larceny deep sample (Edith, Maria, and Tara) each victimized someone known to them. Winnie stole from her parents, as she had done several times in the past few years. Up to the age of 16, Winnie was a model student, but when she met Sam, she began to use drugs and to steal from the parental household.

Larceny Case 3, Winnie. On five occasions and over a period of several months, Winnie, white and 18, stole silverware from her parents and sold it to a coin dealer. She carried out the thefts with her husband. They sold the silver for $200 although it was valued at close to $30,000. Winnie said she "was desperate. . . . I took the silver so I could get some money so [Sam and I] could be together. [My] parents were

planning to send me to [a nearby state], and I didn't want to do that."
This was Winnie's first arrest.

Speaking for himself and his wife, Winnie's father said to the probation officer, "As far as we are concerned, Winnie doesn't exist. We don't want to see or hear from her. This was the last straw." Winnie and her husband each received a suspended sentence and three years' probation.

Edith

Another woman who knew her victims was Edith, a white woman in her mid-twenties. The circumstances surrounding Edith's burglaries were similar to Geoff's and Lennie's in that she committed several burglaries over a short time span to support a drug habit [female larceny case 4]. Unlike them, however, she burglarized the households of those she knew in the neighborhood. While out on bond awaiting trial, she was arrested for other offenses. Like Lennie, she talked to officials to reduce her sentence (a note in the file suggests that she cooperated with federal drug investigators in identifying drug traffickers). Edith had a long record of previous arrests and convictions, totaling about fifteen, and was sentenced to serve five years. Edith was the lone woman in the larceny deep sample to receive time to serve. A seasoned street woman, making her living by thefts, burglaries, and prostitution, supplemented by the welfare benefits she received for her three children, Edith's burglaries were not discounted in seriousness because she knew her victims.

Maria

Maria victimized someone she knew, and she benefited from the known-person discount.

Larceny Case 6, Maria. With two accomplices (a young man and young woman), Maria, 17 and Puerto Rican, stole items from an elderly man's house late one night. The victim, in his early sixties, knew the two women because they had been to his apartment "looking for handouts," and he took pictures of them because he did not trust them. On the night of the incident, he answered his doorbell and let the three in. After he asked them why they were there, Maria told him to be quiet or he would be cut with a knife. He ran to the bathroom to escape. After the three left, he discovered that his wallet, with credit cards and driver's license, was missing. This was Maria's first arrest; she and her female accomplice each received a three-month suspended sentence. There is no record of what happened to the male accomplice.

The police officers were initially skeptical of the elderly victim's story: they wondered why he "just happened" to have photographs of the two young women, and they suspected (I think) that he was buying sexual services from Maria and her female friend. The victim was not questioned fully, nor was a police report filed until a week after the incident, even though he had called the police immediately after. Apparently, one of Maria's accomplices boasted of the crime to someone in the neighborhood, and this person called the police. The police began to see the incident more as a "real crime" when the informant put the elderly man's victimization in a new light.

Tara

Like Maria, Tara's male victim was not entirely credible to the police, judge, or prosecutor. Tara was hitchhiking one night and recalled, "This drunk guy picked me up and asked me to come over and have drinks. He passed out. I was stuck there. I was loaded myself." The man's story conflicted with Tara's. He said that when he saw track marks on her arm and realized that she used drugs, he took her from his apartment and dropped her off on a street corner. Although their stories conflict, a common thread is seen in what had happened by the next morning.

Larceny Case 2, Tara. The male victim awoke to find his apartment had been burglarized while he slept. Cash, credit cards, coats, jewelry, and prescription drugs were gone. In his initial statement, the victim told police that the value of the items was $36,000; later, he reported the value at $2,000. Tara was arrested the next day when a third party, her boyfriend's friend, was discovered using one of the stolen credit cards. Tara also told this third party that she had some leather coats to sell. Although she admitted stealing the credit cards, Tara said that the victim "didn't have anything [worth taking] anyway." Tara was described as "having a drug problem" and needing cash to buy cocaine. White and 26, she had several convictions for drug possession and larceny. She received a three-year suspended sentence. Her accomplice, a boyfriend, had recently been convicted of dealing drugs, although there was no information in the clerk's docket book about him for this offense.

The probation officer described Tara as "dependent and insecure," led astray by her boyfriend, and worried that she might be jailed. Although she pled guilty to first-degree larceny, the victim's initial inflating of the value of the stolen items and his inviting Tara to his apartment rendered the crime less serious.[9] On sentencing day, for example, Tara's defense attorney said, "We see a number of crimes. This [one] does not rank high in the scale of crimes that people might get upset about."

Men Victimizing People They Do Not Know

When Maria's and Tara's offenses are compared to Tyrone's and Roger's, their matched pairs, we can see the effect of victim-offender relations in constructing crime seriousness.

Tyrone

Tyrone's robbery was similar to Maria's in that it occurred late at night, there were three people involved, and the victim was threatened. Tyrone and two accomplices, however, robbed a woman on the street [male larceny case 6]. He had recently been convicted for a sixth-degree larceny. For the instant offense he received a short suspended sentence.

One difference between Maria's and Tyrone's offenses was the alacrity with which the police responded to the female victim of Tyrone's robbery in comparison to their more hesitant response to the elderly male victim in Maria's. The female victim was treated as a victim of a "real robbery." As in "real rape" (Estrich 1986) real robbery is constructed from the circumstances of the offense and the character of victim-offender relations. Tyrone's victim was robbed on the street by three men she did not know, but Maria's victim seemed partly responsible for his victimization. Despite differences in the early phases of police response, I judged their harms to be similarly serious.

Roger

Tara's matched pair is Roger, whose offense I judged to be more serious than hers:

Larceny Case 2, Roger. With a male accomplice and a female accomplice acting as a lookout, Roger broke into a residence and stole items valued at several thousand dollars. Among the stolen items were guns, a television set, jewelry, a wristwatch, and cash. Roger, white and 25, had an extraordinarily long record, totaling more than fifty convictions since he was 16. He has been in and out of jail nine times serving sentences. For this offense, he was sentenced to one year, to be served consecutively with another sentence he had received. Although Roger's male accomplice was also arrested, there was no information in the docket book on his sentence. The female accomplice was not implicated and was not arrested.

On sentencing day, the prosecutor said, "The state would be seeking a lot greater time [because of Roger's extensive prior record] had it not been for the circumstances of this case." The circumstances were the state's evidentiary problems.

Workplace Crime and Fraud

The remaining larcenies were four occupational crimes and a welfare fraud.[10] With one exception, the defendants were not stealing to support a drug habit. These were "real" larcenies, meaning that they were not robberies or burglaries for which the state had a weak case.

Prish

Only one occupational crime was committed by someone in a white-collar job. Prish, the only woman in the deep sample to have a four-year college degree, was convicted of embezzling a large sum of money.

Larceny Case 5, Prish. A 50-year-old white woman, Prish embezzled more than $125,000 from her employer, a car dealer, over a five-year period. While working as the company's bookkeeper and office manager, she falsified records by making fictitious journal entries and removing information on sources of income. Prish denied that she had embezzled the funds, and during the pretrial period she secured a new bookkeeping job from another car dealer in the area. There was no obvious motive for the theft — no gambling or household debt — and Prish had never been arrested before. She received a five-year suspended sentence and was ordered to pay her employer back for the money she embezzled.

Prish's embezzlement puzzled the probation officer supervising her case, who said Prish was a "frumpy-looking housewife in a cotton dress" and "a model probationer . . . always showing up on time and making all appointments." The officer could not be sure whether Prish was "an excellent con artist or telling the truth."

Scott

Another occupational crime was carried out by Scott and two accomplices, who were caught stealing oil from a school.

Larceny Case 1, Scott. Scott, white and 32, and two male accomplices stole oil valued at more than $3,500 from a New Haven school by pumping it from the school's tank to Scott's truck. They were able to pull off the job because one accomplice, a white man in his early fifties, was a security guard for the school. As part of a plea-bargain agreement, Scott was ordered to relinquish his truck to the City of New Haven, which planned to use it for the police department's bomb-disposal unit. About the offense Scott said, "I would like to get my truck back. I've learned my lesson to respect the property of others."

Scott was fined $2,840 and lost the use of his truck, a more severe penalty than his accomplices received (a $1,840 fine for the "insider" security guard and $1,340 for the other accomplice). In both Scott's and Prish's cases, the sentencing judges lectured the defendants for their transgressions of trust. Each judge made a point of saying that the defendants deserved to be incarcerated and were lucky to receive a suspended sentence.

June

Scott was matched to June, who took close to $4,000 in welfare money to which she was not entitled [female larceny case 1]. June had never been arrested before. She received a one-year suspended sentence, was placed on a five-year term of probation, and was ordered to pay back the money.

Joe and Darrell

Joe's and Darrell's thefts were carried out at their jobs. Darrell took coats and materials in the course of his employment as a driver [male larceny case 4]. His employer felt that he had been "sucked in" by a co-worker, who had orchestrated the thefts. Joe stole money and checks from a safe in a utilities company, where he worked nights as a janitor.

Larceny Case 4, Joe. Joe, 29 and black, worked as a custodian. One night he stole more than $3,200 in cash and more than $44,000 in checks from a safe at the New Haven Water Company. One of Joe's work responsibilities was to clean around the safe. When first questioned, Joe denied the theft; however, there were security cameras on the premises, and a film recording showed him leaving the company twice in one evening with a canvas bag. Joe later admitted that he took the cash and checks at the end of his normal cleaning shift. He was sorry that he had taken the checks from the safe and said that "the money was all spent." Three years after the theft, he was killed in an incident "over drugs." First arrested at 19, Joe had been convicted four times in the past, served time in jail, and was on parole at the time of this larceny. He received four years to serve.

One sees a sad, desperate quality to Joe's act. The theft took some planning, and yet he was apparently unaware of the camera surveillance. Joe's and Darrell's offenses represent forms of occupational crime carried out by members of the working class and the working poor (see also Mars 1982).

Judgments of Larceny Seriousness

Of the seven matched pairs, two men (Lennie and Geoff) had many illegalities consolidated in one larceny conviction. I judged their cases to be more serious than those of the women with whom they were paired (see appendix 5). For a third pair (Tara and Roger), I judged the man's offense as the more serious: his was the more typical burglary, with victim(s) unknown to him. For two pairs, the women's offenses registered greater seriousness: Prish's embezzlement was far more serious than Darrell's coat thefts, and Edith's burglaries were somewhat more serious than Joe's theft of cash and checks. For two pairs, I judged the offenses to be comparably serious: June's and Scott's theft of money or goods from a state entity seemed equivalent,[11] as did Maria's and Tyrone's robberies. Taking these judgments of seriousness into account, there was no larceny pair that raised a question of sentencing disparity in my mind.

Racial Dynamics in Larceny Seriousness

The role of race in constructing seriousness was more muted for the larcenies than for the robberies. Victim vulnerability and transgression of trust were more salient. However, within the limits of a small sample, I wonder whether the masking qualities in some men's cases have a racial dimension. Specifically, a conviction for a first-degree robbery normally means one robbery incident, whereas a conviction for a first-degree larceny could stand for many illegal acts, including burglaries and robberies. Considering these asymmetries in the light of the racial composition of the men's deep sample (of robberies, 58 percent black; of larcenies and burglaries, 43 percent), white men's cases may wrongly appear to be less serious than those of black men's.

In the New Haven felony court, a larceny felony conviction can mean several things: a robbery or burglary, for which the state's case is weak; multiple property incidents consolidated in one case (more so for men); welfare fraud (more so for women); or moderate-to-serious forms of occupational crime. Neither "sneaky thrills" (Katz 1988), nor petty fraud, nor shoplifting (Steffensmeier 1980) characterize these cases. Such labels may be more appropriate for larcenies prosecuted in nonfelony courts. But even there, a category such as petty theft (as used in Kruttschnitt 1980–81) can include an array of deceptively packaged and diverse harms.

As in the deep-sample robberies, so too for the larceny cases: women were more likely than men to victimize someone they knew. That relationship may discount seriousness, though not consistently. Feminist scholars have called attention to a "domestic discount"[12] — a less serious quality attached to men's assaulting women they know than to their assaulting women they do not know. Such downgrading in seriousness is seen in the response of police and court officials to men's sexual and physical abuse of girlfriends, spouses, and acquaintances (Estrich 1986; Ferraro 1989; Frohmann 1991; Stanko 1982).[13] My sample suggests a parallel for some women prosecuted for larceny and robbery, although it comes with this caveat: ambiguity surrounds a woman lawbreaker's role when she knows her victim. "Knows" for women includes sexual contact, not simply familiarity or a familial relation. When women harm adults they know,[14] their acts can be perceived as more serious if they betray vulnerable victims, or as less serious when the victims are not credible. Of the four women who knew their larceny victims, for two (Tara and Maria), the victims were not fully credible to the police. For two (Edith and Winnie), however, they were.

Although more women than men victimized a person they knew, more men victimized a workplace organization they knew. Thus, the known-unknown dichotomy fails to capture the ways in which both persons and organizations can be known to lawbreakers. An occupational crime is often committed against an organization known to a lawbreaker, often his or her employer. The betrayal of trust by an employee in an occupational crime is similar to that by a person who steals from someone he or she knows. In both instances, victims may be easy marks.

For some time sociologists have noted the effect of victim-offender relationships on the construction of crime seriousness. The variable characteristic of these relationships has been described in terms of social or relational distance (Black 1976), known or unknown (Vera Institute of Justice 1977; National Crime Victimization Survey data), or a person or organizational victim (Weisburd et al. 1991). Although seriousness can be understood partly from these relationships, a better way to define it is to identify the social significance attached to a relationship — for example, whether it is an employer-employee or parent-child relationship of trust, or a violation of familiarity.

In comparison with other offenses analyzed (robbery, interpersonal violence, drugs), less is known about the social organization of larcenies. That is a pity. An understanding of how seriousness is constructed when persons or organizations are victimized or when businesses or state entities are victimized engenders a more sophisticated conceptualization of common and white-collar crime. The second most common of common crimes for which people are arrested in the United States (after drunk driving), larceny may not seem as interesting or fearsome to scholars or the general public as robbery, interpersonal violence, and drug offenses. Yet larceny is no less rich sociologically.

Notes

1. The distinctions between robbery, burglary, and larceny are that a robbery involves using or threatening to use a weapon; a burglary is unlawful entry in a building or dwelling with the intent to commit a crime; and a larceny is the taking, obtaining, or withholding of an owner's property.

2. Mather (1979) found the same pattern in the Los Angeles felony court. Cases that were factually burglaries were allowed to be pled as larcenies. During the research period, relatively few burglaries were prosecuted in the JD court.

3. See table A-I.1 (app. 1) for a review of the penal code.

4. Of the four men in the wide sample ordered to pay restitution, three committed occupational thefts, and one defrauded the City of New Haven. But of the twelve women ordered to pay restitution, three committed welfare fraud, and one, an embezzlement. Eight other women committed fraud of some sort, but I could not tell from the clerk's records if these were against businesses or state entities.

5. Again, PSI information reveals that higher proportions of men and women (86% and 43%) had been convicted in the past.

6. As noted in chap. 2, GA-6 is the New Haven court that disposes of all misdemeanors and less serious felonies.

7. Lennie's quoted remarks are taken from a transcript produced by the police department.

8. Her husband was the first juvenile in Connecticut to have been criminally prosecuted for homicide.

9. The circumstances of this offense resemble what Maher's prostitute informants call "viccing" a date (Maher and Curtis 1992), though this term is not part of New Haven street argot. *Viccing* refers to taking money or goods (such as a watch) from clients, as the women say, "robbin' dates."

10. Occupational crimes are committed against one's employer or by using one's occupational expertise: they are one form of white-collar crime. See Daly (1989d) for a review of white-collar crime definitions and their applicability to men and women.

11. Note, though, that Scott's theft evoked far more ire from the sentencing judge than did June's welfare fraud, for which another judge gave no moral censure (see chap. 10).

12. I first heard this term used by Elizabeth Rapaport (1992) and want to credit her innovation.

13. In a review of the literature, Delbert Elliott (1989) suggests that such discounting is not confined to men's victimizing women but applies generally across a range of harms involving people who know each other. I agree with Elliott's appraisal but would keep gender relations in the frame.

14. When children are harmed, the same discount may not apply.

7 Interpersonal Violence

I have been living under constant harassment. If the state can't control him, how can I?
— Sharon, Assault Case 2

There was blood — my blood — all over the apartment. I was very lucky. I must have a tough skull.
— Ted's victim, Homicide Case 4

I know I didn't do it, and [my wife and children] told them I didn't do it; but I got found guilty of it.
— Jack, Risk-of-Injury Case 1

[I] murdered the wrong person. . . . I should have killed my husband.
— Edie, Homicide Case 2

In this chapter I explore a spectrum of interpersonal violent acts: homicide, assault, arson, and risk of injury. Although the details are diverse, most men's and women's actions conform to what scholars term *impulsive* (Block 1987, 34) or *hot-blooded* (Rapaport 1991, 380–81) acts. The circumstances of the violence are similar except for risk of injury. Differences emerged in the weapon used and whether the victim survived or died.

As Carolyn Block observes (1987, 33–35), "Homicide is not one . . . but several kinds of crime," keyed to what started the conflict: an assault, a robbery, a burglary, or a rape. Most of the deep-sample violence cases arose from ongoing disputes between persons who knew each other. Even arson, I was surprised to learn, is a type of intimate (or domestic) violence, with fire as the weapon. Most interpersonal harms were *not* planned: they were not *cold- blooded* (though the implied meaning of this term can be questioned).[1] Of the four offenses, the least bounded is risk of injury. Under Connecticut law, the risk-of-injury statute contains a broad set of behaviors (see appendix 1, table A-I.1), but a prosecuted case is normally rape or attempted rape or the physical abuse of a minor (a person under sixteen years of age).

Research on gender differences in interpersonal violence is most developed for homicide, a body of work that reveals several patterns.[2] Women account for a small share (about 10 percent) of homicide arrests. They are more likely to kill their intimates (spouses or partners) than men — who are more likely to kill acquaintances or strangers — and the victims of women's homicides are more likely to have initiated the violence than are the victims of men's homicides. These situational and relational differences can be explained, in part, by the fact that fewer women's homicides occur in the course of robberies, burglaries, or rapes. Instead, women's homicides occur in their own or the victim's residence, while men's homicides occur more frequently outside residential settings. Men are more likely both to kill men and to be killed by men. Very high proportions of men's and women's homicides (90 percent or more) are intraracial, with black and latin populations constituting a disproportionate share of victims and offenders.

Studies of the situational and sequencing dynamics of homicides suggest that male offenders are more likely to instigate the violence that eventually leads to the killing of a victim,[3] while the *victims* of women's homicides are more likely to initiate the violence that leads to their deaths. This pattern has led some scholars (for example, Dobash and Dobash 1984; Jurik and Gregware 1991) to challenge the generality of Luckenbill's (1977) "impression management" model of victim and offender "moves," which can escalate to a more violent level. The "standard situational time frame" of analysis, which normally focuses on the *immediate* circumstances surrounding a homicide, is too narrow to elucidate women's homicides. When women kill someone they know, there is usually a history of violence: they have been beaten in the past. Nancy Jurik and Peter Gregware (1991) encapsulate gender differences in homicide this way: "The symbolic contest, image-saving dimensions of interpersonal violence" are more characteristic of men's homicides, and the "strategic, life-saving dimensions" are more frequent in women's. Further, they note that although men's homicides may be characterized by a "mutual agreement" to use violence to settle disputes, women's homicides have less of this consensual character because more victims initiate the violence.[4]

How might gender-based patterns for homicide apply to other acts of interpersonal violence? With the exception of risk of injury,[5] we should see similar patterns. For risk of injury, a woman's physical or sexual abuse of a child may be more likely when she is abused or controlled by a mate (Stark and Flitcraft 1988).[6] Overall, we should expect to see more women than men acting in self-defense and within a history of violence with victims. That pattern, coupled with a greater likelihood that men will initiate physical aggression, may construct men's violent acts as "more serious" than women's.

There is an added dimension to consider. Hilary Allen's (1987a, 1987b) research in London's crown courts suggests that the reports of court officials of women's violence tend "toward the exoneration of the offender" by neutralizing the woman's guilt, responsibility, and dangerousness (1987a, 82), with more attention given to the psychological states of women than men. Allen finds that women are less likely to be viewed as a danger to the community. Their acts are more easily excused as unintentional or are "naturalized" as something that any woman would do under the same circumstances. An intriguing point Allen makes is that *feminist* discourse about women's violent crime parallels the discourse of court officials: "Feminist discussions . . . view criminal women as more victims than aggressors, more sinned against than sinning, more to be pitied than blamed" (Allen 1987a, 93).

Allen's research signals difficulties in interpreting ambiguous violent acts. As readers of these events, we fill in a good deal about power, harm, mental states, and culpability. Previous research, especially research generated by feminist scholars, prepares us to see women's acts as spawned by victimized circumstances, and thus as less heinous and more defensible than men's. *And perhaps they are.* At the same time, as I suggested in chapter 3, some harmed and harming women's acts may be viewed as dangerous. The more general point to make is that seriousness judgments are rooted in cross-cutting relations of gender, class, race, age, and sexuality. It may not be possible to separate these relations — or the social locations of the parties involved — from a judgment about the seriousness of a "violent act."[7]

Docket Book Variables

As in cases of robbery and larceny, the average length of the potential incarceration time for interpersonal violence convictions was the same for men and women: about 166–176 months in the wide and deep samples (table 7.1). In the wide sample, about 30–35 percent of all convictions were for *B* felonies; a small proportion (4–8 percent) were to the most serious *A* felonies, and about 15 percent were to misdemeanors. The remaining convictions were for less serious and unclassified felonies.[8] More men than women received time to serve (over 70 percent of the men versus just under 60 percent of the women). The average length of sentence for those receiving time was the same for men and women in the wide sample (about five years), but the deep-sample women's sentences were shorter than the men's.

The deep-sample selection process increased the share of defendants represented by private attorneys, decreased the average age for women, slightly increased the black share of men, and decreased the proportion of men detained pending trial. The offense composition of the deep-sample cases is a compromise between different wide-sample distributions for men and women. For men, there are more homicides

Table 7.1 Statistical Data on Men's and Women's Interpersonal Violence (from clerk's docket book, police records, and penal code statutes)

	Interpersonal Violence			
	Men*		Women**	
	Wide (N = 61)	Deep (N = 17)	Wide (N = 50)	Deep (N = 17)
Age (median, yr)	26	28	29	24
Race or Ethnicity				
Black	56%	70%	68%	65%
Latin	11	6	8	12
White	33	24	24	24
Attorney				
Public defender	70%	53%	82%	71%
Private	30	47	18	29
Pretrial Status				
Incarcerated or detained	53%	41%	46%	47%
Out on bail	39	53	44	53
Promise to appear	8	6	10	0
Bail Amount (median)$^\triangle$	$18 K	$20–$25 K	$15 K	$15 K
Pled Guilty	97%	94%	98%	100%
Prior Record				
Has been convicted in New Haven felony court or was on probation or parole at the time of the offense?				
yes	13%	0%***	6%	6%***
Severity				
Potential time (mo), convicted offense$^\triangle$	178%	166%	176%	176%
(std. dev.)	(157)	(90)	(134)	(100)
Sentence (*In-Out*)				
Received incarceration sentence to serve time? yes	74%	71%	58%	59%
Sentence (*Time*)				
Length of sentence (mo), only cases receiving incarceration$^\triangle$	46	60	48	39
(std. dev.)	(58)	(43)	(61)	(37)
Types of Violence				
Homicide	11%	23%	30%	23%
Assault	57	47	48	47
Arson	18	12	16	12
Risk of injury	13	18	6	18

$^\triangle$Denotes that these variables may have a smaller number of cases.
*Except where indicated by a triangle, the measures are of N = 61 and N = 17 in the wide and deep samples, respectively. Bail amounts were shown in the clerk's records (or were relevant) for N = 39 and N = 13 men in the wide and deep samples, respectively. Convicted offense severity and incarceration time averages *exclude* trial cases: two in the wide sample, one in the deep sample.
**Except where indicated by a triangle, the measures are of N = 50 and N = 17 in the wide and deep samples, respectively. Bail amounts were shown in the clerk's records (or were relevant) for N = 33 and N = 15 women in the wide and deep samples, respectively. Convicted offense severity and incarceration time averages *exclude* trial cases: one in the wide sample, none in the deep sample.
***From the PSI, where more complete prior criminal history was given, the percentage of defendants previously convicted was 71% and 65%, respectively.

in the deep sample and somewhat fewer assault cases; for women, there are fewer homicides and more cases of risk of injury.

Coded Elements of the Violence Narratives

Men's and women's interpersonal violence was similar along the following dimensions (see appendix 4): Most acted alone and took active or equal roles. Both men and women harmed young to middle-aged men they knew of the same race or ethnicity as themselves. They carried some type of weapon (more guns for men, more knives for women) and used these and such "other weapons" as a golf club, baseball bat, hammer, and fire (arson).[9] Victims died or were injured in most incidents. Violence arose from two major sources: ongoing conflicts or violence with victims (partners, children, friends) and situational rage or arousal. Drunkenness featured in a minority of incidents, though for more male than female defendants (seven and three, respectively). In only two men's and two women's cases had both the defendant and the victim been drinking. Compared to Allen's (1987b, 128–29) research, for these interpersonal violence cases the same proportion of men and women (about one-fourth) had some type of psychological evaluation for the instant offense.

As in the robbery and larceny samples, when women had accomplices, they were more likely to act with *male* accomplices (as were men), and they were more likely to work with boyfriends or mates. Three women but no men took secondary roles in the incident. Key areas of gender difference were that more women's violent acts took place where the women lived, more men initiated the violence, and more women acted to defend themselves from violent victims. In incidents arising from ongoing disputes with partners or former partners, for five women, all had been beaten by their partners, whereas for three men, all had beaten their partners. These gender differences for fatal and nonfatal violent episodes are like those found in the homicide literature (see notes 2 and 3).

Violence Narratives

In describing and comparing the violent acts, I have ordered them according to my judgments of the least to the most serious: those in which (1) the defendant's actions were largely a fending off of violent victims, (2) the defendant's actions reflected a mutuality of aggression — although some defendants claimed to be fending off violent victims, (3) the defendant initiated the violence toward adults, and (4) the defendant victimized children. Recall that with the exception of one defendant (Jack, who was convicted of risk of injury), all the deep-sample defendants entered guilty pleas. (For the precise charges they pled to, see appendix 1, table A-I.3.)

Fending Off Violent Victims
Shane, Sharon, Carrie, and Jean

One man and three women were reacting to violent victims. Shane was responding to gang members' threats, while the women were defending themselves from violent men who were former partners.

Assault Case 6, Shane. Shane shot at a group of gang members, injuring one. Shane had been intimidated and humiliated by the gang members on several occasions. He decided to bring a gun to school and keep it in his locker should gang members approach him again. One day, as Shane was leaving his high school, gang members confronted him: one punched him in the face. Shane went back into the school to get his gun. When he was again approached by gang members, he fired into the group, hitting one of them. Shane, 17 and black, said he was "fed up" with the situation and that he had no choice but to react the way he did — otherwise, gang members would continue to harass him. He received a suspended sentence.

Shane, and not the injured gang member, was viewed by state officials as the victim in this case. Described as a model student, a member of student government, and a "well-mannered, soft spoken young man" by the probation officer, Shane had never been arrested before. His act, though considered "very serious" by the judge, was excused by the judge as "something he had to do to protect himself."

The circumstances surrounding the women's incidents were remarkably similar: all three had recently broken off relations with abusive partners.

Assault Case 2, Sharon. Taking a handgun from a nearby flowerpot, Sharon shot the victim, a former boyfriend and father of one of her children. The victim, Tim, 33 and black, was hospitalized for several days. Tim came to Sharon's house drunk and threatened to hurt her if she did not let him in. Finding the door unlocked, he came into the kitchen, and it appeared to Sharon that he had a weapon in his jacket. He said he wanted to give the children some money, saying "All I got is the kid."

Sharon, 28 and black, said she called the police "many a times" on the victim. Just after the shooting, she said that "he had whispered close to me that he was going to use a machine gun on me the next day . . . that he was definitely going to kill me with a machine gun." Sharon maintained her innocence, saying, "I have been living under constant harassment. If the state can't control him, how can I? Why should I leave my home because of him?" She received a suspended sentence.

Assault Case 8, Carrie. At noon one day Carrie was arguing with Chuck, with whom she had lived for ten years. He had recently moved out. Witnesses reported that Carrie was yelling at him to leave her alone and that she was crying. Chuck attempted to hit Carrie three times with his car. She pulled a pistol from her purse and fired three shots at the car. Chuck, 51 years old and black, was not injured. Carrie, black and 38, felt she was provoked by Chuck; she had already called the police three times that day. Chuck had beaten Carrie in the past; once she was hospitalized eleven days from a beating. She received a suspended sentence.

Jean stabbed a drunken former boyfriend, who had been beating her for several hours [homicide case 4]; she received thirty months to serve. Unlike Sharon and Carrie, Jean was unlucky in that her victim died.[10] In the next group of fatal and nonfatal assaults, the contexts and histories of the violence are similar. The main axis of seriousness turns less on the defendants' actions and more on whether the victims survived.

Mutual Aggression

Mindful of the debates surrounding mutuality of aggression, especially when women are defending themselves from abusive mates,[11] I want to be clear about my use of the term. By *mutuality* I do not assume that the two parties were equal in their use of force or in initiating the violence, although parity is possible. I mean that the parties agreed that violence was one way to settle the score.

Mutual Aggression with Elements of Defense

For two women (Lonnie and Claire) and two men (Earl and Wes), it was difficult to determine whether the violence was agreed to or whether the defendant was acting to fend off a violent victim. In Lonnie's case, there were some elements of self-defense.

Homicide Case 3, Lonnie. During an argument and fist fight in which the victim, Spike, black and 35, punched Lonnie in the face and broke into a bedroom to get a pair of his pants, Lonnie stabbed him. Spike left the apartment and walked up the street a short way before collapsing on the sidewalk. Lonnie and Spike had recently broken off their relationship of several years. He had come to Lonnie's house to get some things from the bedroom, which was locked. Lonnie had refused to let him into the room. They argued while others watched and tried to break up the fight. Before the stabbing, Lonnie swung a knife at Spike, demanding that he leave the apartment. When police officers arrived, they heard her say, "You keep that son of a bitch away from me because the next time I am going to kill him." A 44-year-old black woman, Lonnie claimed she never hit the victim, and when she saw all the blood in the apartment, she assumed it was hers. She received 3½ years to serve.

Although there was a history of violence between her and Spike, Lonnie's stabbing seemed to be more than fending him off. Her actions reflect Coramae Richey Mann's (1988, 48) observation that some women in domestic homicides "were the victors in the domestic fight," not acting solely to defend themselves.[12] In classifying these acts, I found myself seeing more self-defensive elements in the women's violence, filling in gender asymmetries in physical strength and threats of violence. Only after several readings could I see the self-defensive elements in the men's acts. These were buried in the narrative, as in Earl's case, where I initially overlooked the victim's coming at him with a pair of scissors.

Homicide Case 3, Earl. Using a gun, Earl, 49 and black, killed a male associate of his son one morning. The victim, black and 23, was arguing with Earl's son over paying for an air conditioning unit. When he heard about the fight, Earl drove his car to his son's apartment. Earl said, "When I got there, my son was bleeding and his jaw was broken. He [the victim] came at me with some scissors and I fired once. I don't remember firing three times. I never [wanted to] hurt anybody. I still think about it." In a somewhat different version of the offense (supplied by the prosecutor's office), Earl was said to have "pulled the pistol" when "the victim reached for his rear pocket." He received seven years to serve.

Wes was initially provoked by a victim who had punched him while he was driving [homicide case 2]. He got angry, challenged his friend to fight, and stabbed him, receiving nine years to serve. In Claire's case, she and other family members had been fighting her sister's boyfriend for much of the day. Using a golf club, Claire swung at the victim, killing him [homicide case 1]. She said that he "swung at me [with a pipe] but missed. . . . I didn't hit him to kill him, just to defend myself." She received 7½ years to serve.

In these four cases, the defendants claimed to be fending off violent victims. Lonnie's claims seemed to be most persuasive to me, and perhaps also to the sentencing judges. Her punishment was less (3½ years to serve) than the other three (seven to nine years to serve).

Mutual Aggression with No Elements of Defense

For Maurice, Nellie, and Alice, the scenario was mutual aggression with no elements of self-defense, but the victim sustained greater injury than the defendant.

Assault Case 3, Maurice. Maurice shot Ollie, 26 and black, hospitalizing him for five days. The week before Maurice and Ollie had fought; Ollie believed that he had won the fight and that Maurice "was embarrassed because a lot of people were around." The afternoon of the shooting, Ollie was walking home from work and ran into Maurice, who pulled out a gun and shot it "while a lot of kids were around." Because Ollie did not want to get shot in the back, he turned around. Maurice shot him in the stomach at close range. Maurice, 23 and black, said, "I'll never do it again. I learned a good lesson." He was sentenced to two years and ordered to pay $5,000 in restitution to Ollie.

Dee Dee and Alice had both been fighting other young women, but the reason for the disputes is uncertain. Dee Dee and a female friend had been drinking, fought, and began stabbing at each other [assault case 3]. Both were injured, but the victim was hospitalized in critical condition. Dee Dee was sentenced to serve one year and eight months. Alice, who was arguing with another female teen, slashed at her with a knife and stabbed her in the back [assault case 6]. She received a suspended sentence.

These three violent exchanges are marked by mutual aggression, symmetry of the assailants' size and strength, and offenders and victims who knew one another. Such violence is regarded as routine and not especially serious by the police and the courts (see, for example, Buzawa and Buzawa 1992; Elliott 1989; Ferraro 1989; Ferraro and Boychuk 1992; Vera 1977). In the next set of harms, in which the defendant initiated the aggression, seriousness escalates.

Defendant-initiated Aggression

I have grouped the defendant-initiated violence by the precipitating element (such as arson), and then by whether the violence ended in death or not.

Arson

All four arson cases (Dorothy, Enrico, Nancy, and Wayne) were forms of intimate violence using fire — not fists — as the weapon. Dorothy, 25 and Puerto Rican, set two fires after fighting with her boyfriend.

Arson Case 1, Dorothy. According to the victim, Miguel, his girlfriend, Dorothy, set several fires in their apartment. Miguel came home at

4:00 one morning; he and Dorothy argued. Miguel left to avoid fighting, and when he returned, he found that two fires had been set: one in the living room and another in the bedroom. Miguel asked a neighbor to call the police and then tried to put out the fires. There was no physical injury and little physical destruction. About the fire, Dorothy claimed Miguel was a "liar" because "he made it seem like I did everything." She and Miguel have been together for four years, and he has beaten her in the past. She received one year to serve.

In reading this next case, be aware of how seriousness may be perceived differently when a woman's aggression is directed toward a man (Dorothy's case) and when a man's aggression is directed toward a woman.

Arson Case 1, Enrico. Enrico set fire to a mattress in the basement of the building where his girlfriend, Carla, lived. Enrico and Carla had been arguing all day while at a wedding. When they were returning home in a car with her mother and brother, Enrico scratched Carla in the face. Later, when she was at the hospital to have her injuries checked, her brother saw Enrico leave the family's apartment building just before he smelled smoke. Damage was limited to the basement. Enrico is Puerto Rican and Carla is white; both are in their midtwenties. Enrico had threatened to kill Carla in the past. His attorney said Enrico "denie[s] he had anything to do with this fire" and "feels very strongly about his innocence." He received a suspended sentence.

Note the similarities in Enrico's and Dorothy's arsons: both arose from arguments and seemed impulsive, not planned; the destruction in each was minimal (although later in court it was stressed that many people in Dorothy's apartment building were jeopardized by her act). An aspect of Dorothy's arson not present in Enrico's was her drinking; she and other family members admit that she "becomes wild" when she drinks. Her "losing control" of herself when drinking made her act seem especially dangerous to the judge sentencing her.[13]

Let us consider the role of gender in shaping these stories of harm. Does Dorothy seem to be more of a victim than Enrico? Does it seem that Enrico's claim of innocence is false and that Dorothy's reconstruction of the arson (and her claim of not being fully responsible for it) is true? My reading suggests yes, and yet I wonder, if we were to switch the disputants' gender, would we still see Dorothy as less culpable than Enrico? As readers and observers of personal violence, we fill in the gaps in stories of harm. There is a readiness to see women as less culpable than men for their acts, or at least, to see women's acts as more likely to have arisen from experiences of victimization.[14] Such gender-based attributions are also evident, as we shall see, in the risk-of-injury cases.

For Nancy and Wayne [arson pair 2], there is less ambiguity in judging seriousness: his act was more serious than hers. Nancy set two fires in the apartment she shared with her sister, which gutted the entire apartment. Her history of severe mental problems discounted the seriousness of her arson, and she received a suspended sentence. Wayne set fire to his former girlfriend's apartment after threatening to kill her. He had a long record of convictions, stemming from his drug addiction. Several weeks before the fire, he beat her and held her captive in her apartment. He was sentenced to serve six years.

Robbery Assault

In the robbery-related assaults, the defendants were less likely to know their victims. The assaults arose when victims refused to give up money. One matched pair [Kathleen and Larry, assault pair 1] were co-defendants in an incident. They and an accomplice beat the victim and took some money and valuables; both received suspended sentences. With the other pair [Nellie and Clarence, assault pair 7], the assaults were more serious, and the offense "facts" were ambiguous. Clarence beat a man he knew with a broken bottle and then stole his car [assault case 7]. Arrested a year later on a warrant, he received one year to serve. During the pretrial period, the victim vacillated, saying he was not sure whether Clarence had assaulted him. Nellie and two other women tried to rob a man who had given them a ride home from a bar [assault case 7]. When he resisted, they cut him, hospitalizing him for twelve days. Nellie was sentenced to serve two years, eleven months.[15]

Assault

In an instant, assaultive or threatening behavior can be transformed into a killing. Conversely, a victim may survive. Coupled with fatality is the role of alcohol in constructing seriousness. I found that when violent victims had been drinking, the defendants were viewed positively (as was the case for Sharon, Carrie, and Jean). When both victim *and* defendant had been drinking or when just the defendant had been drinking, seriousness rested on whether the victim had died or survived.

Pete, Georges, and Lester

Three men convicted of assault had been drinking or were drunk at the time of the offense. Pete was thrown out of a bar for being too drunk. He returned with a gun, pointed it to the head of the man who had thrown him out, and fired [assault case 8]. The gun did not go off. He received a suspended sentence. Georges also threatened his victim by firing a gun at her.

Assault Case 5, Georges. Georges went to the house of his former wife, Andrée, one day to take his daughter shopping for a birthday present. Earlier that day he had been to court to finalize their divorce, but he was too drunk to go through with the court proceedings. He went to Andrée's house. Seeing her and his daughter in the car, he said he wanted to take his daughter shopping. His wife refused. He approached the car, pulled out a handgun, and pointed it at her. She drove away as he fired two shots; the car window was shattered. Neither Andrée, 40, nor her daughter, 14, suffered physical injuries. Georges blamed his wife for the incident, saying her unacceptable behavior — lying, not caring for his daughter, and going out on him — drove him to do it. White and 43, Georges came to Connecticut from Québec about fifteen years ago. He received a suspended sentence.

Georges's attempted shooting of his wife offers a good contrast to Carrie's shooting at her former mate: Georges was drunk and initiated the violence, while Carrie was fending off a violent former mate. The two domestic violence cases are worlds apart in situational meaning and defendant culpability, yet they might be scored the same on a well-known measure of family violence, the Conflict Tactics Scale (CTS), developed by Murray Straus and colleagues (Straus 1979; Straus, Gelles, and Steinmetz 1980). Carrie's and Georges's incidents illustrate well the "myth of sexual symmetry" (Dobash et al. 1992) that can be produced by CTS measures of intimate violence. The CTS-generated myth is that husbands are battered as frequently as wives. Rebecca Dobash and colleagues (1992, 79) have challenged the CTS's validity for its "failure to consider intentions, interpretations, and the history of the individuals' relationship." Their concern with context and motive in intimate violence can be applied more generally to other relationships in which interpersonal violence occurs.

By now we should expect to see violent acts downgraded in seriousness by the domestic discount, as happened in Georges's case. Perhaps more surprising is why Pete's act was *not* taken seriously. His age (he was 61) may have precluded jail time, and his drunkenness may have blunted the seriousness. Although both Georges and Pete endangered the lives of their victims, no physical injury resulted. When injuries are visible and documented, the crime appears more serious. This occurred in Lester's assault, in which he slashed a man with a butcher knife, causing a permanent scar on his face [assault case 2], for which he received three years to serve.

Assaulting a Police Officer

As we know, the justice system will not tolerate a challenge to authority in the form of assaulting a police officer or resisting arrest.

In the following pair, the reaction to assaulting the police varied: Andrew's offense was treated more seriously than Latasha's. From the narratives, I could not find a good reason for their different punishments.

Assault Case 4, Andrew. While on his way to play basketball with his friend Bo, Andrew saw two police officers beating Bo. He jumped in and began fighting, kicking one officer in the face and striking a second with a blunt instrument. A crowd gathered to watch the fight. Bo and Andrew fled the scene. In addition to receiving abrasions and contusions, one officer was damaged in his right ear. The other officer's dental bridgework was damaged and two teeth were broken. The officers were trying to arrest Bo for a street robbery he had allegedly just committed. Andrew, 19 and black, described what happened to the judge at sentencing: "I had seen that two police officers had picked [Bo] up and slammed him on the ground. And started beating on him. I came over and asked them to let him up, and they did not do that. So I jumped in at that time." Andrew received four years to serve. Bo was sentenced for assaulting a police officer and for first-degree robbery; he received five years to serve.

Assault Case 4, Latasha. While three male police officers were attempting to question Latasha for having smashed the windows of her former boyfriend's current girlfriend's car, Latasha struck one officer in the nose with a baseball bat and hit another. The two were seriously injured but not hospitalized. Latasha is white and 19. The incident arose because Latasha was angry at her former boyfriend, Terry, with whom she had a son the year before. Terry and his current girlfriend now care for the child, and Latasha accused them of kidnapping her baby. One police officer said that Latasha was "yelling . . . and acting crazy" when he tried to approach her. The mother of Terry's girlfriend said that when Latasha came to her house, Latasha ripped the phone off the wall. She received a suspended sentence and was ordered to pay $2,000 in restitution.

The injuries sustained by the police officers in Andrew's assault were described in great detail, but such detail was missing in Latasha's file. Are we to assume that the officers were not hurt with Latasha's baseball bat? Or perhaps it was embarrassing for them to admit that one young woman had successfully kept three police officers at bay? A key difference in the construction of Andrew's and Latasha's violence was the definition of Latasha's mental state, that she was "crazy." Her acts were treated as the product of a mental instability.[16]

Although the police officers in Andrew's assault may have been injured more seriously, the difference in the pair's sentencing was substantial, especially since Latasha (but not Andrew) had a previous conviction. In the pair-wise disparity analysis (chapter 11), I nominated

Andrew and Latasha as the *sole* pair of the forty deep-sample cases in which the sentencing disparity could not be satisfactorily explained. In light of the state's interests in maintaining police authority, one can understand why Andrew was sentenced to serve four years. More difficult to fathom is why Latasha received no time to serve.

Homicide or Attempted Homicide

Of violence aimed at adults, the next cases are the most serious. Two men (Barry and Ted) and two women (Stacey and Edie) were in this group. Stacey was a pawn in an attempted revenge killing.

Assault Case 5, Stacey. Following her boyfriend's instructions, Stacey attempted to lure a man, Kevin, out of his house by pretending she had been raped. Greg "ripped her blouse and punched her in the face for effect." Stacey went to Kevin and his wife's house, told them she had been raped, and asked for help. The couple became suspicious when Stacey said she had to go outside to get her purse. As she ran out the front door, Greg fired rifle shots at the house. While Stacey had a revolver that Greg had given her, there is no indication in the PSI that she fired it. Greg and Stacey fled in a car; the police followed in a high-speed chase, which ended when Greg's car crashed in a yard. Kevin and his wife were not injured, though there were bullet holes in their truck and front door. Greg claimed that Kevin had recently robbed him, and Kevin said Greg had asked him to kill two people over a drug deal but that he had refused. All are white. Stacey, 28, received one year to serve, and Greg got three years.

Although Stacey was initially arraigned on two counts of attempted murder, she pled to a second-degree assault. Her role as a pawn in Greg's plan to get back at Kevin was acknowledged in the PSI.

In the next case Ted, white and 28, wanted to get rid of his wife, Shelley. He staged the murder to look like a burglary, and it is astonishing that his wife survived the attack.

Homicide Case 4, Ted. When Shelley returned home one evening from work, Ted met her at the door, gave her "a big kiss," and a male accomplice struck her on the head with a hammer. Then Ted tried to strangle her. Shelley said that "there was blood — my blood — all over the apartment. I was very lucky. I must have a tough skull." She also reported that the incident was "a total waste. All he had to do was tell me he wanted a divorce, or he could have left me." All involved are white and in their twenties. Never arrested before, Ted initially denied the murder attempt. He and his accomplice received ten years to serve.

Ted's murder attempt was one of two planned homicides (the other was Stacey and Greg's). Ted had apparently offered $500 to his accomplice. Why he wished his wife dead is uncertain. Reflecting Shelley's explanation, the PSI writer suggests that "[Ted] was gay and wished to pursue that lifestyle. He was afraid that if he attempted to divorce his wife, it would all become public." Ted was the only defendant out of the eighty deep-sample defendants in which sexual orientation was mentioned.

Like Ted's attempt to kill his wife, Edie's stabbing of her stepmother was done to resolve a problem: the victim was an obstacle to the defendant. One difference is that Ted's act was planned, while Edie's arose in a moment of despair.

Homicide Case 2, Edie. Using a statue of Don Quixote and then a knife, Edie hit and stabbed her stepmother one morning. The stepmother, 87 and black, had Alzheimer's disease. Edie had been caring for her for some time. Edie, 60, was described as a "light complected" black female with a long history of depression. After the killing, Edie said, "I just wore out from getting the strength to do those things that [my stepmother] required of me. I never gave in until this happened. Now the stress is off. It was an intolerable situation. She was a very nice lady, but she just wasn't herself." Her husband, a medical professional, did not help care for his in-laws, and later Edie reported, "[I] murdered the wrong person . . . I should have killed my husband." She got ten years to serve.

Edie received the longest sentence of all the women in the deep sample. She had been diagnosed for decades as having depression. Unlike other cases, however, the judge did not interpret Edie's mental problems as cause for mitigation. Indeed, quite the reverse: he believed her to be a threat to herself and others, "particularly her husband."

Recall that only a handful of the interpersonal violence cases had psychological evaluations written. Edie and Ted were among them. Edie was characterized as "severely mentally ill . . . as being delusionary . . . as having chronic suicidal ideation . . . and as continuing to express homicidal thoughts about her husband," while Ted was cast as having "feelings of depression, fear and helplessness . . . and repeatedly expressing suicidal intent if he is convicted." In each case, court officials and psychologists tried to make sense of violence that had not erupted before, as in Edie's case, or that seemed "out of character," as in Ted's. It is not coincidental that both Edie and Ted were among the few middle-class defendants in the violence sample, nor that each is depicted as having "identity problems." For Edie, it was her racial identity as a light-skinned black women desiring to pass as white; for Ted, it was his presumptive heterosexual orientation as a married man desiring to come out safely as gay.[17]

Compared with almost all the other protagonists in the violence sample, there was more detail about Ted and Edie. Their files were thicker, the reports longer. One likely reason is a class- and race-based construction of "normal homicide." As described by Victoria Swigert and Ronald Farrell (1977, 19), the characteristics of the "normal primitive," the criminal stereotype for violent actors, are a class and race (to which I would add gender) composite of these elements: "Little, if any, education and . . . dull intelligence. His goals are sensual and immediate. . . . There is little regard for the future. . . . He has the ten-year-old boy's preoccupation with muscular prowess and 'being a man.'" Wes and Earl fell within the normal primitive classification, as did Barry (below). Ted did not; his deviation from the ordinary homicide,[18] its planned character (with a paid accomplice), set in motion more inquiry, more questioning about his motives for wanting his wife dead. Edie's homicide was also highly atypical, setting in motion a desire to know *why* she killed her stepmother.

It is instructive to compare the non–"normal homicides" with the case of Barry, a young man who beat his uncle to death. Both Barry's and his uncle's backgrounds fit the normal primitive imagery. No psychological evaluation was made of Barry. Instead, the beating is described as an expected outcome of "an almost nonexistent work record, abusing alcohol, and residing in a negative, undesirable living arrangement."

Homicide Case 1, Barry. Using his fists, Barry, 21 and black, beat his 43-year-old uncle to death. The incident occurred late one night when Barry returned to his room, which he shared with his uncle, in a rooming house. He found his uncle on the floor, apparently drunk. Later he told the police that he had slapped his uncle a few times to try to wake him up when he found him on the floor. A witness at the rooming house said he had warned Barry that Barry was "going to kill [his uncle]" if he kept hitting him. After throwing water on his uncle, Barry carried him to their room and laid him on the bed. In the morning, he checked to see whether his uncle was breathing, and thinking he was alive, Barry left the room. About the incident, Barry's mother, a sister of his uncle, said, "[My brother] must have provoked him. Maybe they were out drinking and hanging out. Maybe they were arguing. I know my son didn't kill him. I don't feel bad about my brother. He was always getting into fights. He was not a nice sight to see. He was a drug addict. There was no sorrow when he died." Barry received ten years.

Barry's mother introduced several mitigating circumstances surrounding her son's actions: although he might have been drinking, the victim certainly had been; they might have argued or got into a fight; her brother was disreputable, and his death was no cause for grief.

Her words did not persuade the judge. Of the last mitigating circumstance, differences in the "value" of life, court officials face dilemmas in fashioning a just sentence.[19]

Physical and Sexual Abuse of Children

This fourth group contains some of the most serious deep-sample crimes, as we might expect from previous research. In *The National Survey of Crime Severity* by Marvin Wolfgang and colleagues (1985), offense severity was higher when a parent beat a child than when a husband beat a wife.[20] Unfortunately, Wolfgang and co-workers do not address sexual violence toward children, and they measure seriousness only for parental violence carried out by a male. From their survey results, we can infer that men's violence toward children is viewed as somewhat more serious than their violence toward wives. How do we interpret that difference? Wolfgang and colleagues suggest that seriousness increases when victims are "more vulnerable or weaker" in comparison with offenders (p. 30). A focus on relative size and physical strength accords too much significance to physical size. The more critical ingredient is the abuse of parental power in relations with children who trust and depend on them.

Although not measured by Wolfgang and colleagues, we might assume that parental transgressions of sexual and physical trust (that is, when a child's caretakers have sexual relations with a child) would be viewed as more serious than transgressions of physical trust alone (that is, when a child's caretakers physically abuse a child). Although the latter may include "normal discipline" in some parents' minds, the former cannot be so justified. But what of *women* who physically and sexually abuse children? Are their acts perceived differently than men's?

Over the five-year research period, only three women were convicted of risk of injury in the New Haven felony court. During the same time, about seventy men were convicted for this offense. Thus, the women's share of these cases is very small, only 4 percent. As we examine these cases, it is important to keep in mind their rarity, which may partly explain their sensational quality.

Of the three men convicted of risk of injury in the deep sample, all initiated the aggression; of the three women, two played subordinate roles. The character of women's subordinate role in child abuse, however, can be difficult to assess, as Flo's case suggests.

Over several years, Flo allowed her boyfriend, Skip, to have sexual relations with her young children. Flo, who is white, was 33 when she was arrested. Hers was a celebrated case of an evil woman in the New Haven court during the first half of the 1980s. She and Skip both pled not guilty at trial, but during the trial, she decided to plead guilty in exchange for a suspended sentence with probation. The prosecutor needed her testimony to secure Skip's conviction.

Risk-of-Injury Case 2, Flo. Flo told a counselor that her boyfriend, Skip, white and 40, was pressuring her to allow him to have sexual relations with her children. At the time, her daughter was 9 and her son was 6. Flo did not know what to do because Skip's requests were beginning to sound "reasonable," but she felt her children "might not be into it." The counselor notified the authorities, and the children were examined at a hospital. Flo's daughter's throat culture tested positive for gonorrhea. Both children, however, denied that anything sexual had happened with their mother or her boyfriend in the past six months. Several months later the children went to live with their biological father, who had custody of them. At that time, both children told the police that Skip made them submit to sexual acts while their mother was present.

Further investigation revealed that some years earlier, when the daughter was 5 years old, she was diagnosed with vaginitis. The daughter said that Skip had fondled her when she slept, but a psychological evaluator had dismissed her story, saying she was fantasizing. Although Flo left Skip for a year when this happened, she got back together with him. She told a counselor that Skip had a lot of power over her and that she had problems controlling her children. In return for testifying against Skip, Flo received a suspended sentence. Skip received 9½ years to serve.

It is hard to know how much to attribute to Skip's "power" over Flo. Is this an excuse, or in Liz Kelly's terms (1991, 17), is it another way of "pathologizing women . . . to make them less responsible for their behavior?"[21]

Chris, another women convicted of risk of injury, appeared to be more of a pawn. Her act was characterized as "an act of omission, not commission," in the judge's words, and thus as less serious than that of her husband, who instigated the abuse.

Risk-of-Injury Case 3, Chris. For more than two years, Chris and her husband, Bob, cared for her brother's three children, whose ages at the time were 9 (a girl), 7 (a boy), and 5 (a girl). The older girl said that Bob, white and 36, put his finger in her vagina on many occasions, while the younger girl reported that he did it to her several times. The children said that when Bob did this, their Aunt Chris was present and did not stop him. Described by her mother as a "good person and an obedient daughter," though "easily led," Chris, white and 22, is slightly retarded. She received one year to serve, while her husband, who was convicted of both sexual assault and risk of injury, was sentenced to serve four years.

In Chris's case, her mental slowness was cited by the PSI writer as one explanation for her "going along" with Bob's wishes. Other information in her file (a police report), however, revealed that Chris was not merely an observer to Bob's acts but encouraged and assisted him. That information was not part of the PSI report, which made me wonder whether the PSI writer had overlooked it or chose not to mention it. What can be said with some certainty in these cases is that the men, not the women, initiated the acts. Over time, however, the women aided and assisted the men or attempted to protect them from arrest or conviction.

In the next case, the role of the defendant's wife in the abuse is ambiguous, though she was never arrested. The defendant, Jack, was black and 35. He was convicted in his twenties and served time in jail for killing a man in an after-hours club. He had also been convicted of aggravated assault.

Risk-of-Injury Case 1, Jack. Jack was babysitting for his wife's three children while she attended a funeral in another state. Jack and his wife, Rita, have been together for about nine years; he has fathered two of her children. On the night of the incident, Rita's oldest son, aged 9, called her to say that Jack had beaten the youngest boy, Floyd, aged 5, who was fathered by another man. Jack beat the boy unconscious, using a coat hanger and an electric cord. Rita initially said another man did it, but then changed her story. By the time of the trial, she and Jack said another man had beaten her child. Jack denied the abuse, saying "I know I didn't do it, and Rita and the kids told them I didn't do it; but I got found guilty of it." He was convicted at trial and received the longest sentence of any deep-sample defendant: seventeen years to serve.

Several years before, when Floyd was a toddler, he was abused: burns, bruises, and lacerations were found on his body when Rita brought him to the hospital. Rita initially said that Jack had done it but then named another person. The prosecutor's remarks in this latest incident intimate that although Jack will be incarcerated, the abuse of Floyd may continue. Rita's effort to protect Jack raises questions about the role of women as bystanders in child abuse cases. I would not consider Rita an innocent onlooker, nor as an abused woman cowed by Jack. What, then, is her culpability? Despite some ambiguity in the role played by women in these cases, the crime facts presented by police and psychologists and interpreted by court officials suggested that the men's acts were more serious. Further, some men denied culpability and saw no reason to change their behavior. Compare, for example, Jack's beating of Floyd with Nola's abuse of her child.

Risk-of-Injury Case 1, Nola. Nola brought her four-month old son, her second, to the emergency room at a New Haven hospital. The infant was examined, and the diagnosis revealed "a bilateral skull fracture, bruises on his back, and scarring from old burns on his buttocks and tops of his thighs." At first Nola had said she had left her infant in a carrier on the kitchen table and returned to find him on the floor. Several days later she admitted she was responsible for her son's injuries. She said she was upset with the child, that she had shaken him and thrown him on an air mattress on the floor. The incident occurred while she was visiting her father. She apparently wanted to get away for a couple of days from her husband and first child, who lived in another state. Nola, black and 20 years old, said "I was under a great deal of pressure, and I'm sorry it happened because I am paying now. I'm sorry I'm being classified as other mothers that do this because this was only one time that I just lost control." She received one year to serve. After serving her time, she will resume living with her husband and children.

Nola admitted to abusing her son, and she wanted to improve her parenting skills. Jack, on the other hand, denied that he had beaten Floyd and expressed no desire to improve his relations with him. Nola brought the child into the emergency room seeking help, but in Jack's case, it took a child's phone call to get help.

A striking feature of father-daughter sexual abuse is that it can go on for years, apparently unknown to a wife. Once it is known to her, she may forgive him. The next case illustrates this theme, together with the man's admission of guilt and apparent desire to change.

Risk-of-Injury Case 3, Ralph. Ralph had oral sex with his stepdaughter, Heidi, when she was 11. A year later, they had sexual intercourse. They had intercourse and oral sex for the next three years frequently (perhaps twice a week). Heidi told a school social worker about her stepfather when she was 15. Ralph and Heidi are white. When Ralph's abuse of his stepdaughter was discovered, he was in his midforties. His sexual abuse likely began when he started to live with Heidi's mother, because Heidi recalled that she was "touched" by Ralph when she was 5. Ralph "accept[ed] totally the blame" for this behavior and said the program for sex offenders is helping him. He reported that he and his wife were "working to keep our family together" and that "she wants it that way, and I want it that way." He was sentenced to serve one year.

Would one attribute greater evil or harm to Ralph's acts than to Chris's or Flo's? If so, why? It is likely that Flo, and especially Chris, played a secondary role in the sexual abuse, and for this reason, the women's participation was less serious than Ralph's. Yet, playing a secondary role does not necessarily mean that the woman's act is less serious. Flo's actions can be viewed as similar to Ralph's in seriousness, unless one takes the position that a dominating man controlled her most of the time. Assuming Flo played a secondary role, her participation in the abuse over time constructed her actions as more serious than Nola's, who acted alone in abusing her child. My point is that the meaning of *single* and *multiple* events, and of *primary* and *secondary* roles must be explored, not presumed, in understanding gender and violence toward children.

By switching the members of pairs to reflect similar harms, we can compare Chris's case with Wade's. As the crime narrative will show, Wade's actions were situational and impulsive, though his threats to the victim after the initial incident rendered him a more dangerous character. Unlike Chris's nieces, Wade's niece — his victim — reported the abuse soon after it happened. Her account was believed by her aunt and officials, and Wade's abuse of his niece was more limited in time.

Risk-of-Injury Case 2, Wade. Wade, 30 and black, took six children, all black, to visit a farm on the last day of summer, and during the afternoon he attempted to sexually abuse one of the girls. He also forced the children to drink beer and smoke cigarettes. One of the children was his son (age 6), two were his nieces (one age 10, the other age unknown), one was his nephew (age 12), and two were their friends (both boys, ages 9 and 4). Wade attempted to abuse his ten-year-old niece. He followed her as she scrambled up a hill; he caught her and brought her to the bushes. There he exposed his erect penis, told her, "I'm going to stick it in you," and tried to pull down her pants. She pulled his hair, bit him on the hand, and ran away. Wade threatened to beat her up if she told anyone. Ten days later she told her aunt and then her mother what happened. Several days later, Wade was waiting for her outside school. He refused to speak with the probation officer, saying it was his own business and that he did not like the deal [plea bargain] he was offered. He received two years to serve.

Like Jack, Wade expressed no remorse or concern for the victim. Although his actions arose situationally and were more compressed temporally than Chris's, the probation officer presented him as more of a bad guy in comparison with Chris, who was believed to be mentally deficient and led by a dominating man. In terms of seriousness, I would identify their acts as comparable.

Judging the relative seriousness of men's and women's physical and sexual abuse of children reveals the outer edges of our ability to make gender comparisons. Even if we had the widest possible variation from a large number of cases, the differences between men's and women's bodies and the sociosexualized meaning attached to their bodies strands the comparative exercise on the shoals of sexual difference. For example, could a woman's exposing her breast and genitals to a child have the same aggressive meaning as a man's exposing his penis and threatening to do something with it? As we grasp the details of these offenses, the outer edges of our ability to quantify seriousness and culpability become apparent. Is a woman's "going along with" her mate's desire to have sexual relations with her children more serious than a woman throwing an infant down, causing a skull fracture? These child abuse cases raise questions not only for gender-neutral punishment schemes, but also for schemes based on proportionate harm.

Comparing Seriousness in Interpersonal Violence

In comparing seriousness for the seventeen pairs, I switched the members of some pairs to afford the most meaningful comparisons (see appendix 5).[22] I judged nine pairs to be similar in seriousness; in one pair, the woman's offense was somewhat more serious. For the remaining seven pairs, I judged the men's offenses to be more serious, with two being far more serious than the women's. These judgments in seriousness held across each major form of violence — that is, no one offense type contributed disproportionately to judgments of similar or greater seriousness.

For the racial dynamics of the incidents, 85 percent were intraracial, and 70–75 percent involved family members, friends, or acquaintances of the defendants. There were therefore insufficient numbers of interracial cases to make comparisons. Nor was it possible to compare race differences in those sentenced for homicide: during the research period, no white woman was convicted of homicide, and only a small percentage of white men were (15 percent). The racializing of violence was evident in other ways. Many black men's and black women's interpersonal violent acts were regarded as "expectable" displays of impulsive violence. For some black women, the act was understood to be a sensible response to a violent victim, while for some black men, the act appeared senseless and unprovoked. White men's and women's acts were somewhat less impulsive.[23]

Recall that these men and women were arraigned and convicted on similar statutory charges. Thus, the gender-based patterns in the nature and seriousness of their acts are all the more compelling. I judged 40 percent of the men's interpersonal offenses to be more serious than the women's largely on the basis of the sources of aggression. Men's violence was more likely to be initiated by the men themselves (twelve cases), not by victims or in the context of mutuality. Women's violence was more likely to be characterized by victim-initiated aggression, mutuality of aggression, or being under the influence of a male accomplice (ten cases). All the women in ongoing disputes with victims had been abused by the "victims" in the past, while the men in such disputes had abused their victims in the past.

Judgments of seriousness involve complex contexts and circumstances. Elements in constructing seriousness in violence cases — level of injury, victim-offender relations, vulnerable victims, histories of abuse — may be identified, but they cannot be toted up in a linear, additive way. For example, men's abuse of partners or children in the past can downgrade seriousness for a current offense (as it did for Georges's attempt to shoot his wife and as it did in the case of Enrico's arson), but it can also upgrade seriousness (as in Wayne's arson and Jack's beating of his stepson). Similarly, women harmed by their victims in the past may be treated sympathetically (Jean, Sharon, and Carrie), or not (Dorothy and Lonnie). Situational dynamics, such as a defendant's drunkenness or mental health problems, may or may not mitigate seriousness; women's mental problems downgraded the seriousness of their acts in some cases (Nancy and Latasha), but not in others (Edie and Dorothy).

The New Haven cases do not support Allen's (1987b, xi) general claim that "a woman appearing before the criminal court is about twice as likely as a man to be dealt with by psychiatric rather than penal means." Her specific findings — that for homicide convictions women were four to five times more likely than men to receive a psychiatric disposal (1987b, 128) and that women's acts were more likely to be trivialized or excused — are also not evident in my sample. For her sample of interpersonal violence and other offenses (robbery, larceny, and burglary), Allen found that 33 and 20 percent of women's and men's cases, respectively, had a psychiatric report written (1987b, 129). My deep-sample figures (excluding drugs) were 19 and 13 percent for women and men, a smaller percentage point difference than hers. I *do* find that of the nondrug cases, twice as many women had ever had a psychological evaluation written on them than men (44 versus 22 percent) and psychological problems were more often mentioned in the PSI (53 versus 28 percent).

Despite the more "troubled" profile developed in the women's cases, psychological problems did not exonerate or excuse women's interpersonal violence or other harms in the New Haven felony court to the same extent that Allen found in the London courts. Our different findings can be traced in part to a more marked fracturing of gender by race and ethnicity in United States urban courts. The typical episode of violence in the New Haven felony court was an escalation of an argument between two black people who knew each other. Whether the defendant was a male or female, the court neither exonerated the violence, nor found it exceptional. Another reason for our different findings lies in organizational routines: the London crown courts may have resources to gather mental health histories. In New Haven, there was neither money, interest, nor time to explore the psychodynamics of violence in these cases. Such an understanding or curiosity about violence was reserved for a handful of mostly middle-class defendants.

Anticipating the pair-wise disparity analysis in chapter 11, I found that of the seventeen pairs of interpersonal violence, seven initially raised a disparity question in my mind. For all but one, the disparity could be explained by differences in prior record, role in the offense, age or mental competency, interests of justice, or some combination of these reasons. For the pair of Andrew and Latasha, I felt the sentencing disparity could not be explained.

For many of these violence cases, it was uncertain what really happened and not easy to compare culpability or seriousness. Sources of ambiguity were the defendants' claims to be acting in self-defense, women's "acts of omission" in the abuse of children, and ad hoc characterizations of the defendants' mental states (as "crazy" or "had been drinking"). The gaps in the stories of violence allow us, as readers and observers, an opening in the story line that we try to complete. Cross-cutting relations of class, race, age, and especially gender will be essential in how we make sense of the violence.

Notes

1. See Rapaport's (1991, 380–81) discussion of the death penalty, the law of homicide, and the "moral grading" of "hot-blooded" and "cold-blooded" violence.

2. In summarizing the literature, I draw from Block (1987), Angela Browne (1987), Browne and Kirk Williams (1989), and Martin Daly and Margo Wilson (1987), and reviews of the literature by Nancy Jurik and Peter Gregware (1991), Jurik and Russ Winn (1990), Coramae Richey Mann (1988), Wilbanks (1982), Wilson and Daly (1992). Although much is known about homicide, note that the statistical patterns given in the literature are of homicides for which victim-offender relations are known to the police. Michael Maxfield (1989) suggests that such a focus ignores an increasing proportion of homicides where victim-offender relations cannot be determined.

3. I draw especially from Jurik and Gregware's (1991) review and from Browne (1987), Daly and Wilson (1987), Luckenbill (1977), and Richard Felson and Henry Steadman (1983). A growing feminist literature on the situational dynamics of aggravated assault and homicide, from the point of view of battered women, has been central to redefining concepts and changing elements of the law on homicide (see Coker 1992; Dobash and Dobash 1984; Gillespie 1989; Klein 1982; Kurz 1989; Schneider 1986).

4. Or as Rebecca Dobash and Russell Dobash (1984, 285) put it, male-centered research on violence sees "violent episodes as some sort of gun fight at the OK Corral."

5. Risk of injury contains a wider set of potential ways in which adults can harm minors. These can be impulsive (as in beating a child) or long-term (as in the

sexual abuse of children). Age-based relations of trust and power in families, coupled with gender relations, spawn a variety of harms not easily termed situational, impulsive, or premeditated forms of violence.

6. Although there are several fine studies on the sexual and physical abuse of children (e.g., Kelly 1988; Russell 1984), they center on memories of victims (or survivors), usually female, of what happened and their coming to terms with the abuse. See Kelly's (1991) review, in which she discusses problems for feminist analyses of violence by and between women. The few studies available suggest that women constitute a very low portion of sexual abusers (3%–7%), men initiate abuse in a "family-ring" situation, and women's role is secondary (Kelly 1991, 17–18).

7. Although I have already suggested this possibility in judging crime seriousness for the robbery narratives, I underscore it even more for interpersonal violence without economic gain. I suspect that most observers need to know the gender, age, and relational history (at a minimum) of offenders and victims in interpersonal violent acts to be able to judge the seriousness of a harm.

8. See table A-I.1 (app. 1) for a review of the penal code.

9. Normally, criminologists separate guns, knives, etc., from personal weapons, which are defined as fists and feet. It is appropriate that penises be added explicitly to the list of personal weapons.

10. Jurik and Gregware (1991) find a similar reaction in another jurisdiction (Phoenix, Arizona). Probation officers acknowledged, "You rarely get probation . . . [when] *someone has died*" (p. 32, emphasis in original). They held women legally responsible for violence ending in death (though perhaps with a reduced sentence), even when the woman was a longstanding victim of abuse (p. 33).

11. This debate has been aired on several occasions when Murray Straus meets his critics at professional meetings or in scholarly journals. In counting and analyzing violence with the Conflict Tactics Scale, Straus, Gelles, and Steinmetz (1980) assume gender-neutrality in the strength of a "hit" and in the perceptions of violence. Straus's critics point out that violence cannot be measured in a genderneutral way, nor can it be assumed that victims' perceptions of danger are genderneutral. See Kurz (1989), Dobash et al. (1992), and Straus (1991) (and replies) for a review of these themes and recent airing of the debate.

12. Mann (1988, 48) also says that when she reported this and other findings about domestic homicide at the American Society of Criminology annual meeting, women in the audience challenged her analysis because it minimized the role of previous abuse by the man in the relationship. Evidence for both forms of violence (i.e., fending off violent victims and the mutuality of violence) is present in my sample. Jurik and Winn (1990, 229) have proposed the term *self-help* to describe women's role in domestic homicides.

13. That reaction is at variance with how men's behavior is downgraded in seriousness when they drink. For example, in Scully's (1990) study of men convicted of (and imprisoned for) rape, she found that some men *discredited* women who had been drinking, making them more responsible for the rape, while others *justified* or excused the rape when the men were drinking.

14. There may well be a gender-based difference in perception here, as well, with men observers being more sympathetic or understanding toward the men in the stories of intimate violence than women might be.

15. A sentence of less than three years may be modified at a later time on a defense attorney's motion and a judge's ruling; such modification could be for entering a drug treatment program. Defendants can also waive the PSI when sentences are less than three years. I saw no evidence in the file that Nellie's sentence was modified, but one deep-sample woman's drug case was (see chap. 8, discussion of Penny's case).

16. Latasha and Nancy, the woman who set fire to her apartment, had both been denied access to their children. In an argument with her sister just before she set the fire, Nancy was angry that her sister would not pick up her son for a weekend visit. Corroborating Allen's (1987a, 1987b) research, Latasha's and Nancy's maternal-based anger "naturalized" their acts as something any woman might do.

17. The psychological report for Edie noted that her first suicide attempt occurred around the same time an uncle called her a "Negress," and that she felt "unique and set apart from the rest of the black community." The PSI for Ted described him as saying that he "was not a homosexual" but admitting that "many of his friends were homosexual" and that he went to a well-known homosexual bar regularly.

18. Ordinary homicides were described in clinic records used by Swigert and Farrell (1977, 19) as occurring "in bars where arguments . . . result in aggressive encounters." They also occur when men's masculinity or courage is challenged or when men are humiliated by their mates' infidelity.

19. Whatever court officials do, they can be accused of doing the wrong thing. They can agree that the victim was not a "worthy" person (as Barry's mother claimed) and reduce the defendant's punishment. But such a sentence makes it appear that the court places a different value on victims' lives based on their worthiness. Conversely, judges can argue that "we value all lives equally" and decide to punish the defendant severely. Given the largely intraracial composition of interpersonal violent acts, these lose-lose sentencing situations ought to be confronted by scholars who study race-of-victim discrimination.

20. Wolfgang et al. (1985, vi–vii). The wording of the offenses and their severity is as follows: A parent beats his young child with his fists; as a result the child dies (47.8). A man stabs his wife; as a result, she dies (39.2). A parent beats his young child with his fists; the child requires hospitalization (22.9). A man beats his wife with his fists; she requires hospitalization (18.3). As noted earlier, these measures of seriousness create a false sense of numerical precision. As Duncan (1985, 185–93) points out, (among other problems) there is no standard unit in the scale. The scenes were generated in the following manner: "Respondents were given a description of a crime, 'A person steals a bicycle parked on the street,' and told that the seriousness of this crime [had a rating of] 10. They were then given a list of other crimes and told to compare them in seriousness to the bicycle theft. If the crime seemed to be twice as serious, they were to rate it at 20," and so on (Wolfgang et al. 1985, vi).

21. Kelly raises this question in the contexts of how men's sexual abuse has been pathologized and feminist challenges to such pathological characterizations.

22. As in previous chapters, my sense of the gestalt of the harm is subjective and is open to question. I invite readers to compare their judgments with mine.

23. The white violence cases seemed especially serious, but it would be a mistake to infer that this greater seriousness was largely the result of the victims being white. One would need to study this question with more cases, contexts, and circumstances of violence — as Baldus, George Woodworth, and Charles Pulaski (1990) have done for "death-eligible" cases.

8 Drug Offenses

The police report is right, but the quantity was wrong. [My husband,] Rennie was cooperative . . . and I understood that Rennie
was the only one to be arrested. He said [to the police] that everything belonged to him, and "I don't know why you have to take my
wife."
— Colleen, speaking for herself and Rennie, Drug Pair 7

I knew this guy and he asked me if I had any coke. I said "No, I
don't sell any." I said I knew who could get him some. . . . and I
brought this guy to [Gloria]. I did her a favor, and she gave me some
coke for it. I asked him if he was a cop, and he didn't answer. I
tried to sell him some baking soda. I never really got into it. I was
doing her [Gloria] a favor.
— Douglas, Drug Case 6

Compared with robbery, larceny, or interpersonal violence, the
information supplied in a police report or presented in the PSI for drug
offenses is sketchy and incomplete. Moreover, the drug narratives lack
the drama of other offenses: vivid victim descriptions are absent, and
the action centers on what the police officer(s) did in making an arrest.

Studies of the adjudication of drug offenses (for example, Myers
1989; Peterson and Hagan 1984) assume that the *quantity* of drugs sold
is a good measure of offense seriousness. Such a view reflects drug
law but cedes too much to it. For example, Martha Myers (1989)
analyzed three types of drug defendants: users, sellers or distributors,
and traffickers. In a Georgia law passed in 1980, trafficking was distinguished from selling "solely by the amount possessed, sold . . . or
distributed. . . . Possession of 28 grams or more of cocaine or 100
pounds of marijuana . . . constitutes grounds for a trafficking prosecution" (p. 297). Myers took these legal categories for granted and
provided no information on what the trafficking cases entailed or what
the defendants had done. A similar problem is evident in Ruth Peterson's and John Hagan's (1984) analysis of a shift in prosecutorial
emphasis from drug users to "big time dealers" in federal courts during
the 1960s and 1970s. "Traffickers and professional drug criminals"
were reconstituted as "villains" in the drug crackdown, while users
were recast as "victims" (p. 58). The authors identified the villains
from notes they saw in the margins of court records *or* when the
defendants' "drug-related criminal activities involved 100 pounds or

more of a narcotic substance," an amount that they conceded was "somewhat arbitrary" but was based on major drug cases in the prosecuting attorney's office (p. 60).[1] There is a Beccarian beauty in defining seriousness by the exact weight and type of drugs: federal sentencing guidelines (U.S. Sentencing Commission 1989, 2.38–2.53) illustrate this exactness with dazzling precision. But where do the numbers come from? What makes a drug case serious?

In the New Haven PSI reports, information is usually given on the number of packets or the gram weights of drugs taken from a suspect or seized with a search warrant,[2] but the amount of drugs may have little bearing on how the court responds to defendants. Two additional elements are involved: the defendant's role and, most important, prior record. Peterson and Hagan's (1984) discussion of the severe response to Leroy "Nicky" Barnes, a major dealer in Harlem, only partly anticipates the point I wish to make. Essential to constructing Barnes as a "Black Major Violator" was his repeated presence in the neighborhood over time and his ability to evade arrest. In a more diluted form, the same logic operates in the New Haven felony court. Although one can determine seriousness from the quantity of drugs, the court's response is based on the combined influences of quantity, prior record, and role in the offense.

Docket Book Variables

The wide-sample defendants were originally charged with several counts of sale or possession of drugs, coupled with, perhaps, the possession of a firearm, but the charges at conviction were homogeneous: one count of possession *or* one count of sale of drugs. For the wide sample, more men (about 80 percent) than women (about 60 percent) were convicted of selling, and thus the average case severity was a bit higher for men (159 months) than women (140 months) in the wide sample.[3] The proportion of men having previous felony convictions and receiving an incarceration sentence was higher. The average length of a jail term was somewhat longer for the men, and a higher percentage of men were incarcerated pending trial. Thus, based on the docket book variables, the wide-sample men's cases suggest greater seriousness (see table 8.1).

In selecting the deep sample, the gap for legal measures was narrowed by my choosing drug *sale* cases for seven of the eight pairs. Average case severity became more similar for men and women, as did the proportions receiving a jail sentence and the percent with previous convictions in the New Haven felony court.

Table 8.1 Statistical Data on Men's and Women's Drug Offenses (from clerk's docket book, police records, and penal code statutes)

| | Drug Offenses | | | |
| | Men* | | Women** | |
	Wide (N = 34)	Deep (N = 8)	Wide (N = 63)	Deep (N = 8)
Age (median, yr)	27	27	29	29
Race or Ethnicity				
Black	65%	63%	54%	63%
Latin	15	25	9	12
White	20	12	37	25
Attorney				
Public defender	59%	88%	56%	50%
Private	41	12	44	50
Pretrial Status				
Incarcerated	44%	63%	22%	38%
Out on bail	41	25	68	62
Promise to appear	15	12	10	0
Bail Amount (median)$^\triangle$	$10 K	$10 K	$10 K	$10 K
Pled Guilty	100%	100%	98%	100%
Prior Record				
Has been convicted in New Haven felony court or was on probation at the time of the offense? yes	38%	38%***	29%	38%***
Severity				
Potential time (mo), convicted offense	159	168	140	168
(std. dev.)	(47)	(34)	(57)	(34)
Sentence (*In-Out*)				
Received incarceration sentence to serve time? yes	56%	37%	29%	50%
Sentence (*Time*)				
Length of sentence (mo), only cases receiving incarceration$^\triangle$	24	35	18	11
(std. dev.)	(14)	(26)	(15)	(3)

$^\triangle$Denotes that these variables may have a smaller number of cases.

*Except where indicated by a triangle, the measures are of N = 34 and N = 8 men in the wide and deep drug samples, respectively. Bail amounts were shown in the clerk's records (or were relevant) for N = 20 and N = 4 men in the wide and deep samples, respectively. There were no trials in the men's drug sample.

**Except where indicated by a triangle, the measures are of N = 63 and N = 8 women in the wide and deep drug case samples, respectively. Bail amounts were shown in the clerk's records (or were relevant) for N = 48 and N = 6 women in the wide and deep samples, respectively. Convicted offense severity and incarceration time averages *exclude* trial cases: one in the wide sample, none in the deep sample. (Note: Deviating from the usual pattern, the one woman found guilty at trial did not receive an incarceration sentence.)

***From the PSI, where more complete prior criminal history was shown, the proportion of men and women previously convicted was 63% and 75%, respectively.

Coded Elements from the Drug Narratives

There were moderate gender differences in the social organization and contexts of the drug offenses (see appendix 5). More women acted with others, often with a spouse or mate. Although some women were part of four-person drug groups, no man was. Somewhat more women than men probably played a secondary role, though direct evidence of women's participation was lacking. Women were somewhat more likely to be involved in selling drugs from a residence, and they were more likely to be arrested during a search of their household.

For most defendants, the quantities of drugs seized were low or very low. Based on estimates from the number of glassine or foil packets found on the defendant or in a search, or the gram weights given in the PSI reports, I identified one man and two women as selling moderate to major quantities of drugs (defined as 11 or more grams of cocaine or heroin).[4] Although probable cause for arrest was based on police surveillance or police undercover or informant buys, in several search-and-seizure arrests, no information was given on how the police had established probable cause. Most drug-law violators were addicted to illegal drugs (63 and 75 percent of men and women, respectively). This level of drug abuse, though high, was not much higher than in the larceny and robbery cases.[5]

Drug Narratives

Three elements construct how the court regards drug cases: the defendant's prior record, the defendant's role in the offense, and the quantity of drugs. A simple lining up of these elements provides a script for the least and the most serious drug cases. Least serious is a defendant with a minimal prior record who plays a secondary role in dealing small amounts of drugs. Most serious is a defendant with previous convictions who plays a primary role in dealing large amounts. Most cases did not fit into these categories, having different combinations and weightings of elements. In the robberies, larcenies, and interpersonal violent acts, a defendant's prior record could amplify the seriousness of the offense, but for these drug cases, a defendant's prior record could be more determining than the quantity of drugs sold.[6] With these elements, I present the drug narratives, organized roughly from the least to the most serious.

Minimal or No Prior Record and/or Secondary Role

Juan's drug selling was among the least serious. He was the only man in the deep sample to play a secondary role in dealing drugs. He had never been arrested before, and the quantity of drugs sold was not even given in the PSI.

Drug Case 4, Juan

During a search of Juan's premises in the early afternoon, the police found narcotics, and Juan admitted that they belonged to him. The police obtained a warrant based on an informant tip and drug purchase from someone living in the neighborhood. Juan, 24 and Puerto Rican, is mildly retarded. He reported to the probation officer that he was paid to sell the drugs: "Someone gave it [cocaine] to me to sell, and I sold it. They would give me $20 to $40 a week. I had been selling for 6 months." He received a two-year suspended sentence.

Juan was paired with Miranda. Comparing their cases shows the effect of different offense elements. Miranda probably played a secondary role in a major dealing operation (although I am unsure of her role), and she had been convicted several years earlier on a drug charge.

Drug Case 4, Miranda

Miranda, in her early forties and from Colombia, was involved in a family-based dealing operation. Through a wiretap, New Haven police suspected that her family was "one of the major distributors" in the New Haven area. Search-and-seizure warrants were carried out at four locations one afternoon: Miranda's residence, that of a girlfriend of one of Miranda's sons, that of another female friend of Miranda's son, and that of a man whose apartment was thought to be under the control of the family. About 80 grams of "white powder" was found in Miranda's house, along with 5 grams of cocaine and $26,000 in cash. She received a two-year suspended sentence.

I could not discern from the PSI what Miranda's role was in the drug dealing operation. Although her 18-year-old son was presumed to be the main operator (he was sentenced to serve 2½ years), I think it unlikely that Miranda was a simple bystander. Miranda's case is a good illustration of problems in designating seriousness: her family was considered a major distributor in the area, and she had been convicted in the past on drug-related charges. Her role in the offense cannot be known from the available information. In light of the size of the drug operation and Miranda's previous conviction, I judged her offense to be somewhat more serious than Juan's, but both defendants appeared to be conduits in drug selling organized by others.

Three cases were close to Juan's in seriousness: two men (Reggie and Carlos) and a woman (Bonnie) were arrested with low quantities of drugs and with no previous arrests. For the matched pair of Bonnie and Reggie, both were white, employed full time, and lived in New Haven suburbs.

Drug Case 2, Bonnie
Bonnie's drug dealing was observed by an undercover police officer at a bar. He met a woman, asked her whether he "could find any cocaine," and she said that if he followed her, she would sell him ½ gram for $60. They went to a parking lot, and while the officer waited, Bonnie returned with a packet of "white powder." The officer paid her $60. Bonnie was arrested several months later on an arrest warrant and received a thirty-five-month suspended sentence.[7]

Drug Case 2, Reggie
Reggie sold two packets of cocaine to an undercover police officer, who paid him $50. The buy was made in July, though Reggie was not arrested until October. Although Reggie admitted using cocaine regularly up to his arrest, he has since stopped using and is seeing a drug counselor. He received a two-year suspended sentence and a $250 fine.

The police forced their way into Carlos's apartment and seized an unknown amount of white powder [drug case 8]. Held two months before being sentenced, Carlos received a two-year suspended sentence. Carlos was matched to Lotty, who was arrested for selling drugs with her husband [drug case 8]. Held a week before being sentenced, she received a one-year suspended sentence. Her husband received a two-year suspended sentence. At sentencing, Lotty's attorney argued that "the only thing [she] did was . . . allow the type of thing to go on in her home." Lotty had been arrested in her teens for shoplifting. She likely played a bystander role in selling moderate quantities of cocaine.

Moderate to Heavy Prior Record, Low Quantities
The pair of Colleen and Rennie is a good bridge connecting the cases above. I selected this pair unaware that they were married and prosecuted for the same incident. Colleen's apparent secondary role made her involvement seem less serious than Rennie's, but more important, Rennie's parole status was at issue.

Drug Pair 7, Colleen and Rennie
The police executed a search warrant for the apartment of Colleen and Rennie. They were both in bed when the police arrived. The basis for probable cause was not given in the file. Colleen was white, Rennie was black; they were married and in their thirties. During a search of

the apartment, a "large number of tin foil and glassine packets were found containing white powder." Subsequent tests showed 2.55 grams of heroin, 1.57 grams of cocaine, and 2.74 grams of marijuana.[8] Also found was a stolen handgun. About the offense, Colleen said, "The police report is right, but the quantity was wrong. [My husband] Rennie was cooperative . . . and I understood that Rennie was the only one to be arrested. He said [to the police] that everything belonged to him, and 'I don't know why you have to take my wife.'" Colleen received a three-year suspended sentence, and Rennie got five years to serve.

Colleen had had six convictions, mostly for prostitution, disorderly conduct, and petty larceny. Rennie was on parole at the time of this offense; he had been released four months earlier after serving time for a burglary. Perhaps because of his parole status, he received a jail term while Colleen was again put on probation. Certainly, the quantity of drugs seized was too low (less than 5 grams of cocaine and heroin) to justify a five-year sentence — the longest sentence any defendant in the drug sample had received. From the file I could not be sure whether Colleen sold drugs. It was apparent, however, that Rennie and Colleen assumed that only he should be arrested.

Five other defendants were arrested for selling small quantities, and they had moderate to heavy arrest records: Marcie (on probation), Rob (several convictions), and Julie, Carl, and Mary (many convictions).

Marcie, black and 26, was living with her mother, her two children, her older sister's three children, and her younger sister and her child. At the time of the offense, her older sister was incarcerated for selling drugs, and her mother had a drug case pending. When Marcie was arrested, she was on probation for possession of cocaine. The PSI described the first arrest but not the second.

Drug Case 6, Marcie
Police executed a search warrant at Marcie and her family's apartment, based on informant information and purchases. During the search, "white powder" was found with trace amounts of cocaine in Marcie's room. Marcie received a suspended sentence for this offense. Soon after, she was arrested for selling cocaine (offense not described in the PSI), for which she was sentenced to serve one year.

Marcie's case is noteworthy for several reasons. After her first arrest for possession of cocaine, the probation officer hoped that drug treatment would be effective. Marcie was viewed as a drug-using minority "victim" who deserved a break (Peterson and Hagan 1984). But a second arrest, only a few months later, for selling cocaine swiftly led to a jail term. I suspect that Marcie's apartment was subject to heightened police surveillance since her mother and sister had also been arrested for selling drugs.

Like Marcie, several of Rob's family members were convicted of drug offenses. Black and 29, Rob became addicted to heroin in his late teens, and over the past five years, he did speedballs (a mix of cocaine and heroin), a habit costing him about $225 a week. He denied being a drug trafficker but claimed to act as a middleman to pay for his habit. His five previous convictions were for public order offenses.

Drug Case 3, Rob

Rob sold an undercover police officer a glassine envelope with white powder, which was later tested as heroin. This buy was made during the early evening in January. About two weeks later, Rob sold one glassine bag of white powder to the same undercover police officer. For each bag, the officer paid $20. More than three months later, Rob was arrested. He received a sentence of nine months to serve.

Carl and Julie [drug pair 1] had a more developed record of previous convictions. Julie was convicted more than a dozen times for prostitution, disorderly conduct, and petty larceny. In this incident she was arrested with about forty heroin and cocaine packets in her possession. She received one year to serve. Carl had been convicted more than ten times, mostly for breach of peace and public order offenses. He sold two packets of cocaine to a police officer and received a suspended sentence of 2½ years. In light of Carl's previous record, he would have been a candidate for a jail sentence. He evaded incarceration largely because the state did not have a positive identification.

It was especially clear from Mary's case that her record of arrests and convictions was a determining factor. The amounts seized were very low.

Drug Case 5, Mary

The police carried out a search-and-seizure warrant at Mary's house. The basis for probable cause was not given in the PSI. Mary had been living in the house with her parents, her grown children, and her boyfriend of many years, Lloyd. She and Lloyd were in their early fifties and black. Both had been convicted many times in the past. The police found twelve white packets of heroin and eight of cocaine. Mary had been on methadone maintenance for fourteen years, and she gave an impassioned plea to the judge that she should be allowed to continue on methadone. The judge sentenced Mary to serve one year and Lloyd to serve 1½ years.

At sentencing, Mary's attorney argued for postponing the sentencing, saying that Mary would suffer side effects from a rapid withdrawal from methadone were she to be imprisoned that day. The judge was sympathetic neither to the medical arguments nor to Mary in light of her history of selling drugs: "In 1959 she was convicted of sale of narcotics; in 1983, she was convicted of selling narcotics. She is unreformed, unrepentant." But there was no indication that he attached greater opprobrium to Mary's behavior than to her boyfriend's, whose sentence was somewhat longer.[9]

Varied Prior Record, Moderate to Major Quantities

The last group of defendants was either arrested for selling relatively large quantities of drugs or could in other ways be considered major dealers. Based on the amount of drugs alone, their offenses were serious, and yet in the court's response, the determination was modified by prior record. Dylan, for example, had been convicted twice in his early twenties for disorderly conduct; in his early thirties, he was observed selling a moderate amount of heroin and cocaine.

Drug Case 5, Dylan

The police observed Dylan selling drugs on three occasions. He was arrested each time but was not prosecuted until the third arrest. The first and second arrests were for varied amounts of heroin and cocaine (unspecified in one arrest, seven packets each in another); the third arrest netted a substantial amount. Dylan had forty-seven aluminum foil packets of cocaine and ten glassine envelopes of heroin, while a co-offender, Adam, had twenty packets of cocaine.

At the third arrest Dylan admitted, "I had it on me so there's nothing I can say to change it. I had just walked out to pick up some cigarettes when I spotted [Adam] and I asked him for a ride across town. That's when the cops rolled in. . . . The weekend was coming up, and it was for me." Dylan received a three-year suspended sentence, as did Adam.

Although Dylan had several previous convictions, the probation officer was optimistic that with drug treatment on probation, Dylan could become "a drug-free individual." Even with moderate drug quantities involved, the response to Dylan was similar to that toward Marcie after her first arrest for possession.

The amount of drugs recovered from Penny's apartment was not substantial, but the comments she made to the probation officer suggested that she was at least a moderate dealer.

Drug Case 3, Penny

Based on an informant tip, informant buy, and police buy, the police executed a search-and-seizure warrant of Penny's apartment. When they arrived, they found four people, one of whom tried to get rid of thirteen packets of heroin. Penny told the probation officer that she had sold drugs for six years and that she viewed dealing to be like a job. She claimed to earn as much as $2,000 a day and said she could make more money dealing drugs than from a regular job. She split her earnings four ways with two women and a man. Penny is black and 25; her accomplices were about the same age or in their late teens (their race was not specified in the PSI). When she was arrested, Penny was on probation for possessing heroin. She was originally sentenced to serve 1½ years, but her sentence was modified to six months. Her accomplices each received a one-year suspended sentence.

The judge was annoyed by Penny's remark in the PSI that drug selling was a good-paying job; he was also put off by her nonchalant attitude toward drug use. A confident and self-possessed woman, Penny expressed no intention to officials that she would stop using drugs.

Of all those in the drug sample, Douglas was clearly involved in major dealing. He had sold a large quantity of cocaine to an undercover police officer on several occasions.

Drug Case 6, Douglas

Three incidents took place over a month's time. In the first, a state undercover officer bought ½ ounce of cocaine for $1,320; in the second, Douglas's apartment was searched and packets of cocaine were found; and in the third, he attempted to sell 1 ounce of cocaine to an undercover state officer for $2,500. Douglas said he was a go-between for a "girl named Gloria and a friend of hers who were big time coke dealers." He reported that "I knew this guy and he asked me if I had any coke. I said 'no, I don't sell any.' I said I knew who could get him some . . . and I brought this guy to [Gloria]. I did her a favor, and she gave me some coke for it. I asked him if he was a cop, and he didn't answer. I tried to sell him some baking soda. I never really got into it. I was doing her [Gloria] a favor." Born and raised in Jamaica, Douglas is 24 years old. He received three years to serve. There was no information about Gloria in the clerk's docket book.

The way Douglas described his dealing — "I never really got into it," and "I was doing [the big-time dealer] a favor" — is reminiscent of the ways in which middle-level managers neutralize white-collar crime (Clinard 1983; Coleman 1989; Sykes and Matza 1957). Like others in the drug deep sample, Douglas did not view selling drugs as wrong:

cocaine and heroin were desirable commodities, and buyers came to him. What was the harm in a regular business transaction?

Comparing Seriousness in Drug Offenses

Comparing seriousness in men's and women's drug cases is more difficult than in interpersonal violence, robbery, and larceny cases. Drug harms are amorphous. Although a neighborhood or city can be viewed as victimized by drug selling or addiction, the victims of drug selling are consumers, not complainants. Also, there is a misplaced aim for precision in trying to link gradations of harm or seriousness to quantities and types of drugs, especially when the amounts seized may only be a small portion of what the seller had on the premises or had access to. Furthermore, information in the PSI about the particulars of the drug offenses was often limited. The defendant's role can be uncertain (as for Colleen and Miranda), and little is revealed about the contexts, relations, or histories in the defendants' drug selling.

Because drug quantity is a seemingly objective standard for comparison, I use that dimension to judge seriousness. Of the eight pairs, I judged four to be of similar seriousness. Two women's cases were more serious than the men's, and two men's cases were more serious than the women's (see appendix 5). Based on the quantity of drugs seized, gender differences were not marked. It was more difficult for me to judge seriousness when a man and woman were arrested for drugs found on their premises (as for Rennie and Colleen, Lotty, and Miranda). Rather than assume that the woman had played a secondary role, I adopted a more stringent standard: unless there was clear evidence of a secondary role, I judged the offense to be similarly serious. I judged Rennie and Colleen's drug offense to be the same, with some uncertainty, and Miranda's to be more serious than Juan's.[10]

Judging seriousness by the quantity of drugs involved does not foreshadow how the court will respond to drug defendants. To be sure, a major dealer (Douglas) did get a three-year term of incarceration, but another man with far lower amounts seized (Rennie) got five years to serve, and yet a third man with moderate quantities (Dylan) got a suspended sentence. Mary and Marcie were each given a year to serve, but the drug quantities were very low or not even recorded. The court's response to these defendants was keyed to a notion of harm based on the *continued* sale and use of illegal drugs after the court had been lenient in giving sentences of probation and drug treatment.

We lack basic information on the character of drug cases prosecuted in criminal courts. Even exemplary studies (Myers 1989; Peterson and Hagan 1984) use such terms as *drug trafficker* and *big-time dealer* with little indication of what the defendants did. Because trafficking is such an evocative concept, it is important to elucidate it and other, similar terms in analyzing drug cases. Precision in citing drug quantity and type — which features in federal sentencing guidelines and in some state legislation — gives a false sense that we can know seriousness through gram-based gradations. When quantities are very high, drug cases are regarded as serious, but after that, the sense of seriousness with which the court views drug cases is linked to other dimensions. In the New Haven felony court, either the defendant's probation status, parole status, or prior record was more often determining than the quantities of drugs recovered.

Gender differences in the structure of drug offenses prosecuted were evident in the wide sample, in which a higher proportion of men than women were convicted of selling drugs. In the deep sample (in which all but one pair involved a drug sale), the men's and women's cases were comparably serious. Moderate gender differences were noted in the social organization and contexts of drug selling. Women were more likely to act with others and to act with mates, spouses, or family members, and women more often sold drugs from their residences than on the street.

Race and ethnicity play a more important role in drug cases than in cases of robbery, larceny, and interpersonal violence. Police intelligence, informant networks, and drug buys are developed from proactive and targeted police work, not just from complainants' calls to the police. Peterson and Hagan's (1984) insight on the construction of minority drug users as victims has merit, but it applies to those with minimal or no previous arrests. A more proactive police policy — with a focus on parts of town, residences, or people — can transform a "minority drug-using victim" to a more loathsome entity: an "unreformed, unrepentant" drug seller. Because the harm in selling drugs is diffuse and amorphous, the relation of race and ethnicity to prior record and policing becomes more important.

Looking toward the pair-wise disparity analysis, I identified two drug pair cases as raising a question of sentencing disparity. The differences for one pair (Dylan and Mary) could be explained by prior record, but the differences for the second (Rennie and Colleen) were partly, though not completely, explained by the man's parole status and the woman's role in the offense.

The relation between the wider world of drug dealing — much of which is undetected or not prosecuted — and drug cases adjudicated in criminal courts is unknown. As researchers investigate the symbolism in "get tough" drug laws or those aimed at the bigger dealers, we must also explore who is routinely policed and prosecuted, what they have done, and what it is exactly that court officials are responding to. The gap between legislative or guideline notions of drug cases and actual cases seems wide indeed.

Notes

1. I suspect that the "100 pounds" refers to marijuana cases, not to narcotics.

2. Throughout this chapter I refer to "drugs" without necessarily specifying the type of drug. In part, this is because the PSI did not always specify it and in part because in all cases where the drug type was mentioned, it was heroin and/or cocaine. There were no arrests in which marijuana or various types of pills were the sole illegal drugs involved.

3. See table A-I.1 (app. 1) for a review of the penal code.

4. The federal sentencing guidelines identify 10 grams or more of heroin as a base-level-16 offense. For comparison, aggravated assault and sexual abuse of a minor are at level 15, which is one notch lower in guideline seriousness.

5. The percentages of those addicted to illegal drugs for men and women, respectively, were: drug cases, 63% and 75%; robbery, 50% and 75%; larceny, 43% and 71%; interpersonal violence, 12% and 29%.

6. The previous convictions could be for drug sale or possession or other offenses to support a drug habit, such as robbery. Ultimately, it is a construction of how the defendant has led his or her life up to the instant offense. Street men and women were most likely to be viewed as disreputable, with a higher level of blameworthiness attached to their drug selling.

7. In the cases of Bonnie, Reggie (below), and several others, there seemed to be a rather long period between an undercover purchase of drugs and the suspect's arrest. Apart from the time it may take to test the substances, I cannot account for this period.

8. Note the precision in gram weights. It reveals how weight is fetishized.

9. Lloyd was on probation at the time of this recent arrest. He was convicted on two counts of the sale of narcotics.

10. I may be portraying these women's drug cases as more comparable to the men's in seriousness than they are, but I would prefer to err on the conservative side in making comparative judgments.

Summary

I set out to determine whether men and women accused and convicted of statutorily similar crimes committed offenses of the same seriousness. Of the forty deep-sample pairs, I judged 48 percent to be comparably serious, but for 40 percent the men's offenses were more serious, and for 12 percent, the women's were. I conclude that for my sample of cases, a portion of the men's crimes was more serious. Although others have asserted that the prosecuted women's offenses are, on average, less serious than the men's, my analysis has documented that claim.

I also noted different types of problems — some subjective and some statistical — in assessing crime seriousness. For robbery, the most behaviorally bounded of the offenses, I learned that coded elements, such as acting alone or using a weapon, were not particularly useful in comparing robbery seriousness. A more effective approach is to examine the gestalt of the harm and the extent to which it conformed or deviated from the elements in a "typical stickup."

For larceny, which in my sample constituted a more varied set of harms and contexts than robbery, I found that a gap existed between what defendants were convicted of and what they actually did. Moreover, I suggested that the social significance of victim-offender relations — not merely the element of victims and offenders known or unknown to each other — is a critical component in understanding seriousness.

For interpersonal violence, I found that although the victim's death, the extent of victim injury, the vulnerability of victims in relation to offenders, and histories of abuse were salient in constructing seriousness, these elements did not operate consistently. Moreover, I suggested that even with details about offense contexts and circumstances, there remained much ambiguity about violent acts, and as a consequence, uncertainty in assessing culpability.

In the drug-law violations I noted that there is a misplaced precision in using the quantities of drug seized as a measure of seriousness. Without a clear victim or loss of property, the harm in drug-law violations is hard to assess. Perhaps for that reason, court officials have based seriousness on the quantity of lawbreaking — that is, the evidence of previous arrests for drug selling — more than on the quantity of drugs sold unless the drug amounts were very high.

For the traditional disparity study, my analysis of the crime narratives suggests that controls for offense severity, even for the exact charges at arraignment and conviction, do not effectively control for variation in women's and men's cases. Moreover, in fashioning new, more meaningful controls, researchers need to pay attention to offense-based variation in what elements will be important in judgments of seriousness. For example, known-versus-unknown victim-offender relations may be a meaningful dichotomy in robberies, but not for larceny or interpersonal violence.

Examining the coded elements for all the offenses (appendix 4, total column), one sees gender differences in the composition of offenses, victim-offender relations, and offense roles. Of the defendants who acted with others, men acted with other men (83 percent), comparatively fewer women acted with women (14 percent), and women's co-defendants were far more likely to be boyfriends or spouses than were the men's co-defendants (50 versus 11 percent).

Excluding drug offenses, which had no victims, a higher proportion of women than men knew their victims (59 versus 38 percent). An added dimension to knowing victims for women convicted of robbery and larceny was having had sexual relations with them. Of the fifteen pairs convicted of larceny and robbery, at least three, and perhaps four, women had had such relations with their victims (Pamela, Maggie, Tara, and perhaps Maria); no man had.

Somewhat higher proportions of men than women took active or equal roles in the offenses (88 versus 75 percent), with differences emerging largely in the interpersonal violence and drug offenses. Of the twenty-five pairs convicted of these offenses, only one man had played a secondary role, whereas six women did. I did, however, note some uncertainty in the determination of women's roles: some could have been playing a secondary role, and some could be *perceived* as playing a secondary role by court officials, when they were in fact playing a more active role. In the child abuse cases, the terms *primary role* and *secondary role* role may be ill-suited in characterizing a woman's culpability.

In addition to concluding that a portion of men's crimes was more serious than women's crimes, I found that a linking of biography and offense rendered some men as most blameworthy and some women as least blameworthy. Highly blameworthy defendants (mostly men) had serious records and time spent imprisoned, or they were on parole at the time of the instant offense. Less blameworthy defendants (mostly women) either acted as pawns or were fending off violent victims and had not been arrested before. These dichotomies capture the extreme ends of the blameworthy distribution, which is overlaid by gender. They do not, however, capture most of the cases, which reside in between.

In weighing the seriousness of the offense, coupled with other factors that may bear on sentencing (for example, the defendant's cooperation with officials, role in the offense, and prior record), I identified one matched pair for which a sentencing disparity could not be explained (Andrew and Latasha). There were two others for which the sentences could be largely though not fully explained (Kate and Casey, Rennie and Colleen). I consider these cases and the broader problems of how to assess punishment disparity in chapter 11.

In parts 2 and 3 I addressed the social histories of defendants, the nature and seriousness of their acts, and sentencing outcomes. In part 4, I analyze the visible and public face of "doing justice": the sentencing ceremony.

IV Justifications for Punishment

Philosophical discussions of punishment ignore gender,[1] and feminist scholars have yet to link gendered punishment practices to philosophical principles. To be sure, feminist scholars have analyzed women as legal subjects and defendants (Allen 1987a, 1987b; Carlen 1983; Daly 1987a, 1989a; Eaton 1986; Edwards 1984; Smart 1985; Worrall 1990), but we have not related official discourse to theories of punishment. In chapters 9 and 10 I bridge feminist and philosophical concerns. I analyze what was said at the sentencing ceremony to see whether the punishment rationales of officials vary in gender-based ways, and if they do, how they vary.

When I first planned this study, I expected that by analyzing the punishment justifications of court officials I would have a window on explaining how gender structured the process. My interests in taking this approach were sparked by Feeley's (1979) book on the New Haven GA-6 court, in which he argued that scholars should study "court officials' conceptions of justice." I reasoned that such conceptions should be visible in the courtroom during the sentencing ceremony. Furthermore, I thought it crucial to study a crystallizing moment, when a defendant's biography and crime are socially constructed and a punishment justified, but this time in a public setting. If nothing else, one could learn the ideas and arguments of court officials about men's and women's cases, a topic about which many have speculated but few have studied systematically. In the next two chapters I explore new empirical ground in learning how women's and men's crimes and punishments are discussed in the courtroom. To anticipate what we may find, I review selected debates and research on punishment.

Punishment Philosophies, Principles, and Practices

Normative debates about punishment are often cast in dichotomous terms: the punishment of past crimes or future crimes, basing punishment on deontological or utilitarian principles, a concern with punishment versus treatment (for example, Scheingold 1984; von Hirsch 1985; U.S. Sentencing Commission 1989). Sentencing practices belie these dichotomies in that they often combine elements of both poles (Ellis and Ellis 1989; Thomas 1979; Wheeler, Mann, and Sarat 1988). In light of sentencing practices, some scholars have proposed a philosophical basis for mixing apparently opposing principles. For example,

Norval Morris (1981, 268) suggests that desert-based criteria should set limits on sentencing (maximum and minimum), but within broad limits, and that sentence fine-tuning should be based on utilitarian grounds. Other hybrids have been proposed.[2]

In the past century, prescriptive practices in the United States and Britain have oscillated between the ideological poles of punishment and treatment (Daly 1989c; Garland 1985; Radzinowicz and Hood 1979; Walker 1980). Although court officials are affected by these ideological shifts (see, for example, Rosecrance [1988] for California and Scheingold [1991] for Washington state), how these shifts affect court practice is less clear. Furthermore, whatever punishment theory and prescriptive practices are in vogue, the state's limited financial resources serve to blunt change. In sum, it is easy to compare normative theories of punishment and their prescriptive practices, but with some exceptions, we lack information on how theories and associated practices are articulated in criminal proceedings.

The table (Introduction, IV, table 1) shows the principles and prescriptive practices of the two punishment poles and a hybrid. Associated with punishment as a categorical imperative (that is, wrongs should be punished because it is right to do so) is the principle of retribution. Retributive or desert-based sentencing schemes have these elements: crime should be punished on the basis of the offense in proportion to other offenses and the offender's culpability.[3] Andrew von Hirsch (1985, chapter 7) suggests that a defendant's previous lawbreaking may form part of the calculus of harm or blame in a desert-based scheme, although he argues that "the adjustment for prior criminal record [should] be a limited one, so that the primary emphasis . . . is on the seriousness of the current crime" (p. 91).[4] Retribution need not translate to tougher penalties or to incarceration as the preferred punishment (von Hirsch 1990; Wasik and von Hirsch 1988).[5] Although a range of sentences is possible (such as fines, restitution, community service), attention has been centered on *where* and *how* to draw the line between incarceration and nonincarceration. The defining value of desert-based schemes is equality of punishment in the aggregate. Such a value is to be achieved by punishing like crimes similarly and in proportion to their harm.

Utilitarians justify punishment as a way to achieve a socially useful benefit — such as turning others away from crime (general deterrence), removing individuals from the community (incapacitation), and changing a lawbreaker's attitude or behavior (special deterrence or rehabilitation). Contingent on the person and the crime, the utilitarian seeks an individualized response. Such a response may be based on concerns for crime control (general deterrence and incapacitation) or for punishing and reforming individuals (special deterrence and rehabilitation). The defining value is fitting the punishment to the crime and the

Table IV.1 Punishment Philosophies and Prescriptive Practices

Deontological

Represented today in desert-based sentencing schemes

Based on principle of retribution: punish the offense, commensurate with the harm and in proportion to other harms, with some consideration of prior record

Types of sentences: fines, restitution, community service, probation, incarceration

Defining value: equality of punishment in the aggregate — punish like crimes the same and in accordance with their harm

Optimal outcome: backward-looking punishment structure based on ranked system of harms with like harms punished the same

Utilitarian

Represented in the last century in three ways:

1. general deterrence: send signal to others that crime will not go unpunished
2. special deterrence and rehabilitation: punish (special deterrence) or treat (rehabilitation) those convicted, with the aim of modifying their behavior
3. incapacitation: remove those convicted from the community to prevent future harms

Based on the utilitarian principle: punish the person or crime to achieve socially useful benefits; extent of treatment or punitive orientation depends on punishment theory

Types of sentences: fines, restitution, community service, probation, incarceration

Defining value: individualized response — fit the punishment to the crime and the person; will produce inequality of punishment in the aggregate

Optimal outcome: forward-looking punishment scheme based on reforming persons, changing their behavior, or preventing them from harming others

Hybrid of Deontological and Utilitarian

Represented in the last century in oscillating principles and practices of penality

Represented today in inter- and intrajurisdictional variability in sentencing policies and practices

Articulated theoretically by Morris (1981): Desert is a limiting principle, i.e., it limits the maximum and minimum sentence, but the fine-tuning is based on utilitarian principles (though incapacitation and some forms of deterrence-based ideas, such as mandatory minimums, are rejected).

Articulated theoretically by Braithwaite and Pettit (1990): Liberty is a defining principle, i.e., one should limit the use of incarceration by the utilitarian aim of increasing dominion.

Types of sentences: fines, restitution, community service, probation, incarceration

Defining value: equality and justice decoupled; other values of parsimony, liberty, and reform may take precedence.

person. Thus, like crimes may be responded to differently. Such a response will generate unequal punishment in the aggregate, but utilitarians suggest that because individuals are differently affected by punishment, substantive justice (or outcome equality) may be achieved.

An example of the mix of deontological and utilitarian principles is Morris's (1981) proposal of using desert as a limiting, not a defining, principle of punishment, and of using utilitarian aims within a broad range of sentencing maxima or minima.[6] (Certain utilitarian aims, such as incapacitation, are not acceptable to Morris, however.) The defining value of this hybrid scheme is a trade-off between equality and other sentencing principles: parsimony, desert, and reform. Morris argues for equality as a guiding principle "unless there are other substantial utilitarian reasons to the contrary" (1981, 267). He proposes that inequality of punishment in the aggregate may be just: "A punishment [can be] both unfair and just," and "principles of justice do not require an equality of punishment" (p. 269). Another hybrid model is John Braithwaite's and Philip Pettit's (1990). This model bears some resemblance to Morris's, but it makes a sustained argument for parsimony in using incarceration and focuses on the benefits of increasing "dominion" as a societal value. Paul Robinson (1992) outlines a hybrid model in which desert structures the *amount* of punishment, but other utilitarian principles could be used to determine the *method* of punishment. Nigel Walker (1991, 130–36) proposes a hybrid model using humanitarianism as a limiting principle.[7]

The Philosophical and the Empirical

How do punishment theories and prescriptive practices relate to actual sentencing decisions? The paucity of research on this question is striking. In the United States, one problem is an absence of data. Without a written judicial opinion on why sentences were imposed or an appellate review, a "jurisprudence of imprisoning" (Morris 1981, 258) cannot be deduced. A second problem is the gap between what sociologists find important to investigate empirically and what legal scholars or philosophers find important. Social science scholars study the reproduction of inequality and social distance (for example, Black 1989), jurisdictional and organizational variability (Eisenstein and Jacob 1977; Nardulli, Eisenstein, and Flemming 1988), the ways that justice "gets done" in exchanges between prosecutors, defense attorneys, and judges (such as Frohmann 1991; Heumann 1978; Maynard 1982, 1984; Mileski 1971; Rosett and Cressey 1976; Sudnow 1965), and sentencing differences (Blumstein et al. 1983; Daly and Bordt 1991; Hagan and Bumiller 1983; Kleck 1981; Wilbanks 1987).[8] Social science studies on how decisions are made, how they vary, and how relations of power are manifest differ from the normative theories of penal justice advanced by such scholars as Hart (1968), Joel Feinberg (1984), Nicola Lacey (1988), and von Hirsch (1985).

Despite the gap between the empirical and philosophical, several works have bridged the two by asking judges how they reached a sentencing decision (Hogarth 1971; Mann, Wheeler, and Sarat 1980; Wheeler, Mann, and Sarat 1988). Wheeler and co-workers (1988) related sentencing justifications of federal judges to themes in the legal and philosophical literature. They found that when federal judges sentence white-collar defendants,[9] they use three principles that combine retribution (or harm-based) and utilitarian (or consequence-based) aims: harm, blameworthiness, and consequence. *Harm* refers to the physical and social injury caused by the offense, and *blameworthiness* to the linking of offense and biography. *Consequence* refers to the general deterrence or "societal effects" of the punishment, as well as to the particular or "personal effects" on the individual punished.[10] The consequences of punishment can conflict: on the one hand, judges want to send a message to others that white-collar crime is serious and should be punished, but on the other hand, the judges know that if they incarcerate a middle-class "good family man," the social costs to his family and community may be high.

Gender and Class in Punishment Philosophies and Practices

Wheeler and colleagues briefly speculated on how harm, blameworthiness, and consequence might apply to white-collar and common crime defendants. They surmised that "notions of general deterrence . . . [would be] given much more play in white-collar cases," whereas in "common crimes, especially those involving violence, notions of incapacitation will be central" (p. 191). I wondered, how does gender fit into this picture?[11]

It is possible to draw analogies between class and gender in sentencing. First, consider how consequence is weighed in sentencing white-collar and common-crime defendants. A judicial concern with the greater social costs of incarcerating a white-collar man is duplicated when good family men and women (especially the latter) are sentenced for common crimes (Daly 1987a, 1989a). Next, consider the findings in previous chapters about gender and blameworthiness. We learned in part 2 that women's social histories showed greater victimization, and their current circumstances suggested somewhat more conventionality. In part 3, I suggested that the ends of the blameworthy distribution were overlaid by gender: the least and most blameworthy defendants were likely to be women and men, respectively.

Gender and class may operate in similar ways in justifying punishment. Specifically, the utilitarian principles that judges use in sentencing white-collar men may be more evident in sentencing common-crime women than men. Conversely, the expectations held by Wheeler and co-workers for the greater role of incapacitation in sentencing common crime, especially violent offenses, may apply more to common-crime men than to women. More generally, from research done on prosecuted and imprisoned women,[12] we might expect women to be viewed as more reformable than men, who may be seen as a greater threat to the community or as not reformable.

Before we plunge into the sentencing transcripts, I would like to reiterate some constraints on my analysis. Because not all of the sentencing transcripts for the deep-sample cases were available (see discussion in appendix 1), I am unable to take a pair-wise comparative approach.[13] My focus is on themes that emerge from analyzing women and men separately. For the court's routines, recall that all the women and all but one man pleaded guilty in sentencing bargains, within which the defendants and court officials usually have little room to maneuver. The precise charge(s) against the defendants are shown in appendix 1, table A-I.3. All the crime narratives and punishments are sketched in appendix 6.

Notes

1. In reviewing this literature, one finds that almost all the authors are men and that the presumptive subject of punishment is men. Although some relations of inequality may feature in philosophers' discussions, gender does not. I suspect that the use of "he" and "him" throughout this body of work reflects a presumptive male before the law. Even when an author uses feminine pronouns in a text (such as Duff 1986), gender is not considered in the analysis.

2. Walker (1991, viii) argues that "the deep waters are where the moral philosophers lurk. . . . A few are amphibious and surface to study the realities of sentencing . . . but some have little or no knowledge of recent penological research on sentencing practice." I was delighted to discover Walker's book after writing a draft of this chapter. In it, he says he wishes "to promote the amphibian way: to lure philosophers onto dry land and penologists into deep water" (p. viii), which is also my aim.

3. Von Hirsch (1985), a desert advocate, uses the term *blameworthiness,* but it is tied more strictly to culpability for the harm, as I define these terms (see the introduction to part 2, n.1). I use the term *blameworthiness* to refer to a broader meaning of the harm in light of the defendant's social history and behavior in the pretrial period, as Wheeler, Mann, and Sarat (1988) do.

4. Some desert advocates have argued against using the prior record in fixing penalties (e.g., Fletcher 1978; Singer 1979).

5. But in practice, the implementation of desert-based sentencing in a law-and-order political context has produced longer sentences (see review by Tonry [1987]

of sentencing in Minnesota and Pennsylvania, based on studies available at that time).

6. Hybrid model ideas were anticipated by Hart (1968), who distinguished between the general justifying aim of punishment, the liability for punishment, and the amount of punishment.

7. Walker (1991, chap. 15) identifies other types of "compromises," including those he terms *jigsaw* and *eclectic*. My aim is not to review philosophical discussions of punishment in detail but rather to sketch their main emphases.

8. Another major sociological trajectory is historical and comparative analyses of punishment and social structure. See David Garland (1990) for a review and Dario Melossi (1993) for a recent example of this tradition.

9. In Wheeler, Mann, and Sarat (1988), the analysis of white-collar offenders was largely one of highly placed lawbreakers who had abused a position of occupational power or trust. White-collar crime, however, has also been defined as an act committed by deceit or fraud, independent of the actor's status (Wheeler, Weisburd, and Bode 1982; Weisburd et al. 1991). My discussion here draws on the term's meaning in Wheeler, Mann, and Sarat (1988).

10. Throughout the study, both the authors and the federal judges they interviewed invariably assumed the subject of punishment was a man, not a woman. In light of the authors' focus on more highly placed white-collar offenders, this male presumption is not surprising. It does, however, raise questions about the impact of gender (and other social relations) in judicial constructions of harm, blameworthiness, and consequence.

11. One may also wonder how race or ethnicity fits into this picture. Wheeler, Mann, and Sarat (1988) do not consider this dimension, but my sense is that *white-collar* refers presumptively to white men and that *common crime* refers to a mix of white and black men.

12. Included here are my interviews with probation officers in a Massachusetts court (Daly 1987a), Allen's (1987a, 1987b) research on the less dangerous quality of women's lawbreaking, Steffensmeier's (1980) summary of themes in the literature, and historical studies of penal policies toward women (Rafter 1990; Schweber 1982), which continue to the present (Carlen 1983; Dobash, Dobash, and Gutteridge 1986; Genders and Player 1987). Recall that during the latter part of the nineteenth century and early part of the twentieth in the United States, black women were not as often placed in the same "reform potential" category as were white women (Rafter 1990).

13. As shown in app. 1, table A-I.3, there were forty-eight defendants for whom transcripts survive (noted with an asterisk by their name). There were just fourteen pairs for whom sentencing remarks have survived for both the man and woman.

9 Justifying the Punishment of Women

Transcripts of sentencing remarks survive for twenty-two women.[1] I analyzed them to describe their content and to see what theories of punishment the court officials used in justifying particular sentences.

Recall that sentencing normally occurs four to six weeks after a defendant has entered a guilty plea or been found guilty. The process is formal and orderly. The prosecutor speaks first: he or she describes the offense, whether there is an agreed recommendation or a sentencing cap, what it is, and why it is appropriate.[2] (Note that in an agreed recommendation, the prosecutor, defense attorney, and judge have agreed on the sentence. It is generally fixed, although a judge might be moved to reduce the length of the sentence depending on what is said in the PSI or on the day of sentencing. With a sentencing cap, defense attorneys may argue for less than the cap.) After the prosecutor speaks, the defense attorney then makes a presentation, normally discussing the terms of the agreed recommendation or sentencing cap and highlighting the defendant's positive qualities. The judge asks whether the defendant has anything to say. Finally, before announcing the sentence, the judge discusses the case and the considerations that he or she has taken into account. Sentencings can be swift, sometimes not more than five minutes, or they can last a half hour or more. When a defendant enters a plea and the plea-bargained sentence is for less than three years' incarceration, the PSI may be waived, and the sentence imposed immediately.

Contour and Context of the Women's Sentencings

There are few surprises on sentencing day: more than 75 percent of the women's cases had agreed recommendations or caps (there was one cap) (see table 9.1). It was rare for defense attorneys to argue for less time when there was an agreed recommendation, although one did, and a second sought a sentencing postponement. For the five women defendants without agreed recommendations, their attorneys argued for suspended sentences or shorter sentences.[3] For six of these seven defendants, plus another who received probation in exchange for testifying against a male co-defendant, defense attorneys made longer, more passionate arguments.

Table 9.1   Features of the Sentencing Process for Women

	N = 22*	% of 22
Incarceration sentence? yes	13	60
Defendant detained during pretrial period? yes (all sentenced to incarceration)	10	45
A speed sentencing? yes	3	14
A plea and sentencing? yes (2 were speed sentencings)	3	14
Agreed recommendation or sentencing cap? yes	17	77
Defense attorney argued for less incarceration time or a suspended sentence? yes (3 were successful)	8	36
Remarks were long, passionate? yes	7	32
Defendant spoke on her behalf: yes If yes, did the defendant admit guilt? yes — 4	4	18
Others spoke on the defendant's behalf? yes (2 spoke against the defendant)	4	18
Defense attorney argued that the defendant had some positive qualities? yes	15	68
Drugs or alcohol were blamed for the defendant's problems? yes	11	50
Defendant was cast as a victim or a pawn in an incident instigated by a co-defendant? yes	4	18
Judge engaged in moralizing and lecturing to the defendant? yes	14	64

Type of moralizing (multiple responses)
General	12
"Your life has been a waste"	5
"Reflect on your life in prison"	2
"Kick your drug or alcohol addiction"	8

Sentencing judge

Kinney	12	Kinney	12	55
Higgins	3	Other judge	10	
Fishman	2			

Purtill, Schaller, Ronan, Hadden, Mulvey (1 each)

	N = 22*	% of 22
Judge was optimistic that the defendant could change, viewed the defendant in a positive light, or noted qualities suggesting the defendant was a "cut above the rest"? yes	10	45
Judge gave a justification for the punishment? yes	19	86

Judges not giving justification were Kinney (1), Mulvey (1), and Purtill (1)

*Based upon 22 sentencing transcripts of the 40 deep-sample women: 3 of 4 homicides, 3 of 8 assaults, 2 of 3 cases of risk of injury, 1 of 2 arsons, 5 of 8 robberies, 4 of 7 larcenies, and 4 of 8 drug offenses.

Drug Case 5, Mary

Mary's sentencing is an atypical instance of a longer sentencing and an impassioned defendant plea. She was convicted of selling drugs but wanted to delay serving a one-year jail sentence. (The word *jail* refers generally to any period of incarceration, whether in jail or prison.) Her boyfriend was also arrested for selling drugs, and he had been sentenced to serve 1½ years some months before. The following case provides a flavor of the exchange between Mary and Judge Kinney, after the defense attorney put a medical doctor on the stand to testify that Mary's health would be jeopardized if she withdrew too quickly from methadone.

> **Judge Kinney:** I am not persuaded by [the doctor's] testimony. The request for continuance is denied. [The judge then asks the prosecutor if he wishes to be heard on sentencing, to which the prosecutor says, "Impose a sentence of one year."]
>
> **Mary** [interjecting]: Your honor, please, please.
>
> **Judge:** I heard you already, Miss —, on whether or not the sentencing should be continued, so I am not interested in hearing anything on that. Do you understand, I don't want to hear you on that. Do you want to say anything with regard to the sentence?
>
> **Mary:** All I am asking is, please, just give me a chance to get off this methadone and do it safely. I have been in Niantic,[4] and . . . I have seen people die there, believe me, because of the lack of medical attention. I know what it's like. . . . I have been through it, I have been through it. . . . No matter what else, I don't want to be sick in prison, and I don't want to die in prison, and that is the God's truth. You have to be brought down in a way [from methadone]. . . . I can't explain it. . . . You've never seen anybody go through withdrawals of it. You wouldn't understand it. All I am asking is that I don't want to go through this.
>
> **Judge:** Miss —, I have already told you. I have listened to you. . . . I have decided that I want to impose sentence today, so don't waste your time on that now. [sentenced to serve one year]

Robbery Case 4, Pat

In six women's sentencings, others spoke about the defendant, four in her favor and two against her. At Pat's sentencing, her social worker and her mother spoke on her behalf. She was convicted of the robbery of an ice cream shop in which she drove the getaway car; she had been released from jail the month before. The social worker wanted to impress upon the judge that Pat and her son had a close relationship, and Pat's mother asked the judge not to "add any more time" on her daughter's sentence.

Pat's social worker: Pat is a very loving, warm person. The relationship [with her son] is tremendous. The love between them is unbelievable, and the strength that both of them have is commendable. As a social worker, I feel that naturally they should be together. . . . I feel like he needs her at home.

Pat's mother: I've been mother and father throughout the years [I've raised my ten children], and I know I went wrong with some of things I said and done and some of the things I taught them. But since she has been away, I have been able to take care of her son . . . but I am not able now to do a lot of things. . . . I am really asking you today to take into consideration that [although] Pat has done a lot of wrong things . . . when she got out she made a deep determination and was doing a lot of right things. . . . I am asking you please if there is any way . . . to bring her back. I am asking you please don't add any more time on the time she has because I feel if you do I may not be around when she gets out.

Pat: I know the courts in the past have been lenient with me. They have given me suspended sentences, probation, halfway house, restitution, all the chances that a person really needs, but at that time when I was getting all the chances, my mind wasn't made up, and I was not rehabilitated. . . . This case today . . . I am more guilty of being with the wrong person than anything else. . . . The last crime I would commit is a robbery. I had no need to. I had a good job, and I just wanted to do the right thing. I am just asking the court — I am not asking — I am begging the court to please just consider this one final time. Give me a chance this last time. Please. [sentenced to serve four years]

Although it was unusual for a woman defendant to speak in court (only 18 percent did), when they spoke, they admitted guilt, expressed remorse, and as the excerpts from Mary's and Pat's sentencing suggest, begged the judge to deliver mercy.

Drug Case 4, Miranda

In contrast to Mary's and Pat's sentencings, which were longer than most and involved vocal defendants, was the other extreme: a courtroom encounter I call a speed sentencing. The three women whose sentencings were brief all received suspended sentences. In one case, Miranda participated in a major drug dealing operation from her household, for which her sons had also been convicted. I would have expected more admonishment from the judge about Miranda's not being a responsible parent, especially since police authorities assumed that her family was among the major drug distributors in the area. Instead, Miranda's was among the shortest women's sentencings.

Judge Mulvey [after hearing both the prosecutor and defense attorney say that the agreed recommendation was satisfactory]: All right. . . . I'm familiar with this entire series of cases. I spent a lot of time with counsel on those matters, and this is an equitable disposition. I'll commit you to the custody of the Commissioner of Corrections for [a two-year suspended sentence].

More court time was spent in Miranda's case *after* the sentence was imposed, discussing how the state would handle the property seized during her arrest and the arrests of her family members.

In most sentencings, defense attorneys argued that their women clients had some positive qualities, and in half the sentencings, drugs or alcohol were blamed for the women's problems. In two cases the woman was cast as the real victim, and in two others, a male co-defendant was portrayed as the major instigator. In most sentencings, the judge took the occasion to lecture the defendant about how she had led her life up to that point and her problems with drugs or alcohol. The moralizing was more likely directed to women convicted of robberies, larcenies, and drug offenses, whose lawbreaking reflected a street women path. Illustrative of judicial lecturing and moralizing are the sentencings of Kate, Pamela, and Pat, all of whom were convicted of robbery. For Kate, the judge focused on why she should leave the street life.

Robbery Case 1, Kate

Judge Kinney: It would appear from this presentence report that for a long period of time you've been abusing narcotics and abusing alcohol, which has led to some serious physical and health problems for you. . . . If you continue that kind of abuse, your life span is going to be substantially shortened. You're 36 years of age now. I would think that at this point in your life you would come to the realization this is not the kind of life you can continue. . . . Unless you grab hold of your life and make . . . a change in your lifestyle, you're headed for either very serious health problems that will lead to your not being around any longer or to extensive incarceration. . . . I hope you'll give serious thought to changing your life direction while you're incarcerated this time. [sentenced to serve two years]

The judge was prescient in thinking that Kate's lifestyle was a threat to her health. A year later, Kate was stabbed by a man who intervened in a fight she was having with a woman; she died the next day.[5]

Robbery Case 3, Pamela

For Pamela, the judge focused on how her recent drug addiction was making a waste of her life. She was one of a handful of women who had attended college.

> **Judge Kinney:** It really is a shame to see somebody like you before the court today. . . . You [are] a classic example of the kind of damage that's caused to a person's life by narcotics addiction. . . . You've wasted what could have been a very rewarding and successful life. . . . You have a long time ahead of you, and you can make it either something worthwhile or a total waste as the past few years have been for you. [suspended sentence]

Robbery Case 4, Pat

Toward Pat, who had recently been diagnosed HIV positive, the judge mixed censure and sympathy for "a wasted life."

> **Judge Kinney:** I don't believe you are a vicious person. . . . You are a loving and a kind person and a caring person, and you have real affection for your son, and you should. But you are a criminal also. . . . You are 35 years of age now. Almost an entire life devoted to criminal offenses and drug abuse. And it's a wasted life . . . because you are not a stupid person. You are a person of average or clearly above average abilities, and you should have made more of your life than you have. . . . I feel sorry for you.

When the judge moralized, he would acknowledge a woman's positive qualities (Pat is a "caring person [who has] real affection for [her] son") or express optimism for her future (he hoped Pamela would "straighten out" her life because "it's not over"). There were ten women (45 percent) for whom such positive remarks were made during the sentencing. Of this group, seven received jail sentences, whereas of the twelve women for whom positive remarks were not made, six were jailed. Therefore, an optimistic or positive appraisal of a woman's character was not necessarily associated with suspended sentences.

I explored whether Mileski's (1971) insight on "situational sanctioning" applied to these sentencings. Mileski observed that when defendants received suspended sentences, they were more likely to be reprimanded in court or to be subject to more judicial lecturing. My analysis of the women's sentencings does not bear this out: judges were about as likely to engage in moralizing or lecturing when women received suspended or incarceration sentences (66 versus 61 percent).[6]

Justifications and Theories of Punishment

I read the sentencing transcripts many times before I could identify the category (or categories) in which a sentencing justification fell. In contrast to interview research that analyzes what judges *say* they think about in sentencing, I was analyzing what judges *actually said* in the courtroom.[7] What I found was that judges combine various punishment theories. For example, the general deterrence aim of punishment — to send a signal to others that crime will not go unpunished — may shade into a desert- or retribution-based rationale. The following two examples demonstrate the mixing of punishment principles in courtroom discourse.

Homicide Case 1, Claire

One was the sentencing of Claire, a young woman who killed a man with a golf club. Her defense attorney reported that Claire "is unlike any other client I have had. She has no prior criminal involvement. She realizes she has to go to prison. The question is, What would be a fair and appropriate sentence?" The judge replied:

> **Judge Kinney:** The court has certain responsibilities in cases like this, no matter how good a defendant may appear. . . . Those responsibilities . . . involve condemnation by the court, which speaks for the community, of conduct which results in the taking of a life. It is conduct that will not be tolerated in this society, and it is conduct the court is obliged to condemn. And the only way the court can condemn it, aside from the brief remarks at sentencing, is by the court's sentence, which would indicate not only to the person being sentenced but to others how strongly society condemns this kind of conduct. [sentenced to serve 7½ years]

The judge's remarks contain general and special deterrence themes within a desert-based logic. The court's "obligation to condemn" (desert-based or retribution) merges with the "court's sentence [showing] . . . to the person being sentenced" (special deterrence) "[and] to others how strongly society condemns this . . . conduct" (general deterrence).

Arson Case 1, Dorothy

Another example of the merging of general and special deterrence with retributive themes was Dorothy's sentencing. She set two fires in her apartment after having had a fight with her boyfriend.

> **Judge Kinney:** This could have been . . . a disastrous type of incident for the people that lived in the house — undoubtedly something you didn't give a moment's thought to at the time you did this. But

how many times do we pick up the paper and read about fires that are started by people motivated like you to retaliate against somebody else for some grievance that result in serious injuries or deaths to people. . . . This is the kind of conduct that we have an obligation to try to stop. The only way that we know how to do it is to incarcerate people that commit offenses like this, and this is the reason you are being incarcerated today: to demonstrate to you and hopefully to demonstrate to other people who might be inclined to do the same thing that this conduct is not going to be tolerated. [sentenced to serve one year]

The judge said, "This is the kind of conduct we have an obligation to stop" (retribution, special deterrence, and perhaps, incapacitation). The way to stop it is by incarcerating defendants, for two reasons: "to demonstrate to [the defendant] . . . and other people" (special and general deterrence, respectively) that setting fires in retaliation for grievances "is not going to be tolerated."

Like the federal judges interviewed by Wheeler, Mann, and Sarat (1988), the justifications of the New Haven judges cannot be neatly compartmentalized in ways that legal or moral philosophers theorize. Utilitarian and deontological themes are interwoven with this practical judicial logic: it is a benefit to society (utilitarian) to punish wrongs commensurate with their harm (deontological-retributive). Put another way, the forward-looking (utilitarian) justification is made with reference to the backward-looking (retributive) calculation of deserved punishment.[8]

Justifying Jail
The two most frequent modes of justifying jail were retribution and special deterrence (table 9.2). As seen in Claire's and Dorothy's cases, retribution was joined with general and special deterrence. For two other defendants, retribution was combined with incapacitation, and in another two, retribution was the main focus even though other punishment theories were present.

Retribution
Robbery Case 6, Wendy
Wendy's sentencing illustrates a retributive focus, together with special deterrence and rehabilitation elements. She and a male accomplice robbed a gas station one evening, and she used a sawed-off shotgun. Wendy's defense attorney made an impassioned plea to the court to reduce the length of her sentence. His remarks centered on her status as a mother.

Table 9.2 Justifying Punishment for Women

	Received an Incarceration Sentence		Total in the Transcript Analysis
	Yes	No	
Robbery	4	1	5
Larceny	1	3	4
Violence	6 (1 time served)	3	9
Drugs	2	2	4

Justifying incarceration: Of the 13 women sentenced to serve time, the types of justifications were as follows:

Retribution focus or coupled with special deterrence, general deterrence, incapacitation, and/or rehabilitation (Chris, Claire, Dorothy, Edie, Edith, Pat, Wendy)	7
Special deterrence with focus on prior record (Kate, Mary, Nellie, Penny, Susan); "punished enough" (Jean)	6

Justifying nonincarceration: Of the 9 women who received suspended sentences with probation, the types of justification(s) used were as follows:

[No justification given, but inferred retribution *a:* not serious harm (Miranda); retribution *b:* restitution (Kathleen, June) 3]	
Retribution *a:* Minor harm, minor role (Pamela, Sharon) retribution *b:* restitution (Prish)	3
Special deterrence and rehabilitation: "Punished enough" or good prospect for drug treatment (Lotty, Tara)	2
Other reason: prosecutor needed the defendant's testimony to convict a co-defendant (Flo)	1

Defense attorney: I just would emphasize that someone who is a mother of a young child . . . this has been particularly telling for her. This 3½ year sentence . . . for someone who has never been through this system before . . . [is too high]. . . . I can only throw her on the mercy of the court. . . . To the extent that the court sees fit to give her a lesser sentence than the sentence agreed upon, I ask that you do so.

A church pastor spoke on Wendy's behalf, saying, "Any kind of mercy you could show to her, we would appreciate. I have known her all her life. She has been very cooperative. It is unfortunate." Judge Kinney then said:

Miss —, I'm satisfied . . . that you, in fact, are remorseful over your involvement in this situation. Unfortunately, remorse or regret

. . . does not do an awful lot to mitigate the seriousness of the offense. Armed robberies are extremely serious offenses. . . . [They] have become a scourge of modern urban society, and it is incumbent upon the court to do something to try to address this problem. . . .

The impact that an armed robbery has on the people who are robbed [is substantial]. People are terrified. It is a terrifying incident for them. . . . It is the potential for injury. It is the terror that is inflicted upon people confronted with guns where money is demanded that makes it such a serious offense.

We have pretty well determined, at least I have . . . that sentences for armed robberies should start at five years' imprisonment. I think that is an appropriate penalty for very serious incidents. Now, I recognize . . . that this is a very substantial penalty. But I'm persuaded that it should be. . . .

You do have a good background. . . . I notice[d] . . . that you did not finish school, and there is no question in my mind but that [this has] severely limited . . . meaningful employment to you. . . . I'm thoroughly satisfied that your motivation for . . . this incident was your involvement with narcotics. . . .

[Although] the court thinks in terms of a five-year penalty for armed robbery, recognizing that there are some redeeming qualities in you, recognizing also that you have a young child that you apparently care for, I indicated to counsel that I was interested from a rehabilitative point of view in seeing [whether] you could do something to meet your addiction. And I'm willing to reduce the ordinary sentence that I would impose in an armed robbery to give you the opportunity to do that.

The judge imposed the agreed recommendation of 3½ years in jail with in-patient drug treatment ordered after Wendy's release as a condition of probation.

I excerpted from Wendy's sentencing at length to illustrate several features of the sentencing ceremony. First, several theories of punishment are introduced: "Armed robberies are extremely serious offenses" (retribution), "[the court] should try to address this problem" (retribution and special deterrence), and "from a rehabilitative point of view" (rehabilitation). Second, the defense attorney will surround a woman with family responsibilities if she has children or if there is something positive that can be said about her caring for others. Third, in Wendy's case, the judge announced his going rate for armed robbery — five years' imprisonment — which he adjusts depending on the defendant's prior record, elements of the offense, and potential for reform. Fourth, the judge took the occasion to make his sentence symbolic: he was not just sentencing Wendy that day, he was also speaking to the general public about robbery as the "scourge of modern urban society." Finally, although the judge acknowledged Wendy's redeeming qualities, he did not respond to the defense attorney's plea to reduce her sentence.

Several interpretive questions arise from Wendy's sentencing. With some exceptions, I cannot know who the audience was on sentencing day. The judge may have used Wendy's sentencing for symbolic ends because there were more spectators than usual or perhaps because there was a class visiting. As I analyzed the transcripts, I wondered about the role of the audience (not just the general public, but also state workers) in the judge's use of time and the courtroom as an "educational theater" (Nettler 1990, 19). Another problem of interpretation is classifying the judge's justification. Although he mentioned rehabilitation, I saw this as secondary to his emphasis on retribution. Cases like Wendy's reveal an ambiguity in judicial justifications that resists easy categorization.

Homicide Case 2, Edie

Edie's sentencing illustrates a combination of retribution and incapacitation arguments. Edie, aged 60, stabbed her stepmother to death one morning. Her sentencing was lengthy and poignant: her defense attorney pointed out Edie's history of severe depressions, her exemplary life as a good mother, her care of her father and stepmother, her recent economic losses, and that she had no history of violence.

> **Defense attorney:** She was an exceptional mother. She was a responsible wife. And that, despite having had 38 years of severe psychiatric problems. . . . Because of all the stresses she . . . had, she wasn't able to sufficiently resist the impulse, the breaking of her thin veneer of defense mechanisms in dealing with that stress.
>
> [She was] involved in a lot of social organizations . . . assisted her father . . . assisted the victim. She took them shopping . . . to all their doctors' appointments. She looked after them. She cleaned. She cooked. She drove them places. . . . Despite all the problems she had, she managed to hold it all together, to function as a wife and mother, a citizen in the community, a caretaker of all of her elderly relatives, and exhibited a great deal of concern and responsibility. . . .
>
> During the past couple of years . . . there have been severe financial setbacks for a professional family. She was the wife of a doctor. . . . At a time in life when a lot of people are able to sit back and enjoy the fruits of a long hard struggle, she lost everything . . . through some tax problems that her husband was involved in. She lost the family home. She lost the place she lived, was forced to give away or sell many of her possessions. . . . All that was

really left was a minimal existence, really through no fault of hers and despite her best efforts.

The day before this offense, she . . . was told that her father . . . would have a lengthy stay [in the hospital]. She had sole responsibility for the preceding week and a half for the care of a woman who was . . . suffering from Alzheimer's disease.

Edie's exemplary history as a good mother and heroic caretaker for her father and stepmother, coupled with her age and long history of severe depressions, cut a sympathetic figure. The defense attorney's argument, however, did not reduce the ten-year sentence the judge had in mind. He was concerned with a remark Edie gave in a psychiatric evaluation: "I murdered the wrong person. . . . I should have killed my husband." Edie's honesty about a major source of her frustration and anger (her husband's verbal abuse and his refusal to help her care for her father and stepmother) may have led the judge to justify a long sentence with an incapacitation element in mind:

> **Judge Kinney:** The court has had occasion to sentence several women recently for homicide, and it is not a happy chore by any means. The taking of a human life is among the most serious offenses that the court sees here for sentencing. Unlike the cases the court has sentenced recently, this case doesn't have any of the aspects of justification or excuse that existed in those other cases.
>
> . . . The victim . . . was, despite her handicaps . . . entitled to live out her natural life without it being terminated prematurely. So that the homicide is a situation that the court has to condemn by its sentence and has to provide an appropriate punishment. . . . At this point . . . she is able to control her behavior . . . but I'm thoroughly satisfied that she is mentally ill, that she is suicidal, that she is homicidal, and that she constitutes a serious threat to other persons, particularly her husband, but to other persons as well, and a threat to herself. . . . If she were free to control her own affairs, I'm confident that that would lead to further tragedy, either for herself or for other persons. [sentenced to serve ten years]

Note the judge's reference to Edie's homicide as not having elements of justification or excuse, an atypical homicide in light of women who fight back from abusive men. The next case, Jean's killing of a former mate, may be what the judge was thinking of.

Special Deterrence

Jean is one of six women whose sentencings reflected special deterrence themes. Hers was one of three cases in which judges took into consideration the time served awaiting trial. Toward Jean, Judge Kinney said on sentencing day that she had already been "punished enough," and he noted her exemplary behavior during the pretrial period at the Niantic prison for women. By the time of the plea, she had been incarcerated for about fourteen months for having stabbed a drunken and abusive former partner. Describing the incident as "spontaneous, not planned in any way on [Jean's] part," the judge sentenced her to a short jail term,[9] which, with good time and time served, would make her eligible for release, "if not today, in the very near future, and I think that would be appropriate," he said. He noted further, "I'm satisfied you are not a danger to others or to the community in general. And I wish you well in your future life." Despite the judge's apparent generosity, I am struck by the fact that Jean was prosecuted at all, and that she served more than a year of time in jail for defending herself from a violent victim.

Robbery Case 1, Kate

More typically, special deterrence justifications included the judge's recitation of a woman's accumulating prior record, the breaks she had received from the court in the past, and the need now for the woman to reflect on her life and turn it around. Such themes featured in the sentencings of Kate and Mary, as we have seen, and in the sentencings of Susan, Penny, and Nellie. For example, note the judge's remarks when Kate was sentenced for robbery:

> **Judge Kinney:** We don't sentence an awful lot of women in this court as opposed to male offenders. But of the ones we do, you have as extensive a prior record as I've seen in some . . . time. Granted, much of it is for misdemeanors, but since 1967 you've been continuously in difficulty of one type or another. The offense, although the victim did not sustain serious injury, was a serious offense. Any kind of street robbery is, and certainly a robbery that involves the use of a weapon by any one of the participants is an extremely serious offense and demands some period of incarceration. . . . You're living on the streets and involved in one difficulty after another. The more you come back here on serious offenses, the more time you're going to end up serving at Niantic. [sentenced to serve two years]

Although the judge mentioned that "a robbery . . . is an extremely serious offense and demands some period of incarceration," the retributive theme was secondary to his repeated emphasis on Kate's previous lawbreaking.[10]

Robbery Case 2, Susan

Susan and a male accomplice robbed a convenience store one evening, one of several robberies they had committed that month. Susan's defense attorney noted that "there are relatively few women in our system other than those who may have committed a homicide who are receiving a sentence as lengthy as my client. It will give her time to reflect on what she has done, and . . . on how she is going to go about turning herself around." Susan's sentence was indeed long, the longest any woman had received for robbery during the research period. Judge Kinney's response was terse:

> **Judge Kinney:** I am not terribly optimistic [about your future]. You've got a . . . kind of tough background that you have to overcome. You can do it. You are only 20 years of age. . . . You've got to straighten your life out a little bit. Otherwise, you are going to spend a lot of time locked up. [sentenced to serve eight years]

Drug Case 3, Penny

Penny was convicted of selling drugs, and the judge was annoyed with her because she had admitted she could make more money from selling drugs than working a regular job. In part, her attitude of thumbing her nose at the law moved the judge to conclude that incarceration was warranted.

> **Judge Hadden:** [She] feels she's able to make more money dealing drugs than she is working. I guess that's probably so, but unfortunately for her it's against the law. I guess one can make more money robbing banks than working. As long as you don't get caught. Maybe it's a pretty good way to make a living, I don't know. But still it's against the law. . . . She is very candid about the way she makes her living. [There is] no indication that she's going to correct her situation. The only reason she's not freebasing cocaine is because she doesn't have any more money, according to [the PSI]. I think that it does call for some incarceration. [initially sentenced to 1½ years, modified to serve six months]

Drug Case 5, Mary

Judge Kinney's reaction to Mary displayed a more personalized animosity than was usual for him. A month before this sentencing, he had granted Mary a continuance to begin serving her sentence. On her sentencing day, he said to her defense attorney, who had requested that Mary be heard, "Well, I hope she does so in a more respectful way than when she left here [a month ago]." The judge was not persuaded by Mary's or a doctor's arguments that she needed a four-month continuance to detox from methadone:

> **Judge Kinney:** I am familiar with Miss — . I have been familiar with her for many years. . . . She has been incarcerated many times, as

long as 20 years ago. I recognize her problem. . . . Whenever she's able, she involves herself in the sale of narcotics. That's a dirty business. . . . It goes back 20 years. . . . In 1959, she was convicted of the sale of narcotics. In 1983, she was convicted of selling narcotics. She is unreformed, unrepentant. [sentenced to serve one year]

Mary's sentence had little to do with the particulars of the harm. Instead, the judge was irritated that she was "unreformed" after twenty years of coming before the criminal courts.

Justifying Nonjail

Judges used desert-based arguments in justifying suspended sentences. They focused on the woman's minor offense role or on the greater culpability of others. At times, they ordered the defendant to pay back money illegally obtained. For only two women were notions of rehabilitative treatment emphasized, and in both instances the judge expressed optimism that the women would succeed in a treatment program. One woman did not fit any of these categories: this was Flo, the celebrated evil woman in the New Haven court during the research time period.

Risk-of-Injury Case 2, Flo

Flo and her boyfriend, Skip, went to trial on charges that she had allowed him to sexually abuse her children. During the trial, the prosecutor decided he wanted to ensure Skip's conviction. Thus, in return for her testimony against Skip, Flo was promised a probation term. Newspaper coverage of Flo's sentencing was headlined: "Sex abuse sentence 'deal with devil'" — phrasing that the reporter took from the prosecutor's remarks at Flo's sentencing:

> **Prosecutor:** I was really afraid that if I could not have Flo testify . . . [the jury] might acquit [the boyfriend], and I thought that would be a travesty. . . . Basically what you have to do in a case like this is . . . make a deal with the devil, so to speak. The problem I have is that she . . . made a deal to save her own skin and that really bothers me because . . . she was more concerned with the co-defendant than she was with her kids. . . . She was [more] concerned with her own welfare than that of her children and that bothers me to this day.

The prosecutor continued by characterizing Flo as unstable and having psychiatric problems, although he believed she posed no danger to other children "on the street":

Prosecutor: Flo is emotionally unstable. There are some problems with drug abuse. . . . I think her problems go a lot deeper. . . . She has deep-rooted psychiatric or psychological problems. [Some people think] we should not let an abuser back on the street to victimize other children. I don't see this case as that type. I don't see her as a classic child sexual abuser. I saw her more as a person who was easily led by a more domineering person, and that was Skip. I don't see her with a problem on the street lurking around in parks trying to pick up little kids. I don't think she should be around little children. I don't think she should have custody of her children.

The prosecutor seemed to think that a "classic child sexual abuser" is "on the street" or "lurking around in parks," when the more likely circumstance is in a parental or familial context.[11] Before announcing his sentence, the judge gave his reasons for accepting the suspended-sentence bargain. At the same time, he argued that Flo should be incarcerated (no doubt to mollify a concerned public) and delivered a harsh "situational sanction":

Judge Ronan: Everyone . . . recognizes the heinous and outrageous nature of the episodes and actions on the part of this defendant and her companion. . . . This defendant is at the very least, in the eyes of the court, as culpable and as responsible as [Skip] for the abusive sexual acts inflicted on her very own children. Nonetheless, the experienced professional judgment of [the prosecutor] after partially trying this was properly and capably exercised. . . . Make no mistake, Mrs. —, you should go to prison and you should never again have custody of your children, and that is the opinion of the court. [suspended sentence]

As memorable, dramatic, and intriguing as Flo's case was, both in the press and the courthouse, it was unusual.[12] The more typical situations in which women received probationary sentences were when their lawbreaking was thought to be minor, or, in one instance, not even wrong; when they could pay back money taken; when they had served some time pending trial and the judge thought they had been punished enough; and when they were viewed as good candidates for drug treatment.

Assault Case 2, Sharon

In Sharon's case the court exonerated the defendant while still subjecting her to a felony conviction. It is instructive to compare this case with Jean's. Their offense circumstances were the same: both acted to fend off a violent man. Like Jean, Sharon was a good family woman, supporting her family with a job and having no prior record. The different responses to Jean (sentenced to time served, 2½ years) and Sharon (suspended sentence) were based on what happened to the victim. In Jean's case, the victim died, and Jean served time, but when the victim survived, as in Sharon's case, the court was almost apologetic for prosecuting the case.

In an extraordinary move, at Sharon's sentencing, the prosecutor said to the judge, "With counsel's permission, I'd like to pass a copy of [the victim's] criminal record for your Honor to view in connection with these proceedings." The defense attorney continued on the same theme, saying, "If this case had come up for trial, the defense of self-defense would have been raised. If your Honor looks at [the victim's] prior record, it will indicate that he has harassed and indeed assaulted in his previous history and a lot of that criminal history has to do with my client." In imposing sentence, the judge affirmed the prosecutor's and defense attorney's remarks, saying that Sharon was "trying and with a very high degree of success to maintain herself in the community with her children. . . . She's been regularly employed and [in light of] her troubled background, she's done a good job with her life." He added:

> **Judge Higgins:** I note also the [prosecutor's] submittal of the [victim's] extensive criminal record. I assume some of those charges came about as a result of his relationship with her. It's been stormy over the years. I think she's a woman that we can all place a hopeful investment in. So I'll accept the recommendation [of probation]. . . . Probation isn't any problem really for the person who has a firm resolve to lead a good life. And I can only conclude that she has that, based on the lack of her prior record and that [in spite of her] troubled circumstances she's . . . a nurse's aide and she's done very well. I think that she ought to know that the court takes into account the bad prior records of people when I sentence and we also take into account the good prior record, and this is what she's benefit[ing from] now. [suspended sentence]

The judge concluded the sentencing with what certainly was a magnanimous gesture in his mind: "I'm going to have his prior record attached to the presentence investigation . . . because it isn't often that you see a victim's record attached and I think, as in this case, . . . it has significance in some sentencing procedures and probably ought to be attached — ." The prosecutor interrupting by saying "I agree," which ended the sentencing. Sharon was out on bail pending trial, and thus, unlike Jean, she did not serve jail time for defending herself from a violent intimate.

Robbery Case 3, Pamela

Of the nine women receiving nonjail sentences, only three had been convicted in the past. It is useful to see how judges justify nonjail sentences for those with previous convictions.

Pamela was involved in robbing a man she knew. In fact, she had dated him, and he visited her while she was held in Niantic pending trial. The prosecutor noted:

> **Prosecutor:** The defendant does have a lengthy prior criminal history . . . [but] the majority of her arrests are prostitution related. It's unfortunate that [she] finds herself in the lifestyle that she does. . . . She did extremely well in high school, received a scholarship to college and threw all of that away through the use of narcotics. . . . Ordinarily . . . I would be seeking a period of incarceration for [someone] involved in an armed robbery. There were mitigating factors [in this case] — her participation was not to the extent of her companion, she did fully cooperate with the police . . . and she has no record of this type of offense.

The judge affirmed the prosecutor's mitigating factors, adding several others: she had already served time in jail pending trial, and she had begun working as a secretary after being released:

> **Judge Kinney:** In addition to the factors that counsel have mentioned that . . . justify a suspended sentence, I know that you spent a period of some months confined at Niantic in lieu of bond before I reduced your bond so that you could be out. Taking all those things into consideration . . . you're entitled to a suspended sentence at this time. . . . You have a good job now. Please keep it. Do what you can to straighten out your life. [suspended sentence]

The elements helping Pamela were her cooperation with the police in identifying the co-defendant, her lack of a previous arrest for a violent offense, her time already spent in jail, and her successful effort to secure a job in the pretrial period.

Larceny Case 2, Tara

Tara, who stole goods from a man's apartment while he was asleep, was described by her attorney as not having "the strongest constitution in the world. In fact, she is a very fragile person, which is either a product of or the cause of the problems she has had." The victim had received money from his insurance company. Thus, there was an indication that he had already been compensated for most of his losses. The defense attorney also stressed that Tara had a one-year-old child, had enrolled in a mental health center, and was participating in a methadone maintenance program. The judge acted on these biographical elements in justifying a suspended sentence.

Judge Fishman: It is really unfortunate that somebody's life can be wasted, wasted in the usual sense and wasted in the colloquial sense. Anyone who has been abusing substances since age 13 consisting of marijuana, alcohol, acid, speed, pills, cocaine, heroin — I would think there must be somebody watching over her in that she's still alive. I suppose that she should be grateful for that and begin from there.

. . . The argument for a suspended sentence is well made, and I have read the report [from the mental health counselor] . . . and [it] has confirmed much of what I thought about this case. The . . . insurance company . . . has paid [over $4,000] on the claim. . . . It would appear that restitution is unrealistic and that the accused has no skills that are compensated for in the marketplace at a high rate. . . . I'm going to impose a suspended sentence. I'm going to impose certain conditions of probation that must be strictly adhered to.

The judge's admonition that probation conditions "must be strictly adhered to" is commonly made by judges imposing suspended sentences. Such sentences are not granted easily.

Larceny Case 1, June

Two women who received suspended sentences committed forms of white-collar crime. Neither had been arrested before, and both were expected to pay restitution. Over several years, June collected $3,784 in welfare funds to which she was not entitled. I expected to see a good deal of judicial moralizing toward her, but moralizing did not occur at sentencing. Instead, June's was a speed sentencing, with court time spent in exchanges between prosecutor, defense attorney, and defendant in taking a guilty plea. After taking her plea, the judge asked June several questions before imposing the sentence:

Judge Kinney: Anything you want to say?
June: No.
Judge: Will you be able to make these payments?
June: Yes.
Judge: The agreement is accepted. The accused is sentenced [to a suspended sentence with probation, a special condition being to pay back the welfare funds she had taken].

Larceny Case 5, Prish

Prish received a suspended sentence for embezzling more than $125,000 from her employer. The judge felt that the agreed recommendation was too lenient:

> **Judge Kinney:** This was obviously a calculated offense that occurred over an extensive period of time, and it involved a large sum of money. . . . Well, the court intends to accept the recommendation that the state has made, but I would tell you this, Mrs. —, I consider you a very fortunate person today . . . because in the absence of a recommendation . . . I probably would . . . impose some period of incarceration. So I think you have got a lot to be thankful for today. [suspended sentence, condition of probation to pay back money owed to employer]

The judge's remarks to Prish are a good example of situational sanctioning: sentence leniency was toughened with judicial sternness. By contrast, when jail time was imposed on the women: sentence harshness was tempered with positive remarks about the defendant's character.

Judicial justifications in sentencing women drew largely on retributive and special deterrence themes. General deterrence, incapacitation, and rehabilitation were less frequently invoked. Judicial justifications may combine several theories of punishment, used in equal measure or with varied emphasis. In justifying jail, the judges focused on harm-based themes, and where relevant, on the woman's record of previous arrests and convictions. In justifying suspended sentences, the judges also registered harm-based concerns: the harm was not serious enough to warrant incarceration, there was a way to repay the state or victim by restitution, and the defendant had already been punished enough for the offense. I expected to see more rehabilitation arguments for the women but did not find them.

The sentencings did not evince sexist or racist characterizations of women by court officials. To be sure, a woman's experience with the process may be different, and what court officials say outside the courtroom may be different. With the exception of Chris, who was described as childlike by her defense attorney, exemplary "paternalist"[13] comments were not evident, nor — with the exception of three women — was there much support for the evil woman thesis that officials will react more punitively when women not only deviate from expectable female conformity by committing a crime but when they commit a male-typed offense.

Three of the twenty-two women were described as being a danger to others (Edie, Flo, and Pat), and three women reflected evil woman themes (Edie, Flo, and Mary). For Edie and Flo, the judges focused on the danger the women posed to immediate family members and the women's transgressions of caretaking responsibilities. Although Mary's drug selling was not viewed as a danger to the community, her previous record and challenges to the judge suggested to him that she was unreformed and unrepentant.

My research in this court and two others (Daly 1987a, 1989a) leads me to suggest that the paternalism and evil woman concepts should be laid to rest. These concepts first appeared as claims without empirical support (for example, Nagel and Weitzman 1971; Reckless and Kay 1967; Simon 1975). No one has yet shown their explanatory merit.[14]

A more useful line of analysis is to explore the ways in which courtroom discourse reflects *gendered presuppositions* of crime and justice. Like Mary Eaton (1986), I find that one common presupposition is the domestic division of labor and the vaunted "good family woman." Unlike Eaton and other scholars who have conducted research on British courts (for example, Carlen 1983), I am not persuaded that surrounding women with familial and maternal imagery, at times in heroic terms, necessarily harms women. Eaton and others argue that such familial imagery restricts the range of possibilities for womanhood (excluding, for example, single women, those not in heterosexual couplings, and those without children). This argument may be right in the abstract, but it is less so in actual court practices — at least in United States courts, with which I am familiar. When there are good family women, their labor for others is affirmed. But women who are not considered to be good family women are not penalized for this status.[15] Such women are rendered deviant more by their previous and current lawbreaking and less so by how they care for children. The question of women's care for others and how it might be recognized in justice system decisions is important and contentious. I return to it in chapter 12. For now, I make this point: we should expect to find gendered presuppositions in courtroom discourse and actions, but we should *explore* whether such presuppositions harm or adversely affect some women. Although we know that gendered presuppositions harm women in some legal contexts (such as the victims in rape cases), we should not assume that they harm all (or even most) women in all contexts.

In addition to the domestic division of labor, I noted another set of presuppositions. Of women I could classify, half were viewed as reformable or as being more victimized than victimizing. Although court officials used rehabilitation arguments infrequently, they made more positive judgments about the women's *character* (table 9.3).[16] As I noted before, three women were viewed as a danger (Edie, Flo, and Pat), but three others were each described as *not* being a danger or as being more of a victim (Sharon, Jean, and Chris). And although for

Table 9.3 Judgments of the Women's Character*

	Jail	Nonjail	Total	% of 22
Hardened, unreformed, committed to the street life	7	0	7⎫	45
A danger to others	2	1	3⎭	
Not a danger; more of a victim	2	1	3⎫	41
Could be rehabilitated; reformable	1	5	6⎭	
Uncertain how to classify	1	2	3	14
Total	13	9	22	100

	Black	White	Latin
Hardened, unreformed, committed to the street life	3	2	2
A danger to others	2	1	0
Not a danger; more of a victim	2	1	0
Could be rehabilitated; reformable	5	1	0
Uncertain how to classify	0	1	2
Total	12	6	4

*See table IV.3 (part 4 summary) for judgments of character by pathway categories, which lists the defendants.

seven women their previous lawbreaking cast them as beyond the reach of reform (Nellie, Dorothy, Kate, Susan, Edith, Penny, and Mary), six others were viewed as reformable, and judges were optimistic they could change (Wendy, Kathleen, Pamela, June, Tara, and Lotty). (For three women — Prish, Miranda, and Claire — I could not determine what the officials' character assessments were, but the women were not viewed as a danger, and their previous lawbreaking was nonexistent or slim.)

Here, then, is an instance where some gendered presuppositions — of reformability and victimization — do not necessarily harm women, unless one wishes to argue that the optimism of officials toward some women is a patronizing gesture. As we would expect, the judgments of the women's character were related to their pathways to felony court (see table 2 in the summary for part 4). With one exception, street women were viewed as unreformable and hence deserving of jail time. Although most of the harmed and harming women were viewed as unreformable or a danger, two were cast as victims or as reformable. The potential for reform was often (but not always) linked to the women's previous lawbreaking. Reformability and victimization were as evident for black women as white (there were too few latin women in the sample to make a judgment). As we shall see in the next chapter, officials were far less optimistic that the men could change.

Notes

1. The potentially disastrous effects of a retired court stenographer's refusal to transcribe his notes were alleviated somewhat in that all offense types are represented in the surviving remarks (see app. 1 for discussion). I cannot claim that the surviving sentencing remarks are representative of the group of forty. I can say that they reflect an assortment of offenses and that along with other variables of interest (e.g., sentence outcome, pathway category, race and ethnicity), their distributions are similar to the forty cases. The impact of the missing data was apparent for one dimension of the sentencings, especially for the men: the surviving remarks contain fewer sentencings conducted by Judge Kinney, to whose courtroom the reluctant stenographer was normally assigned (cf. app. 1, n.1, with table 2.1).

2. During the research period, there were only two women prosecutors and one woman defense attorney who spoke with any frequency in the court — too few to be able to analyze gender differences, if any, in the legal arguments made by counsel.

3. Of the five women without agreed recommendations (Claire, Edie, Jean, Chris, and Pat), the sentences were reduced somewhat for two women (Jean and Chris) from what the judge had initially intended.

4. Niantic is the sole prison for women in Connecticut. It houses pretrial detainees and those sentenced to incarceration.

5. As described in a news clipping in the file, Kate and other people were drinking in her room at the YMCA at the time of the incident.

6. My findings for the men, however, do support Mileski's research, as I discuss in the next chapter.

7. See John Conley and William O'Barr (1987) for a review of different methods of studying judicial decision making. My analysis of the transcripts is similar to O'Barr and Conley (1985, 675–76) in that I focus on "naturally occurring institutional speech" but with "significantly larger units of data" and without attention to the details of conversational analysis. Because I was not present in the courtroom during these sentencings, my analysis is another step removed from the ethnographies of courtroom interaction or plea bargaining that use conversational analysis (Atkinson and Drew 1979; Maynard 1984).

8. In this regard, Walker (1991, 79) suggests that some "modern retributists" (such as von Hirsch and Duff) cannot themselves escape a utilitarian justification for retribution-based punishment: that it has a "beneficial effect" on people.

9. There was no agreed recommendation in Jean's case, but the judge had been thinking of a 3-year term of incarceration. On the day of sentencing, he reduced it to 2½ years so that Jean was sentenced to time served and would be released soon after the sentence was imposed.

10. It could be argued that the judge's concern with incarcerating the repeat offender reflects incapacitation elements, as well.

11. Reviews by Kee MacFarlane (1978) and Kelly (1991) suggest that men's sexual abuse of children more likely takes place in a family- or kin-based setting,

as do the relatively rare instances of women's sexual abuse. The "classic child sexual abuser" refers to a category largely populated by men.

12. Recall that Flo was one of only three women convicted of risk of injury during the five-year period. However rare, this is precisely the sort of case that the public and court workers will draw upon to buttress the claim that "women get a break" in the criminal courts.

13. By *paternalist* I mean a female paternalist or chivalry argument, which focuses on protecting women from the harshness of jail, trivializes a woman's lawbreaking, or views women as childlike.

14. Let me be clear on this point: I am not saying that comments about the need to protect women do not arise. Nor am I saying that perhaps, from time to time, some women will not be severely rebuked (although I remain puzzled about what constitutes "male-dominated" crime). I am saying that the paternalism and evil woman concepts are not especially useful in analyzing officials' reactions to women's deviance.

15. I am suggesting here that caring for others can serve to mitigate a sentence, but the absence of care does not aggravate a sentence.

16. Judgments of character and blameworthiness overlap in that the highly blameworthy defendants will not be viewed as having reform potential. However, the character judgment focuses more on expectations for the defendant's future behavior (e.g., that it will change or is modifiable).

10 Justifying the Punishment of Men

Sentencing remarks survive for twenty-six men with a good assortment of the major types of offenses. I analyzed the men's sentencings to describe their content and to see how judicial justifications were linked to theories of punishment.

Men's Sentencings and Gender Differences

As we saw for the women, there are few surprises for the men on the day of sentencing (table 10.1). More than 90 percent came to court with an agreed recommendation or a cap on the sentence (there were five caps). Six sentencings were characterized by defense attorney arguments to reduce the sentence: this group comprised three defendants with caps, two without an agreed recommendation, and one with an agreed recommendation.[1] Longer, more passionate remarks were made by the defense for five of these sentencings. There were five speed sentencings, and six where the time was largely spent on the judge's taking the defendant's guilty plea before sentencing (two of these were speed sentencings).

Eight men spoke to the judge. Most of them did not admit guilt or express remorse. In five cases, others spoke on each man's behalf. Most defense attorneys (two-thirds) offered some positive remarks about their client. In about one-third of the cases, a defendant's alcoholism or drug addiction was cited as his major problem. Few men (8 percent) were cast as victims or pawns in an offense. In a little more than half of the cases, the judge spoke directly to the man, typically castigating him for the wrongfulness of the act and its harm to the victims and the community. The judges were generally not optimistic about the men's future: only one-fifth had some hope that the men would change. Finally, just two-thirds of the judges offered a sentencing justification. Two judges (Martin McKeever and Joseph Purtill) did not normally offer a justification for punishment.

Several gender differences are evident in the sentencings. First, Judge Kinney was involved in fewer of the men's (27 percent) than the women's (55 percent) sentencings. That difference may explain the somewhat greater judicial lecturing of the women; certainly it played a role in the greater likelihood that a justification was offered in the women's sentencings. Second, a somewhat lower share of the women than men went into the sentencing proceeding with an agreed

Table 10.1   Features of the Sentencing Process for Men

	N = 26*	% of 26
Incarceration sentence? yes	16	61
Defendant detained during pretrial period? yes (12 were sentenced to incarceration)	14	54
A speed sentencing? yes	5	19
A plea and sentencing? yes (2 were speed sentencings)	6	23
Agreed recommendation or sentencing cap? yes	24	92
Defense attorney argued for less incarceration time or a suspended sentence? yes (3 were successful)	6	23
Remarks were long, passionate? yes	5	19
Defendant spoke on his behalf: yes If yes, did the defendant admit guilt? yes — 3	8	31
Others spoke on the defendant's behalf? yes	5	19
Defense attorney argued that the defendant had some positive qualities? yes	17	65
Drugs or alcohol were blamed for the defendant's problems? yes	9	35
Defendant was cast as a victim or a pawn in an incident instigated by a co-defendant? yes	2	8
Judge engaged in moralizing and lecturing to the defendant? yes	14	53

Type of moralizing (multiple responses)
General	13
"Your life has been a waste"	1
"Reflect on your life in prison"	1
"Kick your drug or alcohol addiction"	6

Sentencing judge

Kinney	7	Kinney	7	27
Hadden	5	Other judge	19	
McKeever	3			
Purtill	3			
Schaller	2			
Higgins	2			
Celotto, Fishman, Norcott, Testo (1 each)				

	N = 26*	% of 26
Judge was optimistic that the defendant could change, viewed the defendant in a positive light, or noted qualities suggesting the defendant was a "cut above the rest"? yes	5	19
Judge gave a justification for the punishment? yes	17	65
Those not giving justifications were McKeever (3), Purtill (2), Schaller (1), Fishman (1), Testo (1), and Kinney (1)		

*Based upon 26 sentencing transcripts of the 40 deep-sample men: 1 of 4 homicides, 7 of 8 assaults, all 3 cases of risk of injury, both arsons, 6 of 8 robberies, 4 of 7 larcenies, and 3 of 8 drug cases.

recommendation or cap (77 versus 92 percent). Thus, counsel representing the women were somewhat more likely to argue for less jail time or a suspended sentence, and the women's sentencings were somewhat more likely to have longer, passionate exchanges. Third, although drugs and alcohol were cited as the defendant's main problem for a higher proportion of women than men (50 versus 35 percent), the judges offered more optimistic and positive remarks toward the women than to the men (45 versus 19 percent). Finally, unlike the women, the men's sentencings confirmed Mileski's (1971) insight on situational sanctions. Judges were more likely to lecture to those male defendants receiving nonjail than jail sentences (70 versus 44 percent).

Judicial Silence

Mileski has provided examples of how defendants who did not receive incarceration were treated sternly or situationally sanctioned by the judges. Because the court she studied (the New Haven GA-6 court) disposed of misdemeanors and less serious felonies, a relatively low proportion of defendants there received jail sentences (14 percent) compared to those in the felony court (60 percent for the deep sample). In contrast to showing situational sanctions, giving examples of the absence of judicial commentary is challenging because silence is harder to represent.

Judges were silent on the men's transgressions in 35 percent of the sentencings, in contrast to 14 percent of the women's. Of the nine cases where the judges said nothing, two men were first-time offenders, three had a long history of previous lawbreaking, and four had one or two previous convictions. I turn to this last set of cases and focus on the sentencings of Wade, Enrico, and Antonio.

Risk-of-Injury Case 2, Wade

Wade had taken six children to a farm and during the day, tried to sexually abuse one of the girls. He also forced the children to drink beer and smoke cigarettes, and he drove in a reckless way to scare them. After the girl reported him, Wade threatened her. On the day of Wade's sentencing, no court official denounced his behavior or even suggested that it was wrong:

> **Prosecutor:** Mr. — entered a plea of guilty, and . . . there was an agreed recommended sentence placed on the record which was to be five years, suspended after two years with five years' probation and a special condition that the defendant have no contact with the victims in the incident. . . . The facts of the case involved the allegation of the defendant engaging in conduct which created a risk of injury to the morals of his niece, who was under the age of

16. . . . I would ask your Honor to accept the agreed recommendation.

Defense Attorney: My client gave very little information to the Probation Department. . . . Mr. — stands here today and is not pleased with the disposition. However, we are prepared to go forward.

[When asked by the judge whether he had anything to say, Wade replied:]

Wade: I only wish to ask that perhaps you could see fit to give me less probation. Because I feel that my future is now based in Connecticut. It will limit my [plans] as far as returning to school. . . . I really wanted unconditional probation, but they would not give it to me. I only ask you consider less than five years' probation.

Judge McKeever: The probation, I'm sure, can be transferred to wherever you desire to go. I would not consider anything less. If there is nothing further to be — would you look at me, please. If there is nothing further to be said by anyone, the sentence of the court is that you be committed to [sentenced to serve two years].

I wondered why no court official offered a negative word to Wade. Was it because they did not think the attempted sexual abuse was that serious? Or was no one else present at the sentencing (such as the mother of the victim or the victim herself)? Perhaps the officials saw no redeeming qualities in Wade and thought it a waste of time to talk about the wrongfulness of his act. This case may also have seemed routine, like many others that week, and Wade's actions seemed unremarkable. Mileski (1971, 530) suggests that courtroom encounters are routinized and that a judge's work is unceremonial, and thus, we should not expect judicial chastisement in cases like Wade's. Yet I cannot help thinking there is more to this silence than simply a giving up on offenders.[2]

Another example of judicial nonreaction was Enrico's plea and sentencing for arson. Enrico denied he had done anything wrong, but the evidence is strong that he set fire to some mattresses in the house where his girlfriend lived. Although no one was injured and there was no damage to the house, Enrico's arson was one of a series of violent acts toward his girlfriend. On the day of sentencing, Judge Purtill took Enrico's guilty plea, to which Enrico offered the following refrain to several queries: "I love my mother and grandmother." At the end of the plea process, the defense attorney asked Enrico, "You want to end the case now, is that right?" and Enrico replied yes. His attorney asked again, "You don't want to come back next week or next month?" and Enrico said no. The judge chimed in to be sure that Enrico wished to waive the PSI, saying, "Okay, you have a right to that and you are giving up that right; is that correct?" and Enrico replied yes. The judge then said, "All right. The court will then proceed to impose sentence in this matter." After imposing a one-year suspended sentence, Judge Purtill did not tell Enrico that his threatening behavior was unacceptable, nor did he warn Enrico to stay away from the victim.

Robbery Case 6, Antonio

A third case was Antonio's, who with two accomplices broke into a house where adults and children were present, demanding money and drugs. McKeever was again the sentencing judge:

> **Prosecutor:** [Although] he states he has cooperated [with the state] . . . his statement ended abruptly because all of a sudden he couldn't remember who the people were. . . . It is obviously a serious offense, entering into someone's home, especially with children present. Guns were used at that time. . . . I would ask your Honor to impose the sentence [cap].
>
> **Defense Attorney:** Mr. — deeply regrets his involvement in this affair. He blames all of his problems on his drug addiction. . . . He wishes to marry the mother of his children at the first possible time that it is available to him. . . . He has a job waiting for him. . . . Mr. —'s family is here. They're very supportive of him. They're very concerned about his being away from his family, and they have told me that they will assist him in helping to make sure that this never occurs again.

Judge McKeever asked Antonio whether he had anything to say, and Antonio said no. The judge replied: "That being the case — would you look at me, please. It is the sentence of the court . . . ," and the judge imposed a sentence of six years to serve.

Enrico denied that he had done wrong; Antonio believed the state did nothing to reward him for providing the names of his accomplices; and Wade refused to talk with the probation officer for the PSI. Wade told the probation officer, "[My] personal life is [my] own business," and he expressed displeasure with the plea agreement. Perhaps judges find it a waste of time to speak to defendants who neither admit guilt nor respect the legal system.

Larceny Case 6, Tyrone

Mileski (1971, 519) suggests that "the court takes relatively little care with its failures, more care with its newcomers." Yet even some first-timers in felony court were not rebuked by the judges, as the remarks in the plea and sentencing of 17-year old Tyrone show. Tyrone pled to a fifth-degree larceny; the evidence reveals that he acted as a lookout in a street robbery of a woman late one night:

Prosecutor: At about 1 A.M. [the female victim] exited her automobile and was confronted by a youth who asked her for money. He produced a knife, took $7, and then ripped a gold chain off her neck, which was apparently valued at over $250. [When] he did this, two other youths were across the street. [The victim] identified Tyrone as one of the youths.

After accepting the plea, the judge immediately sentenced Tyrone: "The court will accept the plea negotiated and agreed upon sentence and will [sentence you to a six-month suspended sentence]." No discussion followed the sentencing except a remark by Tyrone's attorney to the judge that Tyrone and his mother planned to "go down to probation" the next week [so that Tyrone] could "sign in with the Probation Department." I wondered why the judge did not use the occasion to caution Tyrone about his future behavior.

Larceny Case 2, Roger

It is easier to understand why judges said little to men like Roger, Lennie, and Casey, men who had heavy prior records. On the day Roger was sentenced for a first-degree larceny, he was already serving a three-year sentence for other larceny and forgery convictions. Both the prosecutor and the defense attorney noted weaknesses in the state's case against Roger, and because of these evidentiary problems, the agreed sentence was one year on top of Roger's current sentence. Except to note that in light of Roger's previous criminal record, "the state would be seeking a lot greater time," there was little opprobrium levied against Roger's lawbreaking (he had burglarized a residence and then attempted to fence the stolen items). The judge's reaction:

Judge Fishman: The court has listened to counsel, and I have read the presentence report. So the court has the background of the accused fairly well in mind, and I'm satisfied that the indication that the court gave pertaining to sentence was appropriate, taking into consideration all the factors that have been brought to my attention. Therefore, the court sentences the accused to [one year, to be served consecutively with another sentence].

Roger's sentencing remarks were among the shortest, and his prior record was the longest of all the deep-sample men.

Lennie's previous lawbreaking was also substantial. On the day Lennie was sentenced in felony court for stealing a car, he was sentenced in another court to serve 6½ years for "a variety of charges" (burglaries, selling drugs, and a purse snatch). Lennie's cooperation with the police in identifying others led the state to agree to a one-year sentence on the motor vehicle theft to be served concurrently with the 6½-year term already imposed. Beyond the sentencing agreement and its rationale, none of the court officials had much to say. Lennie's attorney suggested that "the court go along with the agreement. I have nothing further to add at this point." When Judge Kinney asked Lennie whether he had anything to say, Lennie said no, after which the judge imposed one year to serve, concurrent with another sentence, without further comment.

Robbery Case 1, Casey

Casey is a third seasoned lawbreaker who received no judicial remonstrance. He committed a robbery in which he knocked down a store clerk and took $55 from the register. At least the prosecutor and defense attorney acknowledged that Casey had caused harm and had done something wrong:

> **Prosecutor:** As far as physical injuries to the victim, she received a contusion to the neck and a cervical sprain, but . . . the psychological damage was a lot more severe. This is by far the most serious crime [he has committed], and he deserves every minute of the ten years. . . .
>
> **Defense Attorney:** This is the first time [Casey] has been in court on any type of offense involving personal injury to anyone, and he attributes that to his use of crack, which is known to cause aggression[3] and is highly addictive. He stated frankly he did a lot of things that he wasn't proud of. . . . Although he didn't recall the offense in detail . . . he is remorseful. He felt he was hurting people, and he needed help.

Judge McKeever asked Casey whether he had anything to say, to which Casey said, "No, sir." The judge said, "It is then the sentence of the court that you be [sentenced to serve ten years]," without offering further remarks or reflections on the case.

Courtroom Drama

Five of the men's sentencings were poignant and passionate, and in all of them, other people spoke on the defendant's behalf. Recall that Judge Kinney was uncharacteristically angry toward Mary, who tried to postpone the start of serving a jail sentence so that she could be eased off methadone. He displayed the same behavior in sentencing Andrew, the young man who had assaulted two police officers and said he was acting to defend his friend. But this time, Judge Kinney directed his anger to Andrew's attorney. Although I cannot be sure, I wondered whether this attorney nettled the judge because he was Mary's attorney as well.

Andrew was an exemplary student in high school, and his attorney planned to have several witnesses speak to Andrew's good character on the day of sentencing. Less than a week before, the sentencing date was moved to a day earlier, and thus, the defense attorney argued for a continuance to a day when his witnesses could appear. Early in the sentencing, the attorney ran into trouble when he suggested that another judge could handle the sentencing if Judge Kinney was obliged to be absent. The judge's reply was uncompromising: "I'll impose sentence, Mr.—. No one else. Me." The judge continued, "I certainly would listen to these distinguished people, [but] the likelihood of their influencing a decision with respect to sentencing, it just does not exist."

The dauntless attorney tried a different tack. In describing the incident, he suggested that the police officers' injuries were not as serious as they said they were. Judge Kinney exploded: "Now for you to stand there and try to minimize the injuries that Detective — received . . . is the most foolhardy of sentencing arguments I have heard here in a long time. [If y]ou want to persist, go ahead." The attorney continued, "I'm trying to say that I don't think the injuries can be classified as extremely serious. This is the argument I'm trying to make." The judge replied: "I fully understand the argument you are trying to make. I'm still amazed, but I fully understand it." Just before the judge sentenced Andrew to a term of four years to serve, he said, "Andrew, all I can say to you is for a few moments, you have ruined probably the best years of your life — your youth." To which Andrew asked, "Why did you say that?" The judge answered, "Because you are going to spend it incarcerated, and it is unfortunate."

Homicide Case 1, Barry

Barry's sentencing was poignant in that his mother and other family members had forgiven him for beating his uncle to death, but the prosecutor and judge were not as forgiving. The prosecutor opened with an observation:

> **Prosecutor:** This was extreme indifference to human life. . . . This is not a case where you mix alcohol with a small argument and things get out of control. . . . This was a little bit more. . . . To put it quite bluntly, he beat his uncle to death.

Barry's defense attorney spoke at length about Barry's youth, his lack of resources, his placement in special education classes, his having to move from his mother's home because she was denied housing support, and his love-hate relationship with his uncle, for whom he would care when the man collapsed from drinking binges. At the time of the fatal beating, Barry and his uncle shared a room in a rooming house, and Barry came home to find his uncle passed out on the corridor floor. Barry's welfare department caseworker spoke on his behalf: "I would see him on the street, and he was always very considerate and cordial to me. . . . He never made a ruckus. . . . He appeared to be a gentleman." This poignant tale of Barry's circumstances did not move the judge, who argued that despite Barry's youth and "handicaps he operates under . . . society demands substantial incarceration when someone takes another's life." He sentenced Barry to ten years.

Sentencing Justifications and Theories of Punishment

Justifying Jail

Retribution was the most frequently invoked justification, coupled with special deterrence themes and less frequently with general deterrence and incapacitation (table 10.2).[4] For the relatively fewer cases that drew upon special deterrence themes alone, the sentence was based on the defendant's previous lawbreaking, not the immediate harm. I turn to these cases first.

Special Deterrence

Assault Case 7, Clarence

Clarence entered the house of the male victim one evening, beat him with a bottle, and stole his car keys and car. The facts of the case were in dispute because the victim later reported that Clarence was probably not the man who assaulted him. The prosecutor described Clarence as having an "extensive record . . . including eight misdemeanor convictions — all with suspended sentences" and noted that Clarence "apparently has a drinking problem." Clarence's attorney pointed out that the victim had changed his mind about who the offender was and then described Clarence's background:

> **Defense attorney:** Mr. — is a product of a deprived family background. His mother is a chronic alcoholic. At . . . 12 he was placed in a children's center and then at a training school . . . for six years. He was denied during his formative teen years the benefit of any role model, either father or mother. . . . He wants to be a more solid person, a more responsible citizen.

The defense attorney then argued for a reduction in the agreed recommendation from twenty months to one year to serve. She introduced a minister who worked with incarcerated men to help rehabilitate them. "I believe in the grace that is given to us. And I believe that something wonderful can happen from it," the minister said. And in a exchange with the judge, who asked, "Do you feel convinced that [Clarence] is sincere in what he says to you?" the minister replied, "I feel something very genuine is moving in his life."

Table 10.2 Justifying Punishment for Men

	Received an Incarceration Sentence		Total in the Transcript Analysis
	Yes	No	
Violence	9	4	13
Robbery	4	2	6
Larceny	2	2	4
Drugs	1	2	3

Justifying incarceration: Of the 16 men sentenced to serve time, the types of justifications used were as follows:

[No justification given, but inferred retribution and special deterrence (Casey, Antonio); special deterrence alone (Lennie, Roger, Simon, Wade) 6]	
Retribution focus or coupled with special deterrence, general deterrence, incapacitation, and/or rehabilitation (Andrew, Barry, Jack, Lester, Maurice, Ralph, Ron)	7
Special deterrence, focus on prior record (Wayne, Rennie), or "need to be stopped cold" (Clarence)	3

Justifying nonincarceration: Of the 10 men who received suspended sentences, the types of justification used were as follows:

(No justification given, but inferred retribution a: not serious harm [Enrico, Tyrone]; retribution b: restitution [Larry] 3)	
Retribution a: minor harm, minor role (Richie, Shane); retribution b: restitution (Scott)	3
Retribution and special deterrence (Carlos, Georges)	2
Other, state reason (evidentiary problems) (Carl, Charles)	2

To surround Clarence with greater rehabilitative potential, his attorney said, "One thing I forgot to mention . . . Clarence plans to marry in the near future when he is released. [This woman] . . . is a strong force in his life, something to anchor his better qualities." In sentencing Clarence, the judge said that although Clarence's previous lawbreaking was "not the most serious, I would have to conclude that you have got to be stopped cold so that this pattern does not continue":

> **Judge Higgins:** Maybe if someone had stopped you earlier cold, given you a turn in jail, it might not have gone on. But you see, judges have a lot of hope for many people that come before them that rehabilitation can work. I think you have some positive things in your life. . . . I have to express the hope on behalf of society

that you have learned the lesson that has got to be learned by you. There are people who are willing to help you, but they cannot do the job for you. . . . The only one that is going to do it, bottom line, is Clarence. But if he does not make that personal commitment, all the rest of the actions by all the good people who want to help are for naught.

Clarence interjected, saying "I am securing my G.E.D. and when I get out, I want to go to college. I am going to make plans." Judge Higgins sentenced Clarence to one year to serve. After imposing sentence, the judge said to Clarence, "Rehabilitation is only effective when it is wanted by the person who is undergoing the program," and reminded him, "If you come back in here again, a judge [won't] have any difficulty in rationalizing a long term in prison." The sentencing ended on a positive note with the judge saying, "One of the reasons I reduced the time from 20 months to 12 months [is that] I have hope for you." The judge's logic was that Clarence needed a short period in jail to be "stopped cold," and perhaps then he would start to lead a more law-abiding life. The local minister and Clarence's future wife stood as informal social control sentinels, whom the judge hoped would keep Clarence out of trouble.

Drug Case 7, Rennie

Compared to Clarence, whose previous lawbreaking was described as "not the most serious," Rennie's and Wayne's prior records were more extensive. At their sentencings, little was said about their convicted offense. Rennie, who was convicted of selling narcotics, had three previous felony convictions. The prosecutor noted that "[drug] treatment is not a viable alternative for [him], and he has reached the point where a lengthy period of incarceration is the only answer." Rennie's attorney attempted to put Rennie's lawbreaking in a more sympathetic light by suggesting that after he "couldn't pass the test" to get into the marines, "he became heavily addicted to drugs and that seems to be his downfall." Further, the defense attorney suggested hopefully, "I noticed that he is becoming of age, close to 34, that they say is a time when most people . . . eventually will kick the habit." The judge's remarks were brief but clear:

Judge Celotto: All right. You have a drug habit, or you had one. I don't know that you beat it yet, but you're beginning to have some time in prison. And I hope that it [drugs] is not available there, and I hope that is going to be a help to you in getting rid of that problem. [sentenced to serve five years]

Rennie's five-year jail sentence for selling drugs was longer than others. The sentence reflected his previous record and parole status, not the offense harm itself.

Arson Case 2, Wayne

Wayne set fire to his girlfriend's apartment, causing extensive damage. The prosecutor gave some attention to Wayne's continuing threats on the victim's life and to the economic loss suffered by the insurance company. She also emphasized Wayne's "lengthy criminal record. . . . he really hasn't had any steady jobs. He hasn't made any significant contribution to the community. . . . Mr. — has demonstrated that he has no regard for human life or property and that his past record . . . merits absolutely no consideration by the court." Wayne's attorney briefly touched on the seriousness of the harm: "[He] was involved in a crime that's one of the most serious . . . we can think of and has a tremendous potential for loss of human life in addition to property damage." The thrust of the defense attorney's remarks was on Wayne's potential for employment when released from jail and his regular attendance at Alcoholics Anonymous and Narcotics Anonymous programs while being held pending trial. Special deterrence themes predominated in the judge's remarks, with passing reference to incapacitation and retribution:

> **Judge Hadden:** Mr. —'s past history is apparently sprinkled with substance abuse, alcohol and/or drugs. He has got to realize that the law does not recognize that as an excuse or a justification for criminal conduct. Whether he'll continue in prison to avail himself of [drug counseling programs] is entirely up to him. . . . If he can accept and accomplish some of those things that prison terms are . . . intended to accomplish — that is, deter him from committing further crimes and . . . encourage him to undertake a course of treatment, self-re-evaluation, and self-improvement because it isn't going to be any therapist talking to him that's going to cure him or is going to change the course of his life. Wayne is the only one that's going to change the course of Wayne's life, and whatever we do here now has been with the hope that this will be an assist to him as well as to serve society's demand for punishment for a crime committed.

Judge Hadden started with a rationale that mixed special deterrence and incapacitation: "to deter him from committing further crimes." He then emphasized special deterrence ("to encourage him to undertake a course of treatment," with a jail term being "an assist to him"). The judge concluded on a retributive note, "to serve society's demand for punishment for a crime committed." All the court officials, and especially the judge, focused on Wayne's drug addiction and previous lawbreaking, revealing a concern to punish the actor and less the act.

Retribution

Prosecutors and judges more often focused on the extent of physical injury or psychological harm caused by the defendant's act. Although the harm was emphasized, it was placed in the context of a defendant's previous lawbreaking, his positive qualities, or the halo of girlfriends, female kin, or other social controls surrounding him. Therefore, most of the sentencings that drew on retribution also contained special deterrence themes. The sentencing remarks for Barry, Lester, Maurice, and Ralph illustrate how harm-based justifications can be expanded or contracted depending on qualities of the individual.

I have already presented one segment of Barry's sentencing. Here I excerpt another in which the prosecutor and judge highlight the victim's injury. An effective way to dramatize a victim's injury is by showing a photograph of the victim, which the prosecutor did at Barry's sentencing. The judge was clearly affected:

Homicide Case 1, Barry

> **Judge Hadden:** There isn't any question but that he beat his uncle to death. It is as simple as that. The picture shows the results of the beating. Why he did it I don't know. . . . But the evidence was clear he did do it — he has taken a life. And he has a steady prior record. . . . I recognize that he is relatively young, and that is something one has to take into consideration . . . but I think he has to do substantial time in prison for what he did here.

Assault Case 2, Lester

Similarly, in sentencing Lester, who slashed at his victim's face, causing a permanent scar, the prosecutor and judge focused on the victim's physical injury. Oddly, however, at another point in the sentencing, the prosecutor said that the moderately lenient sentence (three years to serve) was "based on the lack of serious physical injury in this assault."[5] The prosecutor described Lester's harm as a "kind of ridiculous and senseless incident," attributing it to Lester's "lack of insight." The defense attorney picked up on the theme of Lester's "very limited intellectual capacity" and "alcohol problem." She held out some hope that Lester would "get a hold of the alcohol problem" and saw "a significant bright spot for him: his girlfriend . . . [who] provides some guidance . . . and, more importantly, insight." In sentencing Lester, Judge Kinney cited his many negative qualities: "It would be difficult for anybody to call you a good citizen or a person that makes a worthwhile contribution to society. . . . You're not employed. . . . You abuse alcohol regularly. You are not doing much to make a mark in the world for yourself except hurting other people." The judge then focused on the assault and lectured Lester on changing his life:

> **Judge Kinney:** This was a serious incident. There's absolutely no excuse for reacting like this to someone refusing your request for money. This man's been left with a serious permanent scar. . . . Clearly this is an offense that requires a significant period of incarceration. And based on your prior record, there's nothing that I see that would mitigate [your] sentence. Maybe [your defense attorney] is right that there's some future for you when you're released, that this girlfriend can do something to help. But basically, Mr. —, you've got to help yourself, and that requires that you do something to address your alcohol problem. . . . If you want to spend the rest of your life [in prison], then continue what you've been doing for the past few years. If you want to do something different with your life, it's up to you to make an effort to do it. [sentenced to serve three years]

Compared to the sentences of Barry and Lester, those of Maurice and Ralph reflected a more positive evaluation of their background and character, coupled with retributive themes.

Assault Case 3, Maurice

Maurice pled guilty to shooting a man he knew in the stomach, requiring the victim to be hospitalized for five days. The victim had beat up Maurice the week before. The prosecutor's remarks downgraded the seriousness of Maurice's harm in a novel way. He expressed surprise that a man in his twenties, who lived in New Haven "in the area he does," had never been arrested before:

> **Prosecutor:** [As to] the defendant's background . . . the thing that jumps out . . . is the fact that the defendant is 23 years old and has no previous arrest record at all. And obviously that was a strong consideration in my reaching this plea bargain. I think for somebody to live in New Haven as long as he has, in the area he does, without accumulating any record certainly has to go to his credit. However, the problem is that he did arm himself with a gun. . . . He almost killed the victim. . . . [The victim] does have a record, but not serious.

The defense attorney picked up on the prosecutor's positive judgment of Maurice by noting his graduation from vocational technical school and attendance at a community college for two years. "He has no prior involvement whatsoever with the law — a spotless record up until this incident." He concluded that "it [was] an uncharacteristic act on the part of my client. . . . It will not be repeated."

In justifying a sentence of two years to serve and $5,000 as partial restitution for the victim's injuries, Judge Hadden began by noting the harm itself. He then considered how the harm was mitigated by Maurice's lack of a prior record:

> **Judge Hadden:** What Mr. — did, under any circumstances, calls for a period of incarceration. The [length of] incarceration depends on other factors. One of the primary factors is his prior record and his background. And other than this incident, he has a good record. And I recognize that there was some provocation. . . . When I take into consideration his good record and the fact that he had some provocation . . . I think . . . the agreed recommendation is . . . reasonable. If it were not for his good record . . . we would be talking about two or three times the amount of time that he is going to receive.

Risk-of-Injury Case 3, Ralph

Ralph's sentencing reveals the same judicial logic seen in Maurice's: the harm must be punished by serving some time, but the length of incarceration is based on other elements of the defendant's character, previous lawbreaking, and potential for reform. Ralph had repeated sexual contact and intercourse with his stepdaughter from the time she was 11 to 15 years old. He was especially contrite at sentencing — more than any other man for whom sentencing remarks survive. Although a sentencing cap had been set for two years to serve, his defense attorney argued that one year was sufficient. Ralph's attorney described his client as "very distraught, very shameful, very guilt-ridden, very depressed, aware of the gravity of what he had done" from "the first day Mr.— walked into my office." He continued:

> **Defense attorney:** Other than this particular regressive behavior, he has not only been a hard worker but a very gentle, nice man. . . . He and his wife have both worked hard to keep the marriage together. . . . She is here today. . . . They are looking to the future. He did grow up in a rather emotionally deprived background with his parents battling all the time and not holding out much love to him. He is very contrite. . . . He has been very depressed. . . . He has gone through immense pain. I have seen that and his shame as to not only what he has done to his stepdaughter but the rest of his family.

Ralph was apologetic and remorseful in court, saying: "I realize a grave injustice that I have brought upon my family. The pain and the anguish. I wish this would never happen again. I feel that it won't. . . . I realize that I have caused everyone a great deal of trouble."

Judge Kinney's remarks focused first on the need to impose a jail sentence for the harm, and then on his justification for the sentence length:

Judge Kinney: This is a difficult case. Not . . . in terms . . . of whether or not incarceration is called for because that is not a problem for the court. Length of incarceration is more of a problem.

This activity involved extensive and serious sexual contact over a long period of time. . . . This young lady has probably experienced some significant harm. It is [not] unusual to see somewhat ambivalent attitudes expressed by victims of offenses like this. They want vindication and punishment. On the other hand, they have some sympathy for the defendant. Almost invariably this is the kind of offense that the court sees committed by people who are sick or at least emotionally disturbed.

It is important . . . to the victim's recovery . . . that some type of incarceration is imposed. I think it is also important . . . that the values that society traditionally espouses . . . be vindicated by an incarceration sentence. It goes without saying that this is the kind of conduct that is universally condemned. It is morally reprehensible conduct. . . .

I think [the defendant] is remorseful, and he should be, of course. I don't think Mr. — is beyond rehabilitation, and I expect . . . that there will never probably be a repetition of this kind of conduct in the future. . . . I recognize the impact that an incarceration sentence will have on the defendant's family. . . . [Except] for this kind of activity, the defendant has lived an otherwise decent law-abiding life, supported his family, has been regularly employed, and all of this is to his credit.

. . . Frankly, the court intended as it came out on the bench this morning to impose the [cap], two years' incarceration. I have changed my mind. What [the defense attorney] suggests to the court is reasonable and . . . accomplishes the ends of justice. [sentenced to serve one year]

Ralph's sentencing was one of three in which judges imposed less jail time based on information they received on the day of sentencing. Ralph's attorney was persuasive in his argument to the judge, Ralph admitted his guilt and expressed remorse, and the judge saw potential for Ralph's reform from both his admission of responsibility and having the support of a loyal wife. In Ralph's case, as in others where girlfriends or future wives were mentioned, the women are typically assumed to be positive forces for the men's reformation. Consider, in contrast, the women defendants, whose boyfriends or husbands were assumed to be negative forces, leading them toward lawbreaking.

Celebrated Cases

Two men's sentencings were especially dramatic and memorable: Andrew's and Jack's. Andrew's assault of two police officers elicited judicial concerns for retribution, general deterrence, and special deterrence.

Assault Case 4, Andrew

> **Judge Kinney:** This assault . . . is an absolutely vicious, unjustified, inexcusable assault. . . . There is absolutely no justification for brutal assaults of this nature. If I thought this was planned or calculated in any way, I would be sitting here imposing a sentence of 10 years on Andrew, not 4 years. I am satisfied that it happened on the spur of the moment without any planning, but that does not excuse it. . . .
>
> I understand that Andrew has a good background. . . . He did reasonably well in school, other people think highly of him, he has not been in difficulty before. I understand all that. And all of those things were taken into consideration by me when I decided what period of incarceration was appropriate. If Andrew had a prior record, if he were not the kind of young man that stands before me today, he would be getting a substantially greater sentence than he is.
>
> But this was a vicious assault. I have an obligation to punish that kind of assault. To give notice to Andrew, to give notice to other people that we're not going to tolerate this kind of conduct on our streets. [sentenced to serve four years]

Andrew's was the only man's sentencing that evinced a clear general deterrence theme ("to give notice to other people that we're not going to tolerate this . . . conduct"). As in several other cases (such as Maurice's and Ralph's), although the judge was convinced that incarceration was deserved, the length of time was based partly on the nature of the harm ("impulsive type reaction, not planned or calculated") and partly on Andrew's prior record and social history ("a good background, other people think highly of him, not been in difficulty before"). Andrew's case was sensitive and celebrated because respected members of the community came to speak on his behalf, his behavior seemed out of character in light of his performance in school, and his reason for assaulting the police officer was that he believed the police were assaulting his friend.

Risk-of-Injury Case 1, Jack

Jack was the only defendant in the deep sample to have been convicted at trial. He was described by the prosecutor as "a poor excuse for a human being . . . a coward . . . a dangerous person." Jack beat five-year-old Floyd unconscious using a coat hanger and an electric cord. The prosecutor described *his* reaction to Jack's beating and tried to imagine Floyd's:

> **Prosecutor:** The crime is an absolutely terrible one. The image of this little child hiding under a chair as this man pursued him with various weapons to beat him is a very haunting one. . . . I don't have to go into the details about the crime. It is absolutely terrible. . . . The . . . injuries were horrible. I have been . . . a prosecutor for almost a dozen years, and there were only a few types of crimes which actually make you physically ill. And this case is that type. It just makes you sick to your stomach.

The prosecutor suggested that the "purpose of our laws is to protect and to punish, and there is no group . . . that deserves more protection than children." Further, he argued, "Every day that this man is in jail, the world is a better place." The themes of retribution and incapacitation were echoed by the judge. The defense attorney tried to suggest that proof of Jack's abuse of Floyd was circumstantial and that Jack "remained consistent in his denial of the beating of Floyd." Jack maintained his innocence on sentencing day, saying to the judge:

> **Jack:** Your Honor, I'm not guilty of the charge I have been found guilty of. I know there is nothing to do now. And like at first, I was offered 6 years suspended after 2, but . . . I did not do the crime. I would have took [the sentence bargain] and kept my life [from] being spent in prison for a long period of time. . . . But . . . the jury did not want to hear it. I'm not guilty, your Honor. So, that is all that I have to say.

The circumstances surrounding Floyd's abuse are cloudy and uncertain: it is likely that Jack and his wife had harmed Floyd in the past, and for that reason the judge said he "shared [with Jack's attorney] the anxiety about Floyd's welfare in the future. . . . Certainly the mother . . . has been far from a responsible, dutiful parent." It is difficult to determine whether Jack's denial had some merit or whether he had no moral compass.

At sentencing, Judge Schaller emphasized retribution and incapacitation:

> **Judge Schaller:** I take into account that the victim . . . is a 5-year-old child, who is certainly helpless. . . . And the court takes into account . . . that Jack . . . appears to be a person from whom the

community deserves a maximum of protection. His inability to function normally and his propensity for violence causes [us] to prevent a recurrence of similar behavior — to isolate him for as long as possible.

. . . A slightly ameliorating [factor] . . . is that many of his actions have been more the result of total lack of control as a person as opposed to a deliberate malice. . . . I frankly can't find any other redeeming feature in his history. . . . The court feels that the sentencing goals to be served here are punishment and isolation of Mr. —. . . . I see . . . no real hope that anything . . . is likely to happen that will reduce his dangerousness to other people, given situations in which he is under some stress or out of control. . . . I think . . . there is a great likelihood it would happen again. [sentenced to serve seventeen years]

Judge Schaller's clarity in his sentencing goals for Jack, "punishment and isolation," suggests that sentencing principles can be clear and certain. In most cases, however, theories of punishment cannot be so precise because neither the harm nor the person can be uniformly marked evil or horrible, on the one hand, or reformable or treatable on the other.

Justifying Nonjail

Of the ten men who received suspended sentences, evidentiary problems were noted for three. In four, the offenses were considered less serious; in two, the defendant was a victim or pawn in an incident instigated by others; in one, restitution was granted. In three sentencings, a man's good record was explicitly mentioned to justify a suspended sentence. Judges and prosecutors drew from such harm-based offense elements as degree of injury, making restitution to the victim, the small quantities of drugs seized, or insufficient evidence to prove a more serious charge. These elements were grafted onto a future bet that the man would stay out of trouble.

Assault Case 6, Shane

In the cases in which a defendant acted largely to defend himself (Shane) or was a pawn in a crime instigated by another man (Richie), judges found it easiest to justify a nonjail sentence. Shane shot at a group of gang members after school one day, injuring one in the arm. The prosecutor noted that Shane "had no prior record . . . was a model student in school . . . and apparently impressed the probation officer as a well-mannered, soft-spoken young man." Further, he suggested, "I don't think we are going to see him again." The defense attorney echoed the prosecutor's positive judgment, and the judge agreed:

> **Judge Purtill:** My comments would be no different from those . . . of the state's attorney and defense counsel. I think the young man was placed in a situation where he felt . . . he had to do something to protect himself. The difficulty is . . . when you take up a firearm, you run the risk of killing people. And fortunately here, no one was injured.[6] . . . It would appear that this young man is not going to be in any type of trouble again. He has a fine record, and I think that the [agreed recommendation] is proper. [sentenced to three years suspended]

Robbery Case 4, Richie

Richie drove the getaway car in a robbery, which he said he had no idea his friend was going to commit. Richie's attorney stressed that "[my client] has consistently denied knowing he was going to rob the [store] on the night in question." He pointed out that Richie "recently got engaged . . . and they plan to marry within the year," that Richie "has a pretty good work record," and that "he is the first to agree that being [with the co-defendant] was a dumb thing." In imposing the sentence, the judge stressed that under normal conditions, Richie would have received some jail time:

> **Judge Kinney:** This is an unusual disposition . . . and the fact you're getting a suspended sentence reflects some reservations [by] the state about the credibility of [the co-defendant]. For two years [while you are on probation] . . . you're going to have a substantial period of time hanging over your head. Make sure you abide by all the conditions of probation and you won't have any difficulty. . . . Stick to your business and your forthcoming marriage, and you'll be better for it. [sentenced to two years and eleven months suspended]

Although court officials used retributive themes, it was also apparent in Shane's and Richie's cases that they assumed the men would stay out of trouble.

Assault Case 5, Georges

Another man whose future was viewed positively was Georges. I suspect that because Georges's violence was aimed at his wife (now his former wife) and because there were no physical injuries, court officials found it easier to excuse him. Moreover, others spoke on Georges's behalf at sentencing (female kin and a friend), and this support helped make him seem less dangerous. Although Georges fired a gun at his wife and daughter while they drove away, the prosecutor minimized the danger by suggesting that Georges was "obviously having marital problems" and that the incident came about because of "the divorce proceedings or pressures brought on by that and also the alcohol problem."

The defense attorney focused on Georges's lack of prior arrests, his steady employment for more than ten years, and the "problems with his marriage, partly related to alcohol and . . . to his wife's alleged infidelity." He stressed that "[Georges] is not a threat to society. He's no longer a threat to his former wife. He's very scared and frightened that he may be subjected to imprisonment." Further, he took exception to a psychologist's characterization of Georges as a "walking time bomb." Georges's daughter-in-law spoke highly of Georges, who babysat for her child: "He's so much better when he has children around him and his family around him. He stays out of trouble." Georges's friend said about his drinking problem: "He's doing real good now. And he doesn't drink when he babysits for the kids. . . . Like I said, I trust him with my kids."

Georges explained that he and his daughter were on good terms, and he was sorry for what he did: "My daughter, she got nothing else against me. She's not mad at me because I did that. I feel very sorry for what happened. I don't know why I did that. I can't remember what I did that for. It was stupid." The judge's comments reflect a denial — apparent throughout the sentencing — that Georges's wife was the target of his gunfire. Female kin and friends emphasized how well Georges got along with children and his daughter. Forgotten was Georges's targeted violence toward his wife. The judge began his sentencing by expressing concern that Georges's shooting was wrong *largely because* he might have hurt his daughter:

Judge Hadden: I think it's come across to you the serious nature of what you did. . . . You may have had a problem with your wife at the time, but you didn't have with your daughter, and she could have been hit just as easily as your wife.

. . . Fortunately no one was hit, nobody was hurt. And I have to take into consideration that you're . . . a man who has never been in any trouble in your life. And you made one reckless, foolish mistake after you had been drinking. . . . It's apparent . . . that you're a hardworking fellow. . . . You were working far beyond the hours one ordinarily would [just before] the incident. You were under some emotional distress because of the breakup of your marriage, and this is what happened. . . .

[As to] the psychological evaluation . . . based on what's been stated here, it seems that's behind you. I hope it is. And you're going to stay away from your wife insofar as that's possible.

After the judge imposed a suspended sentence, he said to Georges, "Good luck — I'm sure you won't be back." In reading Georges's file, I could not share the judge's optimism.

Big Break Cases
Two sentencings were noteworthy in that the judges believed that the men should have received jail time. In Charles's case, there was insufficient proof, and in Scott's, the prosecutor admitted the deal was cut because the prior records of Scott and his accomplices were minimal.

Robbery Case 7, Charles
Charles and an accomplice held up a woman in a parking lot, demanding that she give them her purse. An hour later they attempted to cash a check with the victim's checkbook. Charles said he *found* the checkbook and did not rob the woman. The prosecutor opened by saying, "There were a number of problems of proof in this case which explains the rather lenient disposition." The defense attorney was brief, citing Charles's "caring family . . . meaningful job, and [no] prior involvement with the law." The judge's commentary was brief but harsh:

> **Judge Hadden** [asking the defendant]: Were you here for the sentencing of K — a little while ago? That's what should be happening to you. Do you understand that?
> **Charles:** Yeah.
> **Judge Hadden:** That's where you should be going right now, right through there and down the elevator [pointing to the room holding those in lockup]. Fortunately for you the state recognizes some difficulty in proving the case against you. But we know and you know and I know exactly what you did, and what you did calls for you to go to prison.
>
> But you're getting one big break here, and you better take advantage of it, Mr. — because the next time you come through here you won't be going out those doors [the regular exit door] when you're finished. You will be going through the other door. [five-year suspended sentence, $1,000 fine]

This is a perfect example of situational sanctioning: when a defendant gets a "big break" with a suspended sentence, the judge is verbally tougher.

Larceny Case 1, Scott
The three men who tried to steal oil from a New Haven public school were also subject to situational sanctioning and judicial wrath. Scott, the man in my sample, owned the oil truck; Herb helped load the oil,

and Lee gained access to the oil because he was the school custodian. The prosecutor stated the reasons "we're not asking for time: none of the defendants has any significant prior record . . . and there was not an extremely large quantity of oil involved." The defendants could pay large fines and contributions to charitable organizations; and these amounts covered the value of oil missing. Scott had to turn his oil truck over to the city. The judge's response made it a memorable sentencing:

> **Judge Norcott:** The only consideration for recommendation for a nonincarceration sentence is [their] minimal records. Isn't that true? . . .
>
> Because as far as I'm concerned, this is particularly odious, stealing from a school. It's bad enough to go around and steal from private individuals, but schools are the heart and blood of a city, and that heart and blood are paid for by taxes of individuals. My taxes. I live in New Haven. And it seems to me to be pretty cowardly and a pretty low thing to do, to hit a school. . . . It can only be premised on greed. If you had any kind of criminal records, it seems to me [incarceration is warranted]. . . . Quite frankly, it annoys me. My feeling [is] . . . if there were any kind of reasoning for you to go to jail, you should.

To Lee, the custodian, the judge was especially harsh:

> **Judge:** Your case is a bit different [because] you worked for the City, and that involves a certain feeling of trust. . . . If I stole from the Judicial Department, I would think they would throw me in jail for violating a trust. There's no excuse for that. I think it's a gift of God you're not going to jail, sir.

Judgments of Character

In classifying the judgments of officials of the men's character, I needed to add another category, which I called troublemakers (table 10.3). The seven men in this category were neither unreformed or hardened, nor were they viewed as reformable. Rather, they were seen as troublemakers who needed some sense knocked into them (Andrew, Clarence, Ron, Charles, Carl, Carlos, Simon). Nine men were depicted as unreformed street people, hardened, or a danger to society (Barry, Lester, Casey, Roger, Lennie, Rennie, Wayne, Antonio, Jack). For seven, officials thought the incident was "out of character" or viewed the men as reformable or as victims (Larry, Ralph, Maurice, Georges, Richie, Scott, Shane). The evidence was too sparse to determine what officials thought of Enrico, Wade, and Tyrone.

The hardened or unreformed group largely consisted of street men and some harmed and harming men. Troublemakers were equally

Table 10.3 Judgments of the Men's Character*

	Jail	Nonjail	Total	% of 26
Hardened, unreformed, committed to the street life	8	0	8 ⎫	
A danger to others	1	0	1 ⎬	62
Troublemaker	4	3	7 ⎭	
Not a danger; more of a victim	0	1	1 ⎫	
Could be rehabilitated; reformable	2	4	6 ⎭	27
Uncertain how to classify	1	2	3	11
Total	16	10	26	100

	Black	White	Latin
Hardened, unreformed, committed to the street life	6	1	1
A danger to others	1	0	0
Troublemaker	6	0	1
Not a danger; more of a victim	1	0	0
Could be rehabilitated; reformable	2	4	0
Uncertain how to classify	2	0	1
Total	18	5	3

*See table IV.3 (part 4 summary) for judgments of character by pathway categories, which lists the defendants.

divided between street men and those recently moving into lawbreaking. The men considered reformable came to the court by pathways unrelated to street life. Racial differences were evident in that only three of eighteen black men were viewed as reformable or not a danger, whereas four of the five white men were.

Notes

1. Defense attorneys were successful in reducing the sentences of three men (Clarence, Ralph, and Georges), but not the three others (Barry, Andrew, and Jack).

2. I had too few cases to examine how class and racial and ethnic relations between court officials and judges may have contributed to the lack of commentary. Of the nine cases where no judicial comment was made, however, all but one defendant was black or latin.

3. The defense attorney's assertions here, like the prosecutor's about "classic child sexual abuser" (chap. 9, Flo's sentencing), are good examples of officials' ad hoc, inaccurate claims about behavior.

4. For the nine cases where no judicial justification was given, I cannot be certain what principle of sentencing was operating. I draw from the prosecutor's

and defense attorney's remarks in making an inference. These cases are bracketed in table 10.2.

5. Perhaps the prosecutor needed to minimize the injury to explain a lenient sentence.

6. The judge's reference may be to bystanders in the schoolyard since we know that one of the gang members was injured.

Summary

My analysis of the sentencing remarks yielded surprising and expected results. I was surprised to find that justifications for punishment were not gender-based. For both men and women, the major punishment justifications given in the sentencing ceremony were retribution — that the harm must be punished — and special deterrence — that jail was deserved (or not) because the defendant's prior record was accumulating. I expected to find more use of incapacitation arguments for men, that is, more reference to the need to "protect society" by jailing men,[1] and I expected to see a more explicit use of rehabilitation arguments for women, that is, a focus on the need to correct and reform women's errant behavior. Instead, I found that incapacitation, rehabilitation, and general deterrence were infrequently used. Although I did not discover gender differences in how punishment was justified, I did find gender differences in character judgments, with a higher share of women than men viewed as "reformable" (41 versus 27 percent) (more below).

The sentencing transcripts portion of my study should be viewed as quite exploratory. I am missing about a third of the sentencing remarks and was unable to determine how theories of punishment varied in pair-wise comparisons of the forty deep-sample pairs. Within the limits of my sample, several expected findings emerged.

First, I noted that punishment dichotomies in philosophical theory — utilitarian versus retributive, treatment versus punishment — are often belied by court practices. That is clearly the case for the New Haven felony court: desert-based and utilitarian theories were mixed and combined in one declarative sentence, or in the justification toward one defendant.

Second, the findings on gender-based character judgments should not surprise us, in light of what we learned in previous chapters. The mix of offense and biography in the pathways analysis suggested that the victimization of some women in previous or current relationships, coupled with their greater conventionality and less serious prior record, renders proportionately more women less blameworthy, and hence good candidates for reform. Judges more frequently made positive or optimistic remarks toward the women than the men (45 versus 19 percent). However, such remarks were as likely delivered to women receiving jail and nonjail sentences (the same pattern was apparent for the men).

Table IV.1   Gender and Race in Character Judgments

	Black		White		Latin	
	Women	Men	Women	Men	Women	Men
Unreformed, dangerous, troublemaker	5	13	3	1	2	2
Reformable, no danger	7	3	2	4	0	0
Uncertain	0	2	1	0	2	1
Total	12	18	6	5	4	3

Continuity from earlier chapters is evident in the greater degree of racial and ethnic variability among the men than the women in describing character judgments. Court officials expressed similar levels of optimism that black and white women would change, but they held out little optimism for black men compared to whites (Summary, IV, table 1). Black women did not register as "hardened street criminal" or beyond reform to the same degree as black men did. Nor did black women differ in reform potential from white women. The defendant subgroup most at risk to receive the harshest penalty in this court is not "black" per se, but black men. The pathways categories overlap with the character judgments in expected ways: the street men and women are least likely to be viewed as reformable (Summary, IV, table 2).

In exploring Mileski's (1971) thesis on situational sanctioning, I found that it applied more to the men than the women. That is, judges lectured men to a greater degree when they received nonjail sentences than when they were incarcerated. But for the women, judges lectured or moralized to the majority of women, whether they received jail sentences or not. It is hard to know how much to make of these results because more women in the transcript analysis were sentenced by Judge Kinney, who was more likely to justify his sentence or to lecture defendants. But, coupled with the character judgments, there may be something to this finding. If, as Mileski (1971, 519) suggests, it appears that "the court may . . . abdicate its deterrence role with those it has not been able to deter," then perhaps the court treats women more as "newcomers," hopeful they can be deterred from future lawbreaking.

Another suggestive finding is that when women spoke in court, they more often admitted guilt than men, who more often denied they did anything wrong. If admissions of guilt are one step in the process of taking responsibility for crime (Braithwaite 1989), women are again acting in ways that make them appear as if they have more reform potential.

Table IV.2   Character Judgments by Pathway Categories

Women (N = 22)	Street	Harmed and Harming	Battered	Drug-connected	Other
Hardened, unreformed	Kate Edith Penny Mary	Nellie Susan	Dorothy		
Danger to society	Pat	Edie Flo			
Not a danger, more a victim		Chris	Jean Sharon		
Reformable	Pamela	Tara		Kathleen Wendy Lotty	June
Cannot classify		Claire		Miranda	Prish

Men (N = 26)	Street	Harmed and Harming	Explosive Violent	Bad Luck	Masculine Gaming	Drug-connected
Hardened, unreformed	Lester Casey Roger Rennie Antonio	Lennie Wayne	Barry			
Danger to society			Jack			
Troublemaker	Ron Carl Simon	Clarence		Andrew	Charles	Carlos
Not a danger, more a victim				Shane		
Reformable		Maurice Ralph Scott	Georges	Richie		Larry
Cannot classify	Wade		Enrico		Tyrone	

On the day of sentencing, there is little that defendants or their attorneys can do to change the punishment outcome. Of the 26 men and 22 women, three sentences each were reduced somewhat. These sentences are ceremonies, highly structured and scripted, and compared to Mileski's (1971) observations in the GA-6 court, more of the felony sentencings were degradation ceremonies as Garfinkel (1956) defined them.

From these ceremonies, I saw a punishment logic that worked this way. Harm-based considerations guided judges (and other court officials) in deciding whether incarceration was warranted: when victims died or were thought to be "severely injured," jail time was called for. Although officials initially defined harm by the degree of physical injury or death, the particular character of victim-offender relations, the victims' wishes for punishment, or the possibility of making restitution, there was a point at which neither physical injury nor economic loss could be calculated in a punishment. Moreover, fixing punishment "in proportion to harm," though elegant in principle, is tough to implement when responding to harms ranging from repeated sexual abuse over five years to fighting with police officers in the space of five minutes. A harm-based focus therefore gives way to other judgments about the person and his or her character based on previous lawbreaking and conventionality (employment, marriage, care for others). These markers of stability are infused with gender-, class-, and race-based presuppositions about the defendants' blameworthiness and potential for reform. Sentencing practices in the New Haven felony court evince the Morris (1981) hybrid model of harm-based considerations setting broad ranges, with utilitarian criteria used to fine-tune.

How, then, should these sentencing practices themselves be judged? That is the focus of the next chapter.

Note

1. A preliminary analysis of men convicted of rape in the New Haven felony court shows that incapacitation may be used more often in these cases.

V What Is Just?

11 Difference, Disparity, and Discrimination

In judging the sentencing process, we are normally concerned with three factors: comparability, that similar cases are punished similarly; consistency, that principles are applied evenly; and commensurability, that the punishment seems to be the right response relative to other harms. In this chapter, I focus on comparison and consistency and give some attention to commensurate punishment for diverse harms. First, I recapitulate and expand on some of the findings from previous chapters.

Groups and Gaps: Recapping the Problem

Gender Sentencing Gaps

There appear to be gender-based sentencing gaps in the New Haven felony court. As shown in table 11.1, for the wide sample and without statistical controls, the bivariate gender gap for those sentenced to serve time *(In-Out)* was 29 percentage points. Controlling for offense severity, type of offense, previous felony convictions, race and ethnicity, and detention status, this gap narrowed to 17 percentage points in the multivariate analysis. For the length of the sentence imposed *(Time)*, the bivariate gap was thirteen months, but with the statistical controls, the gap did not narrow, remaining at twelve months. These results indicate that men are more likely to be incarcerated and to receive longer sentences than women.

For the deep sample, the bivariate gender gap for those receiving an incarceration sentence was 10 percentage points. I carried out multivariate analyses of the deep-sample cases, using the original data set and an augmented data set (see table 11.2). The original data set is the same one I used for the wide sample; the augmented one contains new variables, which I fashioned after analyzing the PSI's and the sentencing remarks.[1] The multivariate analysis of the original data showed a gap of 8 percentage points for the *In-Out* decision (not statistically significant), while the analysis of the augmented data set showed no gap whatsoever. For length of sentence, however, there remains a gender gap of twenty to twenty-two months for the original and augmented data sets, which is statistically significant.

Recall that the deep sample is not a random sample drawn from the wide sample; it is a set of statutorily similar cases for pairs of men and women. We would therefore expect to see a substantial reduction

Table 11.1   A Review of Gender Gaps in Sentencing

	In-Out (sentenced to serve time or not)		Time (length of sentence imposed	
	Bivariate (p-pts)	Multivariate (p-pts)	Bivariate (mos)	Multivariate (mos)
Wide sample	29	17*	13	12*
		ORIG AUGM		ORIG AUGM
Deep sample	10	8** 0**	17	22** 20**

p-pts = percentage points
ORIG = original data set
AUGM = augmented data set, which uses new variables created after reading the PSI's and sentencing transcripts. These variables include two measures of prior record (a moderate or a serious record), whether a victim was injured or died, whether the defendant played a primary role, and whether the defendant was a street person. (See table 11.2 for definitions.)
 *From table 2.3(a) and (b), eq. 4
 **From table 11.2

in gender sentencing gaps. This reduction does in fact occur for the *In-Out* decision, especially with the augmented data set, which has better measures for offense-related factors and the defendant's prior record. For the length of sentence *(Time)*, however, the gender gap is not reduced. Thus, the selection of the deep sample had the intended effect of reducing the gender gap in one sentencing outcome but not in another.

Gender-based Variation in Biography and Offense
Although the deep-sample cases were statutorily similar, I judged 40 percent of men's offenses to be more serious than women's and 12 percent of women's offenses to be more serious than men's. About half were comparably serious. Somewhat fewer deep-sample women than men (65 versus 75 percent) had been arrested before, and fewer women than men (25 versus 38 percent) had a serious record of arrests and convictions (more than five). Court workers more frequently linked victimization and criminalization in the women's social histories rather than in the men's, according a less blameworthy quality to some women's acts. Character judgments of the defendants extended on this theme: judges (and other court officials) viewed women as more reformable than men, and judges held out more hope that women would change.

Race and Class in Gender Constructions
Analyzing the wide sample revealed that with the introduction of control variables, black defendants were 11 percentage points more

Table 11.2 Regression Analysis for the Original and Augmented Deep-Sample Data Set

	In-Out 1 = Sentenced to time 0 = No time to serve		Time Length of sentence (in mo)	
	Original	Augmented	Original	Augmented
Sex (male = 1)	.08	−.01	22.3**	20.2**
Severity	.001**	.002**	0.14**	0.14**
Prior record	.12**		−11.5	
Black	.24**	.19*	7.3	5.9
Latin	.21	.25*	40.5**	45.6**
Violence	.38**			
Robbery	.24**			
Drugs	.01			
Moderate record		.21**		0.9
Serious record		.39**		11.2
Injury (1 = yes)		.33**		18.3*
Primary role (1 = yes)		.24**		9.2
Street person (1 = yes)		.22*		
Constant	−.34	−.60	−3.3	−27.8
Adjusted R^2	.37	.49	.17	.17
Mean	.57	.57	44.2	44.2
N of cases	79	79	45	45

**p ≤ .05
*p ≤ .10

Definition of new variables in the augmented data set:

Moderate record: moderate record of convictions (1–5) and incarcerated once; or heavy record of convictions (more than 6)

Serious record: moderate record of convictions (1–5) and incarcerated two or more times; or heavy record of convictions (more than 6) and incarcerated once or more

Injury (yes): the victim died as a result of the incident or the victim was injured (includes restraint and coerced sex)

Primary (yes): the defendant played a sole role in the offense or an equal role with others

Street person (yes): the person's pathway category is street man or woman

likely to be incarcerated than whites — a statistically significant difference — but there were no differences in the length of sentence received. A multivariate analysis of the deep-sample cases again shows a significant race effect for the likelihood of incarceration (see table 11.2).[2] The selection of the deep-sample cases, based on gender matches, did not cause a reduction in racial sentencing gaps. In light of how I selected the deep sample, the appropriate way to examine racial variability is by gender groups. Racial variation among the deep-sample women in pathways, blameworthiness, and character judgments was less than that for men. Racial variation for the men was more marked, because black men were more likely to be concentrated at the top of the punishment hierarchy. They were proportionately more likely to be represented among the street men, less likely to be characterized by the blurred boundaries of victimization and criminalization, and least likely to be viewed as having reform potential. These racial differences for the men arose in large measure because of greater class variation for the men. More white men than blacks or latins had jobs, owned houses, and led conventional or stable working-class lives. Such class variation was less apparent for the women.

With some knowledge of the biographies of the accused men and women, the character of their lawbreaking, and the justifications of court officials for punishment, we can return to the questions I posed earlier in this book. Do the results from the New Haven wide-sample statistical study constitute evidence that women are accorded sentencing leniency? How is race interwoven with gender in shaping the punishment process?

Similar, Different, Disparate, Discriminatory

In addressing questions of sentence variation, I compare cases and outcomes using a pair-wise comparative approach. I begin by defining four categories into which outcomes may fall: *similar, different, disparate,* and *discriminatory.* These terms have been defined and used differently by social scientists, legal analysts, and feminist sociolegal scholars. I briefly discuss their range of meanings.

Early Social Science
Until about a decade ago, social scientists used the terms *disparity* or *discrimination* loosely and interchangeably to mean the same thing: outcomes suggesting that relatively powerless groups were less able to evade apprehension, prosecution, conviction, and more severe punishment. When subgroup differences were statistically significant, the interpretation was that either disparity or discrimination, or both, were evident.

Law
Legal analysts have been less generous in ascribing any nonsimilar treatment to disparity or discrimination. A legal claim of discrimination in punishment is much harder to show or prove, and in recent years appellate review has largely considered the constitutional questions surrounding the death penalty. Under a Fourteenth Amendment constitutional analysis, the legal meaning of discrimination is an inference

of discriminatory purpose by a decision maker. Under Eighth Amendment proportionality reviews, the issue is whether the punishment is out of proportion to the harm. Comparative proportionality review, which considers whether like cases are treated alike, has been confined to the matter of death penalty jurisprudence. In noncapital sentencing, legal analysts tend to focus more attention on disparity that arises from judicial variation than that evidenced in sentencing outcomes for subgroups.

Feminist Legal Theory

The terms *similar* and *different* have an antecedent meaning in feminist legal theory because they refer to the ways gender is conceptualized in social life and law. Feminists are rightly skeptical of making gender comparisons since, as Catharine MacKinnon (1987, 34) suggests, whether feminists claim that women are the same as or different from men, "Man has become the measure of all things." MacKinnon advocates conceptualizing gender not within a difference, but within a dominance framework. Let us see how the terms might be applied to the criminal justice system and to studies of punishment.

A difference approach is based on a male standard with the aim of equal treatment toward men and women. Disparity studies are based on equal treatment assumptions, although it is less clear what the male standard would be in assessing punishment practices.[3] After all, for nearly a century, an ideology of individualized sentencing appears to have rendered no standard at all. A dominance approach is based on a relational standard that acknowledges power differences. The aim is to minimize these power differences, often by taking a substantive justice approach. Within a dominance framework, there may be positive forms of gender disparity. These include an explicit consideration at sentencing of women's care for children (Raeder 1993; Parisi 1982) and of the conditions of women's prison confinement (Rafter 1990).

Recent Social Science

Blumstein and colleagues (1983) provide another set of meanings for disparity and discrimination,[4] which I consider in detail because I have adapted them for my comparative justice metric. *Discrimination* is defined as occurring "when some case attribute that is objectionable (typically on moral or legal grounds) . . . is associated with sentence outcomes after all other relevant variables are adequately controlled" (p. 72).

Disparity occurs when "'like cases' with respect to case attributes"[5] — regardless of their legitimacy — are sentenced differently. As examples, Blumstein and co-workers use the "different weights" that judges may place on case attributes or the "different attributes" judges may use. Differences between judges in the same jurisdiction or in different jurisdictions are also examples of disparity.

These definitions are clarified by the authors' table (from Blumstein et al. 1983, 73):

Legitimacy of Sentencing Criteria	Application of Sentencing Criteria	
	Consistent	Inconsistent
Legitimate	No disparity and no discrimination	Disparity
Illegitimate	Discrimination	Disparity and discrimination

Using the terms of Blumstein and co-workers, *discrimination* refers to the *legitimacy* of the criteria being applied, and *disparity* refers to the *consistency* with which criteria are applied. The focus is on the criteria used in the decision-making process, not on outcomes per se. Discrimination results when illegitimate criteria are applied consistently or inconsistently. Discrimination is also possible when an "otherwise legitimate variable is given an illegitimately large weight" (p. 74).

Disparity arises when legitimate or illegitimate criteria are applied inconsistently. The authors identify race as the "clearest example of an illegitimate criterion," but others might include bail status, type of attorney, and such personal attributes as age and sex (p. 72). "Legitimate" factors can vary, as Blumstein and co-workers discuss when using age and employment status as examples of contentious sentencing factors. Disparity comes in other forms, including the mere appearance of disparity when an observer does not have the same information the judge has, planned disparity in the form of exemplary sentences, and jurisdictional and judicial disparity. Sentencing reformers may not agree on which forms of disparity are acceptable or warranted.

In sum, Blumstein and his colleagues view disparity and discrimination as resulting from the criteria and decision contexts or attributes of decision makers. Their precision in clarifying terms is useful, but it can be difficult to know which term is appropriate in evaluating statistical evidence. For example, using the New Haven study findings, are the statistical sex and race effects evidence of discrimination? Or might they reflect only an apparent disparity since the equations do not accommodate the same information the sentencing judges have? How can we infer from statistical evidence whether one or more judges used legitimate criteria inconsistently or gave different weights to them?[6]

A Comparative Justice Metric

In reviewing the differing uses of the terms *similar, different, disparate,* and *discriminatory,* we find that the jurists leave a good deal of room for decision makers to engage in different, disparate, and even discriminatory behavior — as long as it is not intended; social scientists focus on the extent to which decision makers engage in the consistent application of legitimate criteria; and feminists criticize the equal treatment "difference framework" in light of the pervasive gender inequality in the larger society.

Although aware of its limits, I take an equal treatment approach in analyzing pairs of cases.[7] Specifically, given the seriousness of each crime and the qualities of the defendant's culpability and blameworthiness, I categorize sentencing outcomes as reflecting similar, different, disparate, or discriminatory responses. Although I draw from Blumstein and co-workers in using terms (such as *disparity*), I apply the terms differently by making *pair-wise* (rather than group) comparisons of sentencing *outcomes* (rather than sentencing criteria). My presumptive theory of punishment is retributive in that I use the harm done, the defendant's role in the offense (culpability), and the mix of offense and biography (largely prior record) as making up the initial unit of information to be compared. I do not consider the consequences of the sentences imposed on the defendants.

In comparing the pairs, I began by asking, when is a different response to two defendants acceptable and when does it trouble us. Examples of troubling responses are when two persons convicted of crimes of similar seriousness are punished quite differently; when two persons convicted of crimes of a quite different seriousness are punished similarly; and when justifications used in punishment draw from group-based prejudices associated with class, race, gender, sexuality, or other relations; and when the amount of punishment is either too great or too lenient in relation to the harm.

The *same* response to two defendants convicted of similar offenses is straightforward,[8] but to define an outcome as reflecting a *different* response to two defendants requires that we make a judgment that the harms were sufficiently different to warrant a different response. A different outcome should not trouble us when we are satisfied that the harms were different.

A *disparate* response is more complicated because we have to evaluate whether the punishment or offense characteristics were "quite different." A disparity is often registered when it is not immediately plain why two people have received different punishments for offenses of comparable seriousness or the same punishment for offenses of different seriousness. Further investigation of apparently disparate cases may reveal that one defendant's previous lawbreaking was so much greater than another's that the sentencing difference can be explained.[9] Because the line between a different and disparate response is fuzzy,[10] I give examples of how I have made distinctions.

In addition to judging whether pairs were punished similarly, differently, or whether there was a question of disparity, I identified cases raising a question of justice. A question of justice occurs when punishments seemed too lenient or too harsh — that is, out of proportion to the harm.

For *discrimination,* I refer to the ways prejudice against groups (or toward groups) is applied in an individual case or to a pattern of disparate responses that cannot be explained by legitimate case information. Discrimination may not be known from the information on sentencing outcomes alone.

My comparative justice metric does not include an important element: the subjectivities of the parties involved, especially those of defendants. I suspect that although few judges think they hold prejudicial views toward defendants when they sentence, more defendants think otherwise (Caspar 1972; Matza [1964] 1990).

Analysis of Pairs

I studied the forty deep-sample pairs to determine whether the sentencing responses were similar, different, or raised a question of disparity.[11] Table 11.3 presents the results in which I identified six groups:

1. The offenses were similar, and the defendant pairs received the same sentence ($N=10$).
2. The men's offenses were more severe, and the men received a more severe sentence ($N=9$).
3. The women's offenses were more severe, and the women received a more severe sentence ($N=3$).
4. The men's and women's offenses were of different severity, but they received the same sentence ($N=3$).
5. A disparity question arose when an incarceration sentence versus a suspended sentence was imposed ($N=9$).
6. A disparity question arose in the length of sentence imposed ($N=6$).

For groups 5 and 6, I ordered the pairs beginning with the largest disparity for which the man received the greater punishment and moving to the largest disparity for which the woman did. Although most pairs ($N=25$) did not raise a question of disparity, fifteen pairs did. Of these, nine women received a more lenient sentence, and in six, the men did. In probing these cases further, I was satisfied that the disparity could be explained for twelve. For the remaining three pairs, there were two for which the disparity could largely be explained, though not entirely: in one, the man's jail sentence was eight years longer than the woman's (Casey and Kate, robbery pair 1), and in another the man was jailed for five years while the woman received a suspended sentence (Rennie and Colleen, drug pair 1). There was only *one* pair of the forty for whom I felt the disparity could not be explained satisfactorily: the case in which Andrew received four years to serve for assaulting police officers, while Latasha received a suspended sentence for assaulting police officers (assault pair 4).

The wide- and deep-sample statistical analyses indicate a good deal more disparity than is evident from my pair-wise disparity analysis. In fact, based on the pair-wise analysis, sentencing disparity appears to be negligible in the deep sample.

Similar and Different Responses

Below I present the cases in groups 1–4, which did not raise a question of disparity (see appendix 6 for a summary of the offenses).

Group 1: Similar Response — Same Offense Severity, Same Sentence
Victor and Wendy: Robbery Cases 8 and 6, Sentenced to Three Years and Three and a Half Years, Respectively
This pair illustrates how offenses of comparable seriousness were punished similarly. Each defendant was involved in the robbery of a gas station; each played a participating role, although their accomplice may have had a more directing hand, and each received a similar sentence.

Ted and Edie: Homicide Cases 4 and 2, Both Sentenced to Ten Years
Edie killed her stepmother, and Ted attempted to kill his wife. Although Ted's act was planned and he hired an accomplice to help him, his act and Edie's registered the same level of seriousness and was sentenced the same.

Most defendants in group 1 committed offenses that were relatively less serious than the two pairs above, or they were able to make restitution. Of the ten pairs in this group, six received suspended sentences.

Table 11.3 Pair-wise Disparity Analysis

A. Disparity Question is Not Raised

Offense and Pair No.	M-Name/F-Name	Crime Seriousness	Sentence		Difference	M-F Ratio	Disparity?	Explain?
1. Same offense severity, same sentence; no question of disparity								
Drugs M3/F3	Rob / Penny	same?	M-.75 yr	F-.5 yr	.25	1.5	no	
Assault M3/F3	Maurice / Dee Dee	same	M-2 yrs	F-1.75 yrs	.25	1.14	no	
Assault M1/F1	Larry / Kathleen	same	M-susp	F-susp	0	1.0	no	
Assault M6/F2	Shane / Sharon	same	M-susp	F-susp	0	1.0	no	
Larc M1/F1	Scott / June	same	M-susp	F-susp	0	1.0	no	
Larc M6/F6	Tyrone / Maria	same	M-susp	F-susp	0	1.0	no	
Drugs M2/F2	Reggie / Bonnie	same	M-susp	F-susp	0	1.0	no	
Drugs M8/F8	Carlos / Lotty	same?	M-susp	F-susp	0	1.0	no	
Homi M4/F2	Ted / Edie	same	M-10 yrs	F-10 yrs	0	1.0	no	
Rob M8/F6	Victor / Wendy	same	M-3 yrs	F-3.5 yrs	.50	0.85	no	
2. Men's offense more severe; men's more severe sentence								
Risk M1/F1	Jack / Nola	man more-V	M-17 yrs	F-1 yr	16.0	17.0	no-J	
Homi M2/F4	Wes / Jean	man more-V	M-9 yrs	F-2.5 yrs	6.5	3.6	no	
Homi M3/F3	Earl / Lonnie	man more-S	M-7 yrs	F-3.5 yrs	3.5	2.0	no	
Drugs M6/F6	Douglas / Marcie	man more	M-3 yrs	F-1 yr	2.0	3.0	no	
Larc M3/F3	Geoff / Winnie	man more-V	M-4 yrs	F-susp	4.0	n/a	no	
Larc M2/F2	Roger / Tara	man more-S	M-1 yr	F-susp	1.0	n/a	no	
Assault M2/F6	Lester / Alice	man more	M-3 yrs	F-susp	3.0	n/a	no	
Rob M5/F5	Simon / Toni	man more	M-4 yrs	F-susp	4.0	n/a	no	
Larc M7/F7	Lennie / Laura	man more-V	M-1 yr	F-susp	1.0	n/a	no	

3. Women's offense more severe; women's more severe sentence

Offense and Pair No.	M-Name/F-Name	Crime Seriousness	Sentence		Difference	M-F Ratio	Disparity?	Explain?
Larc M4/F4	Joe / Edith	woman more-S	M-4 yrs	F-5 yrs	1.0	0.8	no	
Arson M1/F1	Enrico/Dorothy	woman more-S	M-susp	F-1 yr	1.0	n/a	no	
Drugs M1/F1	Carl / Julie	woman more	M-susp	F-1 yr	1.0	n/a	no	

4. Different offense severity; same sentence

Offense and Pair No.	M-Name/F-Name	Crime Seriousness	Sentence		Difference	M-F Ratio	Disparity?	Explain?
Assault M5/F8	Georges / Carrie	man more	M-susp	F-susp	0	1.0	no-J	
Drugs M4/F4	Juan / Miranda	woman more	M-susp	F-susp	0	1.0	no	
Larc M5/F5	Darrell / Prish	woman more-V	M-susp	F-susp	0	1.0	no-J	

B. Disparity Question is Raised

Offense and Pair No.	M-Name/F-Name	Crime Seriousness	Sentence		Difference	M-F Ratio	Disparity?	Explain?

5. Incarceration versus jail sentence

Offense and Pair No.	M-Name/F-Name	Crime Seriousness	Sentence		Difference	M-F Ratio	Disparity?	Explain?
Arson M2/F2	Wayne / Nancy	man more	M-6 yrs	F-susp	6.0	n/a	yes	yes-1
Drugs M7/F7	Rennie / Colleen	same?	M-5 yrs	F-susp	5.0	n/a	yes	yes-1,2 ?
Rob M3/F3	Allen / Pamela	man more	M-5 yrs	F-susp	5.0	n/a	yes	yes-1,2
Assault M4/F4	Andrew / Latasha	same	M-4 yrs	F-susp	4.0	n/a	yes	no
Risk M3/F2	Ralph / Flo	same	M-1 yr	F-susp	1.0	n/a	yes	yes-3
Rob M4/F4	Richie / Pat	same	M-susp	F-4 yrs	4.0	n/a	yes	yes-1
Assault M8/F5	Pete / Stacey	man more	M-susp	F-1 yr	1.0	n/a	yes	yes-4
Drugs M5/F5	Dylan / Mary	man more	M-susp	F-1 yr	1.0	n/a	yes	yes-1
Rob M7/F7	Charles / Bell	man more-S	M-susp	F-.33 yr	0.33	n/a	yes	yes-3

(continued)

Table 11.3 (continued)

Offense and Pair No.	M-Name/F-Name	Crime Seriousness	Sentence		Difference	M-F Ratio	Disparity?	Explain?
6. Length of incarceration sentence								
Rob M1/F1	Casey / Kate	man more	M-10 yrs	F-2 yrs	8.0	5.0	yes	yes-1,2 ?
Rob M6/F8	Antonio / Maggie	same	M-6 yrs	F-3 yr	3.0	2.0	yes	yes-1
Homi M1/F1	Barry / Claire	same	M-10 yrs	F-7.5 yrs	2.5	1.3	yes	yes-1
Risk M2/F3	Wade / Chris	same	M-2 yrs	F-1 yr	1.0	2.0	yes	yes-4
Assault M7/F7	Clarence / Nellie	same	M-1 yr	F-2.9 yrs	1.9	0.34	yes	yes-3
Rob M2/F2	Ron / Susan	same	M-2.5 yrs	F-8 yrs	5.5	0.31	yes	yes-1

Codes used for crime seriousness (taken from app. 5):

more-S (somewhat more serious)

more-V (very much more serious)

same? (hard to judge; information sparse)

no-J = no disparity but question of justice

Explanation codes:	N times explained*
1 = prior record	9
2 = role in offense	3
3 = interest of justice, evidence	3
4 = age, mental competency	2

*For the 14 pairs where disparity could be explained; some have more than one explanation.

Group 2: Different Response — Men's Offense More Severe, Men's More Severe Sentence

All the men in group 2 committed offenses of greater severity than the women's, with four of the nine men's offenses being much more severe. For several pairs, the men's previous record of arrests and convictions was long and serious, constructing a heightened blameworthiness to their acts.

Lester and Alice: Assault Cases 2 and 6, Sentenced to Three Years and a Suspended Sentence, Respectively

Lester slashed the face of a man on the street when the man would not give him money; Alice stabbed a friend during a fight. Lester's street life, alcoholism, and injury to the victim constructed his act as more blameworthy than hers.

Jack and Nola: Risk-of-Injury Pair 1, Sentenced to Seventeen Years and One Year, Respectively

Jack was convicted at trial of having beaten his stepson unconscious; Nola had brought her child to the emergency room after throwing it on a mattress.[12] Had Jack pled guilty, he would have received two years to serve.

Wes and Jean: Homicide Cases 2 and 4, Nine Years and Two and a Half Years, Respectively

Wes stabbed his fishing buddy after a day of drinking and fishing, and Jean was fending off a violent victim who had been beating her. Her act had many elements of self-defense, even though Wes also claimed to be acting in self-defense. This pair illustrates problems that are likely to arise in statistical studies of interpersonal violence: women are more likely than men to be fighting off violent victims.

Geoff and Winnie: Larceny Pair 3, Four Years and a Suspended Sentence, Respectively

Geoff's conviction to first-degree larceny masked a far more serious case of several commercial and residential burglaries he had committed, and his record was substantial. Winnie had never been arrested before and stole from her parents.

Group 3: Different Response — Women's Offense More Severe, Women's More Severe Sentence

Edith and Joe: Larceny Pair 4, Four Years and Five Years, Respectively

Edith's burglarizing of several residences was somewhat more serious than Joe's theft of cash and checks from a utilities company, where he worked as a custodian. Although the value of Joe's theft was higher, he victimized an organization, and Edith victimized people in her neighborhood.

Group 4: Mixed Response — Different Severity Offense, Same Sentence
Question of Justice
Two of the three pairs in group 4 raised a question of justice.[13] In both, the defendant's offense was serious, and the punishment was surprisingly lenient. I am not advocating that more people ought to be imprisoned, but I saw in these cases how defendants who are employed and can surround themselves with markers of stability and conventionality are able to evade incarceration.

Georges's Shooting: Assault Case 5, Suspended
Georges's attempted shooting of his former wife (while she and their daughter were driving off to go shopping) was a classic case of domestic violence wherein the man's behavior was excused because of job-related stress and drinking. At sentencing, other family members spoke positively about his steady work record and good behavior with children. The judge did not perceive Georges's act as serious, largely because he pointed the gun toward his wife rather than at his daughter.

Prish's Embezzlement: Larceny Case 5, Suspended Sentence
Prish embezzled a large amount of money from her employer, for whom she had worked for many years. Even the sentencing judge admitted to Prish, "You have got a lot to be thankful for."

Difference or Disparity?

One pair in group 2 (Earl and Lonnie), one in group 5 (Allen and Pamela), and one in group 6 (Barry and Claire; Allen and Pamela) are examples of the difficulties in drawing a line between responses that reflect identifiable case differences and those that raise a question of disparity.

Earl and Lonnie: Homicide Pair 3, Seven Years and Three-and-One-Half Years, Respectively
Earl fatally shot a friend of his son's, and Lonnie fatally stabbed a former boyfriend during an argument. Earl said he saw his bloodied son and thought the victim was going after him with scissors; Lonnie said her former boyfriend had punched her. In this pair I wavered between seeing the outcome as a different response and seeing it as a disparate response. I concluded that Earl's act was more severe and

that Lonnie's was mitigated because of her victim's violence toward her; thus I came to classify the outcome as reflecting an appropriate response to different offenses.

Allen and Pamela: Robbery Pair 3, Five Years and Suspended Sentence, Respectively

While "following orders," those of her cousin, Pamela robbed a man she knew. Allen assisted an accomplice in robbing a woman while she was entering her apartment. The gestalt of the harm in Allen's offense was more serious. Furthermore, Pamela's victim wanted to remain her friend and wanted to help her, while Allen's victim was frightened by this classic case of stranger robbery. Were their offenses sufficiently different to warrant Allen's receiving a five-year jail sentence and Pamela's receiving a suspended sentence?[14] At what point do we register a sense that, although one offense was more serious than another, the penalty difference seems too large?[15]

Barry and Claire: Homicide Pair 1, Ten Years and Seven and a Half Years, Respectively

Barry beat his uncle to death while apparently trying to awaken him from being passed out, and Claire swung a golf club at a man, with whom she and other family members had been fighting that day. Claire's act was viewed by the court as somewhat less serious than Barry's in part because her victim had been fighting with other family members all day and in part because his victim had been severely beaten. Still, did Barry's act merit 2½ years more in jail than Claire's? Because I did not think it did, I classified the pair as raising a question of disparity.

Questions of Disparity

For fifteen pairs a question of disparity was initially raised in my mind. All but two were robberies or forms of interpersonal violence: this fact alerts us to the kinds of offenses where gender disparities may initially appear to be large. Two pairs illustrate how apparent leniency toward either the woman or the man may be satisfactorily explained.

Antonio and Maggie: Robbery Cases 6 and 8, Six Years and Three Years, Respectively

Antonio and Maggie each robbed a household in which the victims were especially vulnerable (children and an elderly man); both played a primary role, though each had an accomplice (two in Antonio's case). I judged their offenses to be comparably serious. Why, then, did Antonio receive three years more? Further investigation finds that

Antonio had been convicted before, while Maggie had never been arrested.[16] I was satisfied that the initial question of disparity could be explained by the differences in Antonio's and Maggie's prior records.

Ron and Susan: Robbery Pair 2, Two and a Half Years and Eight Years, Respectively

Ron and two accomplices robbed a gas station, and Susan and an accomplice robbed a gas station. Susan pushed her victim and pulled her hair, but there appears to have been no victim injury in Ron's robbery. I judged the offense to be comparably serious; why, then, the 5½-year difference between the sentences? Susan's robbery was one of three she had committed that month, whereas Ron's was the first. He had been convicted before for stealing a car and selling marijuana, whereas she had committed several serious violent crimes. Using the public defender's scheme noted by Mather (1979), Susan was among "the meanest" of robbery offenders, whereas Ron seemed more of an "amateur." Differences in prior record and the greater level of blameworthiness in Susan's act explain the disparity.

For most pairs that initially raised a question of disparity, I was satisfied that the disparity could be explained by differences in the defendants' prior records. There were other explanations, however, including the interests of justice or evidence problems (three pairs), age and mental (in)competency (two pairs), and the role taken in the offense (three pairs). I noted offense-based differences in explaining sentence disparity. For the robbery and drug cases, the differences were largely explained by the character of the defendants' prior records. In the violence cases, the more typical explanations were interests of justice, evidentiary problems, age, and mental incompetency.

Evidence Problems

Clarence and Nellie: Assault Pair 7, One Year and 2.9 Years, Respectively

Clarence beat a man while he slept, causing serious injury, and stole his car. Nellie and two other women attempted to rob a man who was giving them a ride home. Nellie cut him severely with a knife, causing serious injury. Her assault appeared to be more brutal than Clarence's; her victim was hospitalized longer. Their prior records were similar in that both had been arrested and convicted on alcohol-related offenses. What explains the two-year difference? Although in both incidents the facts were in dispute,[17] the state had a problem in proving Clarence's assault because his victim later recanted, saying he was not sure that it was Clarence who had assaulted him. Upon closer inspection, Clarence's assault of someone he knew suggested an ongoing dispute between them. I felt that the disparity could be explained by the witness problems the state had, which are linked to the "known-person discount" in interpersonal violence.

Mental Competency
Wayne and Nancy: Arson Pair 2, Six Years and Suspended Sentence, Respectively

Nancy set fire to rooms in an apartment that she shared with her sister, causing the destruction of the entire apartment. Wayne set fire to his girlfriend's apartment, one of several life-threatening acts toward her in the preceding months. I judged Nancy's arson to be less serious than Wayne's because of prior threats to his victim. Yet, I was initially puzzled that Nancy received a suspended sentence. A closer examination of her file revealed a long history of mental problems: she had been in mental institutions during the previous five years and had been released just a month before the arson. The probation officer explained the arson as likely to have resulted from Nancy's failure to take her prescribed medication. Wayne had a serious drug problem and an extensive record of convictions for larcenies and burglaries. His act was constructed as "dangerous"; Nancy's was viewed as a product of a mental imbalance.

Three Troubling Pairs

Three pairs show how combinations of mental (in)competency, the defendant's role in the offense, and prior record coalesce to form a greater penalty for men than for women. In two pairs, I judged the disparity to be mostly, though not fully, explained, whereas in one pair, the disparity could not be explained.

Casey and Kate: Robbery Pair 1, Ten Years and Two Years, Respectively

I judged Casey's robbery to be more serious than Kate's because Casey had injured a store clerk, and Kate and an accomplice had merely threatened to use a weapon while robbing a man on the street. Although Casey robbed a "real" victim — a store clerk unknown to him — Kate robbed a less exemplary victim, a man who was likely seeking a prostitute. Both had serious prior records, though Kate's record was dominated by prostitution, disorderly conduct, and drug offenses; Casey's record included burglaries, larcenies, and assaults. Although Kate's sentence was in line with other deep-sample robberies, Casey's penalty was two years longer.[18]

Rennie and Colleen: Drug Pair 7, Five Years and Suspended Sentence, Respectively

Rennie and Colleen, who were married, were arrested at the same time for selling narcotics; they were in bed when the police entered their apartment with a warrant. The file lacked information on the probable cause for the search warrant; I could not determine whether Rennie acted alone in selling the drugs, although he and Colleen had assumed that he should be arrested and not her. At sentencing, Rennie's five-year sentence was justified by his prior record and continued drug use.[19] He had been released from jail four months before the offense, and the judge viewed the arrest as indicative that "lengthy periods of incarceration are the only answer."[20]

For these pairs, we could explain the sentencing disparities by the greater seriousness of the man's act and prior record (Casey and Kate) and by the greater culpability of the man, the man's parole status, and prior record (Rennie and Colleen). Although I felt that the disparities could be explained (though perhaps not fully), there was one pair for which this was not so.

Andrew and Latasha: Assault Pair 4, Four Years and Suspended Sentence, Respectively

Andrew assaulted two police officers, thinking, he said, that they were beating up his friend. Latasha assaulted two police officers, hitting each of them on the nose with a baseball bat until a third officer intervened in making an arrest. The police described Latasha as "yelling and screaming and acting crazy." They were trying to arrest her for damaging a car. Latasha had been arrested before, Andrew had not.[21] It is hard to understand why Latasha's violence was excused in this incident: she had injured not only two police officers, but earlier in the day she was violent toward the mother of her former boyfriend's new girlfriend. Her attorney said that she was "in need of psychiatric help" and that she had a "history of excessive alcohol use." Her harm was discounted in part because she seemed to be mentally unbalanced and in part because her actions arose while she was resisting arrest. Andrew's assault was viewed as more rational and calculated: he was not resisting an arrest, rather he had intervened when the police were trying to make an arrest.

Latasha's is a good example of how, for some women, mental incompetency may excuse their harm (Allen 1987b). There is another dimension to consider here, as well. Male police officers may find it unacceptable to be lenient to a man who has assaulted or threatened to assault them, whereas it may be somewhat embarrassing for them to admit that a woman was able to assault them.[22] Such a police response has less to do with chivalry than with a masculinist culture in policing (Hunt 1990).

Gender and Race in Interpreting Disparity

In identifying and explaining disparity in the three troubling pairs, my task was made more complex and more interesting because in each pair the man was black and the woman was white. Would we say that the black man was sentenced more harshly because he was a man or because he was a black man? Likewise, would we say the woman was sentenced less harshly because she was a woman or because she was a white woman?

For the one pair for whom I felt that disparity could not be explained, would we call it gender- or race-based or gender- *and* race-based? We could view Latasha's sentence as a result of an act of discretionary leniency, with no racial prejudice directed to Andrew. We could also interpret the sentence Andrew received as reflecting a racial prejudice in responding to black men who assault police officers. Several interpretations are possible, but I see this case as interweaving race- and gender-based elements.

Commensurability for Diverse Harms

My pair-wise analysis suggests that New Haven sentencing was generally consistent and comparable. Yet when examining punishment for different offenses, the sentences imposed did not seem commensurate. As I make this observation, I am struck by the difficulty of devising a punishment metric that would be commensurate — "in proportion to harm" — for the diverse offenses in the deep sample. I am also struck by the craft of engaging in a *proportionality review,* as legal analysts would term it.[23] Whether devising a punishment scale or assessing whether punishment is proportionate for diverse harms, it is useful to ponder those offenses that brought men and women to the New Haven felony court for the *first* time and the sentences they received:

- Andrew's beating of two police officers, injuring them both, in a fight that lasted for perhaps five minutes (four years)
- Ralph's frequent sexual intercourse with his stepdaughter for three years and other sexual abuse for five years (one year)
- Prish's embezzlement of more than $125,000 over five years (suspended sentence; restitution)
- Scott's theft of oil from a school, with two accomplices (suspended sentence; restitution)

- Claire's swinging a golf club at the victim in the midst of a day-long fight between the victim and members of Claire's family (7½ years)
- Jean's stabbing of her abusive former boyfriend, largely to fend off his blows (2½ years; sentenced to time served, about fourteen months)
- Georges's shooting at his wife and daughter, although the bullets missed them (suspended sentence)
- Ted's attempt to kill his wife, with the aid of an accomplice, by strangling her and beating her on the head with a hammer (ten years)
- Nola's throwing her infant son on an air mattress, causing serious injury to the infant's skull (one year)
- Nancy's burning of several rooms in an apartment that she shared with her sister, gutting the apartment (suspended sentence)

Two features of these crimes and punishments are noteworthy. First, there is no relation between the number of transgressions or the duration of the offense and the sentence imposed: Prish's embezzlement and Ralph's sexual abuse, which went on for years, were responded to rather leniently. Even though the breach of employee or parental trust was the object of judicial lecturing and wrath, it did not provoke a heavy penal sanction. By comparison, Andrew's "mistake in judgment" — thinking his friend was being beaten by police officers — was responded to with a heavy penal sanction.

Second, harms occurring between family members are responded to in sharply different ways, ranging from the fully excused to the severely treated. Georges's bullets missed his wife, and Ted's attempt to murder his wife failed: Georges's offense was excused; Ted's was not. Jean's fatal stabbing of her abusive partner ended his attack, and Edie's killing of her stepmother removed her from an intolerable situation: Jean was excused;[24] Edie was not. Nola's physical harm of her child and Nancy's burning of the apartment she shared with her sister were both excused. Harms between family members elicited condemnation of or sympathy toward both the men and women defendants.

For robberies and drug offenses, the role of previous lawbreaking assumes more importance than the harm. Consider these offenses:

- Pat's driving the getaway car in a robbery carried out by her boyfriend (four years)
- Casey's robbery of a convenience store by himself (ten years)
- Rennie's selling small amounts of narcotics (five years)
- Simon's robbing a gang member over a failed drug deal, with an accomplice (four years)

Although we may resist making a comparison between sexual abuse for many years and driving a getaway car in a robbery, or between embezzling money for many years and selling narcotics, it is instructive to see how these harms are decoupled from the sentence imposed. Pat, Casey, Rennie, and Simon were punished not just for what they did but for what they had done before. Prish and Scott were able to make restitution and avoid a penal sanction; Ralph was sufficiently contrite and demonstrated that he was making strides to pull the family back together. The prior record tariff in the robbery and drug cases is a penalty for not staying out of trouble. It can also be viewed as a penalty for poverty and drug addiction.

I began this chapter by reviewing the several gender and race gaps in New Haven felony court sentencing. A statistical analysis of the deep sample showed no gender differences in the likelihood of receiving an incarceration sentence, but it did show differences in the length of sentence. Even with my augmented data set, for which I created new variables after reading the PSI's and sentencing transcripts, gender differences in sentence length persisted.[25] Conversely, a statistical analysis of the deep sample, using the augmented data set, showed race differences in the likelihood of receiving an incarceration sentence (with blacks more likely to be incarcerated than whites), but not for the length of sentence.

I had good reason to think that I could explain the statistical *gender* disparity from differences in offense seriousness (some of the men's crimes were more serious) and the mix of biography and offense (some men were more blameworthy). Further, my analysis of the PSI's and sentencing remarks suggested a partial explanation for the *racial* disparity: a greater level of blameworthiness was attached to black men's than other men's acts, and a lower level of reform potential was granted to them.

Using a comparative justice metric, which focused on a pair-wise analysis of sentence outcomes, I found that twenty-five deep-sample pairs (62 percent) were sentenced in ways that did not raise a question of disparity. For ten pairs, the men's and women's offenses were similar, and they were sentenced similarly; for twelve pairs, the men's or women's offenses were more serious, and they received more severe sentences; and in three pairs, the men and women received suspended sentences for offenses of different severity. For twelve of the fifteen pairs that initially raised a question of disparity, the disparity could be explained fully by differences in prior record, role in the offense, evidentiary reasons, and age or mental competency.[26] In two pairs, the sentencing disparity could largely be explained, but in one it could not be explained at all. Interestingly, as indicated from the deep-sample statistical analysis, the three troubling pairs were composed of a black man and a white woman.

The one pair in which the disparity could not be explained was Andrew and Latasha. My interpretation of the disparity — his receiving four years and her receiving a suspended sentence for assaulting police officers — is that it embodied a combination of gender- and race-based prejudice. Her act was downgraded, and his act was upgraded in seriousness because she was judged "crazy," and he was challenging state authority. As a black man, his act was upgraded in seriousness because he had joined to help his black friend, a robbery suspect, fight the police.

In exploring disparity beyond pair-wise comparison, the punishment picture becomes murkier. The retributivist principle of proportionality is at odds with the ability of some defendants to compensate for harms by making restitution, the ability of some to benefit from the court's selective leniency when crime victims are family members, and the inability of some to evade penal sanctions because they are poor, drug addicted, and have been before the court before.[27]

My comparative justice metric is based on the logic of an equal treatment analysis. Such an approach has been criticized by feminist sociolegal scholars as being rooted in a male standard. It can also be criticized for ignoring questions of whether the overall punishment structure is just and whether the consequences of punishment differ for men and women (for example, incarceration for women is more punitive because the conditions are worse). I consider these issues in the next chapter. Here, I respond briefly to the meaning of the term *male standard*. In the New Haven felony court, there were at least two operative male standards: the more conventional, familied man, and the more disreputable, victimizing, and heavily criminalized man. At least in sentencing *practices,* I did not see one male standard that operated in quite the same way that it may operate in employment practices.

The findings of the pair-wise analysis, when set alongside those of the statistical analysis for the wide sample, suggest two rather different stories about gender disparity in the New Haven felony court. With the pair-wise analysis, I was able to take note of differences in offense seriousness, prior record, and offender blameworthiness for the statutorily similar offenses in the deep sample. In so doing, I identified just one of the forty pairs for which the disparity could not be explained. With the statistical analysis of the deep and the wide samples, a greater level of gender-based disparity was evinced. My analysis leads me to conclude that traditional disparity studies may well give the misleading impression that women are favored in criminal court.

Notes

1. I created and analyzed more variables than those I report here. For example, I fashioned several family variables, such as "has dependents," to see their effect on sentencing. I found, however, that the family variables did not have a mitigating effect on receiving an incarceration sentence nor on the length of sentence. The offense-related and prior record variables had a greater influence.

2. Although there is a *latin* variable in table 11.2, the number of these defendants is too low to draw inferences from this analysis safely.

3. As I suggested in chap. 1, there is a male standard, operating in the criminal code or in guideline systems, as legislators or administrators imagine "the offender" and "his crime." But in evaluating punishment practices, I suspect there are several male standards operating, not just one.

4. Wilbanks (1987) also considers definitional problems, but he focuses on differentiating racism from prejudice and discrimination. He uses the terms *disparity* and *discrimination* interchangeably.

5. Case attributes are defined as a variety of characteristics of (1) offense seriousness, including the type of crime, number of charges, statutory severity, injury or threat of injury, weapon use, value of property stolen, number of accomplices, role of offender, victim vulnerability, victim provocation, victim-offender relation, and intent; and (2) quality of evidence, such as number of witnesses, cooperation of witnesses, existence of evidence, and strength of defendant's alibi (Blumstein et al. 1983, 70).

6. Some time ago Hagan (1977, 173) dealt with questions like these and concluded that "it seems difficult, if not impossible, to determine an empirical content of acts that can be reliably designated as discriminatory." Part of the problem is that acting affirmatively on behalf of a subordinate group can, for members of a dominant group, be the ground for claiming discrimination.

7. As I argue in my conclusion, the method one takes to assess sentencing practices need not be the same as the preferred punishment policy. Advocates of substantive justice policies have not yet identified a way to assess practices.

8. Imagine that these statements were made with reference to pairs of women. Would feminists still be skeptical of the comparative exercise? Perhaps less so, but there would still be questions of racial, ethnic, familial, sexual, and class variability among women. Contemplating the pairs as composed of a man and a woman (without any further information) may generate more skepticism about the comparative exercise, though it is not clear precisely why.

9. This situation is a good example of what Blumstein et al. (1983) refer to as the appearance of disparity to an observer when the judge has more information.

10. During an interview with Washington attorneys and federal judges in the spring of 1992, I asked, "When is a disparity a disparity?" One man (at the time, the solicitor general) replied with confidence: "It's when one person gets a suspended sentence and the other gets a long jail sentence." But one obvious reply is, "What is 'long'?" It is easier to know the more "clear-cut" cases of disparity; less clear is where one draws the line between different outcomes that do not trouble us and those that do.

11. I used the same pairings as in app. 5 on judgments of seriousness.

12. One of the worst penalties for a mother in a child abuse case is losing custody. This did not happen to Nola. After serving some time in jail, she returned to live with her husband and children. There was no movement by state officials to take custody of her children.

13. The third case that raised a question of justice was Jack's. Found guilty at trial, he received seventeen years to serve. He said in court that he was offered a plea bargain in which his sentence would have been two years.

14. Her co-defendant also received a suspended sentence.

15. In further examining these files, it became apparent that although Pamela had several previous convictions (related to prostitution), Allen's previous convictions were far more numerous and serious. Thus, I am certain that the justification that a judge would give would be Allen's developed prior record and Pamela's cooperation with the police. Nonetheless, the issue I want to raise in comparing Pamela and Allen is when the subjective line is crossed from a different to a disparate response.

16. This is a good example of when an additive statistical model of sentencing can do a good job: the presence of a prior record increased the penalty for Antonio. But in cases where the defendant's prior record more thoroughly saturates the meaning of an offender's act, then the additive model does not work as well. There is a third group of cases where prior record both adds a penalty and partly defines the crime's seriousness.

17. Nellie alleged that the victim was trying to rape her and that that was why she cut him.

18. Different judges were involved in the cases: Kinney sentenced Kate, and McKeever sentenced Casey.

19. They were sentenced by different judges: Fishman sentenced Colleen, and Celotto sentenced Rennie.

20. Judge Celotto's response to Rennie's drug use and sale was similar to Judge Kinney's response to Mary's offense (drug case 5): there seemed to be a quality of vengeance in the disposition. Both Rennie and Mary were being punished not for the quantity of drugs they were selling but for returning to the court on new charges.

21. Both were sentenced by Judge Kinney.

22. Obviously, the context of the arrest matters in terms of gender dynamics (see Visher 1983). When the police are moving to control crowds or arresting demonstrators, one would not expect gender to matter as much as other factors in police-citizen encounters.

23. The following discussion is speculative and raises more questions about how a harm-based punishment system would work and what a proportionality review would have to contend with. I do not attempt to assess the sentences with proportionality in mind in this book.

24. *Excused* is perhaps the wrong word here for a woman, who in my view, should not have been prosecuted in the first place.

25. I also conducted the deep-sample analysis of *time* with all seventy-nine cases (I excluded the one trial case), including the defendants receiving suspended sentences and coding their sentences as zero. The average sentence difference for

men and women was ten months in both the original and augmented data sets, and the sex effect was significant in both.

26. Based on my previous research, I expected to see evidence that women's caretaking responsibilities mitigated against incarceration but did not find it.

27. Barbara Hudson (1987) makes a similar point when she suggests that the emphasis in the just-desert model on punishing "the crime" is a gloss and that in fact, certain classes of people continue to be exposed to more severe sentences.

Are men and women sentenced differently for like crimes? To this core question my answer is no — not in the court I studied in the 1980s, even though a statistical study might suggest otherwise. When I carried out a traditional disparity study, analyzing a large data set with control variables, I found statistically significant differences that apparently favored women. But when I used my comparative justice metric, analyzing pairs of cases and using narrative materials, gender differences were negligible. Although the traditional disparity study can be improved with better measures, the narrative materials have an integrity and meaning that cannot be captured by quantifying their parts.

I emphasize the usual caveats that come from a single-jurisdiction study. Although I do not think the results from the New Haven felony court are unique, research in other jurisdictions may confirm or challenge the patterns seen in that court. Because I covered a good deal of ground, it is useful to recapitulate my major findings in these areas: the circumstances bringing men and women to felony court, the content and seriousness of their acts, how their punishments were justified in court, and the racial variation in gender constructions.

Gendered Pathways

Although more than half the men and women in the deep sample grew up in economically precarious circumstances and the majority abused drugs, alcohol, or both, there were important axes of variation. For the women, the leading feminist scenario — that of the street woman — characterized about a third of the sample.[1] These women ran to the street from abusive homes or were attracted to the life of the street; drug addiction and the exigencies of street survival pulled them into prostitution, larcenies, and drug selling. Another women's route was to assault or kill violent intimates. These women, whom I term *battered,* have attracted much media and feminist attention — so much, in fact, that one might think that they represent the average female defendant. Their numbers at the time of my research were relatively small (about 10–12 percent), even though their actions in fending off violent victims raise key questions in feminist legal theory.[2] Other women used or sold drugs in their relations with men or family members (15 percent).

Although the street, battered, and drug-connected woman may be familiar to analysts of women and crime, I have identified another group that has received less scholarly attention. This group comprises harmed and harming women, who made up about a third of the deep-sample women. Their acts were not committed in the pursuit of economic gain, and their violence was spawned within a history of victimization or psychological problems. These pathways are not fixed descriptions of the women but reflect a mix of biography and offense that brought them to court at the time of my study.

When comparing the pathways of women and men, the role of social construction becomes clear: we cannot be sure what part of gender difference is real and what part is amplified or attenuated through social construction. For example, the PSI reports suggested that three times more women than men were either physically or sexually abused while growing up (29 versus 9 percent, respectively) and that more than two times more women than men were described as having psychological problems (53 versus 19 percent). These differences may reflect real differences in women's and men's lives. Simultaneously, they may reflect how experiences are elicited in interactions between a probation officer and a defendant, and how biographical story lines take gendered forms.

I began with the women in the pathways analysis and then turned to the men. In so doing, it was possible to see elements overlooked by theories of crime: the extent to which young women run away from abusive households, the impact and significance for a woman of becoming a mother and caring for a child, a woman's ability to make money by forms of sex work, and gender relations in street and intimate life that put women at great risk of being beaten by men they know. The biographical profiles show women to be more scarred by victimization and more conventional than men.

Compared with the women, there were fewer harmed and harming men, but there were other men's pathways that reflected the costs and excesses of masculinity. Explosively violent men assaulted or harmed others because they were angry or sought to control them. The bad luck men were either used by others or were in the wrong place at the wrong time, and the masculine gaming men acted as junior versions of street men. Even more than the women, some of the street men were hardened by more time incarcerated.

Although men's and women's routes to felony court and the circumstances spawning their lawbreaking varied, there were common themes. More than one-third of the crimes for which women and men were prosecuted were not committed for economic gain. The situations giving rise to these incidents and the reactions of the defendants reveal a process I term the *reproduction of physical and emotional harm*.

For more of the women than the men, the PSI writers depicted the criminalization process as containing explicit links to victimization — whether when growing up in violent households or in adult relations with abusive or dominating men. Therefore, the boundaries between victim and offender were more often blurred in the women's social histories.

An image of blurred boundaries allows a defendant to incorporate a victimized status within a criminalized status. Such a construction can render a defendant's crime less blameworthy, more a product of past or current problems than a chosen course of action. That more women than men could claim a blurred-boundaries image or were described in those terms suggests again a gender difference that is partly real and partly amplified. In theorizing about crime, we cannot work outside gender constructions, but we can be aware of how such constructions work on our theories. In this vein, I share with Allen (1987b, 93) the concern that feminist discussions tend to see "criminal women" as not responsible for their acts, "positioning [them] as victims rather than aggressors." Although the acts of the New Haven women were not neutralized to the same extent that Allen found in the London area courts, the links between victimization and criminalization were more often made for the women than for the men. More such links could be made for the men if the sites of the masculinist domination of boys and men were recognized. These sites for men are not within kin and family life to the same extent as they are for women, but lie in male peer group practices and juvenile and adult institutions. If masculinist structures are founded on the victimization and domination of others, men's claim of a victimized status comes at the price of undercutting their conceptions of manhood.

Gender and Crime Seriousness

From official arrest statistics for broad offense categories, we know that women commit less serious types of crimes than men; for example, the female share of interpersonal violent acts and robberies is low. It has also been asserted that women are involved in the less serious forms of some crimes, such as less serious forms of larceny. Systematic evidence for the latter claim is lacking. Indeed, with the exception of research on homicide and selected white-collar crimes, few have examined the comparative content of men's and women's lawbreaking.

I analyzed women's and men's offenses that were statutorily similar, both at arraignment and conviction. I read the crime narratives in order to code their organizational elements and to compare the level of seriousness. The coded elements revealed that when acting with others, the men's crime groups were all-male and the women's were composed of men and women. Women were more likely to victimize persons they knew and were somewhat less likely to play a primary role in the offense. It was not possible to infer crime seriousness from coded elements alone: although each element (such as *acted alone* or *caused injury*) might be tallied, the gestalt of the harm cannot be grasped in additive terms.

Judgments of crime seriousness are complex and highly nuanced determinations of an incident, coupled with the contexts that led up to it. Can one make such judgments without regard to the gender of those involved? Pair-wise comparisons might have been more persuasive and valid had they been made without a knowledge of the gender of the parties involved. One could construct a gender-neutral scenario, which would not be strained by the switching of the gender of offenders and victims for some types of offenses. These offenses would include drug law violations, those with victims that are organizations or institutions (such as embezzlement and various types of fraud), and offenses where the offender is unseen by the victim (as in most forms of theft from individuals). But for any crime with a face-to-face encounter, the gender of the offender and the victim begins to define the seriousness of the act. This occurs because we read into a crime such power dynamics as relative size, vulnerability, and the ability to inspire fear. For a third group it would not be possible to switch the genders of the parties without straining credulity. The offenses of this group include harms spawned from men's violence toward intimates, whereby the women are fighting back or fending off the blows of violent victims, and men's sexual abuse or violence toward others, their primary targets being women and children.

Women and men accused and convicted of statutorily similar crimes did not, overall, commit crimes of comparable seriousness: a residual 28 percent of men's offenses were more serious than were the women's. An important implication is that the statistical analyses that allege to hold constant the severity of women's and men's offenses do not hold the social seriousness of the acts constant.

Gender and Justifications for Punishment

Studies of how sex and gender are enacted in the criminal courtroom have largely drawn from rape trials or celebrated cases involving women defendants. With some exceptions (Eaton 1986; Lipetz 1984; Mann 1984), documentation of routine men's and women's cases is sparse. From Eaton's and my previous research (Daly 1987a, 1987b, 1989a, 1989b), I was interested to see how familial ties and responsibilities were used in characterizing men and women.

By the day of sentencing, defense attorneys had little room to argue for less time. In their sentencing remarks, they described the defendant's family life when they were able to paint a positive picture of a defendant's care for others or economic support, or when, as was the case for men, they could identify social control exercised by girlfriends and future wives. Even though they might surround defendants with familial imagery when it was positive, impassioned pleas that focused on not incarcerating a familied woman or man were rare. (How family circumstances were discussed during plea bargaining is, of course, another matter. Several judges gave passing reference to this in their remarks.) At sentencing, judges tended to spend more time discussing the offense, and they noted a broader set of biographical elements — not only familial or parental status — in justifying their sentences.

By focusing on the types of justifications that judges used in sentencing, I hoped to identify a gender-based pattern in the response to crime. I had expected to see a "treatment" orientation toward the women and a "punishment" orientation toward the men. I did not find this result. Rather, for both women and men, judges justified their sentences by recourse to theories of retribution and special deterrence. Although a rehabilitation orientation was rare, judges were more optimistic about the women's future and viewed them as having more reform potential than men. Some may read into this judicial optimism a rehabilitation-like posture toward the women, and I am willing to concede that possibility. If, however, we focus on the justifications proffered by judges, we find that rehabilitation arguments were infrequent.

Judicial silence was just as revealing as judicial expression. The judges were less likely to justify the punishment given to the men and a little less likely to moralize or lecture them. In part, this reflects Mileski's (1971) observation that the court has "given up" on its ability to deter repeat offenders. It also reflects judicial differences: some judges were more likely to offer justifications than others. That women more frequently admitted guilt and men more frequently denied it can be interpreted in several ways. Women may be more contrite or remorseful for their acts, or perhaps women know that deferential demeanor may be more effective than a hostile one.

Although little is known about how gender structures criminal courtroom talk for routine cases, I came away from the transcript analysis more aware of the problems involved in framing what I expected to learn and how to interpret it. To be sure, one can view the courtroom as a site of social reproduction — of power relations (class, race, and gender) and of justice rhetorics — as others have (for example, Carlen 1976; Eaton 1986; McBarnet 1981). Less clear is how one relates what is said in the courtroom to the claim that the court reproduces relations of inequality.

For example, in Eaton's (1986, 97) discussion of familial ideology in court discourse, she argues that the court contributes to the subordination of women by endorsing a particular model of family life. In the abstract, the argument is sensible, but in the world of court practice, it may be less so.[3] For example, it does not consider the ironic fact that defense attorney will mobilize familial imagery on behalf of women (and men); so too will defendants (Daly 1989a). If such arguments affirm a woman's labor for others and may serve to mitigate incarceration, then how is it that women suffer gender subordination? Arguments from social reproduction need to be keyed more specifically to how gender relations matter at the site of penality, not at an unspecified or universal site.

I have proposed analyzing gender and courtroom talk by identifying gendered presuppositions; these include relations to kin and family, offense roles, and the prognosis for future behavior. Gendered presuppositions may not work against women defendants, nor may they be in the service of social subordination all the time or even most of the time. Indeed, in the New Haven court, the gender story has proved to be largely one of men's failures, men's greater blameworthiness, and men's somewhat poorer prognosis for change. Measured against the biographies and offenses of men, women looked better.

Race in Gender Constructions

The gender story is also racialized. For all the dimensions I analyzed in the narrative materials, black men stood out as forming the defendant group most at risk to receive the heaviest penalties. Their biographies were least likely to be constructed with the blurred boundaries theme of victimization and criminalization, they were most likely to be categorized as troublemakers or committed to street life, and they were least likely seen as reformable. There were too few latins to make solid comparisons, but generally their collective profile was closer to that of white men than to black men. From the narrative materials, racial differences between women were less apparent. There appeared to be no strong differences in pathways, blurred boundaries of victimization and criminalization, or character judgments.

Understanding racial differences in gender construction must move beyond an analysis of defendants alone. Racial or ethnic and class relations are most powerfully revealed in the composition of those accused of crime, on the one hand, and the state officials, legal commentators, and social science researchers on the other, those who work in the court or study the adjudication process. The varying levels of racial difference that I found in the narrative material of the women and men reflect, in part, this larger set of social relations and the knowledge produced from them. As an example, recall that probation officers said that it was easier to elicit information from the women defendants; they found the men were more guarded. I suspect that more women defendants — both minority-group women and otherwise — are better able to negotiate their subordinated, deviant status with state officials than are minority-group men, who more often contest their deviant status and thus seem recalcitrant.

Devising A Measure of Justice

In the opening chapter, I argued that neither stories nor statistics alone could offer a meaningful measure of justice. I proposed that by oscillating between logico-scientific and narrative modes of reasoning, such a measure might be possible. I am not advocating yet another way of combining quantitative and qualitative methods, as, for instance, Richard Light and David Pillemer (1982) do when they suggest building an "alliance of evidence" with numbers and narrative. Because logico-science and narrative modes are "irreducible to each other" (Richardson 1990, 118), we need to see them as poles from which we can glimpse distinctive representational possibilities. In so doing, we can think more systematically about narrative and more meaningfully about numbers.

The work of oscillation means a commitment to a nonadversarial, nonhierarchical stance about the superiority of logico-science or narrative, although I assume participants will find one pole to be "home" — more familiar. The work of oscillation could redefine the ways we use and interpret numbers, and it might also redefine the ways we locate or frame narratives. Such a method could be applied in many social contexts; here, I consider its possibilities in the justice system.

The Numerical Context

The logico-scientific pole establishes the wider context of the court's work. For research on gender and punishment, it is crucial to know how scholars have selected cases for study. We should be skeptical of the research on accused women when it appears they were chosen for their dramatic or celebrated-case qualities. We should be wary of "voices" research, for example, which reports the many voices of women in prison or elsewhere but which does not report why these women spoke or why the authors decided to select them for their texts. Such research may bring the words and experiences of formerly silenced women to light, but it also contributes to the sensationalizing of crime and punishment.

In addition to depicting context and variation in the court's work, the logico-scientific pole employs a uniform frame for counting and classifying events. That uniformity can be both useful and a hindrance. It is useful in attempting to apply the same criterion (for example, was a weapon used in the crime? or was the defendant abused while growing up?) for all cases. It can also be useful in revealing patterns that a reading of the narratives will not reveal.[4] It can be a hindrance in that certain facts cannot be fitted into the uniform frame. Such elements either become part of an "other" category or are forced into an existing category.

The Narrative

The narrative pole offers depth and meaning. For sociolegal research, it gives us the full texture of the case. We may try to quantify elements in the narrative, but the uniqueness of the crime story (or a person's biography) may resist being captured by the uniform scheme. It is not simply a matter of technical incompetence, for one could code and quantify many details. Rather it is matter of how the story is larger and more meaningful than the sum of its parts. The narrative retains a gestalt that quantification may only approximate or may distort.

Tensions

Justice systems "demand that the criminal law be applied both uniformly and individually" (Nettler 1979, 28). This creates an intractable tension. The concept of uniformity where justice means equality of treatment pushes against the concept of individuality where justice means responding to the specifics of the person and the case. Further, a term such as *equality* has several meanings: numerical (one person, one vote), proportional ("distributing burdens and benefits [on the basis] of some measure of need or desert"), and subjective (distributing burdens and benefits "according to a shifting standard of need, merit, or ability") (ibid., 30–31). The proportional meaning is expressed in desert-based systems, while the subjective meaning is found in individualized systems.

The term *a measure of justice* contains both a moral and an evaluative dimension. The moral dimension — What is the right response? — is recapitulated in the evaluation dimension, how shall we judge the punishment process? Adherents of the logico-scientific and narrative modes of reasoning answer these questions differently; the tensions are displayed in table 12.1.[5]

In the logico-scientific mode, quantification of sentencing outcomes focuses on whether the punishment is uniformly applied. Researchers ask, What is the outcome and why do the outcomes vary? They also attempt to answer those questions by employing a uniform, standardized metric in judging sentencing disparity. The idea of equality is proportional and desert-based. There is interest in developing a stan-

Table 12.1   Tensions in Developing a Measure of Justice

	Measure of Justice	
	Logico-Scientific	Narrative
Empirical Strategy	Quantification focused on whether punishment is the same for selected subgroups after controlling for such sociolegal elements as culpability	Description focused on meaning and process, and on social and organizational contexts of decision making
	Type of data: large data sets, coded elements of offenses, numerical representations of cases and outcomes	Types of data: observations of interactions and conversations; ethnographic or "thick" description; interviews of justice system workers
	Asks: What is the outcome? Why do outcomes vary?	Asks: How does justice get done? What are participants' meanings and conceptions of justice?
	Aim: Devise an objective measure to determine whether the justice system operates on rational-legal principles	Aim: Reveal the ways in which justice system decisions are patterned, but not necessarily rational
Idea of Equality	Assumes proportional equality: benefits and burdens distributed on a measure of need or desert-based criteria	Not specified. One could assume subjective equality: benefits and burdens distributed on the basis of shifting standards of need, merit, ability. Authors' evaluations of justice system processes are bracketed.
Idea of Justice	Apply law uniformly	Apply law individually
Measure of Justice	Numerical representations of social phenomenon focused on disparity and outcome	None outlined. The "jungle" needs to be described (Hawkins 1986), the gestalt of decision making needs to be modeled (Maynard 1982). Justice is contingent, multidimensional, and based on moral sentiments. A measure of justice may be premature or not possible.

dard metric for culpability or crime severity (for example, Baldus, Pulaski, and Woodworth 1986; and von Hirsch and Jareborg 1991).

In the narrative mode, the posture of uniformity is at variance with "a common sense of justice . . . a *gestalten*" (Nettler 1979, 40; emphasis in original), which recognizes contingency in the meaning of social phenomenon in legal contexts. To assess contingency by using a standard protocol is to mismeasure justice. The aim instead is to describe meaning and process, to ask how justice gets done, and to learn how members conceive of and confer meaning to justice. The idea of equality is not specified, though I would assume some notion of subjective equality. I also assume that narrative scholars suggest that the law ought to be applied individually. An evaluation of justice system practices is bracketed; a measure of justice is viewed as premature.

The oscillation I propose between numerical and narrative poles may offer a constructive response to an apparent impasse.[6] Numerical, justice-as-equality researchers need to reflect with more care on the meaning of such concepts as disparity, culpability, blameworthiness, seriousness, equality, and justice. They should also recognize the limits of objectivist analyses of justice. Narrative-reasoning scholars need to develop working standards by which to judge decisions. To describe the undergrowth of the jungle of legal decision making with more care, as Hawkins (1986) suggests, is not enough. We want to know whether the decisions in the jungle are just.

My comparative justice metric used narrative materials within a logico-scientific frame, and I evaluated decisions within the tenets of equal treatment. It is crucial to distinguish equal treatment as a *method* for judging outcomes and equal treatment as a punishment *policy*.[7] At the moment there exists no other method by which to judge sentencing practices but that which relies on equal treatment assumptions.[8]

Implications

In assessing the body of research on gender and sentencing, we face several key questions. To what extent can we rely on statistical data? How do we interpret differences when they arise? A recent study by Darrell Steffensmeier, John Kramer, and Cathy Streifel (1993), together with my research, sheds light on these questions.

Steffensmeier, Kramer, and Streifel point out the many shortcomings of gender disparity studies, citing inadequate measures of offense and prior record as the most crucial. They argue that findings of leniency toward women may stem largely from using poor control variables, a position underscored by my New Haven research. The authors use Pennsylvania guidelines sentencing data for 1985–87 in carrying out the most rigorous and sophisticated statistical study of gender and sentencing to date. They find that with the introduction of control variables, men were 11 percent more likely to be incarcerated than women; there were no differences in the length of sentence. The authors then analyze the judges' justifications for departing from guideline sentences, finding that "judges viewed female defendants as less 'dangerous,' as less culpable than their male codefendants, and as having more responsibilities and ties to the community" (p. 433). Later, they say, "We routinely found ourselves agreeing with the judge's decision and viewing it as 'wise' or warranted" (p. 438).

Their research and mine reached a common conclusion: the most rigorous statistical study (or one that compares statutorily similar offenses) may still find a gender gap in the proportions incarcerated on the order of 10 percentage points. With more information about the cases or judicial reasons for departing from sentence guidelines, however, the gender gap grows smaller. Thus, I would caution policymakers and scholars against using statistical evidence alone in evaluating sentencing practices. If a study finds gender differences, apparently favoring women, the authors should have the additional burden of demonstrating, by a case analysis or other means, that the statistical result is correct. Optimally, researchers should design studies that permit oscillation between logico-scientific and narrative modes of reasoning.

Better empirical approaches are at issue. Another is what sentencing criteria are considered legitimate and what disparities are warranted. Steffensmeier, Kramer, and Streifel suggest (p. 439) that gender differences in criminal involvement, in the danger posed to society, and in the extent of health or psychological problems may be sources of warranted disparity in judicial decision making. My analysis of the deep-sample pairs revealed such patterns in the New Haven court. Yet, how would we react if these elements were used to explain racial disparities?[9]

Commentators agree that race is a clear example of an illegitimate criterion, but they are less certain about others, such as age or gender. That race is viewed as the clearest example of an illegitimate criterion reflects a gesture of redressing the history of white subordination of black people in the United States, shown vividly in criminal law, justice system institutions, and community practices. The available redress is a limited one: men should be punished the same; black men ought not to be punished more than white men for similar offenses. Scholars are less sure about gender because the history and practices of gender subordination differ from those of race. Once indeterminate sentences for women were removed from the criminal codes, women defendants' redress in justice system practices was less certain.[10]

Two subordinated groups — black men (along with other minority group men) and all women — confront the justice system with different relations to it.[11] The relation of men of color to structurally dominant men translated to such heightened methods of formal social control as penal and capital punishment. Women's subordination, practiced daily through heightened informal social and sexual controls with men they know, has translated to less frequent recourse to formal social control. Efforts by liberals to reform the justice system in the United States since the 1960s reflect, in large measure, a desire to redress a history of racial injustice. That history and its policies should not necessarily be applied in the same way to gender. There may be greater justification for race-blind approaches to punishment than those that are gender-neutral.

A Gender-Neutral Policy?

The problem with so-called gender-neutral policies is that they are not neutral but male centered. Here I confine my remarks to how punishment tariffs are fixed and the role of a male standard in shaping punishment policy.

The sharpest example of the failure of gender neutrality is the split-the-difference approach adopted by legislators in California. We might call this method numerical androgyny: increase the penalty for women and decrease it for men, and we have a policy that combines a little of each one. What could be more sensible? Or more perverse? We have already considered some problems of extrapolating too quickly from the numbers. For the sake of argument, however, let us imagine that the average penalty for women was somewhat less than for men. What is the justification for increasing the women's penalty?

I suspect that the California legislators assumed that the logic of racial redress (that men ought to be punished the same; black men ought not to be punished more than white men) should be applied to gender (men and women should be punished the same; women ought not to be punished more than men). Had they *not* extrapolated from race to gender with the same logic of redress, they might have reached a different conclusion: men ought not to be punished more than women. In so doing, women would be the referent, and equality would be achieved by punishing men less than before.

Similarly, when members of sentencing commissions gather to consider the relation between crime and punishment, they ought to ponder who they imagine as the lawbreaker. Is the character of men's and women's lawbreaking in the frame, or are offenses that are carried out by men the norm? Steffensmeier, Kramer, and Streifel (1993, 432) found that a higher proportion of female (29 percent) than male (15 percent) cases received departure sentences. This intriguing finding may suggest a male bias in the guidelines.

What are identified as legitimate sentencing criteria are obviously linked to the punishment principles advocated. Should they be utilitarian or desert-based, or a hybrid? Today, the desert-based equal treatment approach is responding politically to the history of race relations among men. Under this scheme, the state does not guarantee to change anyone's behavior or to reduce crime. The guarantee is merely to impose a similar sentence on those committing similar offenses. There is some honesty and a bit of a charade in this guarantee: the equality stance largely legitimates the state's power to punish.

Applying a desert-based scheme wholesale, without considering its impact on women, may adversely affect them. As Raeder (1993) documents for the federal sentencing guidelines,[12] federal judges have conservatively interpreted the section on family ties and responsibilities as mitigation. Women's care for children, once a lawful consideration in the federal system, is now harder to introduce as mitigation. So long as a person's — that is, a man's or a woman's — care for others serves to mitigate punishment, it is a sound policy. If, however, the lack of caring for others serves to aggravate a penalty, it is a bad policy. Some feminist scholars are concerned that gender-linked notions of appropriate family life can all too easily redound against women. Although plausible, I did not see evidence of this problem in the New Haven court.

Sentencing commissions have considered the impact of guidelines on increasing the size of prison populations, but I have yet to see this issue raised in reference to women's prisons. Some suggest that because prison conditions are generally worse for women, judges ought to take this factor into consideration at sentencing. Such a proposal might awaken consciousness that prisons are also not gender-neutral and that sentencing policy also affects women's prisons.

Apparent sentencing gaps can be closed in several ways. A failure of imagination and a misreading of history is propelling a sentencing policy, based on the logic of racial redress, to be applied in the same way to gender. Increasing the penalties for crimes committed by women because it would give the appearance of equality with men needs to be defended on grounds other than numerical.

There are several directions to take, and they can be taken together. One is to allow for certain criteria, which may be gender-linked, in such sentencing schemes as pregnancy, the care for children, and battering and male domination as they relate to the prosecuted offense. Allowing for gender-linked criteria is not the same as assuming that men's and women's natures differ (the basis of nineteenth- and early twentieth-century policies). It is to assume that some features of men's and women's lives may differ and ought to be acknowledged in sentencing. For those jurisdictions committed to the appearance of equal treatment in sentencing, a second direction is to use women, not men, as the referent group in setting average penalties.

For some time, feminist sociolegal scholars have analyzed the limits of current equality doctrine to improve women's situation. We have also identified the negative consequences of gender-neutral rules and policies. In researching this book, I have found that similar developments are taking place in punishment policies. A logic of gender redress, wrongly extrapolated from the history of race relations, may increase penalties for women. In the name of a restricted notion of equality with men, more women may lose their freedom.

Notes

1. I offer rough estimates of the proportions of women falling into the various pathway groups. Recall that the women's pathway groups were offense-related and that the deep sample contained fewer women prosecuted for drug offenses who were likely to be street women. In chap. 3, I suggested an upper bound in other felony courts of no more than half of the accused women being street women.

2. One could estimate the proportion of accused women in felony court who were involved in incidents with abusive victims. From the New Haven materials, it would be about 40% of women accused of homicide and assault or about 10% of all accused women.

3. Eaton's conviction that familial ideology contributes to the subordination of women and my conviction that it more often confirms women's labor for others has an important cultural referent. Eaton's study was of a suburban London magistrates court, where, it appears, many of the accused were in conventional nuclear families. In New Haven and other urban courts, the heroic family form for women is a single mother caring for her children.

4. For example, not until I coded the victim-offender relationship for all the deep-sample cases did I realize that more women victimized persons they knew.

5. I am describing the emphases of logico-scientific and narrative scholars especially with reference to the punishment literature. A caveat is always in order in such schematics: some narrative scholars may be explicit in stating a normative position, and some logico-scientific scholars may not accept the implied definitions of equality and justice associated with this pole.

6. Because judges and other legal officials often work in the narrative mode, it should not surprise us when they resist logico-scientific schemes, such as the federal sentencing guidelines. Yet, numerical schemes can provide some accountability and guidance.

7. For example, when Hudson (1993) argues that penal policy ought to be part of public policy and that public policy ought to be in the service of social justice, my response is to imagine how we might evaluate such innovative practices: that is, when equal treatment as a method and policy are joined, we have a very limited conception of justice as procedural equality.

8. I am using the term broadly here to include comparable-worth ideas. That is, comparisons can be made of men and women accused and convicted of crimes of comparable severity.

9. In justice system research, when scholars discuss race, they typically refer to racial differences between men. When gender is discussed, men and women of all racial groups are included. For sentencing policy and practices, women of color are visible in and most likely affected by the gender discussion.

10. One recent exception for women defendants is self-defense law (see Schneider 1986).

11. I am confining my discussion here to accused men and women.

12. As von Hirsch (1989) argued, the federal guidelines are not anchored solely in desert principles. The instructions to judges, however, that employment and family ties should not ordinarily be used in sentencing suggests a concern with removing the utilitarian consideration of consequence.

Appendix I
Methods of Gathering Data and Documents

My research began in the summer of 1985. I met with the JD court presiding judge (Frank Kinney), the clerk (Jack Dziekan), and the head of court reporters (Robert Lyman). My initial plan was to compare statistical findings on gender and sentencing with how court officials justified punishment on sentencing day. New Haven felony court records are not computerized; thus, I required access to the clerk's docket book to create a data file. Further, I required assurances from the court reporter that I would be able to obtain transcripts of sentencing remarks taken from 1981 through 1986. With access granted and assurances made, I shaped a research design that called for (1) gathering statistical material on court dispositions for a wide sample of cases, and (2) selecting from the wide sample a smaller set of matched male-female pairs for which I would obtain sentencing remarks and presentence investigation reports (or PSI's). In fall of 1985 Judge Kinney allowed me to observe plea bargaining in chambers, and I began to gain insight into the court's dispositional routines.

Collecting Statistical Data for the Wide Sample

The summer of 1986 was spent in the clerk's office with two research assistants, Rebecca Bordt and Molly Chaudhuri. We had a daunting task: to go through the clerk's docket books and construct a data set from the information in the docket sheets. The docket books are large three-ring binders, about two dozen in all, that have a sheet for each case disposed of in the past ten years. The pages are arranged alphabetically by the defendant's surname. If a person was convicted in 1980 and in 1985, there would be two pages on that defendant in the docket book. The docket sheet contains the defendant's name, birth date, and place of birth; the legal charges for which the defendant was arraigned and arraignment date; date of plea and charges pled to, and sentencing decision; the amount of bail (if known or set); the name of the defendant's attorney; and pretrial motions and decisions of the judge.

We went through the docket books, first coding all the women's cases for which we judged the arrest to have occurred after 1 July 1981 and before 1 July 1986. (I chose a mid-1981 start date because arrests after that date were subject to flat sentencing.) During the five-year research period, there were a total of 189 women's cases disposed of by conviction. Then, after determining the number of men's cases that were disposed of during the same time (a total of 1,854), we went through the docket books again and selected every ninth man's case to yield a sample of 208 men. A four-page coding sheet (with reference to ten additional pages of coding instructions) was prepared for 397 cases.

Variables were coded from the docket sheets directly, and new variables were fashioned. For example, to gauge the seriousness of a case, a set of measures was developed that tapped the statutory severity of the case at arraignment and at conviction. One such measure, *severity* (or potential incarceration time for the offense of conviction), was the maximum number of months of incarceration time the defendant could be subject to upon conviction. With flat sentencing, the maximum allowable penalties for A, B, and C felonies, unclassified felonies, and misdemeanors could be used as an indicator of severity (see table A-I.1). Other variables that tapped the seriousness of the case were the number of counts a defendant was charged with at arraignment and the number pled to upon conviction, and the number of different offense categories charged at arraignment and conviction (for example, charged with robbery and larceny, but convicted of larceny). From the severity of the case variables, in consort with the precise statutory charges at arraignment and conviction, measures were developed to depict patterns of plea bargaining. Analyzing the variables was important to understanding the court's work and for selecting the deep-sample cases.

The clerk keeps no official record of defendants acquitted at trial. Thus, our data set does not have these cases. The docket sheet had no information on the defendant's sex, race, or ethnicity, but we were able to gather these data by working with the New Haven Police Department.

The First Setback in the Research

The summer was productive and rewarding: the wide-sample cases were coded. I could look forward to more observations in Judge Kinney's chambers. Those observations, coupled with my analysis of the wide sample, would move me to the next research stage: selecting the deep sample of cases. It was therefore a major shock to learn in September of 1986 that Judge Kinney had died of a heart attack. This was one of several events over the next few years that slowed me down and forced me to assess the integrity of the project.

Selecting the Deep Sample

I conducted many analyses of the wide sample to determine variation by gender and race or ethnicity and by offense; I also examined the relationship between charges at arraignment and conviction to see whether the charge reduction process was consistent. After many computer runs, I determined

Table A-I.1 Connecticut Criminal Code

Classification	Penalty	Maximum jail time (mo)
Capital Felony	Death	—
A Felony (1)	25 years to life (60 yr)	720
A Felony (2)	Not less than 10 yr or greater than 25 yr	300
B Felony	Not less than 5 yr or greater than 20 yr	240
Unclassified Felony (1)*	Not greater than 15 yr	180
Unclassified Felony (2)	Not less than 3 yr or greater than 10 yr	120
C Felony	Not less than 1 yr or greater than 10 yr	120
Unclassified Felony (3)	Not greater than 7 yr	84
Unclassified Felony (4)	Not greater than 5 yr	60
D Felony	Not less than 1 yr or greater than 5 yr	60
A Misdemeanor	Not greater than 1 yr	12
B Misdemeanor	Not greater than 6 mo	6
C Misdemeanor	Not greater than 3 mo	3

Offenses in the penal code classification:

A felony (1); 720 mo: Felony and arson murder, kidnapping 1st degree

A felony (2); 300 mo: Arson 1st degree

B felony; 240 mo: Manslaughter 1st degree, kidnapping 2d degree, assault 1st degree, sexual assault 1st degree, arson 2d degree, manufacturing bombs, burglary 1st degree, robbery 1st degree, larceny 1st degree, promoting prostitution 1st degree, rioting at a correctional institution, racketeering

Unclassified felony (1); 180 mo: Sale or possession with intent to sell a controlled or narcotic substance

C felony and unclassified felony (2); 120 mo: Manslaughter 2d degree, risk of injury,** sexual assault 2d degree, arson 3d degree, burglary 2d degree, robbery 2d degree, larceny 2d degree, forgery 1st degree, assault on a police officer, promoting prostitution 2d degree, escape 1st degree, inciting to riot at a correctional institution

Unclassified felony (3); 84 mo: Sale or possession with intent to sell a nonnarcotic controlled substance, possession of a narcotic substance

D felony and unclassified felony (4); 60 mo: Assault 2d degree, sexual assault 3d degree, incest, restraint 1st degree, reckless burning, burglary 3d degree, mischief 1st degree, robbery 3d degree, larceny 3d degree (theft of utilities), forgery 2d degree, possession hallucinogenic substance (some exceptions), hindering prosecution, possession or carrying a handgun without a permit, possession sawed-off shotgun, promoting prostitution 3d degree, escape 2d degree, serious false report

A misdemeanor; 12 mo: Negligent homicide, assault 3d degree, threatening, reckless endangerment 1st degree, sexual assault 4th degree, restraint 2d degree, manufacture or possession of burglary tools, trespass 1st degree, mischief 2d degree, larceny 4th degree, misuse of automobile, misappropriation of property, forgery of symbols, interfering with a police officer, destroying evidence, aiding escape, riot 1st degree (noncorrectional institution), gambling

B misdemeanor; 6 mo: Reckless endangerment 2d degree, larceny 5th degree, criminal impersonation, forgery 3d degree, riot 2d degree, breach of peace, public disturbance, public indecency, trespass 2d degree, mischief 3d degree

C misdemeanor; 3 mo: Larceny 6th degree, possession drug paraphernalia, disorderly conduct, obstructing passage, harassment, trespass 3d degree, mischief 4th degree

*For drug offenses, the penalties vary according to whether the defendant is deemed drug dependent or not. If drug dependent, the penalties are lower (maximum of 15 years) than if not drug dependent (maximum of 20 years). During the time of my research, New Haven police and court practices rarely reflected these statutory distinctions: defendants were treated as if they were drug dependent.

**Risk of injury is broadly concerned with harm to minors: it proscribes behavior that "causes or permits any child under . . . 16 years to be placed in a situation [of endangerment], or [have] its health injured, or its morals impaired, or any act likely to impair the health or morals of a child . . . " (Connecticut Penal Code Offenses, §53-21).

that, in general, gender-based variation held across racial and ethnic groups, that plea bargaining worked in a consistent and predictable way, and that my analysis should focus on seven offenses for which gender comparisons were possible: homicide, assault, risk of injury (see table A-I.1 note for definition), arson, robbery, larceny, and drugs.

Table A-I.2 shows the numbers of men and women in the initial and reduced wide samples. Note the sharp gender differences for each offense type. For the reduced wide sample, about 40 percent of women were convicted of drug offenses, while only 22 percent of men were. Homicide, assault, risk of injury, arson, and robbery accounted for 47 percent of women's convictions, but they were close to 70 percent of men's convictions.

Selecting the deep sample correctly was of central importance, and I had several considerations. First, I wanted it to include the seven types of offenses, corresponding roughly to their proportions in the wide sample. Second, I wanted it to comprise "like" cases for women and men. As can be seen in table A-I.2, under the headings for "Matches" and "Near Matches," there were many potential matches — based on legal charges — from which to select. Thus, I designed and implemented a decision protocol to select the deep-sample cases systematically (described in chapter 2).

The final deep sample of forty men and forty women balances several objectives: (1) a set of cases in which men and women are alike with respect to statutory charges, matched as much as possible by age, race or ethnicity, and pretrial status; and (2) a good representation of the range of offenses for which men and women are convicted in New Haven's felony court. The deep-sample cases are shown in table A-I.3, which gives each defendant's pseudonym, the charges, and other information available to me when selecting the cases.

Collecting Data for the Deep Sample

Having selected the deep sample, I required two documents for each case: the remarks made on sentencing day and the PSI report.

Sentencing Transcripts

It is not a simple matter to obtain transcripts of proceedings in the New Haven felony court. At this point the project's second major setback occurred. After retrieving information from the many volumes of the court reporter's daybook for the name of the court reporter assigned to a particular judge on a particular day (another laborious process), I telephoned Robert Lyman in the spring of 1988. Although Lyman had retired as Head of Court Reporters two years before, he worked in Judge Kinney's courtroom and took notes for thirty of the eighty sentencings in my deep sample. I was not prepared for his response to my request for transcripts. He began by apologizing because he remembered that he had assured me that transcripts

Table A-I.2   Wide and Deep Samples

Offense Category	N Women	N Men	N matches* Women	N matches* Men	N near matches** Women	N near matches** Men	N of Cases Deep Sample
Robbery	27	45	10	15	3	3	8/8
Larceny	23	14	11	6	3	2	7/7
Violence							
Homicide	15	7	8	3	1	1	4/4
Assault	24	35	9	6	8	7	8/8
Risk of injury	3	8	1	1	2	2	3/3
Arson	8	11	1	1	3	2	2/2
Drugs	63	34	25	14	3	2	8/8
Total, Reduced Wide Sample	163	154	65	46	23	19	40/40 = 80
Rape	1	24					
Burglary	0	7					
Other***	5	5					
Failure to Appear	3	8					
Violation of Probation	17	10					
Total, Wide Sample	189	208					

Estimated trial rate for the full wide sample is 8% and 3% for men and women, respectively (assuming a 66% conviction rate at trial).

The 189 women are the universe of cases; the 208 men are a random sample from the universe of cases ($N = 1,854$) that were drawn by selecting every ninth case in the clerk's docket books. The actual female share of offenses is estimated to be:

	Actual Female Share (%)
Robbery	6
Larceny	15
Homicide	20
Assault	7
Risk of Injury	4
Arson	7
Drugs	17
Wide Sample	9
Reduced Wide Sample	10

*Matches are identical for arraignment and conviction charges.

**Near matches are similar, but not identical for arraignment and conviction charges (shown further in app. 1, table A-I.3).

***For men, the other category was weapons ($N = 3$), prostitution ($N = 1$), racketeering ($N = 1$); for women, it was obstructing justice (drug-related arrests, $N = 3$), and prostitution ($N = 2$).

Table A-I.3   Deep-Sample Detail

Robbery (8 Pairs)

Pair No. and Names	SEVERITY	Charge of Conviction	INC-ORG	Original Charges	PR	AGE	R/E	ATT	PT
			MATCHES						
1 Casey*	240	1st rob	240	1st rob	no	26	B	PD	inc
Kate*	240	1st rob	240	1st rob	no	35	W	PD	inc
2 Ron*	240	1st rob	480	1st rob consp 1st rob	yes	21	B	PD	oob
Susan*	240	1st rob	480	1st rob consp 1st rob	yes	21	L	PD	inc
3 Allen	240	1st rob	600	1st rob consp 1st rob 2d larc	no	20	B	PD	inc
Pamela*	240	1st rob	600	1st rob consp 1st rob 2d larc	no	30	B	PD	pta
4 Richie*	240	aid 1st rob	240	aid 1st rob	no	32	W	PR	oob
Pat*	240	aid 1st rob	240	aid 1st rob	yes	35	B	PR	inc
5 Simon*	240	att 1st rob	240	att 1st rob	yes	20	B	PD	inc
Toni	240	att 1st rob	240	att 1st rob	no	19	W	PD	oob
			NEAR MATCHES						
6 Antonio*	240	1st rob	540	1st rob consp 1st rob poss shotgun	no	29	L	PR	inc
Wendy*	240	1st rob	300	1st rob poss shotgun	no	25	B	PD	inc

Reason for selecting pair 6: theirs were the closest matched cases involving possession of a shotgun in a robbery.

| 7 Charles* | 60 | 3d rob | 480 | 1st rob aid 1st rob | no | 18 | B | PR | oob |
| Bell | 60 | 3d rob | 240 | 1st rob | no | 25 | B | PD | inc |

Reason for selecting pair 7: theirs were among the least statutorily serious robbery cases where 1st-degree robbery was pled to 3d-degree robbery.

Abbreviations and headings:

SEVERITY	Maximum potential incarceration time (in months) under Connecticut law for conviction charges
INC-ORG	Maximum potential incarceration time (in months) under Connecticut law for original charges at arraignment
PR	Prior record: "Yes" means that the defendant was convicted previously in the New Haven felony court or was on probation or parole at the time of the arrest. Those with a "no" may have been convicted in the past, but in another court or for a misdemeanor.
R/E	Race or ethnicity: B = black L = latin W = white
ATT	Lawyer representing the defendant. PD = public defender, PR = private attorney
PT	Pretrial status: inc = incarcerated pending trial
	oob = out on bond
	pta = promise to appear (same as released on recognizance)

Notes: An asterisk indicates defendants for whom sentencing transcripts survive.

All the defendants' names are pseudonyms.

Offenses are abbreviated throughout; some abbreviations that may not be immediately understandable are: *aid* = aiding and abetting; *att* = attempt to; *consp* = conspiracy to; *marij* = marijuana; *poss* = possession of; *1st, 2d* (etc.) refer to 1st degree, 2d degree (etc.)

(continue

Table A-I.3 (continued)

Pair No. and Names	SEVERITY	Charge of Conviction	INC-ORG	Original Charges	PR	AGE	R/E	ATT	PT
8 Victor	360	1st rob consp 1st rob	792	1st rob consp 2d rob 1st kidnap 3d assault 3d larc consp 3d larc	no	17	W	PD	inc
Maggie	480	1st rob 1st kidnap	1764	1st rob consp 1st rob 1st kidnap consp 1st kidnap 1st burg consp 1st burg 3d larc consp 3d larc att 3d larc 3d assault consp 3d assault	no	21	B	PR	inc

Reason for selecting pair 8: original charges involved a mix of robbery, kidnapping, and assault, though the woman's case adds up to more potential jail time. Based on statutory charges, this case was one of the most serious women's cases at arraignment.

Larceny (7 Pairs)

Pair No. and Names	SEVERITY	Charge of Conviction	MATCHES	Original Charges	PR	AGE	R/E	ATT	PT
1 Scott*	120	2d larc	240	1st larc	no	32	W	PR	oob
June*	120	2d larc	240	1st larc	no	28	B	PR	pta
2 Roger*	240	1st larc	300	1st larc 3d burg	yes	25	W	PR	inc
Tara*	240	1st larc	300	1st larc 3d burg	yes	26	W	PR	oob
3 Geoff	240	1st larc	240	1st larc	yes	19	W	PR	oob
Winnie	240	1st larc	240	1st larc	no	18	W	PD	oob
4 Joe	240	1st larc	240	1st larc	yes	29	B	PD	inc
Edith*	240	1st larc	240	1st larc	yes	25	W	PD	inc
5 Darrell	240	1st larc	240	1st larc	no	45	B	PD	pta
Prish*	240	1st larc	240	1st larc	no	50	W	PR	pta

			NEAR MATCHES						
6 Tyrone*	6	5th larc	360	1st rob 2d larc	no	16	B	PD	oob
Maria	3	6th larc	360	1st rob 2d larc	no	17	L	PD	inc

Reason for selecting pair 6: conviction charges were among the least serious for larceny convictions in comparison to the arraignment charges.

7 Lennie*	12	4th larc (m/v use)	480	1st larc consp 1st larc	no	19	B	PD	inc
Laura	18	4th larc (m/v use) impersonation	240	1st larc	no	28	B	PD	oob

Reason for selecting pair 7: theirs were the closest matched cases that involved the theft (or illegal use) of another's motor vehicle.

(continued)

Table A-I.3 (continued)

Interpersonal Violence
Homicide (4 Pairs)

Pair No. and Names	SEVERITY	Charge of Conviction	INC-ORG	Original Charges	PR	AGE	R/E	ATT	PT
			MATCHES						
1 Barry*	240	1st mansl	720	1st murder	no	21	B	PD	inc
Claire*	240	1st mansl	720	1st murder	no	18	L	PD	oob
2 Wes	240	1st mansl	720	1st murder	no	50	B	PD	oob
Edie*	240	1st mansl	720	1st murder	no	60	B	PD	inc
3 Earl	240	1st mansl	720	1st murder	no	49	B	PD	oot
Lonnie	240	1st mansl	720	1st murder	no	44	B	PR	oob
			NEAR MATCH						
4 Ted	240	consp murder	720	att murder	no	28	W	PR	oot
Jean*	240	1st mansl	720	1st murder	no	37	B	PD	inc

Reason for selecting pair 4: initially, the conviction charge for the man and woman was conspiracy to commit murder. I found, however, that the clerk's records were wrong in showing a conspiracy conviction for the woman (she was convicted of a 3d-degree robbery). I then selected a replacement case, which I thought was a white woman (this was how her race was given in police records), but after obtaining the PSI file, I learned she was black.

Assault (8 pairs)

Pair No. and Names	SEVERITY	Charge of Conviction	INC-ORG	Original Charges	PR	AGE	R/E	ATT	PT
			MATCHES						
1 Larry*	12	3d assault	432	1st kidnap 2d rob poss marij	no	21	B	PR	oob
Kathleen*	12	3d assault	432	1st kidnap 2d rob poss marij	no	18	B	PD	oob

Note: Later I learned that the defendants in this pair were co-defendants in the offense.

Pair No. and Names	SEVERITY	Charge of Conviction	INC-ORG	Original Charges	PR	AGE	R/E	ATT	PT
2 Lester*	60	2d assault	240	1st assault	no	27	B	PD	oob
Sharon*	60	2d assault	240	1st assault	no	28	B	PR	oob
3 Maurice*	240	1st assault	240	1st assault	no	23	B	PR	inc
Dee Dee	240	1st assault	240	1st assault	no	24	B	PD	inc
			NEAR MATCHES						
4 Andrew*	240	assault/po assault/po	492	1st assault 1st assault interfere w/po	no	19	B	PR	oob
Latasha	120	assault/po	750	1st assault 1st assault assault/po assault/po resisting arrest 2d mischief 3d mischief	no	19	W	PR	oob

Reason for selecting pair 4: theirs were the only cases with convictions for assaulting a police officer; original charges are comparable.

Pair No. and Names	SEVERITY	Charge of Conviction	INC-ORG	Original Charges	PR	AGE	R/E	ATT	PT
5 Georges*	240	att 1st assault	1440	att murder	no	43	W	PR	oob
Stacey	120	consp 2d assault att 2d assault	2160	att murder att murder consp murder	no	28	W	PD	inc

Reason for selecting pair 5: theirs were the most closely matched cases that had original charges of attempted murder reduced to assault.

(continued)

Table A-I.3   (continued)

Pair No. and Names	SEVERITY	Charge of Conviction	INC-ORG	Original Charges	PR	AGE	R/E	ATT	PT
6 Shane*	60	2d assault	300	1st assault carry pistol	no	17	B	PR	oob
Alice	60	2d assault	288	1st assault carry weapon poss marij	no	17	B	PD	oob

Reason for selecting pair 6: theirs were the most closely matched cases with weapons charges.

7 Clarence*	240	1st assault	720	1st assault 1st rob 1st larc	no	29	B	PD	inc
Nellie*	240	1st assault	480	1st assault 1st rob	yes	22	B	PD	inc

Reason for selecting pair 7: original and convicted offenses of high severity in a robbery-assault incident.

8 Pete	60	att 2d assault	324	att 1st assault 1st reckless endanger discharge firearm carry weapon	no	61	W	PD	pta
Carrie	48	1st reckless endanger	348	att 1st assault 1st reckless endanger discharge firearm carry pistol	no	38	B	PD	oob

Reason for selecting pair 8: firearms-related incident; original charges differ only in the particular carrying charge.

Arson (2 Pairs)

MATCH

1 Enrico*	60	reckless burning	300	1st arson	no	26	L	PR	oob
Dorothy*	60	reckless burning	300	1st arson	no	25	L	PD	oob

NEAR MATCH

2 Wayne*	240	2d arson	312	1st arson threatening	no	27	B	PD	inc
Nancy	240	2d arson	300	1st arson	no	22	B	PD	inc

Reason for selecting pair 2: theirs were the closest matched cases for charges at arraignment and conviction.

(continued)

Table A-I.3 (continued)

Risk of Injury (3 Pairs)

There was only one exact match. For the remaining cases, men's cases were selected that were the most similar to the women's for the number of counts and indication of sexual assault.

Pair No. and Names	SEVERITY	Charge of Conviction	INC-ORG	Original Charges	PR	AGE	R/E	ATT	PT
1 Jack*	360	risk of inj 1st assault	360	risk of inj 1st assault	no	35	B	PD	inc
Nola	360	risk of inj 1st assault	360	risk of inj 1st assault	no	20	B	PR	inc
2 Wade*	120	risk of inj	600	risk of inj risk of inj risk of inj att 1st sex assault	no	30	B	PD	inc
Flo*	240	risk of inj risk of inj	720	risk of inj risk of inj aid 1st sex assault aid 1st sex assault	no	33	W	PR	ool
3 Ralph*	120	risk of inj	720	risk of inj risk of inj risk of inj risk of inj risk of inj 2d sex assault	no	45	W	PR	inc
Chris*	240	risk of inj risk of inj	360	risk of inj risk of inj risk of inj	no	22	W	PR	inc

Note: Jack was the *only* defendant in the deep sample convicted at trial.

Drug Violations (8 Pairs)

Pair No. and Names	SEVERITY	Charge of Conviction	INC-ORG	MATCHES Original Charges	PR	AGE	R/E	ATT	PT
1 Carl*	180	sale narc	180	sale narc	no	37	B	PD	inc
Julie	180	sale narc	180	sale narc	no	29	B	PD	inc
2 Reggie	180	sale narc	240	sale narc	no	23	W	PR	oo
Bonnie	180	sale narc	240	sale narc	no	25	W	PR	oo
3 Rob	180	sale narc	240	sale narc	yes	29	B	PD	in
Penny*	180	sale narc	240	sale narc	yes	25	B	PD	in
4 Juan	180	sale narc	264	sale narc poss narc	no	24	L	PD	oo
Miranda*	180	sale narc	264	sale narc poss narc	no	42	L	PR	oc
5 Dylan	180	sale narc	360	sale narc sale narc	yes	31	B	PD	pt
Mary*	180	sale narc	360	sale narc sale narc	yes	51	B	PR	oc
6 Douglas	180	sale narc	480	sale narc consp sale narc	yes	24	B	PD	in
Marcie	180	sale narc	480	sale narc consp sale narc	yes	26	B	PD	in

(continue

Table A-I.3 (continued)

Pair No. and Names	SEVERITY	Charge of Conviction	NEAR MATCHES INC-ORG	Original Charges	PR	AGE	R/E	ATT	PT
7 Rennie*	180	sale narc	552	sale narc sale non-narc poss narc poss narc firearm theft	no	33	B	PD	inc
Colleen	180	sale narc	600	sale narc sale narc poss narc poss narc poss non-narc firearm theft	no	33	W	PD	oob

Reason for selecting pair 7: original charges involved drugs and weapons charges. I learned later that each was arrested for the same offense.

| 8 Carlos* | 84 | poss narc | 360 | sale narc
consp sale narc | no | 27 | L | PD | inc |
| Lotty* | 84 | poss narc | 372 | sale narc
consp sale narc
poss non-narc | no | 29 | B | PR | oob |

Reason for selecting pair 8: theirs were the most closely matched cases that were reduced to possession.

of sentencing remarks could be made (at a price, of course, for which I had research funds). But now, he said, he could not do them. Upon pressing him to reconsider his decision, he replied with emotion: "I retired on February 28, 1986, and have no desire to plunge into the morass of the court."

Finding a stenographer to transcribe another's notes is not normally a problem, but in Lyman's case it was. He had taken notes not by machine, but in Pittman shorthand. Unless I could locate someone who knew that method *and* was able to read Lyman's notes, it would not be possible to obtain transcripts of the sentencings. The saga of obtaining sentencing remarks was to continue for the next year and a half. During the early phase, I called a lawyer about right of access to the court and what legal action, if any, I could take. That contact led me to Judge Francis Hennessy (associate judicial administrator for Connecticut). Judge Hennessy suggested that I write a formal request to the new head of court reporters, Sabrina Santoro, which I did in June of 1988. I was told it would take at least three months to complete the request for remarks; thus I waited. When I received no response after about four months, I called Santoro to determine the status of my request. She replied that she was told I no longer wanted the transcripts since no one could be found to transcribe Lyman's notes. I again put in my request for the desired transcripts during the first week of January 1989. It was not until January 1990 that I received the last of the remarks.

I had given up on finding someone to transcribe Lyman's notes, but an energetic graduate student was convinced that for a price someone might be found to transcribe the notes. This student, Matthew Maly, worked for several months to locate a transcriber. His search was international; from contacts in the United States and Canada, we learned of a highly esteemed court reporter, a Bahamian named Samuel Fitz-Henley. We wrote Fitz-Henley with a copy of Lyman's handwritten notes and a transcript so that he could determine whether it would be possible to transcribe them. He told me Lyman's writing was difficult to read and that the amount of time it would take to transcribe the notes would be great — three times longer than normal — and even then accuracy could not be assured.

Fitz-Henley recommended a colleague in California, a retired man who knew Pittman shorthand. I contacted this person, Joseph Sweeney, to see whether he could do the job. My hopes were again raised, but several weeks later I received discouraging news. Sweeney found that the notes were "not well written" and that he would not be able to translate them. He suggested that Lyman "should be called upon to transcribe [the notes] if he is still living and able to function normally."

There was one way to have circumvented the sentencing notes problem: I could have selected the deep sample based upon the person taking notes, thus eliminating those cases where Lyman was the stenographer. This option was not an acceptable one from a social research viewpoint. Although I would have wished to have all eighty transcripts, the forty-eight that survived contain a good representation of the offenses and defendants adjudicated and are a fair reflection of the sentencing judge.[1]

Presentence Investigation Reports

After several meetings with Judge Frank Hennessy, the Judicial Department's legal counsel, and the director of adult probation, we reached agreement on my access to the PSI's. From January 1989 through the spring of that year, my research assistant, Rebecca Bordt, and I worked in the Probation Department office two to three days each week, retrieving information for the deep-sample cases.

I began analyzing the PSI's during the summer of 1989. Over the next year, I organized the PSI and sentencing documents along five dimensions. First, I wrote a biography for each defendant from information in the file. I then coded each PSI completely, using variables such as experiences growing up, education and work experience, current family situation, previous arrests or convictions, and problems with drug or alcohol addiction. Third, I wrote a crime narrative, drawing from both the PSI and sentencing remarks. Then, I described the explanations for the defendant's behavior that were given by defendants or their family members, probation officers, judges, prosecutors, and defense attorneys in the PSI or sentencing remarks. Finally, I analyzed the sentencing remarks, focusing on their organization, what was said, and which theories of punishment were used.

Limits of the Data

There are three limitations to my data and documents. First, the statistical analysis of sentencing is drawn largely from data available in the clerk's docket book. Although I am satisfied with the quality and ingenuity of the variables constructed, some are not optimal. Moreover, the number of cases for subgroup analyses, especially for latin defendants, is small. Second, PSI reports may be incomplete or inaccurate in other ways. Information gathered to sketch a defendant's social history — such as interviews with a defendant, his or her family members, and the crime victim; discussions with previous employers or teachers of the defendant; and interpretations of psychological reports — all had been filtered through a probation officer's eyes and ears. Although there are well-known limitations to PSI's (Rosecrance 1985; Spencer 1984), I am not sure that a sociologist's portrait of a defendant would be any more accurate (see introduction to part 2). Finally, the sentencing remarks reflect the public face of justice; they do not reveal the negotiation processes that encapsulate the defendant and the case in particular ways. Rather, the remarks show the outcome of these processes, orchestrated for the benefit of defendants and spectators.

Despite the disadvantages of statistical evidence, PSI reports, and official sentencing talk, each has strengths. Had I not been able to use or rely upon these data, I would have had to sit in the courtroom every day for five years to gather sufficient information to analyze gender differences in sentencing — which was not a feasible research design. The clerk's docket books offered a good starting point to identify cases. Although the PSI may be incomplete and distorted in any number of ways, it contains the information available to court officials when they make decisions. For example, Judge Kinney told me that "you don't get a lot out of the PSI that you don't already know," meaning that the document was redundant with his knowledge of the offense and the defendant's social history. Where the document can be remiss, he told me, is in not showing the weaknesses of the state's case. Finally, the public face of justice in the sentencings — the commentary offered by court officials on sentencing day — is the modern version of a state's guillotine. Articulated for journalists, citizens, and defendants, court officials' statements may be "a bit of charade," as Heumann says. Yet they remain the only official record we have of how the state legitimates and justifies its power to punish.

Note

1. In addition to Lyman's thirty sentencings, notes could not be found for two sentencings taken by other stenographers. The distributions for the surviving transcripts are:

		Women (N=22)	Men (N=26)
Offense:	robbery	23%	23%
	larceny	18	15
	violence	41	50
	drugs	18	12
Race or Ethnicity:	black	55	69
	latin	18	12
	white	27	19
Judge:	Kinney	55	23
	other judge	45	77

Appendix II
Sentencing Analysis

Table A-II.1 displays the definitions, codings, and distributions for sentencing variables, and tables A-II.2 and A-II.3 provide added analyses for gender and race. Defendants convicted at trial are excluded. Caution is advised in interpreting the results for the latin defendants because their numbers are low. Additional commentary and interpretation are given at the end of the appendix.

Table A-II.1   Independent Variables: Definitions, Codings, and Means

		Women (N = 160)	Men (N = 147)
Independent Variables			
Severity: Maximum potential incarceration time for conviction charges (in mos)	Mean (s.d.)	190 (100)	172 (118)
Prior Record: Has been convicted in the New Haven felony court or was on probation or parole at the time of the offense:			
yes	1	23%	29%
no	0	77	71
Offense for which the defendant was convicted			
Violence (homicide, risk of injury, arson, assault)	1	31%	40%
Robbery	1	17	28
Drugs	1	39	23
Omitted category (larceny)	0	13	9
Defendant's race or ethnicity			
Black	1	56%	57%
Latin	1	11	13
Omitted category (white)	0	33	30
Type of **Attorney**			
Public defender	1	69%	71%
Privately retained	0	31	29
Judge: Judge presiding in the case			
Kinney	1	53%	48%
All other judges	0	47	52
Detain: Defendant was incarcerated during the pretrial period:			
yes	1	36%	54%
no	0	64	46

Table A-II.2 Sex Effect and Other Variables within Racial and Ethnic Groups

A. *In-Out* decision: 1 = incarceration time to serve
0 = no time to serve

	Black		White		Latin	
	Eq. 3	Eq. 4	Eq. 3	Eq. 4	Eq. 3	Eq. 4
Sex (male = 1)	.23**	.22**	.15*	.13	.16	.21
Severity	.001**	.001**	.001**	.001**	.0004	.0004
Prior record	.23**	.19**	.35**	.21**	.07	.10
Violence	.32**	.30**	.03	−.17	.54**	.51**
Robbery	.32**	.26**	−.003	−.18	.43*	.41
Drugs	.12	.14	−.23*	−.24*	−.11	−.14
Att'y (PD = 1)		−.08		.13		
Judge (Kinney = 1)		.03		−.03		
Detain (yes = 1)		.33**		.44**		−.09
Constant	.06	.02	.11	.15	.16	.19
Adjusted R^2	.25	.34	.28	.43	.38	.37
Mean	.66	.66	.45	.45	.58	.58
N of cases	173	173	98	98	36	36

**p ≤ .05
*p ≤ .10

Note: Using the rule of thumb that there should be at least five cases for each variable, eq. 4 for Latins was run with seven variables.

B. *Time:* Time sentenced to serve (in months)
(only those having to serve time)

	Black	White	Latin
Sex (male = 1)	14.5**	25.5	10.5
Severity	0.3**	0.2	0.1**
Prior record	11.4	48.0**	123.7**
Violence	26.2*	29.0	
Robbery	1.4	34.0	
Drugs	1.3	−2.1	
Constant	−48.0	−47.9	−7.9
Adjusted R^2	.50	.23	.77
Mean	40.2	43.1	45.6
N of cases	114	44	21

**p ≤ .05
*p ≤ .10

Note: The variables for *attorney, judge,* and *detain* have no effect on the *Time* outcome; thus the equation with the smaller set of variables is shown for black and white defendants. Because the number of latins is low, the equation was run with three variables.

Table A-II.3 Effect of Race or Ethnicity and Other Variables within Gender Groups

A. *In-Out* decision: 1 = incarceration time to serve
0 = no time to be served

	Women		Men	
	Eq. 3	Eq. 4	Eq. 3	Eq. 4
Black	.14*	.07	.23**	.12
Latin	.14	.17	.18	.07
Severity	.002**	.001**	.001**	.0005*
Prior record	.23**	.16*	.29**	.24**
Violence	.25**	.20*	.13	.12
Robbery	.19	.10	.13	.11
Drugs	−.004	.005	−.15	−.10
Attorney (PD = 1)		−.06		.16*
Judge (Kinney = 1)		.01		−.05
Detain (yes = 1)		.33**		.21**
Constant	−.09	−.06	.30	.24
Adjusted R²	.23	.30	.21	.30
Mean	.44	.44	.73	.73
N of cases	160	160	147	147

**p ≤ .05
*p ≤ .10

B. *Time:* Time sentenced to serve (in months)
(only those having to serve time)

	Women	Men
Black	12.2	−6.0
Latin	23.3	−8.3
Severity	0.33**	0.2**
Prior record	12.0	40.4**
Violence	19.3	47.7**
Robbery	−9.7	43.7**
Drugs	1.5	18.1
Constant	−57.5	−51.0
Adjusted R²	.50	.38
Mean	33.5	46.8
N of cases	71	108

**p ≤ .05
*p ≤ .10

Note: The variables for *attorney, judge,* and *detain* have no effect on the *Time* outcome. Thus the equation with the smaller set of variables is shown.

Additional Commentary

The results in tables A-II.2 and A-II.3 clarify how achieving statistical signif-icance is dependent in part on sample size. For example, in the women's equation in table A-II.3*b*, the R-squared (or explained variation) is quite high, but only one variable, *severity*, is significant. Several other variables appear to have a strong influence (that is, latin, prior record, and violence), but the coefficient size was not large enough to achieve significance. Simi-larly in table A-II.2*b*, the equation for white defendants shows that white men were sentenced, on average, 25.5 months longer than were white women; the coefficient neared but did not reach statistical significance. For the black defendants, black men were sentenced, on average, 14.5 months longer than black women, and the coefficient was statistically significant.

For the regressions reported in appendix 2 and chapter 2, the effect of the offense severity and prior record variables is what we would expect. Defendants who had previously been convicted in felony court and whose cases were more severe (in a statutory sense) were more likely to be sen-tenced to serve time, and their sentence lengths were longer. With some exceptions, the effect of the offense prosecuted was what we would expect: compared with larceny, defendants convicted of violent offenses (homicide, risk of injury, arson, and assault) and robbery were more likely to be sen-tenced to serve time and to have longer sentences. Those convicted of drug and larceny offenses were sentenced similarly.

The exceptions for the effect of offense type are seen when the sample is broken down by gender and race or ethnic groups. For the *In-Out* decision for white defendants (table A-II.2*a*), those convicted of drug offenses were less likely to be incarcerated than those convicted of larceny. Interpersonal violence and robbery convictions were sentenced no differently than larceny for whites. In fact, the sign of the coefficient suggests that again larceny convictions were responded to more harshly. For the *Time* decision for women, the robbery effect was also unexpected: a negative sign to the coef-ficient, though not significant, suggests no differences in sentence lengths for women sentenced for larceny and robbery.

The type of attorney representing defendants had no effect on sentencing for the larger sample but did when the sample was broken down by gender and race. Men represented by public defenders were more likely to receive time to serve; such differences were not evident for women (table A-II.3*a*). There were no judge effects in the equations.

In predicting whether the defendant would receive an incarceration sen-tence, the variable having a strong and consistent impact was whether or not the defendant was incarcerated in the pretrial period. This finding is in line with previous research: judges use similar criteria when deciding to in-carcerate defendants pending trial and after conviction. Yet the fact that defendants were detained in the pretrial period had no effect on the length of sentence.

Appendix III

Deep-Sample Social History Profile

The following tabulation is based on information in the PSI's, supplemented by information on probation intake forms, notes in the file, and the sentencing remarks. There are two sets of tables. The first shows PSI information for the 80 defendants. For some tables in this set, the response "do not know" (DNK) is largely a consequence of a PSI not having been written on the defendant. The second set is of the 66 (34 women and 32 men) for whom a PSI was written. Unless otherwise indicated, the percentage applies to the number on that line.

	Women		Men	
	N	(N = 40)	N	(N = 40)
Age when offense was adjudicated (yr)				
Median	25		27	
Range	17–60		16–61	
Race or Ethnicity				
Black	23	58%	26	65%
Latin	5	12	4	10
White	12	30	10	25
N of Children in Hhold Growing Up				
1	5		1	
2–3	10		8	
4–5	5		8	
6–8	4		9	
9 or more	4		6	
Cannot determine or changed	12		8	
Average N of children	4.3		5.7	
Evidence of Abuse or Neglect of Defendant or Siblings?				
Yes	12	30%	3	8%
No or DNK	28		37	
Years of Schooling Completed				
High school dropout	23	58%	24	60%
High school or GED	9		11	
Post–high school training	2		1	
Some college	3		2	
Four-year college degree	1		1	
DNK	2		1	

(continued)

	Women		Men	
	N	(*N* = 40)	*N*	(*N* = 40)
Given Birth or Fathered a Child?				
Yes	25	63%	16	40%
No or DNK	15		24	
Had Responsibilities for Care or Economic Support of Dependents at Time of Offense?				
Yes	15	38%	9	23%
No or DNK	35		31	
Addicted To or Abuses Drugs or Alcohol?				
Yes, drugs	13 ⎱		11 ⎱	
Yes, alcohol	4 ⎰	65%	8 ⎰	55%
Yes, drugs and alcohol	9		3	
No or DNK	14		18	
Evidence that Defendant Has Psychological or Mental Problems?				
Yes	19	48%	10	25%
No or DNK	21		30	
Prior Record				
Never arrested	14	35%	10	25%
1–5 previous arrests or convictions	16	40	15	38
More than 5 arrests or convictions	10	25	15	38
Previous adult incarceration (excludes pretrial detention)				
Never incarcerated	26	65.0%	20	50%
Incarcerated once	7	17.5	6	15
Incarcerated two or more times	7	17.5	14	35
Age of First Arrest or Contact with Juvenile or Criminal System (yr)				
Under 13	1 ⎱		2 ⎱	
13–14	0 ⎰	5%	1 ⎰	25%
15–16	1		7	
17–18	11 ⎱	35	7 ⎱	28
19–20	3 ⎰		4 ⎰	
21–22	3 ⎱	25	3 ⎱	22
23 or older	7 ⎰		6 ⎰	
N/A (never arrested)	14	35	10	25
Median (of those arrested before)	17–18		17–18	
Institutionalized as a Teen (i.e., in a juvenile home, reformatory, or mental institution)				
Yes	6	15%	8	20%
No or DNK	34		32	

The following tables show information *only* for those defendants for whom a PSI was written ($N = 34$ women; $N = 32$ men)

	Women		Men	
	N	(N = 34)	N	(N = 32)
Family Circumstances Growing Up				
One-parent family				
Mother	9⎫	50%	12⎫	44%
Mother's kin	8⎭		2⎭	
Two-parent family				
Mother and father	11⎫		15⎫	
Mother and stepfather	3⎬	47%	2⎬	53%
Other	2⎭		—⎭	
Cannot determine	1		1	
Economic Circumstances Growing Up				
Comfortable middle class	2⎫	44%	1⎫	34%
Stable working class	13⎭		10⎭	
Precarious	18	53	18	56
Cannot determine	1		3	
Knew Biological Father or Father Played Role in Upbringing?				
Yes	11	32%	17	53%
Defendant Abused or Neglected by a Parent or Caretaker				
Yes	10	29%	3	9%
Do Any of the Defendant's Siblings Have an Arrest Record?				
Yes	10		5	
N/A (no sibs)	5		1	
Yes, of those with sibs		34%		16%
Defendant's Parent(s) or Caretaker(s) Have an Arrest Record?				
Yes	3	9%	3	9%
Defendant's Parent(s) or Caretaker(s) Addicted to Alcohol or Narcotics?				
Yes	12	35%	6	19%
Mother	(6)		(2)	
Father	(4)		(3)	
Both parents	(2)		(1)	
Defendant Ran Away from Home or Juvenile Institution?				
Yes	9	26%	3	9%
Feelings toward Parent(s)				
Positive	8	24%	10	31%
Strained	13	38	8	25
Cannot determine	13	38	14	44

(continued)

	Women		Men	
	N	(*N* = 34)	*N*	(*N* = 32)
Education, Employment, and Family				
Has Vocational Training?				
Yes	10	29%	6	19%
Ever Enrolled in College?				
Yes	4	12%	3	9%
Employment Record				
None or sporadic	23	68%	18	56%
Steady jobs or off-and-on steady	11		14	
Age at First Birth or Fathering of Child (yr)				
13–14	2⎫	18%	0⎫	0%
15–16	4⎭		0⎭	
17–18	2⎫	15	3⎫	19
19–20	3⎭		3⎭	
21–22	6⎫	32	1⎫	25
23 or older	5⎭		7⎭	
N/A (has no child[ren])	12	35	18	56
Median age	21		23	
Defendant Ever Abused by a Partner or Spouse?				
Yes	10	29%	1	3%
Defendant Admitted Abusing a Partner or Spouse?				
Yes	0		2	6%
Drug and Alcohol Use				
Age When Drug or Alcohol Abuse Began (yr)				
Under 13	0⎫		1⎫	
13–14	3⎬	21%	1⎬	19%
15–16	4⎭		4⎭	
17–18	2⎫	15	1⎫	19
19–20	3⎭		5⎭	
21–22	5⎫	24	0⎫	3
23 or older	3⎭		1⎭	
Not specified	2		5	
N/A (not drug or alcohol abuser)	12	40	14	59
Median (where known, users only)	19–20		17–18	
Drug or Alcohol Abuse Began with Defendant's Association with a Partner or Spouse?				
Yes	7		0	
No	15		18	
N/A (not drug or alcohol abuser)	12		14	
Yes, of drug or alcohol abusers		32%		0%

	Women		Men	
	N	(N = 34)	N	(N = 32)
Prior to Offense, Defendant Ever Try Alcohol or Drug Treatment?				
Yes	16		3	
No	6		13	
Cannot determine	0		2	
N/A (not drug or alcohol abuser)	12		14	
% yes of drug or alcohol abusers		72%		19%
Psychological Profile				
Defendant Ever Received Psychological Evaluation?				
Yes	14	41%	8	25%
Probation Officer Characterized Defendant's Intelligence?				
Yes	9	26%	13	41%
If yes, how characterized?				
Slow or retarded	0		7	
Below average	2		0	
Average	0		3	
Higher than average, has potential, or is intelligent	7		3	
What Problems Are Noted by Psychologists, Counselors, or Family Members?				
Aggressive	4⎫		3⎫	
Suicidal	3⎪		0⎪	
Aggressive and suicidal	1⎪		0⎪	
Depressive	4⎬	psych	2⎬	psych
Manic depressive	2⎪	53%	0⎪	19%
"Nervous"	3⎪		0⎪	
Schizophrenic	1⎪		0⎪	
Regressed sex offender	0⎭		1⎭	
Immature, "primitive"	0⎫	mental	2⎫	mental
Mentally retarded (excludes "slightly")	0⎭	0%	2⎭	12%
Not specified precisely	1		0	
Total with a problem noted	19	56%	10	31%
Defendant Ever Tried to Commit Suicide?				
Yes	5	15%	1	3%
Circumstances at Time of the Offense				
Employed at Time of Offense?				
Yes	6	18%	10	31%
On State Aid at Time of Offense?				
Yes	14	41%	6	19%

(continued)

	Women		Men	
	N	(N = 34)	N	(N = 32)
Who Was Defendant Living with?				
Mother	1		10	
Mother and father	1		1	
Female kin	3	nonfamilied	0	nonfamilied
Male kin	0	20%	1	44%
Various family members	0		1	
Alone	2		1	
Defendant's child only	6		0	
Mother or father and defendant's child	4	familied	0	familied
Partner or spouse and child	5	71%	6	34%
Partner or spouse	9		5	
Cannot determine	3		7	
Person Caring for Child(ren) When Defendant Is at Liberty?				
Defendant	11		0	
Child's mother and the defendant	0		6	
Defendant's mother or parents	3		1	
Child's father	1		0	
Other kin	3		0	
Cannot determine	0		1	
% cared soley by defendant of those with child(ren)		61%		0%
N/A (child[ren] are grown)	4		7	
N/A (has no child[ren])	12		17	
Who Usually Cares for Children When Defendant Is Not at Liberty?				
Defendant's mother or parents	7			
Child's father	3			
Other kin	3	(Q not relevant for the men)		
Cannot determine	1			
N/A (child[ren] grown)	4			
N/A (has no children)	12			
N/A (defendant never incarcerated)	4			

Appendix IV
Coded Elements of Crime Narratives

	Robbery		Larceny		Violence		Drugs		Total	
	M	F	M	F	M	F	M	F	M	F
1. *Social Organization*										
Acted alone	1	1	2	2	14	12	5	3	22	18
Acted with others	7	7	5	5	3	5	3	5	18	22
Number of Offenders										
Acted alone	1	1	2	2	14	12	5	3	22	18
Two	4	7	2	4	2	3	3	3	11	17
Three	3	0	3	1	1	2	0	2	7	5
Gender Composition of Offenders										
All male	7	0	4	0	2	0	2	0	15	0
All female	0	1	0	1	0	1	0	0	0	3
Mixed	0	6	1	4	1	4	1	5	3	19
Acted with boyfriend or girlfriend, spouse	0	1	0	3	1	4	1	3	2	11
Friend(s)	7	6	5	2	2	1	2	2	16	11
N/A (acted alone)	1	1	2	2	14	12	5	3	22	18
Defendant's role										
Active or equal role	5	6	6	5	17	14	7	5	35	30
Secondary role or following orders	3	2	1	2	0	3	1	3	5	10
2. *Victim-Offender Relations*										
Defendant knew the victim*	0	3	0	3	12	13	N/A		12	19
Defendant may have known the victim**	2	0	0	1	2	2			4	3
The defendant did not know the victim	6	5	4	1	3	2			13	8
Organizational victim only	0	0	3	2	0	0			3	2
Organizational victim?										
Yes	4	4	3	2	0	0	N/A		7	6
Type: state entity	0	0	2	1					2	1
business	4	4	1	1					5	5
Gender of Victim										
Male	3	5	0	2	11	10	N/A		14	17
Female	4	3	2	0	6	4			12	7

(continued)

	Robbery		Larceny		Violence		Drugs		Total	
	M	F	M	F	M	F	M	F	M	F
Mixed	1	0	0	1	0	3			1	4
N/A (org. victim only)	0	0	3	2	0	0			3	2
Cannot determine	0	0	2	2	0	0			2	2
Incident was										
Intraracial	4	2	0	2	14	15	N/A		18	19
Interracial	1	5	1	0	3	2			5	7
N/A (org. victim only)	0	0	3	2	0	0			3	2
Cannot determine	3	1	3	3	0	0			6	4
Age of victim										
Under 16 yrs	0	0	0	0	3	4	N/A		3	4
16–39	5	5	1	1	9	10			15	16
40 and over	1	1	1	2	5	3			7	6
Mixed ages	1	0	0	0	0	0			1	0
N/A (org. victim only)	0	0	3	2	0	0			3	2
Cannot determine	1	2	2	2	0	0			3	4

3. *Weapon Used and Victim Injury*
Weapon used

	Robbery		Larceny		Violence		Drugs		Total	
Gun	4	5	0	0	5	3	N/A		9	8
Knife	1	2	1	1	1	6			3	9
Gun and knife	1	0	0	0	0	0			1	0
Other	1	0	0	0	7	6			8	6
Fists	1	1	1	0	4	2			6	3
None	0	0	5	6	0	0			5	6
Defendant used or carried a weapon (excludes fists and penis)?										
Yes	5	4	1	1	11	13	N/A		17	18
Victim injury										
Died	0	0	0	0	4	4	N/A		4	4
Coerced sex	0	0	0	0	1	2			1	2
Injured	1	2	1	0	7	6			9	8
Other	3	1	0	0	1	0			4	1
None	4	5	6	7	4	5			14	17

4. *Other*
Location of incident

	Robbery		Larceny		Violence		Drugs		Total	
Street	2	2	1	3	4	1	4	2	11	8
Commercial est.	4	4	1	2	1	0	0	0	6	6
Residence	1	1	4	1	9	14	4	6	18	22
Other	1	1	1	1	3	2	0	0	5	4
N/A	0	0	0	0	0	0	0	0	0	0
Occupational crime? yes	0	0	3	1	0	0	0	0	3	1

(continued)

	Robbery		Larceny		Violence		Drugs		Total	
	M	F	M	F	M	F	M	F	M	F
5. *Co-Defendant Sentence*										
Defendant's sentence relative to other(s)										
N/A (acted alone)	1	1	2	2	14	12	5	3	22	18
No data or not known	0	2	4	2	0	0	1	0	5	4
Defendant's sentence lower	4	2	0	1	1	3	0	3	5	9
Defendant's sentence higher	2	1	0	0	0	0	1	1	3	2
Defendant's sentence same	1	2	1	2	2	2	1	1	5	7

Victim-offender relations: *family member, friend, or acquaintance; **by sight or from the neighborhood

Appendix V

Pair-wise Judgments of Offense Seriousness

Offense and Pair No.	Defendant Names	Same Seriousness	Man's More Serious	Woman's More Serious
Robbery				
M1/F1	Casey, Kate		x	
M2/F2	Ron, Susan	x		
M3/F3	Allen, Pamela		x	
M4/F4	Richie, Pat	x		
M5/F5	Simon, Toni		x	
M6/F8	Antonio, Maggie	x		
M7/F7	Charles, Bell		x-S	
M8/F6	Victor, Wendy	x		
Larceny				
M1/F1	Scott, June	x		
M2/F2	Roger, Tara		x-S	
M3/F3	Geoff, Winnie		x-V	
M4/F4	Joe, Edith			x-S
M5/F5	Darrell, Prish			x-V
M6/F6	Tyrone, Maria	x		
M7/F7	Lennie, Laura		x-V	
Violence				
Homicide				
M1/F1	Barry, Claire	x		
M2/F4	Wes, Jean		x-V	
M3/F3	Earl, Lonnie		x-S	
M4/F2	Ted, Edie	x		
Assault				
M1/F1	Larry, Kathleen	x		
M2/F6	Lester, Alice		x	
M3/F3	Maurice, Dee Dee	x		

(continued)

Offense and Pair No.	Defendant Names	Same Seriousness	Man's More Serious	Woman's More Serious
M4/F4	Andrew, Latasha	x		
M5/F8	Georges, Carrie		x	
M6/F2	Shane, Sharon	x		
M7/F7	Clarence, Nellie	x		
M8/F5	Pete, Stacey		x	
Arson				
M1/F1	Enrico, Dorothy			x-S
M2/F2	Wayne, Nancy		x	
Risk of injury				
M1/F1	Jack, Nola		x-V	
M2/F3	Wade, Chris	x		
M3/F2	Ralph, Flo	x		
Drugs				
M1/F1	Carl, Julie			x
M2/F2	Reggie, Bonnie	x		
M3/F3	Rob, Penny	x?		
M4/F4	Juan, Miranda			x
M5/F5	Dylan, Mary		x	
M6/F6	Douglas, Marcie		x	
M7/F7	Rennie, Colleen	x?		
M8/F8	Carlos, Lotty	x?		

x-S somewhat more serious
x-V very much more serious
x? hard to judge; information sparse

Seriousness judgments for the pairs

	Same Seriousness	Man's More Serious	Woman's More Serious	
Robbery	4	4	0	
Larceny	2	3	2	
Violence (homicide, assault, arson, risk of injury)	9	7	1	
Drugs	4	2	2	
Total N of pairs	19	16	5	40
	48%	40%	12%	100%

Appendix VI
Deep-Sample Crimes and Punishments

The cases are organized by crime and within crime for each matched pair. They are paired according to their listing in appendix 5 and table 11.3, which differs in some cases from their initial pairing, as shown in appendix 1, table A-I.3.

Key: After each name, the race or ethnicity — black (B), white (W), or latin (L) — and age. After each crime, the pathway category, and previous record: moderate = 1–5 previous arrests or convictions; serious = 6 or more arrests or convictions. In parentheses after the prior record, the number of times previously incarcerated as an adult; 4 = 4 or more. The complete sentence is given in months, followed by the time sentenced to probation and probation conditions, if any.

Robbery

Robbery Pair 1: Casey (B, 26) and Kate (W, 35)

Casey. Entered a convenience store, asked the clerk for an item, and hit her on head with a blunt instrument. Victim fell to the floor, sustaining neck and ear injuries. He took about $55 from the cash register. Another employee observed him and was able to pick him out in a photo identification. Street; serious (4); 120 months flat.

Kate. With a female accomplice, waved down a man driving a car, opened the car door, and pulled him out; the accomplice put a knife to his back. Both women demanded his wallet and car keys. A police officer saw the three, and recognizing Kate, he stopped. The two woman fled, but the officer chased Kate and arrested her. Street; serious (4); 60 months suspended after 24 months, probation 36 months, no conditions.

Robbery Pair 2: Ron (B, 21) and Susan (L, 21)

Ron. With two male accomplices, robbed a gas station one evening. Wearing masks, the three entered the station, said they had a gun, and announced a stickup. They fled on foot carrying a cash drawer, taking about $125. A police officer saw them, and with the aid of a second officer, arrested them on the scene. Street; moderate (1); 96 months suspended after 30 months, probation 36 months, no conditions.

Susan. With a male accomplice, robbed a gas station, taking $385 in cash and the female clerk's purse. This was one of three robberies she had committed in the previous month with her accomplice. She used a sawed-off shotgun, pushed a female clerk, and pulled her hair. Harmed and harming (drugs); moderate (1); 144 months suspended after 96 months, probation 60 months, no conditions.

Robbery Pair 3: Allen (B, 20) and Pamela (B, 30)

Allen. Acted as a lookout while his male accomplice robbed a woman while she was entering her apartment one evening. The accomplice put his arm around the victim's neck, attempted to grab her purse, and then threatened her with a gun. She relinquished her purse, which contained $12. Harmed and harming; serious (3); 60 months flat.

Pamela. While Reinhart, a friend, was driving the car, Pamela's male "cousin," who was sitting in the back, put a handgun to Reinhart's head. He told him to stop the car and told Pamela to take money from his pocket; about $40–$50 was taken. Pamela said she was only carrying out her cousin's orders. Street; serious (1); 48 months suspended, probation 36 months, drug treatment.

Robbery Pair 4: Richie (W, 32) and Pat (B, 35)

Richie. Drove the getaway car in the robbery of a convenience store late one evening. He alleged he was giving his male friend a ride to the store to buy some cigarettes. In the robbery, Richie's friend drew a knife and demanded money; he took a total of $55. Bad luck; moderate (1); 35 months suspended, probation 24 months, no conditions.

Pat. Drove the getaway car in the robbery of an ice cream parlor late one evening. She was in the car while her male accomplice was in the shop. He brandished a gun, ordered two employees and a customer to the back of the store, and took $800. Police later saw the car and arrested the couple. Street; serious (4); 120 months suspended after 48 months, probation 60 months, no conditions.

Robbery Pair 5: Simon (B, 20) and Toni (W, 19)

Simon. With a male accomplice, attempted to rob Wayne in an alleyway on the morning of Christmas Eve day. A witness reported that there were two men "running around the projects with a shotgun and a handgun." The incident stemmed from a gang dispute of uncertain origin, but a failed drug deal may have been at issue. Street; moderate (1); 96 months suspended after 48 months, probation 36 months, no conditions.

Toni. Attempted to rob a jewelry store. Toni came into the shop and left but returned a short time later. While being shown some items, she pulled out a handgun and demanded money from the female clerk. The clerk refused and later said she thought it was a practical joke. Toni left frustrated. The clerk was able to identify the make of her car. Harmed and harming (drugs); first arrest (0); 48 months suspended, probation 36 months, psychological counseling.

Robbery Pair M6, F8: Antonio (L, 29) and Maggie (B, 21)

Antonio. With two male accomplices, forced his way into a household early one evening with six adults and four children present. Brandishing guns and a knife, the three demanded money and drugs, but the household members said that they had none. One adult was struck. The victims surrendered some money, and the apartment was ransacked for more. About $520 in jewelry, cash, and other household items was taken, including $5 from a baby's bank. Street; moderate (1); 120 months suspended after 72, probation 48 months, no conditions.

Maggie. Wearing a ski mask and with a male accomplice, forced her way into the victim's house in the late afternoon. She knew the elderly victim, Max, having worked for him as a housecleaner and companion. When Max tried to flee, the male accomplice slashed him in the hand. The two demanded bankbooks; Maggie took Max's wallet and then ransacked the house. A total of $102 was taken, along with other valuables, including a mink coat. Max was forced into his car and taken to a bank to make a cash withdrawal. He was later dropped off on the street. Other; first arrest (0); 60 months suspended after 36 months, probation 36 months, no conditions.

Robbery Pair 7: Charles (B, 18) and Bell (B, 25)

Charles. With a male accomplice, "accosted" a woman in a parking lot, threatened her with a handgun, and demanded that she give them her purse. They fled with her purse, which contained $10 in cash, a checkbook, and other items. About an hour later, they attempted to cash one of the victim's checks for $300. Masculine gaming; first arrest (0); 60 months suspended, probation 60 months, no conditions, $1,000 fine.

Bell. With a male accomplice, robbed Effie, a man she knew, on the street. Her accomplice gave Effie a severe karate blow that hospitalized him for a day. He lost $825 of his vacation money. Harmed and harming (alcohol); serious (1); 12 months suspended after 4 months, probation 24 months, pay victim one-half of medical expenses.

Robbery Pair M8, F6: Victor (W, 17) and Wendy (B, 25)

Victor. With two male accomplices, robbed a gas station at dawn during the summer. One accomplice tied up the middle-aged male clerk; all three stole an unknown amount of money from the clerk and from the station's register. Victor took a knife from the clerk and took money from his pocket. Harmed and harming; moderate (0); 36 months flat.

Wendy. With a male accomplice, robbed a gas station at around midnight in January. The two initially tried to purchase an item on entering the store. The male clerk noticed that Wendy was holding a sawed-off shotgun while her accomplice, Mo, ordered him to turn over the money. About $700 was taken. Drug-connected; moderate (1); 120 months suspended after 42 months, probation 36 months, drug treatment.

Larceny

Larceny Pair 1: Scott (W, 32) and June (B, 28)

Scott. With two male accomplices, stole oil valued at more than $3,500 from a New Haven school by pumping it from the school's tank to his truck. One accomplice was a security guard at the school. Harmed and harming (unclear link); moderate (0); 24 months suspended, probation 60 months, $2,840 in restitution and charitable contributions, loss of truck.

June. Over several years, illegally received $3,784 in funds from Aid to Families with Dependent Children (AFDC). She was employed while receiving aid. Other; first arrest (0); 12 months suspended, probation 60 months, pay back $3,784 owed.

Larceny Pair 2: Roger (W, 25) and Tara (W, 26)

Roger. With a male accomplice and a female accomplice who acted as a lookout, broke into a residence and stole items valued at several thousand dollars, including guns, a television set, jewelry, a wristwatch, and cash. Street (hardened); serious (4); 12 months flat.

Tara. After being picked up while hitchhiking, she and the male victim went to his apartment. He passed out. When he awoke, he found that items were stolen while he slept: cash, credit cards, coats, jewelry, and prescription drugs at a total value of about $2,000 were gone. Tara was arrested the next day when a third party, her boyfriend's friend, was discovered using one of the stolen credit cards. Harmed and harming (drugs); moderate (0); 36 months suspended, probation 36 months, drug treatment, psychological counseling.

Larceny Pair 3: Geoff (W, 19) and Winnie (W, 18)

Geoff. The file contained seven separate offenses: four thefts from businesses and three household burglaries. The business thefts were valued at $11,000. While released on bond for the thefts, Geoff and a male accomplice burglarized (or attempted to burglarize) the households. One victimized couple thought that he or his accomplice had poisoned their dog. Street (hardened); serious (1); 120 months suspended after 48 months, probation 60 months, drug treatment.

Winnie. On five occasions and over a period of several months, stole silverware from her parents and sold it to a coin dealer. She carried out the thefts with her husband. They sold the silver for $200, although it was valued at close to $30,000. Drug-connected; first arrest (0); 24 months suspended, probation 36 months, psychological counseling.

Larceny Pair 4: Joe (B, 29) and Edith (W, 25)

Joe. Stole $3,200 in cash and $44,000 in checks from a safe in a utilities company, where he worked nights as a janitor. When first questioned, he denied the theft, however, security cameras had filmed him leaving the company with a canvas bag twice in one evening. Street; moderate (1); 48 months flat.

Edith. Broke into several residences and stole more than $2,000 in goods from each. In one burglary, she worked alone; in a second, she worked with a female accomplice. Both times she burglarized houses in her family's neighborhood. Street; serious (1); 60 months flat.

Larceny Pair 5: Darrell (B, 45) and Prish (W, 50)

Darrell. With a male co-worker, stole coats and materials while employed as a driver, selling them to several outlet stores. The items were valued in excess of $5,000. Employer sees Darrell as having been "sucked in" by his accomplice. Bad luck; first arrest (0); 24 months suspended, probation 24 months, $400 restitution to employer.

Prish. Embezzled more than $125,000 from her employer, a car dealer, over a five-year period. While working as the company's bookkeeper and office manager, she falsified records by creating fictitious debits and credits. Other; first arrest (0); 60 months suspended, probation 60 months, $128,000 restitution to employer.

Larceny Pair 6: Tyrone (B, 16) and Maria (L, 17)

Tyrone. With two male accomplices, participated in a robbery of a woman who was walking from her car to her apartment one night. The victim identified Tyrone as one of two males across the street, while the third came up to her, showed a knife, took $7 in cash, and ripped off her gold chain. Masculine gaming; moderate (1); 6 months suspended, probation 24 months, no conditions.

Maria. With a male and female accomplice, stole items from an elderly man's house late one night. The victim, in his early sixties, knew the two women. He let the three in; Maria told him to be quiet or he would be cut with a knife. He escaped to the bathroom. When the three left, he discovered that his wallet, with credit cards and driver's license, was missing. Harmed and harming (drugs); first arrest (0); 3 months suspended (no probation).

Larceny Pair 7: Lennie (B, 19) and Laura (B, 28)

Lennie. While driving around with his friends one evening, stole a car. Driving the car the next day, he spotted a woman in her driveway and decided to steal her purse. He hit the woman on the back of the head and grabbed the purse. Harmed and harming; serious (2); 12 months flat.

Laura. With her husband, stole a car. The police arrested them after a "high-speed chase" and found drug paraphernalia in the stolen car. Laura used another woman's license (taken in a purse snatch), falsely identifying herself to the police as that woman. Street; moderate (0); 18 months suspended, probation 12 months, no conditions.

Interpersonal Violence: Homicide

Homicide Pair 1: Barry (B, 21) and Claire (L, 18)

Barry. With his fists, beat his middle-aged uncle to death. Barry returned to his room, which he shared with his uncle in a rooming house, and found his uncle on the floor, apparently drunk. He said he "slapped" his uncle a few times to try to wake him up. Explosively violent; moderate (2); 240 months suspended after 120 months, probation 60 months, no conditions.

Claire. With a golf club, Claire swung at the victim, a boyfriend of her sister's, hitting him in the back of head. The victim had been arguing with Claire and family members throughout the day. She said she was defending herself. Harmed and harming (alcohol); moderate (0); 180 months suspended after 90, probation 36 months, no conditions.

Homicide Pair M2, F4: Wes (B, 50) and Jean (B, 37)

Wes. Stabbed his friend, who had punched him while he was driving the car and punched him again after he stopped the car. They had been fishing and drinking all day. Wes was angry because the first punch almost made him lose control of the car. When they got out of the car to fight, Wes thought his friend was going to stab him so he pulled his knife and stabbed him first. He left the victim by the side of the road. Explosively violent; serious (0); 108 months flat.

Jean. Stabbed John, a former boyfriend, during an argument in which he was drunk, slapped her, and ripped out her telephone. One of her children, who witnessed the incident, told police that his mother and John had been arguing "for quite some time" before the stabbing. Battered; first arrest (0); 120 months suspended after 30 months, probation 36 months, no conditions.

Homicide Pair 3: Earl (B, 49) and Lonnie (B, 44)

Earl. With a gun, killed a male associate of his son one morning. The victim was arguing with Earl's son; hearing about the fight, Earl drove to his son's apartment, and confronted the man. He saw his bleeding son and thought the victim was coming after him with a weapon. Explosively violent; serious (1); 84 months flat.

Lonnie. During an argument and fist fight in which the victim, Spike, punched her in the face and broke into a bedroom to get a pair of his pants, Lonnie stabbed him. Spike left the apartment and walked up the street a short way before collapsing on the sidewalk. Battered; moderate (0); 120 months suspended after 42 months, probation 36 months, psychological counseling.

Homicide Pair M4, F2: Ted (W, 28) and Edie (B, 60)

Ted. With a paid accomplice, attempted to kill his wife. As Ted met his wife at the door, the male accomplice struck her on the head with a hammer. Then Ted tried to strangle her, but she survived. Explosively violent; first arrest (0); 120 months flat.

Edie. With a statue and then a knife, hit and stabbed her aged stepmother one morning. The stepmother had Alzheimer's disease, and Edie was caring for her for some time. After the killing, Edie took the train to New York City and spent the day there before checking into a mental hospital. Harmed and harming (psychological problems); first arrest (0); 240 months suspended after 120 months, probation 60 months, psychological counseling.

Interpersonal Violence: Assault

Assault Pair 1: Larry (B, 21) and Kathleen (B, 18)

Larry and Kathleen. With a third person, beat a male victim, took $45, and ripped gold chains from his neck. They forced the victim to drop his pants and take his shoes off before letting him out of the car. The incident likely arose from a failed drug deal; there were no apparent injuries. Larry: Drug-connected; moderate (0); 3 months suspended, probation 12 months, $100 restitution to victim. Kathleen: Drug-connected; moderate (0); 3 months suspended, probation 12 months, $100 restitution to victim.

Assault Pair M2, F6: Lester (B, 27) and Alice (B, 17)

Lester. Slashed at the male victim's face with a butcher knife, wounding him from the left ear to the mouth. The victim fell unconscious and now has a scar on his face. Lester was angry when the victim, whom he did not know, refused to buy him a pint of liquor. Street; serious (2); 60 months suspended after 36 months, probation 36 months, no conditions.

Alice. While arguing with another female teenager, slashed at her with a knife and stabbed her in the back. The incident occurred around noon, apparently in the victim's house. Harmed and harming (alcohol); moderate (0); 36 months suspended, probation 36 months, no conditions.

Assault Pair 3: Maurice (B, 23) and Dee Dee (B, 24)

Maurice. Shot Ollie in the stomach at close range, hospitalizing him. The week before, Maurice and Ollie fought, and Ollie won. Maurice confronted him with a gun and shot him. Harmed and harming (unclear link); first arrest (0); 72 months suspended after 24; probation 60 months, $5,000 restitution to victim.

Dee Dee. While drinking with a female friend, Dee Dee fought and stabbed at her. No reason was given for the fight. Both women were injured, but the victim was hospitalized in critical condition. Harmed and harming (alcohol); moderate (2); 48 months suspended after 20 months, probation 36 months, psychological counseling.

Assault Pair 4: Andrew (B, 19) and Latasha (W, 19)

Andrew. On seeing two police officers beating his friend Bo, jumped in and began fighting, kicking one officer in the face and striking a second with a blunt instrument. A crowd watched the fight. Both officers were injured; they were trying to arrest Bo for a street robbery he had allegedly just committed. Bad luck; first arrest (0); 120 months suspended after 48 months, probation 36 months, no conditions.

Latasha. Struck a police officer in the nose with a baseball bat and hit another. The two were seriously injured but not hospitalized. A third officer intervened to make the arrest. The police were trying to question Latasha for having smashed the windows of a car owned by her former boyfriend's current girlfriend. Harmed and harming (alcohol); moderate (0); 24 months suspended, probation 36 months, alcohol treatment, psychological counseling, $2,000 restitution.

Assault Pair M5, F8: Georges (W, 43) and Carrie (B, 38)

Georges. Shot twice at his former wife's car as she drove away with their daughter. The car window was shattered, but no one was physically injured. Georges had wanted to take his daughter shopping for a birthday present, but his former wife refused permission. Explosively violent; first arrest (0); 60 months suspended; probation 60 months, alcohol treatment, avoid victim contact, and no possession of firearms.

Carrie. During an argument with her former boyfriend in which she was yelling at him to leave her alone, the boyfriend attempted to hit her three times with his car. She pulled a pistol from her purse and fired three shots at the car but did not injure him. Battered; serious (2); 12 months suspended, probation 24 months, $250 fine.

Assault Pair M6, F2: Shane (B, 17) and Sharon (B, 28)

Shane. Shot at a group of gang members, injuring one. The incident occurred in a school yard. On the day of the shooting, the gang members confronted Shane, and one punched him in the face. Shane got a gun from his school locker, and when he was approached by gang members, he fired at the group. Bad luck; first arrest (0); 36 months suspended; probation 24 months, no conditions.

Sharon. With a handgun taken from a nearby flowerpot, shot a former boyfriend, hospitalizing him for several days. He had come to Sharon's house drunk and threatened to hurt her. He came into the kitchen, and Sharon thought he had a weapon in his jacket. Battered; first arrest (0); 6 months suspended, probation 18 months, no conditions.

Assault Pair 7: Clarence (B, 29) and Nellie (B, 22)

Clarence. Went to the house of his friend, Bertie, late one night, beat him with a broken bottle, took his car keys, and stole his car. Bertie's mother identified the assailant, whom she saw leaving the house. Arrested a year later on a warrant, Clarence said he did not do it. Bertie agreed, saying his mother's eyesight was bad. Harmed and harming; serious (3); 48 months suspended after 12 months, probation 36 months, no conditions.

Nellie. With two female accomplices, severely "cut" Robert, who was giving them a ride home from a bar. They stopped for one of the women to urinate, and when she returned, the three women grabbed Robert and tried to reach in his pockets. He resisted. He was found in a parking lot bleeding heavily from the head and neck area and was hospitalized for twelve days. Harmed and harming (alcohol); moderate (1); 84 months suspended after 35 months, probation 36 months, no conditions.

Assault Pair M8,F5: Pete (W, 61) and Stacey (W, 28)

Pete. After being thrown out of a bar for being too drunk, Pete returned with a gun and pointed it at the head of the man who threw him out. He attempted to fire the gun, but it did not go off. Three people pinned him to the floor until the police arrived. Street (hardened); serious (4); 30 months suspended, probation 36 months, alcohol treatment, psychological counseling.

Stacey. Following the instructions of her boyfriend, Greg, Stacey attempted to lure a man, Kevin, out of his house by pretending she had been raped. As she ran out the front door, Greg fired rifle shots at the front door where Kevin and his wife were standing. Stacey and Greg drove away; a police chase ended when their car crashed in a yard. Street; serious (1); 48 months suspended after 12 months, probation 36 months, no conditions.

Arson

Arson Pair 1: Enrico (L, 26) and Dorothy (L, 25)

Enrico. Set fire to a mattress in the basement of the building where his girlfriend, Carla, lived. They had been arguing earlier in the day, and he scratched her face. While she was having her injuries checked at a hospital, her brother saw Enrico leave their apartment building just before he smelled smoke. Damage was limited to the basement. Explosively violent; moderate (0); 12 months suspended, probation 24 months, no conditions.

Dorothy. Set several fires in an apartment she shared with her boyfriend. He came home late, and they argued. He left, and when he returned, he found that fires had been set in the living room and the bedroom. There was no physical injury and little physical destruction. Battered; moderate (0); 60 months suspended after 12 months, probation 36 months, psychological counseling, alcohol treatment.

Arson Pair 2: Wayne (B, 27) and Nancy (B, 22)

Wayne. Set fire to the apartment of his former girlfriend, Anna, causing extensive damage. Three weeks before he had come to her apartment, abusing and threatening her. On the night of the fire, he called Anna, threatened to kill her, and said he didn't care about the police. While at a friend's house, Anna received a call that her apartment was on fire. Harmed and harming; serious (4); 72 months flat.

Nancy. Set two fires in the apartment she shared with her sister Ellie while she was away. One fire was in the bedroom and another in the kitchen. The fire gutted the entire apartment. Harmed and harming (psychological problems); moderate (0); 60 months suspended, probation 60 months, psychological counseling, placement in a halfway house, takes prescribed medication.

Risk of Injury

Risk-of-Injury Pair 1: Jack (B, 35) and Nola (B, 20)

Jack. While his wife was away and he was caring for the children, Jack beat his stepson unconscious using a coat hanger and an electric cord. Another child called the mother, who was in another state, to tell her what had happened. Explosively violent; moderate (2); 204 months flat.

Nola. Threw her four-month-old son on an air mattress, causing a skull fracture and bruises. At the emergency room, the infant was found to have scars from old burns on his buttocks and the tops of his thighs. Harmed and harming (psychological problems); first arrest (0); 60 months suspended after 12 months, probation 60 months, psychological counseling.

Risk-of-Injury M2, F3: Wade (B, 30) and Chris (W, 22)

Wade. While taking six children on a picnic, attempted to sexually abuse one of the girls, a niece. He followed her as she scrambled up a hill, caught her, and brought her into some bushes. He exposed his penis, told her he was "going to stick it" in her, and tried to pull down her pants. She pulled his hair, bit him on the hand, and ran away. He threatened to beat her up if she told anyone, but she told her aunt. He continued to threaten her by waiting for her after school. Street (hardened); serious (2); 60 months suspended after 24 months, probation 60 months, no contact with family or victim.

Chris. Over several years, while babysitting for her nieces and nephew, allowed her husband, Bob, to sexually abuse the children. The children said that when Bob did things to them, their aunt was present and did not stop him. Harmed and harming (psychological problems); first arrest (0); 36 months suspended after 12 months, probation 36 months, stay away from victims' family.

Risk-of-Injury M3, F2: Ralph (W, 45) and Flo (W, 33)

Ralph. Had oral sex with his stepdaughter when she was 11, and then, a year later, sexual intercourse. They had intercourse and oral sex for the next three years on a frequent basis. The girl reported the abuse to a school social worker when she was 15. Harmed and harming (unclear link); moderate (0); 84 months suspended after 12 months, probation 60 months, treatment program for sex offenders.

Flo. Allowed her boyfriend, Skip, to have sexual relations with her children. There was evidence of Skip's sexual abusing one of the children several years before, but it was dismissed by a psychologist as the child's fantasizing. Harmed and harming (psychological problems); first arrest (0); 54 months suspended, probation 60 months, drug treatment, psychological counseling.

Drug Offenses

Drugs Pair 1: Carl (B, 37) and Julie (B, 29)

Carl. With a male accomplice, sold two packets of cocaine for $50 to an undercover police officer. Street; serious (2); 30 months suspended, probation 36 months, no conditions.

Julie. Police officers approached her on the street and told her to open her jacket to see if she was concealing anything. A change purse fell from her left arm. Police found heroin and cocaine in forty-two cellophane and foil packets. Street; serious (2); 12 months flat.

Drugs Pair 2: Reggie (W, 23) and Bonnie (W, 25)

Reggie. Sold two packets of cocaine for $50 to an undercover police officer. Drug-connected; first arrest (0); 24 months suspended, probation 24 months, $250 fine.

Bonnie. Sold ½ gram of cocaine ($60) to an undercover police officer. Other; first arrest (0); 35 months suspended, probation 36 months, no conditions.

Drugs Pair 3: Rob (B, 29) and Penny (B, 25)

Rob. On two different occasions, sold an undercover police officer a glassine envelope with white powder ($20), which was later tested as heroin. Street; moderate (0); 9 months flat.

Penny. Police executed a search-and-seizure warrant of Penny's apartment. They found four people there, one who was trying to get rid of thirteen packets of heroin. Street; moderate (0); originally 36 months suspended after 18 months, modified to 6 months, with drug treatment.

Drugs Pair 4: Juan (L, 24) and Miranda (L, 42)

Juan. Police searched Juan's apartment and found an unspecified amount of narcotics. Bad luck; first arrest (0); 24 months suspended, probation 36 months, vocational rehabilitation.

Miranda. Police executed search-and-seizure warrants at four locations, including Miranda's residence. They found 80 grams of white powder containing traces of cocaine, along with 5 grams of cocaine, and $26,000 in cash. Drug-connected; moderate (0); 24 months suspended, probation 36 months, no conditions.

Drugs Pair 5: Dylan (B, 31) and Mary (B, 51)

Dylan. Police arrested Dylan on three occasions for selling drugs. The first and second arrests were for varied amounts of heroin and cocaine (unspecified in one arrest, seven packets each of heroin and cocaine in another); the third arrest was for forty-seven aluminum foil packets of cocaine and ten glassine envelopes of heroin. Street; moderate (0); 36 months suspended, probation 36 months, drug treatment.

Mary. Police carried out a search-and-seizure warrant at her house, finding twelve white packets of heroin and eight of cocaine. Street; serious (4); 12 months flat.

Drugs Pair 6: Douglas (B, 24) and Marcie (B, 26)

Douglas. Two drug transactions and a police search occurred. Sold ½ ounce of cocaine ($1,320) and then 1 ounce of cocaine ($2,500) to an undercover state officer. Douglas's apartment was searched and an unspecified number of cocaine packets were found. Street; moderate (0); 96 months suspended after 36 months, probation 36 months (sentence later modified to serve 20 months), no conditions.

Marcie. Police executed a search warrant at her apartment, finding white powder with trace amounts of cocaine. Drug-connected; moderate (0); 60 months suspended after 12 months, probation 36 months, no conditions.

Drugs Pair 7: Rennie (B, 33) and Colleen (W, 33)

Rennie and Colleen. Police executed a search warrant of their apartment, finding a "large number of tinfoil and glassine packets containing white powder." Subsequent tests showed 2.55 grams of heroin, 1.57 grams of cocaine, and 2.74 grams of marijuana. Rennie: Street; serious (4); 60 months flat. Colleen: Street; serious (3); 36 months suspended, probation 36 months, drug treatment.

Drugs Pair 8: Carlos (L, 27) and Lotty (B, 29)

Carlos. Police executed a search warrant and forced their way into Carlos's apartment after getting no response to knocking on the door. An unspecified amount of white powder and evidence was seized. Drug-connected; first arrest (0); 24 months suspended, probation 24 months, no conditions.

Lotty. Police executed a search-and-seizure warrant of Lotty and her husband's apartment, finding 150 milligrams of cocaine, 35 grams of white powder with traces of cocaine, and two joints of marijuana. Drug-connected; first arrest (0); 12 months suspended, probation 36 months, no conditions.

References

Abrams, Kathryn. 1991. "Hearing the call of stories." *California Law Review* 79 (4): 971–1052.

Adelberg, Ellen, and Claudia Currie (eds.). 1987. Too Few to Count. Vancouver: Press Gang.

Alder, Christine. 1986. "'Unemployed women have got it heaps worse': Exploring the implications of female youth unemployment." *Australian and New Zealand Journal of Criminology* 19:210–25.

Allen, Hilary. 1987a. "Rendering them harmless: The professional portrayal of women charged with serious violent crimes." In Pat Carlen and Anne Worrall (eds.), Gender, Crime and Justice, pp. 81–94. Philadelphia: Milton Keynes.

———. 1987b. Justice Unbalanced. Philadelphia: Open University Press.

Allen, Judith. 1989. "Men, crime, and criminology: Recasting the questions." *International Journal of the Sociology of Law* 17:19–39.

American Friends Service. 1971. Struggle for Justice. New York: Hill and Wang.

Arnold, Regina. 1990. "Processes of victimization and criminalization of black women." *Social Justice* 17(3): 153–66.

Atkinson, J. Maxwell, and Paul Drew. 1979. Order in Court: The Organization of Verbal Interaction in Judicial Settings. London: MacMillan.

Baldus, David C., Charles A. Pulaski, Jr., and George Woodworth. 1986. "Arbitrariness and discrimination in the administration of the death penalty: A challenge to state supreme courts." *Stetson Law Review* 15(2): 133–261.

Baldus, David C., George Woodworth, and Charles A. Pulaski, Jr. 1990. Equal Justice and the Death Penalty. Boston: Northeastern University Press.

Bartlett, Katharine T., and Rosanne Kennedy (eds.). 1991. Feminist Legal Theory. Boulder: Westview.

Beccaria, Cesare. [1764] 1986. On Crimes and Punishments. Trans. David Young. Indianapolis: Hackett.

Beirne, Piers. 1991. "Inventing criminology: The 'science of man' in Cesare Beccaria's Dei delitti e delle penne (1764)." *Criminology* 29(4): 777–820.

Bell, Susan G., and Marilyn Yalom. 1990. Revealing Lives: Autobiography, Biography, and Gender. Albany: SUNY Press.

Berkmann, Miriam. 1986. "Profile of Judge Frank J. Kinney, Jr., Superior Court of Connecticut." Sentencing Principles Seminar, Guggenheim Program in Criminal Justice, Yale Law School.

Bickle, Gayle S., and Ruth D. Peterson. 1991. "The impact of gender-based family roles in criminal sentencing." *Social Problems* 38(3): 372–94.

Black, Donald J. 1970. "Production of crime rates." *American Sociological Review* 35(4): 733–48.

———. 1976. The Behavior of Law. New York: Academic.

———. 1979. "Common sense in the sociology of law." *American Sociological Review* 44: 18–27.

————. 1989. Sociological Justice. New York: Oxford University Press.

Block, Carolyn Rebecca. 1987. Homicide in Chicago. Chicago: Center for Urban Policy, Loyola University of Chicago.

Blum, Linda. 1991. Between Feminism and Labor: The Significance of the Comparable Worth Movement. Berkeley: University of California Press.

Blumstein, Alfred, Jacqueline Cohen, Susan E. Martin, and Michael H. Tonry (eds.). 1983. Research on Sentencing: The Search for Reform, vol. 1 (of 2 vols.). Washington, D.C.: National Academy Press.

Boritch, Helen. 1992. "Gender and criminal court outcomes: An historical analysis." Criminology 30(3): 293–325.

Braithwaite, John. 1989. Crime, Shame and Reintegration. Cambridge: Cambridge University Press.

Braithwaite, John, and Philip Pettit. 1990. Not Just Deserts: A Republican Theory of Criminal Justice. Oxford: Oxford University Press.

Brenzel, Barbara. 1983. Daughters of the State. Cambridge: MIT Press.

Brown, Elizabeth Mills. 1976. New Haven: A Guide to Architecture and Urban Design. New Haven: Yale University Press.

Browne, Angela. 1987. When Battered Women Kill. New York: Free Press.

Browne, Angela, and Kirk Williams. 1989. "Exploring the effect of resource availability on the likelihood of female-perpetrated homicides." Law & Society Review 23(1): 75–94.

Bureau of Justice Statistics (BJS). 1987. "Sentencing outcomes in twenty-eight felony courts" (by Mark A. Cunniff). Washington, D.C.: U.S. Department of Justice, Office of Justice Programs.

————. 1989. "Correctional populations in the United States, 1987." Washington, D.C.: U.S. Department of Justice, Office of Justice Programs.

————. 1990. "Profile of felons convicted in state courts" (by Patrick A. Langan and John M. Dawson). Washington, D.C.: U.S. Department of Justice, Office of Justice Programs.

————. 1991. "Tracking offenders, 1988" (by Jacob Perez). Washington, D.C.: U.S. Department of Justice, Office of Justice Programs.

————. 1992. "Women in jail, 1989" (by Tracy L. Snell). Washington, D.C.: U.S. Department of Justice, Office of Justice Programs.

————. 1993. "Survey of state prison inmates, 1991" (by Allen Beck, Darrell Gilliard, Lawrence Greenfield, Caroline Harlow, Thomas Hester, Louis Jankowski, Danielle Morton, Tracy Snell, and James Stephan). Washington, D.C.: U.S. Department of Justice, Office of Justice Programs.

Burkhart, Kathryn. 1976. Women in Prison. New York: Popular Library.

Buzawa, Eve S., and Carl G. Buzawa (eds.). 1992. Domestic Violence: The Changing Criminal Justice Response. Westport, Conn.: Auburn House.

Cain, Maureen (ed.). 1989. Growing Up Good. Newbury Park: Russell Sage.

————. 1990. "Towards transgression: New directions in feminist criminology." International Journal of the Sociology of Law 18:1–18.

Campbell, Anne. 1991. The Girls in the Gang. 2d ed. New York: Basil Blackwell.

Carlen, Pat. 1976. Magistrates' Justice. London: Martin Robertson.

————. 1983. Women's Imprisonment. Boston: Routledge and Kegan Paul.

————. 1988. Women, Crime and Poverty. Philadelphia: Open University Press.

Carlen, Pat, Diana Christina, Jenny Hicks, Josie O'Dwyer, and Chris Tchaikovsky. 1985. Criminal Women. Cambridge: Polity.

Caspar, Jonathan. 1972. American Criminal Justice. Englewood Cliffs, N.J.: Prentice-Hall.

Chapman, Jane Roberts. 1980. Economic Realities and the Female Offender. Lexington, Mass.: Lexington Books.

Chesney-Lind, Meda. 1989. "Girls' crime and woman's place: Toward a feminist model of female delinquency." *Crime & Delinquency* 35(1): 5–29.

———. 1992. "Patriarchy and prisons: A critical look at trends in women's incarceration." In Marie-Andrée Bertrand, Kathleen Daly, and Dorie Klein (eds.), Proceedings of the International Conference on Women, Law, and Social Control. Vancouver: International Centre for Criminal Law Reform and Criminal Justice Policy.

Chesney-Lind, Meda, and Noelie Rodriguez. 1983. "Women under lock and key: A view from the inside." *Prison Journal* 63(2): 47–65.

"City, suburbs worlds apart." *New Haven Register,* 15 June 1992. (Second of a four-part series on the U.S. census.)

Clinard, Marshall. 1983. Corporate Ethics and Crime. Beverly Hills: Russell Sage.

Cohen, Albert J. 1955. Delinquent Boys. Glencoe, Ill.: Free Press.

Coker, Donna K. 1992. "Heat of passion and wife killing: Men who batter/men who kill." *Southern California Review of Law and Women's Studies* 2(1): 71–130.

Coleman, James. 1989. The Criminal Elite: The Sociology of White Collar Crime. 2d ed. New York: St. Martin's.

Conley, John M., and William M. O'Barr. 1987. "Fundamentals of jurisprudence: An ethnography of judicial decision making in informal courts." *North Carolina Law Review* 66(3): 467–507.

Cullen, Francis T., Bruce G. Link, and Craig W. Polanzi. 1982. "The seriousness of crime revisited: Have attitudes toward white-collar crime changed?" *Criminology* 20(1): 83–102.

Daly, Kathleen. 1987a. "Structure and practice of familial-based justice in a criminal court." *Law & Society Review* 21(2): 267–90.

———. 1987b. "Discrimination in the criminal courts: Family, gender, and the problem of equal treatment." *Social Forces* 66(1): 152–75.

———. 1989a. "Rethinking judicial paternalism: Gender, work-family relations, and sentencing." *Gender & Society* 3(1): 9–36.

———. 1989b. "Neither conflict nor labeling nor paternalism will suffice: Intersections of race, ethnicity, gender, and family in criminal court decisions." *Crime & Delinquency* 35(1): 136–68.

———. 1989c. "Criminal justice ideologies and practices in different voices: Some feminist questions about justice." *International Journal of the Sociology of Law* 17:1–18.

———. 1989d. "Gender and varieties of white-collar crime." *Criminology* 27(4): 769–94.

———. 1991. "Of numbers and narrative." Paper presented at the annual meeting of the Law & Society Association, June.

———. 1992. "Women's pathways to felony court: Feminist theories of lawbreaking and problems of representation." *Southern California Review of Law and Women's Studies* 2(1): 11–52.

Daly, Kathleen, and Rebecca Bordt. 1991. "Gender, race, and discrimination research: Disparate meanings of statistical 'sex' and 'race effects' in sentencing." Department of Sociology, University of Michigan.

Daly, Kathleen, and Meda Chesney-Lind. 1988. "Feminism and criminology." *Justice Quarterly* 5(4): 497–538.

Daly, Kathleen, Shelley Geballe, and Stanton Wheeler. 1988. "Litigation-driven research: A case study of lawyer/social scientist collaboration." *Women's Rights Law Reporter* 10(4): 221–40.

Daly, Martin, and Margo Wilson. 1987. Homicide. New York: Aldine de Gruyter.

Delgado, Richard. 1989. "Storytelling for oppositionists and others: A plea for narrative." *Michigan Law Review* 87:2411–41.

Devlin, Mark. 1985. Stubborn Child. New York: Atheneum.

Dobash, R. Emerson, and Russell Dobash. 1984. "The nature and antecedents of violent events." *British Journal of Criminology* 24(3): 269–88.

Dobash, Russell P., R. Emerson Dobash, and Sue Gutteridge. 1986. The Imprisonment of Women. New York: Basil Blackwell.

Dobash, Russell P., R. Emerson Dobash, Margo Wilson, and Martin Daly. 1992. "The myth of sexual symmetry in marital violence." *Social Problems* 39(1): 71–91.

Duff, R. Anthony. 1986. Trials and Punishments. New York: Cambridge University Press.

Duncan, Otis Dudley. 1985. Notes on Social Measurement: Historical and Critical. New York: Russell Sage.

Eaton, Mary. 1986. Justice for Women? Philadelphia: Open University Press.

Edwards, Susan S. M. 1984. Women on Trial. Manchester, U.K.: Manchester University Press.

Eisenstein, James, and Herbert Jacob. 1977. Felony Justice: An Organizational Analysis of Criminal Courts. Boston: Little, Brown.

Elliott, Delbert. 1989. "Criminal justice procedures in family violence cases." In Lloyd Ohlin and Michael Tonry (eds.), Family Violence, vol. 11 of Crime and Justice: A Review of Research, pp. 427–80. Chicago: University of Chicago Press.

Ellis, Ralph D., and Carol S. Ellis. 1989. Theories of Criminal Justice: A Critical Appraisal. Wolfeboro, N.H.: Longwood Academic.

Emerson, Robert M. 1983. "Holistic effects in social control decision-making." *Law & Society Review* 17(3): 425–55.

Estrich, Susan. 1986. "Rape." *Yale Law Journal* 95(6): 1087–184.

Farber, Daniel A., and Suzanna Sherry. 1993. "Telling stories out of school: An essay on legal narrative." *Stanford Law Review* 45:807–55.

Feeley, Malcolm M. 1979. The Process Is the Punishment. New York: Russell Sage.

Feeley, Malcolm M., and Deborah L. Little. 1991. "The vanishing female: The decline of women in the criminal process, 1687–1912." *Law & Society Review* 25(4): 719–57.

Feinberg, Joel. 1984. Harm to Others. New York: Oxford.

Felson, Richard B., and Henry J. Steadman. 1983. "Situational factors in disputes leading to criminal violence." *Criminology* 21(1): 59–74.

Ferraro, Kathleen J. 1989. "Policing woman battering." *Social Problems* 36(1): 61–74.

Ferraro, Kathleen J., and Tascha Boychuk. 1992. "The court's response to interpersonal violence: A comparison of intimate and nonintimate assault." In Eve S. Buzawa and Carl G. Buzawa (eds.), Domestic Violence: The Changing Criminal Justice Response, pp. 209–25. Westport, Conn.: Auburn House.

Fineman, Martha. 1991. The Illusion of Equality: The Rhetoric and Reality of Divorce Reform. Chicago: University of Chicago Press.

Finnegan, William. 1990. "Out There," pts. 1 and 2. New Yorker (10 Sept. and 17 Sept.).

Flanagan, Timothy J., and Kathleen Maguire (eds.). 1992. Sourcebook of Criminal Justice Statistics 1991. Washington, D.C.: U.S. Department of Justice, Bureau of Justice Statistics.

Flanagan, William, and Maureen McLeod (eds.). 1983. Sourcebook of Criminal Justice Statistics 1982. Washington, D.C.: U.S. Department of Justice, Bureau of Justice Statistics.

Fletcher, George P. 1978. Rethinking Criminal Law. Boston: Little, Brown.

Frankel, Marvin. 1972. Criminal Sentences. New York: Hill and Wang.

Freed, Donald. 1973. Agony in New Haven. New York: Simon and Schuster.

Freedman, Estelle. 1981. Their Sisters' Keepers: Women's Prison Reform in America, 1830–1930. Ann Arbor: University of Michigan Press.

Frohmann, Lisa. 1991. "Discrediting victims' allegations of sexual assault: Prosecutorial accounts of case rejections." Social Problems 38(2): 213–26.

Garfinkel, Harold. 1956. "Conditions of successful degradation ceremonies." American Journal of Sociology 61:420–24.

Garland, David. 1985. Punishment and Welfare. Gower: Hants, England.

———. 1990. Punishment and Modern Society. Chicago: University of Chicago Press.

Gelsthorpe, Loraine, and Allison Morris. 1988. "Feminism and criminology in Britain." British Journal of Criminology 28(2): 93–110.

Genders, Elaine, and Elaine Player. 1987. "Women in prison: The treatment, the control and the experience." In Pat Carlen and Anne Worrall (eds.), Gender, Crime and Justice, pp. 161–75. Philadelphia: Open University Press.

Gilfus, Mary E. 1992. "From victims to survivors to offenders: Women's routes of entry and immersion into street crime." Women & Criminal Justice 4(1): 63–89.

Gillespie, Cynthia K. 1989. Justifiable Homicide: Battered Women, Self-Defense, and the Law. Columbus: Ohio University Press.

Gross, Hyman. 1979. A Theory of Criminal Justice. New York: Oxford University Press.

———. 1981. Introduction to sec. 4 on Desert. In Hyman Gross and Andrew von Hirsch (eds.), Sentencing, pp. 237–42. New York: Oxford University Press.

Gross, Hyman, and Andrew von Hirsch (eds.). 1981. Sentencing. New York: Oxford University Press.

Gruhl, John, Susan Welch, and Cassia Spohn. 1984. "Women as criminal defendants: A test for paternalism." Western Political Quarterly 37:456–67.

Hagan, John. 1974. "Extra-legal attributes and criminal sentencing: An assessment of a sociological viewpoint." Law & Society Review 8:357–83.

———. 1977. "Finding 'discrimination': A question of meaning." Ethnicity 4:167–76.

Hagan, John, and Kristin Bumiller. 1983. "Making sense of sentencing: A review and critique of sentencing research." In Alfred Blumstein, Jacqueline Cohen, Susan E. Martin, and Michael H. Tonry (eds.), Research on Sentencing: The Search for Reform, vol. 2, pp. 1–54. Washington, D.C.: National Academy Press.

Hagedorn, John M. 1988. People and Folks. Chicago: Lake View.

Hall, Stuart, Chas Critcher, Tony Jefferson, John Clarke, and Brian Roberts. 1978. Policing the Crisis: Mugging, the State, and Order. New York: Holmes & Meier.

Hamilton, V. Lee, and Steve Rytina. 1980. "Social consensus on norms of justice: Should the punishment fit the crime?" American Journal of Sociology 85(5): 1117–44.

Harris, Anthony R. 1977. "Sex and theories of deviance: Toward a functional theory of deviant type-scripts." American Sociological Review 42(1): 3–16.

Hart, H. L. A. 1968. Punishment and Responsibility: Essays in the Philosophy of Law. New York: Oxford University Press.

Hawkins, Keith. 1986. "On legal decision-making." Washington and Lee Law Review 43(4): 1161–242.

Heidensohn, Frances M. 1985. Women and Crime. New York: New York University Press.

Heilbrun, Carolyn. 1988. Writing a Woman's Life. New York: Ballantine.

Heumann, Milton. 1978. Plea Bargaining. Chicago: University of Chicago Press.

Hogarth, John. 1971. Sentencing as a Human Process. Toronto: University of Toronto Press.

Horowitz, Ruth. 1983. Honor and the American Dream. New Brunswick: Rutgers University Press.

Hudson, Barbara. 1987. Justice through Punishment: A Critique of the "Justice" Model of Corrections. London: MacMillan.

———. 1993. Penal Policy and Social Justice. Basingstoke: Macmillan.

Hunt, Jennifer C. 1990. "The logic of sexism among police." Women & Criminal Justice 1(2): 3–30.

Jurik, Nancy C., and Peter Gregware. 1991. "A method for murder: The study of homicides by women." In James Holstein (ed.), Perspectives on Social Problems, vol. 4, pp. 179–201. Westport, Conn.: Jai.

Jurik, Nancy C., and Russ Winn. 1990. "Gender and homicide: A comparison of men and women who kill." Violence and Victims 5(4): 227–42.

Katz, Jack. 1988. Seductions of Crime. New York: Basic Books.

Kelly, Liz. 1988. Surviving Sexual Violence. Minneapolis: University of Minnesota Press.

———. 1991. "Unspeakable acts." Trouble and Strife 21:13–20.

Kitsuse, John I., and Aaron V. Cicourel. 1963. "A note on the use of official statistics." Social Problems 11:131–38.

Kleck, Gary. 1981. "Racial discrimination in criminal sentencing: A critical evaluation of the evidence with additional evidence on the death penalty." American Sociological Review 46:783–805.

Klein, Dorie. 1982. "The dark side of marriage: Battered wives and the domination of women." In Nicole Hahn Rafter and Elizabeth Anne Stanko (eds.), Judge, Lawyer, Victim, Thief, pp. 83–107. Boston: Northeastern University Press.

Kruttschnitt, Candace. 1980–81. "Social status and sentences of female offenders." Law & Society Review 15:247–65.

————. 1982a. "Women, crime, and dependency." *Criminology* 19:495–513.

————. 1982b. "Respectable women and the law." *Sociological Quarterly* 23:221–34.

Kurz, Demi. 1989. "Social science perspectives on wife abuse: Current debates and future directions." *Gender & Society* 3(4): 489–505.

Lacey, Nicola. 1988. State Punishment, Political Principles, and Community Values. New York: Routledge and Kegan Paul.

Laslett, Barbara. 1990. "Unfeeling knowledge: Emotion and objectivity in the history of sociology." *Sociological Forum* 5:413–33.

Leonard, Eileen. 1982. Women, Crime, and Society. New York: Longman.

————. 1983. "Judicial decisions and prison reform: The impact of litigation on women prisoners." *Social Problems* 31(1): 45–58.

Light, Richard J., and David B. Pillemer. 1982. "Numbers and narrative: Combining their strengths in research reviews." *Harvard Educational Review* 52(1): 1–26.

Lipetz, Marcia J. 1984. Routine Justice: Processing Cases in Women's Court. New Brunswick, N.J.: Transaction Books.

Luckenbill, David F. 1977. "Criminal homicide as a situated transaction." *Social Problems* 25(2): 176–86.

————. 1980. "Patterns of force in robbery." *Deviant Behavior: An Interdisciplinary Journal* 1:361–78.

————. 1981. "Generating compliance: The case of robbery." *Urban Life* 10(1): 25–46.

McBarnet, Doreen J. 1981. Conviction: Law, the State and the Construction of Justice. London: MacMillan.

McCleary, Richard, Barbara C. Nienstedt, and James M. Erven. 1982. "Uniform Crime Reports as organizational outcomes: Three time series experiments." *Social Problems* 29(4): 361–72.

MacFarlane, Kee. 1978. "Sexual abuse of children." In Jane Robert Chapman and Margaret Gates (eds.), The Victimization of Women, pp. 81–109. Beverly Hills: Russell Sage.

MacKinnon, Catharine. 1987. Feminism Unmodified. Cambridge: Harvard University Press.

Maher, Lisa. 1993. "In the name of love: Women and initiation to illicit drugs." Paper presented at the British Criminology Conference, July.

Maher, Lisa, and Richard Curtis. 1992. "Women on the edge of crime: Crack cocaine and the changing contexts of street-level sex work in New York City." *Crime, Law, and Social Change* 18:221–58.

Mann, Coramae Richey. 1984. "Race and sentencing of female felons: A field study." *International Journal of Women's Studies* 7:160–72.

————. 1988. "Getting even? Women who kill in domestic encounters." *Justice Quarterly* 5(1): 33–51.

Mann, Kenneth, Stanton Wheeler, and Austin Sarat. 1980. "Sentencing the white collar offender." *American Criminal Law Review* 17:479–500.

Mars, Gerald. 1982. Cheats at Work: An Anthropology of Workplace Crime. Boston: Allen and Unwin.

Mather, Lynn. 1979. Plea Bargaining or Trial? Lexington, Mass.: Lexington Books.

Matthews, Roger, and Jock Young (eds.) 1986. Confronting Crime. Newbury Park: Russell Sage.

Matza, David. [1964] 1990. Delinquency and Drift. New Brunswick, N.J.: Transaction.

Maxfield, Michael G. 1989. "Circumstances in supplementary homicide reports: Variety and validity." *Criminology* 27(4): 671–95.

Maynard, Douglas W. 1982. "Defendant attributes in plea bargaining: Notes on the modeling of sentencing decisions." *Social Problems* 49:347–60.

———. 1984. Inside Plea Bargaining. New York: Plenum.

Meierhoefer, Barbara S. 1992. The General Effect of Mandatory Minimum Terms. Washington, D.C.: Federal Judicial Center.

Melossi, Dario. 1993. "Gazette of morality and social whip: Punishment, hegemony, and the case of the USA, 1970–92." *Social and Legal Studies* 2(3): 259–79.

Messerschmidt, James W. 1993. Masculinities and Crime. Lanham, Md.: Rowman & Littlefield.

Michigan Law Review. 1989. Symposium, Legal Storytelling. Vol. 87.

Mileski, Maureen. 1971. "Courtroom encounters: An observation study of a lower criminal court." *Law & Society Review* 5(4): 473–538.

Miller, Eleanor. 1986. Street Woman. Philadelphia: Temple University Press.

Miller, Jody A. 1993. "Gender and power on the streets: The ecology of street prostitution in an era of crack cocaine." Department of Sociology, University of Southern California.

Miller, Walter B. 1958. "Lower class culture as a generating milieu of gang delinquency." *Journal of Social Issues* 14:5–19.

Millman, Marcia. 1975. "She did it all for love: A feminist view of the sociology of deviance." In Marcia Millman and Rosabeth Moss Kanter (eds.), Another Voice, pp. 251–79. Garden City: Anchor.

Moore, Joan W. 1978. Homeboys. Philadelphia: Temple University Press.

———. 1991. Going Down to the Barrio: Homeboys and Homegirls in Change. Philadelphia: Temple University Press.

Morris, Norval. 1981. "Punishment, desert, and rehabilitation." In Hyman Gross and Andrew von Hirsch (eds.), Sentencing, pp. 257–71. New York: Oxford University Press.

Myers, Martha. 1987. The Social Contexts of Criminal Sentencing. New York: Springer-Verlag.

———. 1989. "Symbolic policy and the sentencing of drug offenders." *Law & Society Review* 23(2): 295–315.

Naffine, Ngaire. 1987. Female Crime: The Construction of Women in Criminology. Boston: Allen and Unwin.

Nagel, Stuart, and Lenore Weitzman. 1971. "Women as litigants." *Hastings Law Journal* 23:171–81.

Nardulli, Peter F., James Eisenstein, and Roy B. Flemming. 1988. The Tenor of Justice. Urbana: University of Illinois Press.

Nettler, Gwynne. 1979. "Criminal Justice." *American Review of Sociology* 5:27–52.

———. 1984. Explaining Crime. 3d ed. New York: McGraw-Hill.

———. 1990. "Definition of crime." In Delos H. Kelly (ed.), Criminal Behavior, 2d ed., pp. 11–22. New York: St. Martin's Press.

Newburn, Tim, and Betsy Stanko (eds.). 1994. Just Boys Doing Business? London: Routledge.

New Haven Special Commission on Poverty. 1983. "The extent, distribution, and causes of poverty in New Haven." Phase 1 report. City of New Haven.

O'Barr, William M., and John M. Conley. 1985. "Litigant satisfaction versus legal adequacy in small claims court narratives." *Law & Society Review* 19(4): 611–701.

Odubekun, Lola. 1992. "A structural approach to differential gender sentencing." *Criminal Justice Abstracts* 24(2): 343–60.

Parisi, Nicolette. 1982. "Are females treated differently? A review of the theories and evidence on sentencing and parole decisions." In Nicole Hahn Rafter and Elizabeth Anne Stanko (eds.), Judge, Lawyer, Victim, Thief, pp. 205–20. Boston: Northeastern University Press.

Peterson, Ruth D., and John Hagan. 1984. "Changing conceptions of race: Towards an account of anomalous findings of sentencing research." *American Sociological Review* 49(1): 56–70.

Pollak, Otto. 1950. The Criminality of Women. Philadelphia: University of Pennsylvania Press.

Radzinowicz, Leon, and Roger Hood. 1979. "Judicial discretion and sentencing standards: Victorian attempts to solve a perennial problem." *University of Pennsylvania Law Review* 127:1288–349.

Raeder, Myrna. 1993. "Gender and sentencing: Single moms, battered women, and other sex-based anomalies in the gender-free world of the federal sentencing guidelines." *Pepperdine Law Review* 20(3): 905–990.

Rafter, Nicole Hahn. 1982. "Hard times: Custodial prisons for women and the example of the New York State Prison for Women at Auburn, 1893–1933." In Nicole Hahn Rafter and Elizabeth Anne Stanko (eds.), Judge, Lawyer, Victim, Thief, pp. 237–60. Boston: Northeastern University Press.

———. 1990. Partial Justice: Women, Prisons and Social Control. 2d ed. New Brunswick, N.J.: Transaction.

Rapaport, Elizabeth. 1991. "The death penalty and gender discrimination." *Law & Society Review* 25(2): 367–83.

———. 1992. "When is a domestic homicide a capital crime? Gender differences in America's death row." Paper presented at the annual meeting of the Law and Society Association, May.

Reckless, Walter C. 1961. The Crime Problem. 3d ed. New York: Appleton-Century-Crofts.

Reckless, Walter, C., and Barbara Ann Kay. 1967. The Female Offender. Washington, D.C.: President's Commission on Law Enforcement and Administration of Justice.

Remick, Helen (ed.). 1984. Comparable Worth and Wage Discrimination. Philadelphia: Temple University Press.

Resnik, Judith, and Nancy Shaw. 1980. "Prisoners of their sex: Health problems of incarcerated women." In Ira Robbins (ed.), Prisoners' Rights Sourcebook: Theory, Litigation and Practice, vol. 2, pp. 319–413. New York: Clark Boardman.

Rhode, Deborah. 1989. Justice and Gender: Sex Discrimination and the Law. Cambridge: Harvard University Press.

Richardson, Laurel. 1990. "Narrative and sociology." *Journal of Contemporary Ethnography* 19(1): 116–35.

Robinson, Paul. 1992. "Desert and prevention: Hybird principles." In Andrew von Hirsch and Andrew Ashworth (eds.), Principled Sentencing, pp. 41–53. Boston: Northeastern University Press.

Romenesko, Kim, and Eleanor M. Miller. 1989. "The second step in double jeopardy: Appropriating the labor of female street hustlers." *Crime & Delinquency* 35(1): 109–35.

Rose, Arnold M., and Arthur E. Prell. 1955. "Does the punishment fit the crime? A study in social valuation." *American Journal of Sociology* 61:247–59.

Rosecrance, John. 1985. "The probation officers' search for credibility: Ball park recommendations." *Crime & Delinquency* 31(4): 539–54.

———. 1988. "Maintaining the myth of individualized justice: Probation presentence reports." *Justice Quarterly* 5(2): 235–56.

Rosenbaum, Marsha. 1981. Women on Heroin. New Brunswick: Rutgers University Press.

Rosett, Arthur, and Donald R. Cressey. 1976. Justice by Consent: Plea Bargains in the American Courthouse. New York: J. B. Lippincott.

Rossi, Peter H., Jon E. Simpson, and JoAnn L. Miller. 1985. "Beyond crime seriousness: Fitting the punishment to the crime." *Journal of Quantitative Criminology* 1(1): 59–90.

Rossi, Peter H., Emily Waite, Christine E. Bose, and Richard A. Berk. 1974. "The seriousness of crimes: Normative structure and individual differences." *American Sociological Review* 39:224–37.

Russell, Diana. 1984. The Secret Trauma: Incest in the Lives of Girls and Women. New York: Basic Books.

Scheingold, Stuart. 1984. The Politics of Law and Order. New York: Longman.

———. 1991. The Politics of Street Crime. Philadelphia: Temple University Press.

Schlossman, Steven, and Stephanie Wallach. 1978. "The crime of precocious sexuality: Female juvenile delinquency and the Progressive Era." *Harvard Educational Review* 48(1): 65–94.

Schneider, Elizabeth M. 1986. "Describing and changing: Women's self-defense work and the problem of expert testimony on battering." *Women's Rights Law Reporter* 9(3–4): 195–225.

Schweber, Claudine. 1982. "'The government's unique experiment in salvaging women criminals': Cooperation and conflict in the administration of a women's prison. The case of the Federal Industrial Institution for Women at Alderson." In Nicole Hahn Rafter and Elizabeth Anne Stanko (eds.), Judge, Lawyer, Victim, Thief, pp. 277–303. Boston: Northeastern University Press.

Scully, Diane. 1990. Understanding Sexual Violence. Boston: Unwin Hyman.

Seidman, David, and Michael Couzens. 1974. "Getting the crime rate down: Political pressure and crime reporting." *Law & Society Review* 8:457–93.

Sellin, Thorsten, and Marvin E. Wolfgang. 1964. The Measurement of Delinquency. New York: Wiley.

Simon, Rita. 1975. Women and Crime. Lexington, Mass.: Lexington Books.

Singer, Richard G. 1979. Just Deserts: Sentencing Based on Equality and Desert. Chicago: University of Chicago Press.

Smart, Carol. 1976. Women, Crime, and Criminology: A Feminist Critique. Boston: Routledge and Kegan Paul.

———. 1985. "Legal subjects and sexual objects: Ideology, law, and female sexuality." In Julia Brophy and Carol Smart (eds.), Women-in-Law, pp. 50–70. Boston: Routledge and Kegan Paul.

———. 1989. Feminism and the Power of Law. New York: Routledge and Kegan Paul.

———. 1990. "Feminist approaches to criminology or postmodern woman meets atavistic man." In Loraine Gelsthorpe and Allison Morris (eds.), Feminist Perspectives in Criminology, pp. 70–84. Philadelphia: Open University Press.

Spencer, J. William. 1984. "Conducting presentencing investigations: From discourse to textual summaries." Urban Life 13(2–3): 207–27.

Spohn, Cassia, Susan Welch, and John Gruhl. 1985. "Women defendants in court: The interaction between sex and race in convicting and sentencing." Social Science Quarterly 66:178–85.

Stanko, Elizabeth A. 1982. "Would you believe this woman? Prosecutorial screening for 'credible' witnesses and a problem of justice." In Nicole Hahn Rafter and Elizabeth Anne Stanko (eds.), Judge, Lawyer, Victim, Thief, pp. 63–82. Boston: Northeastern University Press.

Stark, Evan, and Anne H. Flitcraft. 1988. "Women and children at risk: A feminist perspective on child abuse." International Journal of Health Services 18(1): 97–108.

Steffensmeier, Darrell J. 1980. "Assessing the impact of the women's movement on sex-based differences in the handling of adult criminal defendants." Crime & Delinquency 26(3): 344–57.

Steffensmeier, Darrell, John Kramer, and Cathy Streifel. 1993. "Gender and imprisonment decisions." Criminology 31(3): 411–46.

Straus, Murray A. 1979. "Measuring intrafamily conflict and violence: The Conflict Tactics (CT) Scales." Journal of Marriage and the Family 51:75–88.

———. 1991. "Discipline and deviance: Physical punishment of children and violence and other crimes in adulthood." Social Problems 39(2): 133–54. (See replies by Kurz, Loseke, and McCord, and Straus's reply in the same issue.)

Straus, Murray A., Richard J. Gelles, and Susan K. Steinmetz. 1980. Behind Closed Doors: Violence in the American Family. Garden City, N.Y.: Doubleday.

Sudnow, David. 1965. "Normal crimes: Sociological features of the penal code in a public defender office." Social Problems 12(3): 255–76.

Sullivan, Mercer L. 1989. "Getting Paid": Youth Crime and Work in the Inner City. Ithaca: Cornell University Press.

Swigert, Victoria Lynn, and Ronald A. Farrell. 1977. "Normal homicides and the law." American Sociological Review 42:16–32.

Sykes, Gresham M., and David Matza. 1957. "Techniques of neutralization: A theory of delinquency." American Sociological Review 22:667–70.

Taylor, Carl S. 1990. Dangerous Society. East Lansing: Michigan State University Press.

Temin, Carolyn Engel. 1973. "Discriminatory sentencing of women offenders: The argument for ERA in a nutshell." American Criminal Law Review 11(2): 355–72.

Thomas, D. A. 1979. Principles of Sentencing. 2d ed. London: Heinemann.

Tonry, Michael H. 1987. Sentencing Reform Impacts. Washington, D.C.: U.S. Department of Justice, National Institute of Justice.

U.S. Sentencing Commission. 1989. Guidelines Manual. Sec. 3E1.1 (Nov.).

Vera Institute of Justice. 1977. Felony Arrests: Their Prosecution and Disposition in New York City's Courts. New York: Vera Institute of Justice.

Visher, Christy A. 1983. "Gender, police arrest decisions, and actions of chivalry." *Criminology* 21(1): 5–28.

Vogel, Lise. 1993. Mothers at Work: Maternity Policy in the U.S. Workplace. New Brunswick, N.J.: Rutgers University Press.

Vold, George B., and Thomas J. Bernard. 1986. Theoretical Criminology. 3d ed. New York: Oxford University Press.

von Hirsch, Andrew. 1985. Past or Future Crimes. New Brunswick: Rutgers University Press.

———. 1989. "Federal sentencing guidelines: Do they provide principled guidance?" *American Criminal Law Review* 27(2): 367–90.

———. 1990. "The politics of 'just deserts'." *Canadian Journal of Criminology* 32:397–413.

von Hirsch, Andrew, and Andrew Ashworth (eds.). 1992. Principled Sentencing. Boston: Northeastern University Press.

von Hirsch, Andrew, and Nils Jareborg. 1991. "Gauging criminal harm: A living-standard analysis." *Oxford Journal of Legal Studies* 11(1): 1–38.

Walker, Nigel. 1991. Why Punish? New York: Oxford University Press.

Walker, Samuel. 1980. Popular Justice. New York: Oxford University Press.

Wasik, Martin, and Andrew von Hirsch. 1988. "Non-custodial penalties and the principles of desert." *Criminal Law Review* 1988:555–72.

Weisburd, David, Stanton Wheeler, Nancy Bode, and Elin Waring. 1991. Crimes of the Middle Classes: White-Collar Offenders in the Federal Courts. New Haven: Yale University Press.

Wheeler, Stanton, Kenneth Mann, and Austin Sarat. 1988. Sitting in Judgment. New Haven: Yale University Press.

Wheeler, Stanton, David Weisburd, and Nancy Bode. 1982. "Sentencing the white-collar offender: Rhetoric and reality." *American Sociological Review* 47(4): 641–59.

Widom, Cathy Spatz. 1989. "Child abuse, neglect, and violent criminal behavior." *Criminology* 27(2): 251–71.

Wilbanks, William. 1982. "Murdered women and women who murder." In Nicole Rafter and Elizabeth Stanko (eds.), Judge, Lawyer, Victim, Thief, pp. 151–80. Boston: Northeastern University Press.

———. 1987. The Myth of a Racist Criminal Justice System. Pacific Grove: Brooks/Cole.

Wilson, Margo I., and Martin Daly. 1992. "Who kills whom in spouse killings? On the exceptional sex ratio of spousal homicides in the United States." *Criminology* 30(2): 189–215.

Wolfgang, Marvin E., Robert J. Figlio, Paul E. Tracy, and Simon I. Singer. 1985. The National Survey of Crime Severity. Washington, D.C.: U.S. Government Printing Office.

"Women's Self-Defense Law." 1986. *Women's Rights Law Reporter* 9(3–4) (special issue).

Worrall, Anne. 1990. Offending Women. New York: Routledge and Kegan Paul.

Young, Alison. 1992. Untitled ms. on feminism, postmodernism, and criminology. Lancaster, England: Department of Law, University of Lancaster.

Young, Jock. 1988. "Radical criminology in Britain: The emergence of a competing paradigm." *British Journal of Criminology* 28(2): 159–83.

Zedner, Lucia. 1991. Women, Crime and Custody in Victorian England. New York: Oxford University Press.

Zimring, Franklin E. 1981. "Making the punishment fit the crime: A consumer's guide to sentencing reform." In Hyman Gross and Andrew von Hirsch (eds.), Sentencing, pp. 327–34. New York: Oxford University Press.

Zimring, Franklin E., and James Zuehl. 1986. "Victim injury and death in urban robbery: A Chicago study." *Journal of Legal Studies* 15(1): 1–40.

Index

Santoro, Sabrina, 283
Sarat, Austin, 37, 40n2, 174n3, 175n9, 175n11, 184
Schaller, [Barry] Judge, 27, 178, 202, 218–19
Scott, 119–20, 121, 123n11, 222–23, 223, 229, 242, 251, 253, 279, 305
Scully, Diane, 148n13
Sentencing: racial disparity in, 5, 13nn3–4, 234–36, 251, 253–54, 263–64, 268–69; gender gaps in, 5–11, 25–32, 233–34, 251, 253–54, 261–64, 267–69; equal treatment in, 8–11, 270–71; feminist concerns about, 8–9, 11; policy problems in, 8–11; relation of punishment philosophy to, 10, 20, 172–73, 213–17; split-the-difference approach to, 10–11; in New Haven Felony Court, 21; percentage incarcerated by sex and race, 28, 29–30, 31; time incarcerated by sex and race, 28, 30–32, 256–57n25, 288–90; process of, 177; of women, 177–99; for drug offenses, 179, 180–81, 190–91, 211–12, 250, 252; of robbery cases, 179–82, 184–87, 189–90, 194, 205, 207, 220, 222, 241, 247–49, 252; of arson cases, 183–84, 212; of homicide cases, 183, 187–88, 208–9, 212–13, 241, 245, 246–47; justifications for, 184–96, 209, 210, 219–22, 230, 261–63; and special deterrence, 188–91, 209–13; of risk-of-injury cases, 191–92, 203–4, 215–19, 245; of assault cases, 192–93, 209–11, 213–15, 217, 219–22, 245, 246, 250–51; of larceny cases, 194–96, 205–7, 222–23, 245–46; and character judgments, 197–98, 223–24, 227–29; of men, 201–30; judicial silence toward male defendants, 203–7; harm-based considerations in, 230; pair-wise disparity analysis of, 240–54; and commensurability for diverse harms, 251–53; analysis of, 287–90
Seriousness of crime: statutory status of, 88–89; gender differences in,

88–90, 165–67, 260–61; sociological meaning of, 89–90; and female victims, 89–90, 108; elements associated with, 90; robbery, 93–96, 106–8, 165; and gestalt of the harm, 99; racial dynamics in, 106–7; larceny, 120–22, 165; violent crime, 144–47, 165; drug offenses, 161–63, 165; pair-wise judgments of, 300–301
Sex differences. *See* Gender
Sexual abuse of children, 140–45, 148n6, 191–92, 200nn11–12, 203–4, 215–17, 312–13
Shane, 76–77, 129, 219–20, 223, 229, 242, 281, 310
Sharon, 55, 60, 124, 129–30, 134, 146, 192–93, 197, 229, 242, 280, 310
Similarity, definition of, 236–40
Simon, 98–99, 223, 229, 242, 252, 253, 278, 303
Simon, Rita, 109n14
Simpson, Jon, 89, 90, 95, 108
Smart, Carol, 11
Special deterrence, 188–91, 209–13, 227
Split-the-difference approach, to sentencing, 10–11
Spohn, Cassia, 13n4
Stacey, 137, 243, 280, 311
Stanko, Betsy, 82n10
Steadman, Henry, 147n3
Steffensmeier, Darrell, 175n12, 267–69
Straus, Murray, 135, 148n11
Street men, 66–71
Street women, 45–47, 49–51, 57–60, 258
Streifel, Cathy, 267–69
Substance abuse, 45–48, 51–53, 56–57, 65, 66–71, 79, 294–95. *See also* headings beginning with Drug
Susan, 52–53, 60, 99–100, 108, 189–90, 198, 229, 244, 248, 278, 303
Sweeney, Joseph, 284
Swigert, Victoria, 139, 149n18

Tara, 117, 120, 122, 166, 194–95, 198, 229, 242, 279, 305